LITERATURE AND IDEAS SERIES
Irving Howe, General Editor

Helaine Newstead teaches in the English Department at Hunter College of the City University of New York, and has taught at Columbia University. A former recipient of a Guggenheim fellowship (for studies on the Tristan legend), she is also Vice President of the International Arthurian Society and President of its American branch; Chairman and a life member of the Columbia University Faculty Seminar on Medieval Studies; and a frequent contributor to such scholarly journals as PMLA, Romance Philology, Speculum, Journal of English and Germanic Philology, and Medium Aevum. In 1964 a testimonial issue of Romance Philology was dedicated to her.

Chaucer and His Contemporaries

ESSAYS ON MEDIEVAL LITERATURE AND THOUGHT

Edited with Introduction by
HELAINE NEWSTEAD

A FAWCETT PREMIER BOOK
Fawcett Publications, Inc., Greenwich, Conn.
Member of American Book Publishers Council, Inc.

The illustration on the cover of this volume is "Dancing on Christmas Eve," a woodcut from *The Nuremberg Chronicle* by Hartmann Schedel, Nuremberg: Anton Koberger, 1493. Reproduced by permission of The Pierpont Morgan Library, New York.

Library of Congress Catalog Card Number 68-31468

First Fawcett Premier printing, April, 1968

Published by Fawcett World Library,
67 West 44th Street, New York, New York 10036
Printed in the United States of America

Contents

Chaucer and His Contemporaries

Introduction

THE FOURTEENTH CENTURY in England was a time of turbulence and strife. The Hundred Years' War with France, the devastating outbreaks of the Black Death, and the Peasants' Revolt of 1381 left deep social and economic scars. Even the stabilizing influence of the church was diminished by the existence of rival popes in Rome and Avignon and by growing evidence of corruption among the clergy.

Yet, despite these disasters, it was an age of affluence and brilliant achievement in art, learning, and literature. Architecture, sculpture, painting, carving, and metalwork all flourished under the patronage of royalty, the great nobles, and church prelates, especially in the reigns of Edward III (1327–1377) and Richard II (1377–1399). The development of the English wool trade with the Continent brought economic prosperity to cities and towns, and wealthy citizens helped to foster the arts by benefactions and bequests to local churches and religious orders. Elsewhere, in different parts of the country, castles and handsome manor houses were constructed by knights and prosperous merchants. During the course of the century the universities were significantly expanded by the foundation of five new colleges at Oxford and seven at Cambridge. In literature, this vigorous flowering of the arts finds a parallel in the emergence of three major poets —Geoffrey Chaucer, William Langland, and the anonymous author of *Sir Gawain and the Green Knight*—whose work represents the range and diversity of English culture during the period.

The fact that all three poets wrote in English means that the language itself had come of age. From the time of the Norman Conquest until the middle of the thirteenth century, English was the language of the conquered native population, French the language of the Norman aristocracy and the governing classes. Latin, of course, was used by the church and the learned professions, as it was throughout Europe. But after the loss of Normandy in 1204 and the somewhat later royal decrees prohibiting the holding of land in both England and France, English gradually regained the ascendancy. By the middle of the fourteenth century, English had become the dominant language of England, considerably simplified in inflections and grammar, and greatly enriched in vocabulary by borrowings from French and by smaller but no less significant contributions from the Scandinavian tongue spoken by earlier invaders in the ninth, tenth, and eleventh centuries. Many Englishmen, however, continued to use French and Latin according to their needs and education, such as Chaucer's friend John Gower, who wrote long poems in all three languages. But the English language current in the fourteenth century was by no means standardized. Regional dialects were markedly different from one another. Most readers today find Chaucer's English readily intelligible because his dialect, that of London and the Southeast Midlands, was the ancestor of modern standard English. But the West Midland dialect of Langland's *Piers Plowman* and the Northwest Midland of *Sir Gawain and the Green Knight* bristle with difficulties, and the general reader usually needs the help of a "translation" or a glossary.

A distinctive poetic tradition also flourished in the West and Northwest Midlands in the fourteenth century, a tradition derived from the old native alliterative meter in which poetry was composed in pre-Conquest England. The basic metrical unit is the four-stress alliterative line, with a strong caesura in the middle, usually unrhymed, but sometimes combined with rhyme. *Piers Plowman,* the works of the *Gawain-*Poet, the alliterative *Morte Arthure* all illustrate the varied and powerful rhythmic effects of alliterative poetry. On the other hand, Chaucer's verse, based on French and Italian models, is rhymed either in couplets or in stanzas. In his earlier poems he uses the octosyllabic couplet, an English adaptation of the French form, current in the Southeast Midlands. His major works, however, are composed in the line that later became the standard for English poetry, the five-stress line generally known as iambic pentameter, which Chaucer probably introduced. Chaucer uses it in couplets or in his own seven-line stanza, the rhyme royal.

Medieval poets were very close to their public, since poetry was intended to be read aloud to a listening audience. The poet, of course, had to anticipate the needs of his listeners, indicating at the outset the kind of literary experience he was offering—dream vision, romance, edifying narrative, comic tale—and unobtrusively guiding them in order to evoke the appropriate responses. The opening stanzas of *Pearl,* for instance, establish the poem as a dream vision and unfold the theme of despairing grief at the loss through death of one who is symbolized by the flawless Pearl. The religious questions raised in the introductory stanzas prepare the audience for the development of these and related ideas in the vision that follows.

A different kind of preparation appears in the *Prologue* to the *Canterbury Tales,* when Chaucer concludes his long series of portraits and informs his listeners:

> Now have I toold you soothly, in a clause,
> Th'estaat, th'array, the nombre, and eek the cause
> Why that assembled was this compaignye
> In Southwerk at this gentil hostelrye
> That highte the Tabard, faste by the Belle.
> But now is tyme to yow for to telle
> How that we baren us that ilke nyght.[1]

Such explicit transitions may strike the modern reader as naive or pedestrian, but they should be understood as technical devices to prepare listeners for a change of direction.

As the quoted passage suggests, it seems to have been customary for the author himself to read his work. In fact, the famous frontispiece in one of the manuscripts of Chaucer's *Troilus* depicts the poet standing in a pulpit reciting his poem to the royal court. But there must have been other readers, and the multiplication of manuscript copies of a work as well as evidence of revisions implies that medieval writers sought more permanence and a wider circulation than the ephemeral reading by the author himself. Because oral presentation was the custom, the best poets create an impression of colloquial and familiar speech even when they are dealing with the most exalted religious themes, as Nevill Coghill shows in his essay on *Piers Plowman* (pp. 236–254).

The practice of oral delivery also made it natural for the author to appear in his own poem as a character or a commentator. But it is important to realize that medieval poets, although they may be identified by name and other characteristics, do not greatly concern themselves with subjective, personal revelations. The themes of the poems are always more significant than the author. Thus, in *Piers Plowman,* the experiences of Will the Dreamer, who is also the author, are best understood as those of every Christian in search of sal-

---

[1] *The Works of Geoffrey Chaucer,* ed. F. N. Robinson (Boston: Houghton Mifflin, 2 ed., 1957), General Prologue, vss. 715–721. All quotations from Chaucer are taken from this edition.

vation in a troubled world. Although the poem includes other incidental references to the author, his family, and his circumstances—all very precious to us today—they are subordinate to its great themes.

Chaucer uses the device of the first-person narrator with consummate virtuosity but never in such a way that the medieval audience could mistake him for the subject of the poem. He moves easily in and out of the narrative, skillfully focusing attention, in the *Book of the Duchess,* upon the grieving Black Knight in the colloquy with the first-person narrator, and in the *Prologue* to the *Canterbury Tales,* upon his fellow-pilgrims. Even when he *seems* to be the subject, as in the *House of Fame* and the *Prologue* to the *Legend of Good Women,* the spirit of self-mockery and the pervasively comic tone in the personal passages establish the proper relationship. In the *House of Fame,* the mighty golden Eagle, transporting the poet in his talons through the air, explains that Jupiter has taken pity on his dull life:

> "Thou herist neyther that ne this;
> For when thy labour doon al ys,
> And hast mad alle thy rekenynges,
> In stede of reste and newe thynges,
> Thou goost hom to thy hous anoon;
> And also domb as any stoon,
> Thow sittest at another book
> Tyl fully daswed ys thy look.
> And lyvest thus as an heremyte,
> Although thyn abstinence ys lyte."
>   (*House of Fame,* vss. 652-660)

Such comfortable jesting, obviously intended for friends, must have delighted the original audiences who knew the poet, but its incidental function is plain in a poem that explores the illusory nature of worldly fame and the follies of those who seek it.

It is hardly surprising, under such conditions, that we should know so little about the poets themselves. A large number of documents about Chaucer are preserved not because he was a great poet but because he was in government service for most of his life. For the others, we must depend on inferences and allusions from the works themselves, linguistic evidence, and scattered references in late and sometimes unreliable sources. Even the Chaucer life-records, copious though they are, contain no direct information about his writings, his education, or his date of birth. Yet from these official documents and the inferences that they yield, a biography of sorts can be constructed.

The poet was born about 1343 into a wealthy London family. His father, John, was a prosperous wine merchant, and the family owned substantial properties. Although not of noble birth, Geoffrey Chaucer was able to make a career in the royal court and in government service. In the earliest record, 1357, he appears as a page in the household of Prince Lionel, a son of the reigning king, Edward III. Later he took part in a military campaign in France and was ransomed by the king. By 1367 he was a member of the king's household and married. In 1369 he began his long and close association with John of Gaunt, fourth son of Edward III and the most powerful noble in England. Between 1368 and 1378, Chaucer made several journeys to France and to Italy, to Florence, Genoa, and Milan in particular, on various diplomatic and financial missions for the king. From 1374 to 1386 he was also Controller of the Customs on Wool in the port of London. After leaving this post in 1386, he represented the county of Kent in Parliament. He was appointed in 1389 Clerk of the King's Works, which meant that he supervised the royal buildings and their maintenance, and two years later he became deputy forester of one of the royal forests in Somersetshire. The three kings who reigned during his lifetime, Edward III, Richard II, and Henry IV, showed their appreciation of his talents and services by generous gifts. In October 1400, Chaucer died in the house in the garden of Westminster Abbey that he had leased in the previous December. He was buried in the Abbey, and in later times other writers were buried near his tomb in what is known as the "Poets' Corner."

These records outline Chaucer's career as a courtier, a diplomat, and a government official who held a variety of responsible positions and who earned the confidence and respect of his royal patrons. Although they contain not a word about his poems, they illuminate certain aspects of his literary activities. Chaucer's public, it is clear, was the brilliant and highly sophisticated royal court. One of his early poems, the *Book of the Duchess,* was written about 1370 to commemorate the first wife of John of Gaunt, Blanche of Lancaster, who died of the plague in 1369. The culture of the court was French, and Chaucer's early works were composed in the French tradition, though of course written in English.

The journey in 1372–1373 that took him to Florence introduced him to the great Italian triumvirate, Dante, Petrarch, and Boccaccio. Dante was dead, but although the other poets were still alive, there is no evidence that the English poet ever met them. Their works, it seems fair to say, changed the course of Chaucer's literary development. Dante's influence is profound though somewhat difficult to define precisely. Chaucer mentions Petrarch with respect and translates one of his sonnets into rhyme royal stanzas in *Troilus*. Boccaccio's influence is more evident and extensive. The most important examples are *The Knight's Tale* and *Troilus*, which are adaptations of two of Boccaccio's long romances. Chaucer must also have responded to the intellectual and artistic stimulation of Florence at this time of cultural glory.

No less significant were Chaucer's travels in provincial England as a result of his government duties. In the course of these travels he seems to have become acquainted with a kind of life very different from that in court circles and with a variety of English folk in different social ranks. Some of this he may have acquired in the cosmopolitan atmosphere of London, but his delighted awareness of rural life and provincial types surely came to him from his English travels.

When the Eagle in the *House of Fame* describes Chaucer's eager absorption in books, he is referring to a characteristic that the official records fail to mention. Chaucer read widely and fruitfully because he loved books. He knew the French writers well, especially the encyclopedic work by Guillaume de Lorris and Jean de Meun, *Le Roman de la Rose,* part of which he translated. He was also familiar with the classical tradition represented in the poems of Ovid and Virgil and the works of other authors read in the Middle Ages. The most significant book for Chaucer, however, was the sixth-century Latin treatise by Boethius, the *Consolation of Philosophy,* which he translated into English prose. No other work so profoundly affected his thinking: its influence was lifelong and pervasive. Chaucer's intellectual interests extended also to the sciences. His knowledge of physics, medicine, alchemy (an early form of chemistry, not necessarily fraudulent), astronomy and astrology not only demonstrates the range of his mind but also reflects the scientific interests of his own time. For his little son Lewis, who was too young to read Latin, he translated a *Treatise on the Astrolabe* into English prose so that Lewis could learn how to use this scientific instrument for astronomical calculations. It is an unpretentious work, Chaucer explains, written for the education of his little son, with simplified problems that he could solve. Chaucer may also be the author of the *Equatorie of the Planetis,* a recently discovered manuscript in English prose dealing with a more advanced level of astronomy.

We are fortunate to have such abundant documentation about Chaucer's life, even though much of it seems to have little direct bearing upon his literary achievements. When we turn to William Langland and the poem *Piers Plowman,* we are confronted with formidable problems because such documents are lacking. *Piers Plowman* is preserved in three versions known as the A, B, and C Texts, and in numerous manuscripts that testify to its continued popularity in the fourteenth and fifteenth centuries, a popularity that extended well into the sixteenth century with printed editions. The A Text is the earliest and shortest version, written about 1370; the B Text, about 1377, is a revision and expansion of A; and the C Text, after 1390, is a revision of B. The dates are conjectural. The manuscripts vary so much among themselves that they suggest an almost continuous process of revision not only by the author but by copyists. The author is generally assumed to be William Langland, and what we know of him consists of autobiographical details in the poem itself and notes in some of the manuscripts added by persons who knew him or knew of him as the author. This fragmentary information implies that he was born about 1332 in the region of the Malvern Hills, the setting of the first vision in the poem. He was educated at his father's expense, probably at the Benedictine Priory in Great Malvern, took minor orders in the church, and went to London. He lived in Cornhill with his wife and daughter, for marriage was not prohibited in minor orders, and earned a meager living by praying and singing psalms for the souls of his benefactors. The date of his death is unknown, though generally supposed to be about 1400. Although he wrote his great work while he was living in London, and vividly described scenes of London life, he chose the language of his birthplace, the West Midlands, and the alliterative meter indigenous to the region.

Since we know so little about the author, it is difficult to determine the audience the poem was intended to reach. The constant revisions imply that even in its own day it was a difficult work in need of clarification. A. C. Spearing's essay (pp. 255–282) shows that the formalized arts of the sermon

were a major influence upon its structure, and it is reasonable
to assume, from the wealth of learned allusions and Latin
tags, that the original audience was composed of clerics and
educated laymen. Langland's views were thoroughly orthodox, but his emotional fervor in behalf of the poor and his
passionate denunciations of corruption among the clergy
probably caused his popularity among revolutionaries. By
1381, the year of the Peasants' Revolt, this aspect of the
poem was familiar enough for John Ball to refer to Piers
Plowman in a letter encouraging the rebels. In a later day,
the poem was used as an argument by those who favored a
separate English church. Social satire, of course, is present but
it is only one component in a work that deals with comprehensive religious issues that the poet considered equally urgent. The poem is undoubtedly difficult to assimilate, especially for the modern reader who must reach through study
the perceptions that were immediately intelligible to the medieval audience, but the experience is richly rewarding.

The third great fourteenth-century poet is still more elu-
sive. We have no clue to his name or identity, but it is assumed that he is the author of the four Middle English
poems preserved in a single manuscript now in the British
Museum, known as Cotton Nero A.x: *Pearl, Purity, Patience,*
and *Sir Gawain and the Green Knight*, to list them in the
order of the manuscript. The date of the manuscript is about
1400, and internal evidence suggests that the four poems
were composed between 1360 and 1395. The dialect is Northwest Midland, and all are written in the alliterative meter,
though *Pearl* and *Sir Gawain* also use rhyme and stanzas.
The four poems, it is true, exhibit differences, but these are
no more startling than those encountered in the works of authors whose identities are known, say, the differences between
Chaucer's *Book of the Duchess* and *The Miller's Tale.*

The poet must have written for a sophisticated and cultivated audience, perhaps one of the great baronial courts in
the Northwest Midlands. He himself was a highly educated
man, familiar with courtly French literature as well as English alliterative poetry, and deeply learned in Scripture and
controversial religious questions. His most notable trait, however, is his sympathetic understanding of the aristocratic life
and his admiration for its highest ideals of civilized conduct.
The concept of "courtesy," as D. S. Brewer shows (pp. 310–
343), is central in his thinking. Among English poets he is dis-

tinguished by a rare sense of form, with a strong interest in symmetrical patterns, evident particularly in *Pearl* and *Sir Gawain*. The confident mastery of language that the poems reveal presupposes the existence of poetic models from which the poet could have learned his craft. Much of this earlier alliterative tradition has now vanished. If, in fact, Cotton Nero A.x itself had been lost or destroyed, the existence of these four masterpieces could never have been known or even inferred. Perhaps the local dialect may have discouraged a wider circulation. Whatever the cause, the poems were miraculously preserved in a single manuscript, unknown until they were rediscovered in the nineteenth century. Because of them, we may glimpse a courtly society sharing the ideals of courtly life everywhere but developing its own individual culture.

The essays and studies in this volume are intended to direct the reader to the works of the poets. They are preceded by two contemporary accounts of events that profoundly affected life in the fourteenth century. Boccaccio's report of the Black Death in Florence in 1348 vividly describes the impact of the terrible plague upon the people in a great city. The outbreaks in England were not greatly different, although we have no comparable account. Froissart relates the events of the Peasants' Revolt of 1381 from his own point of view, which is uncompromisingly hostile to the rebels. The grim experiences are nevertheless honestly recorded, and Froissart's sources of information, if biased, are authentic.

The first group of essays presents some of the concepts familiar to medieval poets and their audiences and therefore are helpful in reading the literature. The essays on Chaucer are concerned primarily with the ideas expressed in his work, especially in the dream visions and *Troilus*. W. W. Lawrence's article on the *Tale of Melibeus* directs attention to Chaucer's interest in medieval discussions of war and peace. The article by the same scholar on *The Shipman's Tale* and E. T. Donaldson's study of "The Idiom of Popular Poetry in *The Miller's Tale*" consider literary questions, the one dealing with Chaucer's modifications of a popular tale to adapt it to the *Canterbury Tales*, the other illuminating one aspect of a comic masterpiece. Virginia Woolf's essay is included not because it is a contribution to scholarship but because it is a sensitive evocation of Chaucer's poetry and what it must have meant in the bleak period of the Paston letters after the poet's death. The other essays on Langland and the *Gawain*-Poet need no special explanation, except to note that they will serve as useful guides in areas where interpretation is difficult or controversial.

—HELAINE NEWSTEAD

PART I

Two Contemporary Voices

The Black Death

GIOVANNI BOCCACCIO

. . . I SAY, THEN, that the years of the beatific incarnation of the Son of God had reached the tale of one thousand three hundred and forty-eight, when in the illustrious city of Florence, the fairest of all the cities of Italy, there made its appearance that deadly pestilence, which, whether disseminated by the influence of the celestial bodies, or sent upon us mortals by God in His just wrath by way of retribution for our iniquities, had had its origin some years before in the East, whence, after destroying an innumerable multitude of living beings, it had propagated itself without respite from place to place, and so, calamitously, had spread into the West.

In Florence, despite all that human wisdom and forethought could devise to avert it, as the cleansing of the city from many impurities by officials appointed for the purpose, the refusal of entrance to all sick folk, and the adoption of many precautions for the preservation of health; despite also humble supplications addressed to God, and often repeated both in public procession and otherwise, by the devout; towards the beginning of the spring of the said year the doleful effects of the pestilence began to be horribly apparent by symptoms that shewed as if miraculous.

Not such were they as in the East, where an issue of blood from the nose was a manifest sign of inevitable death; but in men and women alike it first betrayed itself by the emergence of certain tumors in the groin or the armpits, some of which grew as large as a common apple, others as an egg, some more, some less, which the common folk called gavoccioli. From the two said parts of the body this deadly gavocciolo soon began to propagate and spread itself in all directions indifferently; after which the form of the malady began to change, black spots or livid making their appearance in many

From "First Day," THE DECAMERON by Giovanni Boccaccio. Trans. by J. M. Rigg. Everyman's Library Edition. Reprinted by permission of E. P. Dutton & Co., Inc.

cases on the arm or the thigh or elsewhere, now few and large, now minute and numerous. And as the gavocciolo had been and still was an infallible token of approaching death, such also were these spots on whomsoever they shewed themselves. Which maladies seemed to set entirely at naught both the art of the physician and the virtues of physic; indeed, whether it was that the disorder was of a nature to defy such treatment, or that the physicians were at fault—besides the qualified there was now a multitude both of men and of women who practised without having received the slightest tincture of medical science—and, being in ignorance of its source, failed to apply the proper remedies; in either case, not merely were those that recovered few, but almost all within three days from the appearance of the said symptoms, sooner or later, died, and in most cases without any fever or other attendant malady.

Moreover, the virulence of the pest was the greater by reason that intercourse was apt to convey it from the sick to the whole, just as fire devours things dry or greasy when they are brought close to it. Nay, the evil went yet further, for not merely by speech or association with the sick was the malady communicated to the healthy with consequent peril of common death; but any that touched the clothes of the sick or aught else that had been touched or used by them, seemed thereby to contract the disease.

So marvellous sounds that which I have now to relate, that, had not many, and I among them, observed it with their own eyes, I had hardly dared to credit it, much less to set it down in writing, though I had had it from the lips of a credible witness.

I say, then, that such was the energy of the contagion of the said pestilence, that it was not merely propagated from man to man, but, what is much more startling, it was frequently observed, that things which had belonged to one sick or dead of the disease, if touched by some other living creature, not of the human species, were the occasion, not merely of sickening, but of an almost instantaneous death. Whereof my own eyes (as I said a little before) had cognisance, one day among others, by the following experience. The rags of a poor man who had died of the disease being strewn about the open street, two hogs came thither, and after, as is their wont, no little trifling with their snouts, took the rags between their teeth and tossed them to and fro about their chaps; whereupon, almost immediately, they gave a few turns, and fell down dead, as if by poison, upon the rags which in an evil hour they had disturbed.

In which circumstances, not to speak of many others of a similar or even graver complexion, divers apprehensions and imaginations were engendered in the minds of such as were left alive, inclining almost all of them to the same harsh resolution, to wit, to shun and abhor all contact with the sick and all that belonged to them, thinking thereby to make each his own health secure. Among whom there were those who thought that to live temperately and avoid all excess would count for much as a preservative against seizures of this kind. Wherefore they banded together, and, dissociating themselves from all others, formed communities in houses where there were no sick, and lived a separate and secluded life, which they regulated with the utmost care, avoiding every kind of luxury, but eating and drinking very moderately of the most delicate viands and the finest wines, holding converse with none but one another, lest tidings of sickness or death should reach them, and diverting their minds with music and such other delights as they could devise. Others, the bias of whose minds was in the opposite direction, maintained, that to drink freely, frequent places of public resort, and take their pleasure with song and revel, sparing to satisfy no appetite, and to laugh and mock at no event, was the sovereign remedy for so great an evil: and that which they affirmed they also put in practice, so far as they were able, resorting day and night, now to this tavern, now to that, drinking with an entire disregard of rule or measure, and by preference making the houses of others, as it were, their inns, if they but saw in them aught that was particularly to their taste or liking; which they were readily able to do, because the owners, seeing death imminent, had become as reckless of their property as of their lives; so that most of the houses were open to all comers, and no distinction was observed between the stranger who presented himself and the rightful lord. Thus, adhering ever to their inhuman determination to shun the sick, as far as possible, they ordered their life. In this extremity of our city's suffering and tribulation the venerable authority of laws, human and divine, was abased and all but totally dissolved, for lack of those who should have administered and enforced them, most of whom, like the rest of the citizens, were either dead or sick, or so hard bested for servants that they were unable to execute any office; whereby every man was free to do what was right in his own eyes.

Not a few there were who belonged to neither of the two said parties, but kept a middle course between them, neither laying the same restraint upon their diet as the former, not allowing themselves the same license in drinking and other dissipations as the latter, but living with a degree of freedom sufficient to satisfy their appetites, and not as recluses. They therefore walked abroad, carrying in their hands flowers or fragrant herbs or divers sorts of spices, which they frequently raised to their noses, deeming it an excellent thing thus to comfort the brain with such perfumes, because the air seemed to be everywhere laden and reeking with the stench emitted by the dead and the dying, and the odours of drugs.

Some again, the most sound, perhaps, in judgment, as they were also the most harsh in temper, of all, affirmed that there was no medicine for the disease superior or equal in efficacy to flight; following which prescription a multitude of men and women, negligent of all but themselves, deserted their city, their houses, their estates, their kinsfolk, their goods, and went into voluntary exile, or migrated to the country parts, as if God in visiting men with this pestilence in requital of their iniquities would not pursue them with His wrath wherever they might be, but intended the destruction of such alone as remained within the circuit of the walls of the city; or deeming, perchance, that it was now time for all to flee from it, and that its last hour was come.

Of the adherents of these divers opinions not all died, neither did all escape; but rather there were, of each sort and in every place, many that sickened, and by those who retained their health were treated after the example which they themselves, while whole, had set, being everywhere left to languish in almost total neglect. Tedious were it to recount, how citizen avoided citizen, how among neighbours was scarce found any that shewed fellow-feeling for another, how kinsfolk held aloof, and never met, or but rarely; enough that this sore affliction entered so deep into the minds of men and women, that in the horror thereof brother was forsaken by brother, nephew by uncle, brother by sister, and oftentimes husband by wife; nay, what is more, and scarcely to be believed, fathers and mothers were found to abandon their own children, untended, unvisited, to their fate, as if they had been strangers. Wherefore the sick of both sexes, whose number could not be estimated, were left without resource but in the charity of friends (and few such there were), or the interest of servants, who were hardly to be had at high rates and on unseemly terms, and being, moreover, one and all, men and women of gross understanding, and for the most part unused to such offices, concerned themselves no further than to supply the immediate and expressed wants of the sick, and to watch them die; in which service they themselves not seldom perished with their gains. In consequence of which dearth of servants and dereliction of the sick by neighbours, kinsfolk and friends, it came to pass—a thing, perhaps, never before heard of—that no woman, however dainty, fair or well-born she might be, shrank, when stricken with the disease, from the ministrations of a man, no matter whether he were young or no, or scrupled to expose to him every part of her body, with no more shame than if he had been a woman, submitting of necessity to that which her malady required; wherefrom, perchance, there resulted in after time some loss of modesty in such as recovered. Besides which many succumbed who, with proper attendance, would, perhaps, have escaped death; so that, what with the virulence of the plague and the lack of due tendance of the sick, the multitude of the deaths, that daily and nightly took place in the city, was such that those who heard the tale—not to say witnessed the fact —were struck dumb with amazement. Whereby, practices contrary to the former habits of the citizens could hardly fail to grow up among the survivors.

It had been, as today it still is, the custom for the women that were neighbours and of kin to the deceased to gather in his house with the women that were most closely connected with him, to wail with them in common, while on the other hand his male kinsfolk and neighbours, with not a few of the other citizens, and a due proportion of the clergy according to his quality, assembled without, in front of the house, to receive the corpse; and so the dead man was borne on the shoulders of his peers, with funeral pomp of taper and dirge, to the church selected by him before his death. Which rites, as the pestilence waxed in fury, were either in whole or in great part disused, and gave way to others of a novel order. For not only did no crowd of women surround the bed of the dying, but many passed from this life unregarded, and few indeed were they to whom were accorded the lamentations and bitter tears of sorrowing relations; nay, for the most part, their place was taken by the laugh, the jest, the festal gathering; observances which the women, domestic piety in large measure set aside, had adopted with very great advantage to their health. Few also there were whose bodies were attended to the church by more than ten or twelve of their neighbours, and those not the honourable and respected citizens; but a sort of corpse-carriers drawn from the baser ranks, who called themselves becchini [1] and performed such offices for hire, would shoulder the bier, and with hurried steps carry it, not to the church of the dead man's choice, but to that which was nearest at hand, with four or six priests in front and a candle or two, or, perhaps, none; nor did the priests distress themselves with too long and solemn an office, but with the aid of the becchini hastily consigned the corpse to the first tomb which they found untenanted. The condition of the lower, and, perhaps, in great measure of the middle ranks, of the people shewed even worse and more deplorable; for, deluded by hope or constrained by poverty, they stayed in their quarters, in their houses, where they sickened by thousands a day, and, being without service or help of any kind, were, so to speak, irredeemably devoted to the death which overtook them. Many died daily or nightly in the public streets; of many others, who died at home, the departure was hardly observed by their neighbours, until the stench of their putrefying bodies carried the tidings; and what with their corpses and the corpses of others who died on every hand the whole place was a sepulchre.

It was the common practice of most of the neighbours, moved no less by fear of contamination by the putrefying bodies than by charity towards the deceased, to drag the corpses out of the houses with their own hands, aided, perhaps, by a porter, if a porter was to be had, and to lay them in front of the doors, where anyone who made the round might have seen, especially in the morning, more of them than he could count; afterwards they would have biers brought up, or, in default, planks, whereon they laid them. Nor was it once or twice only that one and the same bier carried two or three corpses at once; but quite a considerable number of such cases occurred, one bier sufficing for husband and wife, two or three brothers, father and son, and so forth. And times without number it happened, that, as two priests, bearing the cross, were on their way to perform the last office for someone, three or four biers were brought up by the porters in rear of them, so that, whereas the priests supposed that they had but one corpse to bury, they discovered that there were six or eight, or sometimes more. Nor,

[1] Probably from the name of the pronged or hooked implement with which they dragged the corpses out of the houses.

for all their number, were their obsequies honoured by either
tears or lights or crowds of mourners; rather, it was come to
this, that a dead man was then of no more account than a
dead goat would be today. From all which it is abundantly
manifest, that that lesson of patient resignation, which the
sages were never able to learn from the slight and infrequent
mishaps which occur in the natural course of events, was now
brought home even to the minds of the simple by the magnitude of their disasters, so that they became indifferent to
them.

As consecrated ground there was not in extent sufficient to
provide tombs for the vast multitude of corpses which day
and night, and almost every hour, were brought in eager
haste to the churches for interment, least of all, if ancient
custom were to be observed and a separate resting-place assigned to each, they dug, for each graveyard, as soon as it
was full, a huge trench, in which they laid the corpses as they
arrived by hundreds at a time, piling them up as merchandise
is stowed in the hold of a ship, tier upon tier, each covered
with a little earth, until the trench would hold no more. But I
spare to rehearse with minute particularity each of the woes
that came upon our city, and say in brief, that, harsh as was
the tenor of her fortunes, the surrounding country knew no
mitigation; for there—not to speak of the castles, each, as it
were, a little city in itself—in sequestered village, or on the
open champaign, by the wayside, on the farm, in the home-
stead, the poor hapless husbandmen and their families, for-
lorn of physicians' care or servants' tendance, perished day
and night alike, not as men, but rather as beasts. Wherefore,
they too, like the citizens, abandoned all rule of life, all habit
of industry, all counsel of prudence; nay, one and all, as if
expecting each day to be their last, not merely ceased to aid
Nature to yield her fruit in due season of their beasts and
their lands and their past labours, but left no means unused,
which ingenuity could devise, to waste their accumulated
store; denying shelter to their oxen, asses, sheep, goats, pigs,
fowls, nay, even to their dogs, man's most faithful companions, and driving them out into the fields to roam at large
amid the unsheaved, nay, unreaped corn. Many of which, as
if endowed with reason, took their fill during the day, and
returned home at night without any guidance of herdsman.
But enough of the country! What need we add, but (reverting
to the city) that such and so grievous was the harshness of
heaven, and perhaps in some degree of man, that, what with

the fury of the pestilence, the panic of those whom it spared, and their consequent neglect or desertion of not a few of the stricken in their need, it is believed without any manner of doubt, that between March and the ensuing July upwards of a hundred thousand human beings lost their lives within the walls of the city of Florence, which before the deadly visitation would not have been supposed to contain so many people! How many grand palaces, how many stately homes, how many splendid residences, once full of retainers, of lords, of ladies, were now left desolate of all, even to the meanest servant! How many families of historic fame, of vast ancestral domains, and wealth proverbial, found now no scion to continue the succession! How many brave men, how many fair ladies, how many gallant youths, whom any physician, were he Galen, Hippocrates, or Æsculapius himself, would have pronounced in the soundest of health, broke fast with their kinsfolk, comrades and friends in the morning, and when evening came, supped with their forefathers in the other world! . . .

SIR JOHN FROISSART

The Peasants' Revolt

1381

. . . WHILE THESE CONFERENCES were going forward there
happened great commotions among the lower orders in England, by which that country was nearly ruined. In order that
this disastrous rebellion may serve as an example to mankind,
I will speak of all that was done from the information I had
at the time. It is customary in England, as well as in several
other countries, for the nobility to have great privileges over
the commonalty; that is to say, the lower orders are bound by
law to plough the lands of the gentry, to harvest their grain,
to carry it home to the barn, to thrash and winnow it; they
are also bound to harvest and carry home the hay. All these
services the prelates and gentlemen exact of their inferiors;
and in the counties of Kent, Essex, Sussex, and Bedford,
these services are more oppressive than in other parts of the
kingdom. In consequence of this the evil disposed in these
districts began to murmur, saying that in the beginning of
the world there were no slaves, and that no one ought to be
treated as such, unless he had committed treason against his
lord, as Lucifer had done against God; but they had done no
such thing, for they were neither angels nor spirits, but men
formed after the same likeness as these lords who treated
them as beasts. This they would bear no longer; they were
determined to be free, and if they laboured or did any work,
they would be paid for it. A crazy priest in the county of
Kent, called John Ball, who for his absurd preaching had
thrice been confined in prison by the Archbishop of Canterbury, was greatly instrumental in exciting these rebellious
ideas. Every Sunday after mass, as the people were coming
out of church, this John Ball was accustomed to assemble a
crowd around him in the marketplace and preach to them.

From THE CHRONICLES OF ENGLAND, FRANCE AND SPAIN by Sir
John Froissart. H. P. Dunster's condensation of the Thomas Johnes
Translation. Dutton Paperback Edition (1961). Reprinted by per-
mission of E. P. Dutton & Co., Inc.

On such occasions he would say, "My good friends, matters cannot go on well in England until all things shall be in common; when there shall be neither vassals nor lords; when the lords shall be no more masters than ourselves. How ill they behave to us! for what reason do they thus hold us in bondage? Are we not all descended from the same parents, Adam and Eve? And what can they show, or what reason can they give, why they should be more masters than ourselves? They are clothed in velvet and rich stuffs, ornamented with ermine and other furs, while we are forced to wear poor clothing. They have wines, spices, and fine bread, while we have only rye and the refuse of the straw; and when we drink, it must be water. They have handsome seats and manors, while we must brave the wind and rain in our labours in the field; and it is by our labour they have wherewith to support their pomp. We are called slaves, and if we do not perform our service we are beaten, and we have no sovereign to whom we can complain or who would be willing to hear us. Let us go to the king and remonstrate with him; he is young, and from him we may obtain a favourable answer, and if not we must ourselves seek to amend our condition." With such language as this did John Ball harangue the people of his village every Sunday after mass. The archbishop, on being informed of it, had him arrested and imprisoned for two or three months by way of punishment; but the moment he was out of prison, he returned to his former course. Many in the city of London envious of the rich and noble, having heard of John Ball's preaching, said among themselves that the country was badly governed, and that the nobility had seized upon all the gold and silver. These wicked Londoners, therefore, began to assemble in parties, and to show signs of rebellion; they also invited all those who held like opinions in the adjoining counties to come to London; telling them that they would find the town open to them and the commonalty of the same way of thinking as themselves, and that they would so press the king, that there should no longer be a slave in England.

By this means the men of Kent, Essex, Sussex, Bedford, and the adjoining counties, in number about 60,000, were brought to London, under command of Wat Tyler, Jack Straw, and John Ball. This Wat Tyler, who was chief of the three, had been a tiler of houses—a bad man and a great enemy to the nobility. When these wicked people first began their disturbances, all London, with the exception of those who favoured them, was much alarmed. The mayor and rich citizens assembled in council and debated whether they should shut the gate and refuse to admit them; however, upon mature reflection they determined not to do so, as they might run the risk of having the suburbs burnt. The gates of the city were therefore thrown open, and the rabble entered and lodged as they pleased. True it is that full two-thirds of these people knew neither what they wanted, nor for what purpose they had come together; they followed one another like sheep. In this manner did many of these poor fellows walk to London from distances of one hundred, or sixty leagues, but the greater part came from the counties I have mentioned, and all on their arrival demanded to see the king. The country gentlemen, the knights and squires, began to be much alarmed when they saw the people thus assembling, and indeed they had sufficient reason to be so, for far less causes had excited fear. As the Kentish rebels were on their road towards London, the Princess of Wales, the king's mother, was returning from a pilgrimage to Canterbury; and when they saw her the scoundrels attacked her car and caused the good lady much alarm; but God preserved her from violence, and she came the whole journey from Canterbury to London without venturing to make any stoppage. On her arrival in London, King Richard was at the Tower; thither then the princess went immediately, and found the king, attended by the Earl of Salisbury, the Archbishop of Canterbury, Sir Robert de Namur, and several others, who had kept near his person from suspicion of the rebels. King Richard well knew that this rebellion was in agitation long before it broke out, and it was a matter of astonishment to every one that he attempted to apply no remedy.

In order that gentlemen and others may take example and learn to correct such wicked rebels, I will most amply detail how the whole business was conducted. On the Monday preceding the feast of the Holy Sacrament in the year 1381, these people sallied forth from their homes to come to London, intending, as they said, to remonstrate with the king, and to demand their freedom. At Canterbury, they met John Ball, Wat Tyler, and Jack Straw. On entering this city they were well feasted by the inhabitants, who were all of the same way of thinking as themselves; and having held a council there, resolved to proceed on their march to London. They also sent emissaries across the Thames into Essex, Suffolk, and Bedford, to press the people of these parts to do the same, in order that the city might be quite surrounded.

It was the intention of the leaders of this rabble, that all the different parties should be collected on the feast of the Holy Sacrament on the day following. At Canterbury the rebels entered the church of St. Thomas, where they did much damage; they also pillaged the apartments of the archbishop, saying as they were carrying off the different articles, "The Chancellor of England has had this piece of furniture very cheap; he must now give us an account of his revenues, and of the large sums which he has levied since the coronation of the king." After this they plundered the abbey of St. Vincent, and then leaving Canterbury took the road towards Rochester. As they passed they collected people from the villages right and left, and on they went like a tempest, destroying all the houses belonging to attorneys, king's proctors, and the archbishop, which came in their way. At Rochester they met with the same welcome as at Canterbury, for all the people were anxious to join them. Here they went at once to the castle, and seizing a knight by name Sir John de Newtoun, who was constable of the castle and captain of the town, told him that he must accompany them as their commander-in-chief and do whatever they wished. The knight endeavoured to excuse himself; but they met his excuses by saying, "Sir John, if you refuse you are a dead man." Upon which, finding that the outrageous mob were ready to kill him, he was constrained to comply with their request.

In other counties of England the rebels acted in a similar manner, and several great lords and knights, such as the Lord Manley, Sir Stephen Hales, and Sir Thomas Cossington, were compelled to march with them. Now observe how fortunately matters turned out, for had these scoundrels succeeded in their intentions, all the nobility of England would have been destroyed; and after such success as this the people of other nations would have rebelled also, taking example from those of Ghent and Flanders, who at the time were in actual rebellion against their lord; the Parisians indeed the same year acted in a somewhat similar manner; upwards of 20,000 of them armed themselves with leaden maces and caused a rebellion, which I shall speak of as we go on; but I must first finish my account of these disturbances in England. When the rebels had done all they wanted at Rochester, they left that city and came to Dartford, continuing to destroy all the houses of lawyers and proctors on the right and left of the road; from Dartford they came to Blackheath, where they took up their quarters, saying that they were armed for the king and commons of England. When the principal citizens of London found that the rebels were quartered so near them, they caused the gates of London-bridge to be closed, and placed guards there, by order of Sir William Walworth, Mayor of London; notwithstanding there were in the city more than 30,000 who favoured the insurgents. Information that the gates of London-bridge had been closed against them soon reached Blackheath, whereupon the rebels sent a knight to speak with the king and to tell him that what they were doing was for his service; for the kingdom had now for many years been wretchedly governed, to the great dishonour of the realm and to the oppression of the lower orders of the people, by his uncles, by the clergy, and more especially by the Archbishop of Canterbury, his chancellor, from whom they were determined to have an account of his ministry. The knight who was appointed to this service would willingly have excused himself, but he did not dare to do it; so advancing to the Thames opposite the Tower, he took a boat and crossed over. The king and those who were with him in the Tower were in the greatest possible suspense and most anxious to receive some intelligence when the knight's arrival was announced, who was immediately conducted into the royal presence. With the king at this time were the princess his mother, his two natural brothers, the Earl of Kent and Sir John Holland, the Earls of Salisbury, Warwick, and Suffolk, the Archbishop of Canterbury, the great Prior of the Templars, Sir Robert de Namur, the Mayor of London, and several of the principal citizens. Immediately upon entering the apartment the knight cast himself on his knees before the king, saying, "My much redoubted lord, do not be displeased with me for the message which I am about to deliver to you; for, my dear lord, I have been compelled to come hither." "By no means, sir knight," said the king. "Tell us what you are charged with, we hold you excused." "My most redoubted lord, the commons of this realm have sent me to entreat you to come to Blackheath and speak with them. They wish to have no one but yourself: and you need not fear for your person, as they will not do you the least harm; they always have respected you as their king, and will continue to do so; but they desire to tell you many things which they say it is necessary you should hear: with these, however, they have not empowered me to make you acquainted. Have the goodness, dear lord, to give me such an answer as may satisfy them, and that they may be convinced that I have really been in your presence; for they have my children as hostages for my return, and if I go not back they will assuredly put them to death." To this the king merely replied, "You shall have my answer speedily"; and when the knight had withdrawn, he desired his council to consider what was to be done; after some consultation, the king was advised to send word to the insurgents, that if on Thursday they would come down to the river Thames, he would without fail speak with them. The knight, on receiving this answer, was well satisfied, and taking leave of the king and his barons, returned to Blackheath, where upwards of 60,000 men were assembled. He told them from the king that if they would send their leaders the next morning to the Thames, the king would come and hear what they had to say. The answer was deemed satisfactory; and the rebels passed the night as well as they could, but you must know that one-fourth of them were without provisions.

At this time the Earl of Buckingham was in Wales, where he possessed large estates in right of his wife; and the common report in London was that he favoured these people: some asserted it for a truth, declaring that they had seen him among them, for there was one Thomas from Cambridge who very much resembled him. The English barons who were at Plymouth, preparing for their voyage, when they heard of the rebellion were fearful lest they should be prevented, and consequently as soon as they could weighed anchor and put to sea. The Duke of Lancaster, who was on the borders between Morlane, Roxburgh, and Melrose, holding conferences with the Scots, also received intelligence of the rebellion, and of the danger he was in, for he well knew his own unpopularity. Notwithstanding this, he managed very satisfactorily his treaty with the Scottish commissioners, who themselves also knew what was going on in England, and how the populace was everywhere rising against the nobility. But to return to the commonalty of England: on Corpus Christi day King Richard heard mass in the Tower of London, after which he entered his barge, attended by the Earls of Salisbury, Warwick, and Suffolk, and some other knights, and rowed down the Thames towards Rotherhithe, a royal manor, where upwards of 10,000 of the insurgents had assembled. As soon as the mob perceived the royal barge approaching, they began shouting and crying as if all the spirits of the nether world had been in the company. With them, also, was the knight whom they had sent to the Tower to the king; for if the king had not come, they determined to have him cut to pieces, as they had threatened him.

When the king and his lords saw this crowd of people, and the wildness of their manner, the boldest of the party felt alarm, and the king was advised not to land, but to have his barge rowed up and down the river. "What do you wish for?" he demanded of the multitude; "I am come hither to hear what you have to say." Those near him cried out, "We wish you to land, and then we will tell you what our wants are." Upon this the Earl of Salisbury cried out, "Gentlemen, you are not properly dressed, nor are you in a fit condition for a king to talk with." Nothing more was said on either side, for the king was prevailed upon at once to return to the Tower. The people seeing this were in a great passion, and returned to Blackheath to inform their companions how the king had served them; upon hearing which, they all cried out, "Let us instantly march to London." Accordingly they set out at once, and on the road thither destroyed all the houses of lawyers and courtiers, and all the monasteries they met with. In the suburbs of London, which are very handsome and extensive, they pulled down many fine houses: they demolished also the king's prison, called the Marshalsea, and set at liberty all who were confined in it; moreover, they threatened the Londoners at the entrance of the bridge for having shut the gates of it, declaring that they would take the city by storm, and afterwards burn and destroy it.

With regard to the common people of London, numbers entertained these rebellious opinions, and on assembling at the bridge asked of the guards, "Why will you refuse admittance to these honest men? they are our friends, and what they are doing is for our good." So urgent were they, that it was found necessary to open the gates, when crowds rushed in and took possession of those shops which seemed best stocked with provisions; indeed, wherever they went, meat and drink were placed before them, and nothing was refused in the hope of appeasing them. Their leaders, John Ball, Jack Straw, and Wat Tyler, then marched through London, attended by more than 20,000 men, to the palace of the Savoy, which is a handsome building belonging to the Duke of Lancaster, situated on the banks of the Thames on the road to Westminster: here they immediately killed the porters, pushed into the house, and set it on fire. Not content with this outrage, they went to the house of the Knight-hospitalers of

Rhodes, dedicated to St. John of Mount Carmel, which they burnt together with their church and hospital.

After this they paraded the streets, and killed every Fleming they could find, whether in house, church, or hospital: they broke open several houses of the Lombards, taking whatever money they could lay their hands upon. They murdered a rich citizen, by name Richard Lyon, to whom Wat Tyler had formerly been servant in France, but having once beaten him, the varlet had never forgotten it; and when he had carried his men to his house, he ordered his head to be cut off, placed upon a pike, and carried through the streets of London. Thus did these wicked people act, and on this Thursday they did much damage to the city of London. Towards evening they fixed their quarters in a square, called St. Catherine's, before the Tower, declaring that they would not depart until they had obtained from the king everything they wanted—until the Chancellor of England had accounted to them, and shown how the great sums which were raised had been expended. Considering the mischief which the mob had already done, you may easily imagine how miserable at this time was the situation of the king and those who were with him. In the evening, he and his barons, together with Sir William Walworth, and some of the principal citizens, held a council in the Tower, when it was proposed to arm themselves and fall by night upon these wretches while they were drunk and asleep, for they might have been killed like so many fleas, as not one of them in twenty had arms: and the citizens were very capable of doing this, for they had secretly received into their house their friends and servants properly prepared for action. Sir Robert Knolles remained in his house guarding it, with more than six-score companions completely armed, who could have sallied forth at a minute's notice. Sir Perducas d'Albret was also in London at this period, and would of course have been of great service, so that altogether they could have mustered upwards of 8,000 men well armed. However, nothing was done; they were really too much afraid of the commonalty; and the king's advisers, the Earl of Salisbury and others, said to him, "Sir, if you can appease them by fair words, it will be so much the better; for should we begin what we cannot go through, it will be all over with us and our heirs, and England will be a desert." This counsel was followed, and the mayor ordered to make no stir; who obeyed, as in reason he ought. On Friday morning the rebels, who lodged in the square of St. Catherine's, before the Tower, begin to make themselves ready. They shouted much and said that if the king would not come out to them, they would attack the Tower, storm it, and slay all who were within. The king, alarmed at these menaces, resolved to speak with the rabble; he therefore sent orders from them to retire to a handsome meadow at Mile-end, where in the summertime people go to amuse themselves, at the same time signifying that he would meet them there and grant their demands. Proclamation to this effect was made in the king's name, and thither, accordingly, the commonalty of the different villages began to march; many, however, did not care to go, but stayed behind in London, being more desirous of the riches of the nobles and the plunder of the city. Indeed, covetousness and the desire of plunder was the principal cause of these disturbances, as the rebels showed very plainly. When the gates of the Tower were thrown open, and the king, attended by his two brothers and other nobles, had passed through, Wat Tyler, Jack Straw, and John Ball, with upwards of 400 others, rushed in by force, and running from chamber to chamber, found the Archbishop of Canterbury, by name Simon, a valiant and wise man, whom the rascals seized and beheaded. The prior of St. John's suffered the same fate, and likewise a Franciscan friar, a doctor of physic, who was attached to the Duke of Lancaster, also a sergeant-at-arms, whose name was John Laige.

The heads of these four persons the rebels fixed on long spikes and had them carried before them through the streets of London; and when they had made sufficient mockery of them, they caused them to be placed on London-bridge, as if they had been traitors to their king and country. The scoundrels then entered the apartment of the princess and cut her bed to pieces, which so terrified her that she fainted, and in this condition she was carried by her servants and ladies to the river side, when she was put into a covered boat and conveyed to a house called the Wardrobe, where she continued for a day and night in a very precarious state. While the king was on his way to Mile-end, his two brothers, the Earl of Kent and Sir John Holland, stole away from his company, not daring to show themselves to the populace. The king himself, however, showed great courage, and on his arrival at the appointed spot instantly advanced into the midst of the assembled multitude, saying in a most pleasing manner, "My good people, I am your king and your lord, what is it you want? What do you wish to say to me?" Those who heard him made answer, "We wish you to make us free for ever. We wish to be no longer called slaves, nor held in bondage." The king replied, "I grant your wish; now therefore return to your homes, and let two or three from each village be left behind, to whom I will order letters to be given with my seal, fully granting every demand you have made: and in order that you may be the most satisfied, I will direct that my banners be sent to every stewardship, castlewick, and corporation."

These words greatly appeased the more moderate of the multitude, who said, "It is well: we wish for nothing more." The king, however, added yet further, "You, my good people of Kent, shall have one of my banners: and you also of Essex, Sussex, Bedford, Suffolk, Cambridge, Stafford and Lincoln, shall each have one; I pardon you all for what you have hitherto done, but you must follow my banners and now return home on the terms I have mentioned," which they unanimously consented to do. Thus did this great assembly break up. The king instantly employed upwards of thirty secretaries, who drew up the letters as fast as they could, and when they were sealed and delivered to them, the people departed to their own counties. The principal mischief, however, remained behind: I mean Wat Tyler, Jack Straw, and John Ball, who declared that, though the people were satisfied, they were by no means so, and with them were about 30,000 also of the same mind. These all continued in the city without any wish to receive the letters or the king's seal, but did all they could to throw the town into such confusion that the lords and rich citizens might be murdered and their houses pillaged and destroyed. The Londoners suspected this, and kept themselves at home, well armed and prepared to defend their property.

After he had appeased the people at Mile-end Green, King Richard went to the Wardrobe, in order that he might console the princess, who was in the greatest possible alarm. But I must not omit to relate an adventure which happened to these clowns before Norwich and to their leader, William Lister, who was from the county of Stafford. At the same time that a party of these wicked people in London burnt the palace of the Savoy, the church and house of St. John's, and the hospital of the Templars, there were collected numerous bodies of men from Lincolnshire, Norfolk, and Suffolk, who, according to the orders they had received, were marching towards London. On their road they stopped near Norwich, and forced every one whom they met to join them.

The reason of their stopping near Norwich was that the governor of the town was a knight, by name Sir Robert Salle, who was not by birth a gentleman; but who, because of his ability and courage, had been created a knight by King Edward: he was, moreover, one of the handsomest and strongest men in England. Lister and his companions took it into their heads that they would make this man their commander. They, therefore, sent orders to him to come out into the fields to speak with them, declaring, in case he refused, that they would attack and burn the city. The knight, considering it was much better for him to go to them than that they should commit such outrages, mounted his horse and went out of the town alone to hear what they had to say. On his approach they showed every mark of respect, and courteously entreated him to dismount and talk with them. He did dismount, and in so doing committed a great folly, for immediately the mob surrounded him, and at first conversed in a friendly way, saying, "Robert, you are a knight and a man of great weight in this country, renowned for your valour; yet, notwithstanding all this, we know who you are; you are not a gentleman, but the son of a poor mason, such as ourselves. Come with us, therefore, as our commander, and we will make you so great a man that one quarter of England shall be under your control."

The knight, on hearing them speak thus, was exceedingly enraged, and eyeing them with angry looks said, "Begone, scoundrels and false traitors, would you have me desert my natural lord for such a company of knaves as you are? Would you have me dishonour myself? I would rather have you all hanged, for that must be your end." On saying this, he attempted to mount his horse; but his foot slipping from the stirrup, the animal took fright, and the mob upon this cried out, "Put him to death." Upon hearing which, Sir Robert let go his horse, and drawing a handsome Bordeaux sword, began to skirmish, and soon cleared the crowd from about him in an admirable manner. Many attempted to close with him; but each stroke he gave cut off heads, arms, feet, or legs, so that the boldest became afraid to approach him. The wretches were 40,000 in number, and he killed twelve of them and wounded many before they overpowered him, which at last they did with their missiles; and as soon as he was down, they cut off his arms and legs and rent his body piecemeal. Such was the pitiable end of Sir Robert Salle.

On Saturday morning the king left the Wardrobe and went

to Westminster, when he and his lords heard mass in the abbey. In this church there is a statue of our Lady, in which the kings of England have much faith. To this on the present occasion King Richard and his nobles paid their devotions and made their offerings; they then rode in company along the causeway to London; but when they had proceeded a short distance, King Richard, with a few attendants, turned up a road on the left to go away from the city.

This day all the rabble again assembled under Wat Tyler, Jack Straw, and John Ball, at a place called Smithfield, where every Friday the horsemarket is kept. There were present about 20,000, and many more were in the city, breakfasting, and drinking Rhenish wine and Malmsey Madeira in the taverns and in the houses of the Lombards, without paying for anything; and happy was he who could give them good cheer to satisfy them. Those who collected in Smithfield had with them the king's banner, which had been given to them the preceding evening; and the wretches, notwithstanding this, wanted to pillage the city, their leaders saying that hitherto they had done nothing. "The pardon which the king has granted will be of no use to us; but if we be of the same mind, we shall pillage this rich and powerful town of London before those from Essex, Suffolk, Cambridge, Bedford, Warwick, Reading, Lancashire, Arundel, Guildford, Coventry, Lynne, Lincoln, York, and Durham shall arrive; for they are on their road, and we know for certain that Vaquier and Lister will conduct them hither. Let us, then, be beforehand in plundering the wealth of the city; for if we wait for their arrival, they will wrest it from us." To this opinion all had agreed, when the king, attended by 60 horses, appeared in sight; he was at the time not thinking of the rabble, but had intended to continue his ride without coming into London; however, when he arrived before the abbey of St. Bartholomew, which is in Smithfield, and saw the crowd of people, he stopped, saying that he would ascertain what they wanted, and endeavour to appease them. Wat Tyler, seeing the king and his party, said to his men, "Here is the king, I will go and speak with him; do you not stir until I give you a signal." He then made a motion with his hand, and added, "When you shall see me make this signal, then step forward, and kill every one except the king; but hurt him not, for he is young, and we can do what we please with him; carrying him with us through England, we shall be lords of the whole country, without any opposition." On saying which he spurred his horse and galloped up to the king, whom he approached so near that his horse's head touched the crupper of the king's horse.

His first words were these: "King, dost thou see all these men here?" "Yes," replied the king; "why dost thou ask?" "Because they are all under my command, and have sworn by their faith and loyalty to do whatsoever I shall order." "Very well," said the king: "I have no objection to it." Tyler, who was only desirous of a riot, made answer: "And thou thinkest, king, that these people, and as many more in the city, also under my command, ought to depart without having thy letters? No, indeed, we will carry them with us." "Why," replied the king, "it has been so ordered, and the letters will be delivered out one after another; but, friend, return to thy companions, and tell them to depart from London; be peaceable and careful of yourselves; for it is our determination that you shall all have the letters by towns and villages according to our agreement." As the king finished speaking, Wat Tyler, casting his eyes round, spied a squire attached to the king's person bearing a sword. This squire Tyler mortally hated, and on seeing him, cried out, "What has thou there? give me thy dagger." "I will not," said the squire: "why should I give it thee?" The king upon this said, "Give it to him; give it to him"; which the squire did, though much against his will. When Tyler took the dagger, he began to play with it in his hand, and again addressing the squire, said, "Give me that sword." "I will not," replied the squire, "for it is the king's sword, and thou being but a mechanic art not worthy to bear it; and if only thou and I were together, thou wouldst not have dared to say what thou hast, for a heap of gold as large as this church." "By my troth," answered Tyler, "I will not eat this day before I have thy head." At these words the Mayor of London, with about twelve men, rode forward, armed under their robes, and seeing Tyler's manner of behaving, said, "Scoundrel, how dare you to behave thus in the king's presence?" The king, also enraged at the fellow's impudence, said to the mayor, "Lay hands on him." Whilst King Richard was giving this order, Tyler still kept up the conversation, saying to the mayor: "What have you to do with it; does what I have said concern you?" "It does," replied the mayor, who found himself supported by the king, and then added: "I will not live a day unless you pay for your insolence." Upon saying which, he drew a kind of scimitar, and struck Tyler such a blow on the head as felled him to his horse's feet. As soon as the rebel was down, he was surrounded on all sides, in order that his own men might not see him; and one of the king's squires, by name John Standwich, immediately leaped from his horse, and drawing his sword, thrust it into his belly, so that he died.

When the rebels found that their leader was dead, they drew up in a sort of battle array, each man having his bow bent before him. The king at this time certainly hazarded much, though it turned out most fortunately for him; for as soon as Tyler was on the ground, he left his attendants, giving orders that no one should follow him, and riding up to the rebels, who were advancing to revenge their leader's death, said, "Gentlemen, what are you about: you shall have me for your captain: I am your king, remain peaceable." The greater part, on hearing these words, were quite ashamed, and those among them who were inclined for peace began to slip away; the riotous ones, however, kept their ground. The king returned to his lords, and consulted with them what next should be done. Their advice was to make for the fields; but the mayor said that to retreat would be of no avail. "It is quite proper to act as we have done; and I reckon we shall very soon receive assistance from our good friends in London."

While things were in this state, several persons ran to London, crying out, "They are killing the king and our mayor"; upon which alarm, all those of the king's party sallied out towards Smithfield, in number about seven or eight thousand. Among the first came Sir Robert Knolles and Sir Perducas d'Albret, well attended; then several aldermen, with upwards of 600 men-at-arms, and a powerful man of the city, by name Nicholas Bramber, the king's draper, bringing with him a large force on foot. These all drew up opposite to the rebels, who had with them the king's banner, and showed as if they intended to maintain their ground by offering combat.

The king created at this time three knights: Sir William Walworth, Sir John Standwich, and Sir Nicholas Bramber. As soon as Sir Robert Knolles arrived at Smithfield, his advice was immediately to fall upon the insurgents, and slay them; but King Richard would not consent to this. "You shall first go to them," he said "and demand my banner; we shall then see how they will behave; for I am determined to have this by fair means or foul." The new knights were accordingly sent forward, and on approaching the rebels made signs to them not to shoot, as they wished to speak with them; and when within hearing, said, "Now attend; the king orders you to send back his banners; and if you do so, we trust he will have mercy upon you." The banners, upon this, were given up directly, and brought to the king. It was then ordered, under pain of death, that all those who had obtained the king's letters should deliver them up. Some did so, but not all; and the king on receiving them had them torn in pieces in their presence. You must know that from the time the king's banners were surrendered, these fellows kept no order; but the greater part, throwing their bows upon the ground, took to their heels and returned to London. Sir Robert Knolles was very angry that the rebels were not attacked at once and all slain; however, the king would not consent to it, saying that he would have ample revenge without doing so.

When the rabble had dispersed, the king and his lords, to their great joy, returned in good array to London, whence the king immediately took the road to the Wardrobe, to visit the princess his mother, who had remained there two days and two nights under the greatest apprehension. On seeing her son, the good lady was much rejoiced, and said, "Ah, ah, fair son, what pain and anguish have I not suffered for you this day!" "Madam," replied the king, "I am well assured of that; but now rejoice, and thank God, for it behoves us to praise him, as I have this day regained my inheritance—the kingdom of England, which I had lost."

This whole day the king passed with his mother, and a proclamation was made through all the streets that every person who was not an inhabitant of London, and who had not resided there for a whole year, should instantly depart; for if any of a contrary description were found in the city on Sunday morning at sunrise, they would be arrested as traitors to the king, and have their heads cut off. This proclamation no one dared to infringe, but all instantly departed to their homes quite discomfited.

John Ball and Jack Straw were found hidden in an old ruin, where they had secreted themselves, thinking to steal away when things were quiet; but this they were prevented doing, for their own men betrayed them. With this capture the king and his barons were much pleased, and had their heads cut off, as was that of Tyler's, and fixed on London-bridge, in the room of those whom these wretches themselves had placed there.

News of this total defeat of the rebels in London was sent throughout the neighbouring counties, in order that all those who were on their way to London might hear of it; and as soon as they did so, they instantly returned to their homes, without daring to advance further.

We must now turn our attention to the Duke of Lancaster, who, during the time of the rebellion in England, had remained on the borders of Scotland, negotiating a peace with the Earl of Douglas, and certain other barons; which business was so ably conducted on both sides, that a truce for three years was agreed to between the two kingdoms. As soon as this truce was concluded, the lords of the two countries visited each other with much respect; and the Earl of Douglas said to the Duke of Lancaster, "My lord, we are well informed of the rebellion of the populace in England, and what peril the kingdom is in from this event; and as we look upon you as a valiant and prudent man, we place at your service five or six hundred spears." The duke did not refuse the offer, and further requested of the earl passports for himself and his people to return through Scotland to Berwick, which were immediately granted. At Berwick, however, the duke was much surprised and enraged at finding the gates closed against him by Sir Matthew Redmayne, the governor, who informed him that his orders were from the king, and that what he had done was very much against his own will. The duke upon this returned to Roxburgh, where the Scottish lords received him courteously; and in order to pay him greater honour, the Earl of Douglas and some other barons delivered up to him the castle of Edinburgh, where he continued to reside until he received intelligence from England authorizing his return, which, to say the truth, was not so soon as he wished. You must know that the duke was thus treated, because it was currently reported through England, during the time of the rebellion, that he had become a traitor to his lord and king, and had turned to the Scottish party.

After the death of Tyler, Jack Straw, John Ball, and several others, the people being somewhat appeased, the king resolved to visit his bailiwicks, castlewicks, and stewardships, in order to punish the principal insurgents, and to recover the letters of pardon which had been forced from him, as well as to settle other matters tending to the peace of the realm. By a secret summons he assembled 500 spears and as many archers, and with them took the road to Kent, in which quarter the rebellion had first broken out. The first place he stopped at was a village called Comprinke; here he ordered the mayor and all the men of the village, to be called, with whom one of his council remonstrated, telling them how much they had erred, and because this mischief, which had nearly proved the ruin of England, must have had some advisers, it was better that the ringleaders should suffer than the whole; his majesty, therefore, demanded, under pain of incurring his displeasure for ever, that those should be pointed out who had been most culpable. When the people heard this, and saw that the innocent might escape by pointing out the guilty, they looked at each other, and said: "My lord, here is one by whom this town was excited." Immediately the person alluded to was taken and hanged, as were seven others. The letters-patent, which had been granted, were demanded back, and given up to the king's officer, who tore them in pieces, saying, "We command, in the king's name, all you who are here assembled to depart every one to his own home in peace; that you never more rebel against the king or against his ministers. By the punishment which has been inflicted, your former deeds are pardoned." The people with one voice exclaimed, "God bless the king and his good council." In the same manner they acted in many other places in Kent, and, indeed, throughout England, so that upwards of 1,500 were beheaded or hanged; and it was not till all this was over, and everything quiet, that the king sent for the Duke of Lancaster from Scotland. . . .

PART II

The Spirit of the Age

Imagination and Thought
in the Middle Ages

C. S. LEWIS

1

THE MAN OF THE Middle Ages had many ignorances in common with the savages of more modern times, and some of his beliefs would certainly suggest savage parallels to an anthropologist. But it would be very wrong to infer from this that he was at all like a savage. I do not only, or chiefly, mean that such a view would depress medieval man beneath his true dignity. That's as may be; some might prefer the Polynesian. The point is that, whether for better or for worse, he was different. He was in a different predicament and had a different history. Even when he thought or did the same things as savages, he had come to them by a different route. We should be quite on the wrong track if we sought the origin, at least the immediate origin, of even the strangest medieval doctrines in what some even call pre-logical thinking.

Here is an example. In a twelfth-century English poem call the *Brut* we read the following: "There dwell in the air many kinds of creatures which shall remain there till doomsday comes. Some of them are good and some do evil." These beings are mentioned to account for the birth of a child for whom no human father could be detected; one of them had in fact begotten Merlin. Now, if we considered this passage *in vacuo,* we might very well suppose that the poet's mind was working just like that of a savage, and that his belief in aerial daemons sprang as directly from a tribal culture as coarse grass from uncultivated soil. In reality, we know that he is getting it all from a book, from Geoffrey of Monmouth's Latin History of the Kings of Britain, and that Geoffrey is get-

Chapter 3 from STUDIES IN MEDIEVAL AND RENAISSANCE LITERATURE (1966) by C. S. Lewis. Reprinted by permission of the Cambridge University Press. This chapter was originally delivered in 1956 as a pair of lectures to an audience of scientists in Cambridge.

ting it from the second-century *De Deo Socratis* of Apuleius, who, in his turn, is reproducing the pneumatology of Plato. Trace that pneumatology back for a few centuries or so and then at last you may come to whatever roots it had in a culture really close to savagery and a thinking possibly pre-logical. But all that is almost as remote from the medieval English poet as it is from us. He tells us about the aerial daemons neither because his own poetic imagination invented them, nor because they are the spontaneous reaction of his age and culture to the forces of nature, but because he has read about them in a book.

Here is another. In a French poem of the fourteenth century Nature personified appears as a character and has a conversation with another personage called *Grâcedieu*. Grace-of-God would, for various reasons, be a misleading translation, so I will call her *Supernature*. And Nature says to Supernature "The circle of the cold moon truly marks the boundary between your realm and mine forever." Here again we might well suppose the savage mind at work; what more natural than to locate the houses of the gods at a reasonable distance and choose the Moon for the gate between their world and ours? Yet, almost certainly that is not what is happening. The idea that the orbit of the Moon is a great boundary between two regions of the universe is Aristotelian. It is based on a contrast which naturally forced itself upon one whose studies were so often biological and psychological, but also sometimes astronomical. The part of the world which we inhabit, the Earth, is the scene of generation and decay and therefore of continual change. Such regularities as he would observe in it seemed to him imperfect; terrestrial nature carried things on, he thought, not always but "on the whole" in the same way. It was clear from observing the weather that this irregularity extended a good way upwards above the surface of the Earth. But not all the way. Above the variable sky there were the heavenly bodies which seemed to have been perfectly regular in their behavior ever since the first observations were made and of which none, to his knowledge, had ever been seen to come into existence or to decay. The Moon was obviously the lowest of these. Hence he divided the universe at the Moon; all above that was necessary, regular, and eternal, all below it, contingent, irregular and perishable. And of course, for any Greek, what is necessary and eternal is more divine. This, with a Christian coloring added, fully accounts for the passage we began with.

Both examples—and it would not be difficult to cite more—point to the same truth, and it is a truth basic for any understanding of the Middle Ages. Their culture is through and through a bookish culture. Millions, no doubt, were illiterate; the masters, however, were literate, and not only literate but scholarly and even pedantic. The peculiar predicament of medieval man was in fact just this: he was a literate man who had lost a great many of his books and forgotten how to read all his Greek books. He works with the rather chancy selection he has. In that way the Middle Ages were much less like an age which has not yet been civilized than like one which has survived the loss of civilization. An exaggerated, but not wholly fake, model would be a party of shipwrecked people setting to work to try to build up a culture on an uninhabited island and depending on the old collection of books which happened to be on board their ship.

Of course this is grossly oversimplified and I must immediately take notice of one complication which may have already occurred to you. Genealogically, and in some measure culturally, the medieval European had roots in the barbarian life of the north and west as well as in Mediterranean civilization. Along that line, it may be said, he had a much closer link with primitive thought than through its far-off echoes in Latin literature. This of course is true. Fragments of indigenous and spontaneous mythology survive; Germanic, in Anglo-Saxon, Old Norse, and Old High German, or Celtic (to some undefined extent) in the French romances. Popular literature, such as the ballads, may throw up more or less disguised fragments of this at quite late periods. But we must insist that these things loom much larger in the popular picture of the Middle Ages than they did in the reality. By the time we reach the High Middle Age all the old Germanic literature has been forgotten and the languages in which it was written are unknown. And as for the ballad and the romance, it is important to realize that both these attractive products are the reverse of typical. It is easy to be deceived here, because it was the ballad and the romance which first excited modern interest in the Middle Ages; medieval studies began there. The reason is simple. These forms appealed to the Romanticism of the eighteenth and nineteenth centuries. Even now many of us were first lured to medieval studies by this romantic attraction. Even now the "man in the street" thinks of the Middle Ages, if at all, in terms of the romances; popular iconography—a joke in *Punch,* an advertisement—wishing to suggest the medieval, depicts a knight in armor riding through desolate country, adding castles, dragons, and distressed damsels *quantum suff*. But the paradox is that the note is one which the real Middle Ages struck only in a minority of ballads and romances and hardly at all in any other form. That boundlessness, indefiniteness, suggestiveness are not the common or characteristic medieval mood. The real temper of those ages was not romantic. The Arthurian stories represent, perhaps, truancy or escape from habitual concerns.

Characteristically, medieval man was not a dreamer nor a spiritual adventurer; he was an organizer, a codifier, a man of system. His ideal could be not unfairly summed up in the old housewifely maxim "A place for everything, and everything in its (right) place." Three things are typical of him. First, that small minority of his cathedrals in which the design of the architect was actually achieved (usually, of course, it was overtaken by the next wave of architectural fashion long before it was finished). I am thinking of a thing like Salisbury. Second, the *Summa* of Thomas Aquinas. And thirdly, the *Divine Comedy* of Dante. In all these alike we see the tranquil, indefatigable, exultant energy of a passionately logical mind ordering a huge mass of heterogeneous details into unity. They desire unity and proportion, all the classical virtues, just as keenly as the Greeks did. But they have a greater and more varied collection of things to fit in. And they delight to do it. Hence the *Comedy* which is, I suppose, the supreme achievement: crowded and varied as a railway station on a bank holiday, but patterned and schematized as a battalion on a ceremonial parade.

You see how this arises naturally from their situation? I described them as literate people who had lost most of their books. And what survived was, to some extent, a chance collection. It contained ancient Hebrew, classical Greek, classical Roman, decadent Roman and early Christian elements. It had reached them by various routes. All Plato had disappeared except part of the *Timaeus* in a Latin version: one of the greatest, but also one of the least typical, of the dialogues. Aristotle's logic was at first missing, but you had a Latin translation of a very late Greek introduction to it. Astronomy and medicine, and (later) Aristotle, came in Latin translations of Arabic translations of the Greek. That is the typical descent of learning: from Athens to Hellenistic Alexandria, from Alexandria to Baghdad, from Baghdad, *via* Sicily, to the university of Paris, and thence all over Europe. . . . A scratch collection, a corpus that frequently contradicted itself. But here we touch on a real credulity in the medieval mind. Faced with this self-contradictory corpus, they hardly ever decided that one of the authorities was simply right and the others wrong; never that all were wrong. To be sure, in the last resort it was taken for granted that the Christian writers must be right as against the pagans. But it was hardly ever allowed to come to the last resort. It was apparently difficult to believe that anything in the books—so costly, fetched from so far, so old, often so lovely to the eye and hand, was just plumb wrong. No; if Seneca and St. Paul disagreed with one another, and both with Cicero, and all these with Boethius, there must be some explanation which would harmonize them. What was not true literally might be true in some other sense; what was false *simpliciter* might be true *secundum quid*. And so on, through every possible subtlety and ramification. It is out of this that the medieval picture of the universe is evolved: a chance collection of materials, an inability to say "Bosh," a temper systematic to the point of morbidity, great mental powers, unwearied patience, and a robust delight in their work. All these factors led them to produce the greatest, most complex, specimen of syncretism or harmonization which, perhaps, the world has ever known. They tidied up the universe. To that tidy universe, and above all to its effect on the imagination, I now turn.

I assume that everyone knows, more or less, its material layout: a motionless Earth at the center, transparent spheres revolving round it, of which the lowest, slowest, nearest and smallest carries the Moon, and thence upwards in the order Mercury, Venus, the Sun, Mars, Jupiter, Saturn; beyond these, all the stars in one sphere; beyond that, a sphere which carries no light but merely imparts movement to those below it; beyond that, the Empyrean, the boundary of the *mundus,* the beginning of the infinite true "Heaven."

No one, as far as I know, has exaggerated the emotional and imaginative difference between such a universe and that which we now believe ourselves to inhabit; but a great many people have misconceived the nature of the difference. The cardinal error (ubiquitous in earlier modern writers, and still clung to by some who should know better today) may be expressed in the following words. "The Earth, both by her supposed size and by her central position, had, for medieval thinkers, an importance to which we now know that she is by no means entitled." Hence, of course, the probable conclu-

sion that their theology—here, once more, pre-logical thinking might be suspected—was the offspring of their cosmology.
The truth seems to me the reverse. Their theology might be
thought to imply an Earth which counted for a good deal in
the universe and was central in dignity as well as in space;
the odd thing is that their cosmology does not, in any obvious
sense, encourage this view.

First, as regards size. That the Earth is, by any cosmic
scale, insignificant, is a truth that was forced on every intelligent man as soon as serious astronomical observations began
to be made. I have already said that Aristotle thought the region above the Moon more divine than the airy, watery, and
earthy realm below it. He also thought it incomparably large.
As he says in the *Metaphysics*, "The perceptible world
around us"—that is, the realm of growth, decay and weather—
"is, so to speak, a nothing if considered as part of the
whole." Later in Ptolemy's compendium, which transmitted
Greek astronomy to the Middle Ages, a more precise statement is made; the Earth, we are told, must, for astronomical
purposes, be regarded as having no magnitude at all, as a
point. This was accepted by the Middle Ages. It was not
merely accepted by scholars; it was re-echoed by moralists
and poets again and again. To judge from the texts, medieval
man thought about the insignificance of Earth more persist-
ently, if anything, than his modern descendants. We even find
quite popular texts hammering the lesson home by those
methods which the scientific popularizer uses today. We are
told how long it would take you to get to the sphere of the
fixed stars if you traveled so many miles a day. The figure
brings the distance out at something near 118 million miles.

Now of course this is a small distance compared with those
of which modern astronomers talk. But we are here considering not the accuracy of the figure but its imaginative and
emotional impact. From that point of view I maintain that
the difference between a million, a hundred millions, and a
million millions, is wholly negligible. All these figures can be
used, manipulated, with equal ease by anyone who can do
simple arithmetic; none of them can at all be imagined in the
sense of "visualized," and those who have most imagination
know this best.

From that point of view, then, the medieval model of the
universe is on a par with the Newtonian (I do not say, with
the modern, for I want to defer the consideration of it). Either will allow you to lose yourself in unimaginable distances,

to sink and say with Leopardi *il naufragar m'è dolce in questo mare*, and to see the Earth as a speck of dust—if, of course, that is the sort of thing you want to do. And now comes the point I really want to make. I have not said that the difference between the medieval and, say, the Newtonian picture was less than our grandfathers supposed. It was quite as great. But it was not the kind of difference we have been taught to expect.

What it really was I can, here and now, only suggest. The thing really needs to be learned not from a lecture but (you are scientists) by an experiment; an experiment on one's imagination. It is a simple one. Go out on any starry night and walk alone for half an hour, resolutely assuming that the pre-Copernican astronomy is true. Look up at the sky with that assumption in your mind. The real difference between living in that universe and living in ours will then, I predict, begin to dawn on you.

You will be looking at a world unimaginably large but quite definitely finite. At no speed possible to man, in no lifetime possible to man, could you ever reach its frontier, but the frontier is there; hard, clear, sudden as a national frontier. And secondly, because the Earth is an absolute center, and Earthwards from any part of this immense universe is downwards, you will find that you are looking at the planets and stars in terms not merely of "distance" but of that very special kind of distance which we call "height." They are not only a long way from the Earth but a long way above it. I need hardly point out that height is a very much livelier notion than distance; it has, the moment it is imagined, commerce with our nerves, with all our racial and infantile terrors, with our pleasures as mountaineers, our love of wide prospects, and a whole vast network of ethical and social metaphors which we could not shake off even if we tried. Now these two factors taken together—enormous but finite size, and distances which, however vast, remain unambiguously vertical, and indeed vertiginous—at once present you with something which differs from the Newtonian picture rather as a great building differs from a great jungle. You can lose yourself in infinity; there is indeed nothing much else you can do with it. It arouses questions, it prompts to a certain kind of wonder and reverie, usually a somber kind, so that Wordsworth can speak of "melancholy space and doleful time" or Carlyle can call the starry sky "a sad sight." But it answers no questions; necessarily shapeless and trackless, patient of no absolute order or direction, it leads, after a little, to boredom or despair or (often) to the haunting conviction that it must be an illusion. Earth and man are, if you like, dwarfed by it, but not much more dwarfed than the solar system, or the galaxy, or anything else. One cannot be, in any very important sense, small where size has ceased to have a meaning. The old universe was wholly different in its effect. It was an answer, not a question. It offered not a field for musing but a single overwhelming object; an object which at once abashes and exalts the mind. For in it there is a final standard of size. The Primum Mobile is really large because it is the largest corporeal thing there is. We are really small because our whole Earth is a speck compared with the Primum Mobile.

I have been speaking so far only of dimensions. But the effect of the old model becomes even more interesting when we consider order. It is not merely very large, it is a whole of finely graded parts. Everything descends from the circumference with a steady diminution of size, speed, power and dignity. This ninefold division is harmoniously crossed by a threefold division. All above the Empyrean is in a special, immaterial, sense "Heaven," full of the Divine Substance. From the Empyrean down to the Moon is the realm of aether —that strange half-matter in which so many different ages have believed, on what seems to a layman very inadequate evidence—changeless, necessary, not subject to Fortune. From the Moon down to the Earth is the realm of air (for they thought the air extended to the moon's orbit), which is also the realm of luck, change, birth, death, and contingence.

You see why I compared it to a building—though indeed any great, complex work of art—*Paradise Lost* or Euclid's *Elements* or Spinoza's *Ethics* or Beethoven's Ninth Symphony—would have done almost as well. It is a structure, a finished work, a unity articulated through a great and harmonious plurality. It evokes not mere wonder but admiration. It provides food for thought and satisfaction for our aesthetic nature. I think everyone will see what I mean if I say that in passing from the Newtonian to the Ptolemaic cosmos one passes from the romantic to the classical. Milton could describe the moon as looking

> Like one that had bin led astray
> Through the Heav'ns wide pathles way.

That hits off admirably the feeling many generations now have had when they look at the night sky: I do not think any ancient or medieval man would have felt so. That particular

charm, the charm of the pathless, was one that the old universe lacked; it had a severer, a more robust attraction and
appealed to a more formal imagination.

After the dimensions and the order, we must consider the
dynamics. I have already said that movement Earthward
from any part of the whole was conceived as movement
downward. In that sense they understood what we would call
gravitation. Thus one philosopher says that if you could bore
a hole through the Earth and drop a stone down, the stone
would come to rest at the center. And in the *Comedy*, Dante
and Virgil come to the center where they find Lucifer embed-
ded and have to climb down his shaggy sides in order to continue their journey to the Antipodes; but Dante finds to his
surprise that after they have passed his waist they have to
climb *up* to his feet. For they have of course passed the center
of gravitation. But they never talk of gravitation. Their way of
describing it is to say that every natural object has a native or
"proper" place and is always "trying" or "desiring" to get
there. When unimpeded, flame moves upwards and solid bodies move downwards because they want to go, you may call it,
"home." Is this animism? Did they really think that all matter
was sentient? Apparently not. They will distinguish animate
and inanimate as clearly as we do; will say that stones, for example, have only being; vegetables being and life; animals,
being, life and sense; man, being, life, sense and reason. The
truth is that their language about inanimate bodies was the
same kind of language that the modern man uses—I mean,
the modern "plain" man, not the modern scientist or philosopher. When a modern says that the stone fell "in obedience to
the law of gravitation," he does not really think there is literally a law or literal obedience; that the stone, on being re-
leased, whips out a little book of statutes, finds the chapter
and paragraph relevant to its predicament, and decides it had
better be a law-abiding stone and "come quiet." Nor did the
medieval man believe that the stone really felt homesick, or
felt at all. Both ways of putting it are analogical; neither
speaker would usually know any way of expressing the facts
except by an analogy.

But of course it makes a great difference to the tone of
your mind which analogy you adopt—whether you fill your
universe with phantom police-courts and traffic regulations,
or with phantom longings and endeavors. The second alternative, which the Middle Ages adopted, is connected with another and more far-reaching doctrine which is not merely

analogical. We are now approaching the junction between their cosmology and their theology. The theology involved is, however, not that of the Bible, the Fathers, or the Councils, but that of Aristotle. Of course they thought it consistent with Christianity; whether they were right in so thinking is not my concern.

The infinite, according to Aristotle, is not actual. No infinite object exists; no infinite process occurs. Hence we cannot explain the movement of one body by the movement of another and so on forever. No such infinite series could, he thought, exist. All the movements of the universe must therefore, in the last resort, result from a compulsive force exercised by something immovable. He thought that such an Unmoved Mover could move other things only by being their end or object or (if you like) target—what he calls their "Final Cause"—not as one billiard ball moves another, but as food moves the hungry man, as the mistress moves her lover, as truth moves the philosophical inquirer. He calls this Unmoved Mover either "God" or "Mind." It moves the Primum Mobile (which of course sets all the inferior bodies in motion) by love. But notice that this does not mean what a Christian would naturally mean by the word. There is no question here of a beneficent Being loving the world He has created and descending to redeem it. God, in Aristotle, moves the world by being loved, not by loving; by being the supremely desirable object. This of course implies not only consciousness but high rationality on the part of that which is moved. Accordingly we find (not now by analogy, but in strictest fact) that in every sphere there is a rational creature called an Intelligence which is compelled to move, and therefore to keep his sphere moving, by his incessant desire for God. It was disputed whether the Intelligence is "in" the sphere as the soul is in the body (in which case the sphere must be envisaged as an eternal and exalted animal) or as a man is in a ship (in which case the corporeal sphere is a kind of instrument). On the whole the second view won. A modern may ask why a love for God should lead to perpetual rotation. I think, because this love or appetite for God is a desire to participate as much as possible in His nature; i.e. to imitate it. And the nearest approach to His eternal immobility, the second best, is eternal regular movement in the most perfect figure, which, for any Greek, is the circle. Hence the universe is kept going by the continual effort of its most excellent parts (each a little slower and feebler than the one above it) to conform their behavior to a model of which they always fall short. That of course is the real meaning of Dante's (often misunderstood) line about "the love that moves the sun and the other stars." Even so, love is perhaps too ethical a word; "appetite" would be better. In this scheme God is the quarry, the Intelligences the huntsmen; God is the mistress, all things else the suitors; God the candle, and the universe the moth.

2

In my last lecture I suggested the experiment of a starlit walk taken with the assumption that Ptolemaic astronomy is true. In order to bring that old model into fuller activity, I now want to recall an experience which, I suppose, everyone has had; that of coming out from some indoor function of pomp and importance, an opera or a debate or a feast, and suddenly looking up at the cold stars above the housetops. What seemed so big while we were inside is all at once dwarfed. The sky is like an ironic comment on this and on all other human concerns. If we remember our Pascal, we may even murmur "The silence of those eternal spaces frightens me." After that, we may rally and hit back and say, still using Pascal, that though we are small and transitory as dew-drops,* still we are dew-drops that can think, which is (we presume) more than can be said for the galaxies. Let us now try to understand why neither of these reactions—neither the initial deflation nor the come-back—was at all likely to occur to a man of the Middle Ages.

He did not think that the spaces he looked up at were silent, or dark or empty. Far from being silent, they were perpetually filled with sweet, immeasurable sound. The vast hollow spheres, turning each at its proper interval inside its superior, gave out a blended harmony. There were various explanations of the fact that we do not hear it. One of the oldest and most pleasing was based on the travelers' tale that those who lived near the great cataract on the Nile were unconscious of its noise. Because they had always heard it, they never heard it. The same would obviously hold true in an even higher degree of the music of the spheres. That is the only sound which has never for one split second ceased in any part of the universe; with this positive we have no negative to contrast. Presumably if (*per impossibile*) it ever did

* Lewis has confused Pascal's *roseau* (reed) with *rosée* (dew). [Ed.]

stop, then with terror and dismay, with a dislocation of our whole auditory life, we should feel that the bottom had dropped out of our lives, but it never does. The music which is too familiar to be heard enfolds us day and night in all ages.

Nor were those high regions dark. The darkness in which the stars (for us) are set is merely the darkness of the long, conical shadow cast by the Earth when the sun is below our feet. They knew, from their theory of lunar eclipses, that the apex of this dark cone must fall well above the moon. Beyond that apex the higher heavens are bathed in perpetual sunshine. In a sense, no doubt, we should say the same. But then we are aware (as they, I think, were not) of the part played by the air in diffusing sunlight and producing the bubble of luminosity which we call day; we have even, in stratospheric ascents, gone high enough to see the blue curtain grow thin at the zenith so that blue turns to black and the night of space almost shows through. They knew that, up yonder, one was above the air, in whatever they meant by aether; they did not know that one would see the sun flaming in a black pit. They thought on the contrary that they would be floating (for Milton is here a medieval) in

> those happie climes that lye
> Where day never shuts his eye,
> Up in the broad fields of the skye.

And these spaces, bright and resonant, were also inhabited. We have already peopled them with the Intelligences who either animate or guide the spheres. Distinct from these, but of course equally immortal and superhuman, are the angels. Their natural habitat is between the Empyrean and the Moon and their number is probably enormous. Unlike the aerial daemons who live between Moon and Earth, they have no bodies —such, at least, was the view that finally prevailed—but are naked minds. We, like them, are rational, but there is a great difference. We have an immediate and intuitive grasp only of axioms and have to seek all other knowledge by the laborious process of discursive thinking. They are wholly intuitive; concepts are as palpable to them as apples or pennies are to us. In fact, their reason is to ours as noon to dusk. Clearly when you look up at a sky peopled by such creatures as these, it is just no good asserting "I am a dew-drop that thinks." The very necessity of "thinking" (as we ordinarily understand the word) is the measure of our inferiority.

Understand that the vast majority of these bodiless minds have no concern at all with us. We touch only the lowest fringe of angelic life. For angelic life also is graded; the word *angel* is, rather unfortunately, used both for the whole lot and also for the lowest rank—just as we use *sailors* sometimes in contrast to ships' officers, but sometimes in a sense that covers all who enable the ship to sail. They are ordered in nine classes which are arranged in three groups of three classes each. The top hierarchy, which consists of the creatures classified as Seraphim, Cherubim, and Thrones, looks exclusively God-wards, absorbed in contemplation of the Divine essence, and unconcerned with the created universe. The next hierarchy (Dominations, Virtues, and Powers) has some responsibility for the general order of nature. The lowest hierarchy deals with human affairs; Principalities with the destiny of nations, Archangels and Angels, in varying ways, with those of individuals. You will notice that even at such a unique crisis as the Annunciation the Mother of Christ was visited only by an Archangel, a member of the lowest class but one. That gets the perspective right. It is this conception, as well as the poet's own genius, which gives to Dante's angels a sublimity and masculinity never captured by later art. It is the loss of this conception which finally vulgarizes the angels into those consumptive girls with wings that figure in so much Victorian stained glass. The full degradation of the Cherub—the fat baby who has played that role ever since Raphael—will perhaps be clearest if we remember that the word probably comes from the same root as *gryphon*. Even for Chaucer a cherub was a creature of fire: not at all "cuddly."

But I must crowd the sky a little more. Medieval man looked up at a sky not only melodious, sunlit, and splendidly inhabited, but also incessantly active; he looked at agents to which he, and the whole earth, were patients. Besides the Intelligences and the angelic hierarchies there are the planets themselves. Each of them is doing things to us at every moment. First, on the physical side, the beams of each planet (which penetrate through the Earth's crust) find the appropriate soil and turn it into the appropriate metal; Saturn thus producing lead, Mars iron, the Moon silver, and so forth. The Moon's connection with silver, and the Sun's with gold, may be real survivals (at many removes) of pre-logical, pictorial, thinking. Venus is, perhaps, a maker of copper because she was, centuries earlier, Kupris, the lady of Cyprus, and that accursed island produced copper in ancient times. Why Saturn made lead, or Jove tin, I do not know.

But of course, as everyone has heard, the planets had a

more than physical effect. They influenced the course of
events and they influenced human psychology. Born under Saturn, you were disposed to melancholy; born under Venus, to
amorousness. At this point, clearly, there is a rich survival of
classical paganism into medieval culture. And of course the
names of the planets, and their representations in art, are
those of the ancient planetary gods. As far as my reading
goes, no one appears to have been at all worried about it.
There was, indeed, a quarrel between the theologians and the
astrologers, but not exactly about that. So far as I know, no
theologian denied the general theory of planetary influences.
The important question, theologically, was whether the planets compelled or merely disposed men to action. If they compelled, then of course there was an end of human freedom
and responsibility. If they merely disposed, then planetary influence, like heredity or health or education, was merely part
of the concrete situation handed over to the individual to do
the best he could with. The theologians were in fact, as so
often, fighting against determinism. Nor were they fighting
against a phantom: in Renaissance times, if not before them,
astrological determinism was very widely accepted. It seemed
(odd as this sounds to us) to have the support of age-old experience and common sense, and the theological resistance
seemed idealistic wishful thinking. In the Middle Ages men's
minds no doubt wavered. The ordinary, moderate, respectable
view was summed up in the maxim *sapiens dominabitur astris*;
a wise man, assisted by Grace, could get over a bad horoscope
just as he could get over a naturally bad temper.

That, as I have said, was the important question on the
theoretical level. On the practical level orthodox people,
while admitting planetary influence, strongly disapproved of
"judicial astrology," the lucrative practice of foretelling the
future. They did not need to deny that some astrological predictions of human behavior might be correct. Planetary influence could not remove free will but it could alter the states
of mind and imagination which free will has to deal with. Any
man can master this psychological raw material and thus re-
fute the prediction; but few men do and therefore the predictions will succeed as regards the majority. Just in the same
way and for similar reasons a modern theologian might say
that Marxian predictions based on economic determinism or
Freudian predictions based on psychological determinism will
usually be true, and true about mass-behavior, but not necessarily about a given individual.

I stress the parallel between astrology and more modern forms of determinism in order to bring out a point which, though I have made it elsewhere, is too important to be passed over. We must never allow ourselves to think of astrology as something that belonged to the romantic or dreaming or quasi-mystical side of the mind; above all, we must not connect it with magic. Astrology was a hard-headed, stern, anti-idealistic affair; the creed of men who wanted a universe which admitted no incalculables. Magic sought power over nature; astrology proclaimed nature's power over man. Hence the magician is the ancestor of the modern practicing or "applied" scientist, the inventor; the astrologer, of the nineteenth-century philosophical materialist. Neither figure, by the way, is specially typical of the Middle Ages. Both flourished as much, if not more, in the ancient and in the Renaissance world.

I have already said that the medieval man thought he was looking up at a luminous universe through the dark shadow of the Earth. He was also looking up at the region of aether through the region of air. The air was the medium through which all the influences from above reached him. The whole air could become healthy or unhealthy as the result of certain conjunctions in the upper sky. Hence a medieval doctor could explain widespread illness by saying "It's due to this influence." If he were talking Italian he would no doubt say *questa influenza,* and that word has stuck. I mention the air, however, not merely to bring in that curiosity but for two other reasons.

First: the air is below the Moon. That is, as you have heard, it is excluded from the region of necessity and regularity. In the air, as on the Earth, you have contingence and the irregular; in the air you have the aerial daemons who can, like men, do either good or evil. Here we come to an important difference between medieval and modern man. The ordinary modern (I do not mean the modern scientist) would regard regularity—or, if you like, monotony—as a symptom of inferiority. The fact that the heavenly bodies always behave in the same way, while men do this and that and change their minds, would be for him presumptive evidence that the former are irrational and inanimate and that we, we "dew-drops" that think, are to that extent their betters. For the same reason, if he believed in the aerial dæmons and the planetary Intelligences, he would probably prefer the daemons. The Middle Ages inherited from the Greeks a very different view. Aristotle in the *Metaphysics* remarks that in a household (he is of course assuming a household with slaves) the free members are precisely those who have least chance to live "at random." The slaves can do that; for the free people "everything is mapped out." It is a surprising picture but, I have no doubt, a true one; all ancient literature goes to show that a house-slave is, of all servants, the least like a robot. But I quote it here for a different reason. Though Aristotle does not make it perfectly clear, scholars are agreed that he is intending to compare the heavenly bodies with the free people and the slaves with us. For the heavenly bodies "everything is mapped out," our liberty to live "at random" marks our inferior status. We, like slaves, have or take "spare time" and in it "potter about," chatting, making love, playing games, cracking nuts or "just sitting"; they, like Aristotle himself, have their strict program.

Secondly, the mediation of celestial influences through the air illustrates a principle that runs through the whole universe. Last time I compared that universe to a great building: I should now like to compare it to a fugue—the orderly and varied reiteration of the same "subject." When Donne says

> On man heavens influence workes not so,
> But that it first imprints the ayre,

he is making one statement of that subject. You have here, you see, a triad in the form: Agent (the planets), Medium (the air), Patient (man, and, in general, Earth). It is a triad which still has its appeal; I suppose that aether, at no very distant period, was accepted because we wanted a medium or go-between. But it appealed very much more strongly in the Middle Ages. The triad is repeated on every level.

First, among the angels themselves. The Middle Ages learned all about their triadic organization from a Latin version of a (probably sixth-century) Greek theologian whom we know as Pseudo-Dionysius. The method by which he dovetails his triadic angelology into his Old Testament, where (by our standards) nothing like it is to be found, is a charming example of the process I mentioned before—the great medieval labor of harmonization and syncretism. He points out that in Isaiah vi the angels are crying out "Holy, Holy, Holy" not (as we might expect) to God but to one another. Why? Obviously because each angel is handing on his knowledge of the Divine Sanctity to the angel next below him. The only exception is the Seraphim. They alone of all creatures apprehend God immediately. But as soon as you reach the Cherubim you have a triad; God as agent, Seraphim as medium, Cherubim as patient. Then below that, Seraphim as agent, Cherubim as medium, Thrones as patient. And then the same triad within the second hierarchy and the third; and of course between the first, second, and third hierarchies as wholes. It is a continual devolution as if God, who in a sense does all things, will yet do nothing immediately which can possibly be done through the mediation of His creatures. And as if even this were not enough, we are then told that within each individual angel, of whatever class, the triad occurs again; each has primary faculties which act through the medium of secondary faculties on tertiary faculties. Thus you get not only triad above triad but triad within triad till the mind is dizzy with them.

All this, within the angelic world itself. But the moment one steps outside that world one finds that it itself, collectively, is part of a vaster triad. For God governs the world through the angels; the whole angelic population, without prejudice to its complex internal triads, is the medium between God as agent and nature (or man) as patient. Just so on Earth a king governs the commons through the barons. But this of course was not, for the medieval mind, a mere analogy. It was the real earthly and social reproduction of the triad. I say "social" to distinguish it from "individual"; for within the individual man, as within the individual angel, the triad is repeated.

It is indeed repeated twice, once on the ethical and once on the psychological level. Ethically (and here, at many removes, they were following Plato) the triad is Reason, Emotion, and Appetite. Reason, seated in the head, governs the Appetites, seated in the abdomen or beneath it, by the aid of the more fully human and civilized emotions which were located in the thorax; such things as shame, honor, pity, self-respect, affection. This ethical triad was accepted for millennia. The effort now sometimes made to lead a civilized life on reason alone, rejecting the emotions, the attempt of the monarchic head to rule the plebeian belly without the aid of that aristocracy in the thorax, would have seemed to Plato a rash venture; like what motorists call "driving on your brakes." It is hard on the brakes and leads to skids. On the psychological level the individual triad depends on the doctrine of the triple soul. But the word *anima* had a larger and less exclusively religious range of meaning than *soul;* "life" would sometimes be a better translation. There is vegetable soul, common to all plants, which gives only life; sensitive soul, which gives life and sensation; and rational soul, by which we think. Man of course has all three: when things are going right inside him, his rational governs his vegetable through his sensitive.

A thirteenth-century author, Alanus, works out the theological, the social, and the individual triads in terms of castle (or citadel), city, and the lands beyond the city walls. These are literally given, of course, in the social one; a king in his citadel, the barons in the city, the peasants in the fields outside. In the individual the head is the citadel, where the empress Sapience keeps her court. In the City of the Breast lives the high baronage of Magnanimity. Outside, in the abdomen, or still more outside, in the genitals, live the common appetites. But it is the theological triad that most concerns us at the moment. The castle of God is the Empyrean, the region beyond the outermost sphere. In the city, in the vast ethereal spaces, dwell the cosmic nobility, the nine orders of angels. Down here on Earth there is a place permitted to us "as to aliens," he says, "outside the wall." [1]

Outside the wall—that is the point. Go back for a moment to the experience I mentioned at the beginning; that of looking up at the stars as you come out from an opera or a feast. The full contrast between the medieval experience and ours is only now apparent. For whatever else we feel, we certainly feel that we are looking *out*; out of somewhere warm and lighted into dark, cold, indifferent desolation, out of a house on to the dark waste of the sea. But the medieval man felt he was looking *in*. Here is the outside. The Moon's orbit is the city wall. Night opens the gates for a moment and we catch a glimpse of the high pomps which are going on inside; staring as animals stare at the fires of the encampment they cannot enter, as rustics stare at a city, as suburbia stares at Mayfair.

I have spoken advisedly of "high pomps." My account so far has perhaps made this complex, densely peopled cosmos a little too severe, made the operations of the spheres and the angels sound, as we should say, "a little too like work." I could correct that more easily if I had slides. I am thinking in particular of one picture which represents the Intelligence of the Primum Mobile itself. It is of course wholly symbolical; they knew perfectly well that such a creature—it had no body—could not be literally depicted at all. But the symbol chosen is delightfully significant. It is a picture of a girl dancing and playing a tambourine; a picture of gaiety, almost of frolic. And why not? These spheres are moved by love, by intellectual desire, never sated because they can never com-

[1] *De Planctu Naturae*, P.L. ccx, *Prosa* iii, col. 444 A, B.

pletely assimilate themselves to their object, and never frustrated because they continually do so to the fullest extent which their nature admits or requires. Their existence is thus one of delight. The motions of the universe are to be conceived not as those of a machine or even an army, but rather as a dance, a festival, a symphony, a ritual, a carnival, or all these in one. They are the unimpeded movement of the most perfect impulse towards the most perfect Object.

A modern mind will of course say that the men of that age fashioned heaven in the likeness of Earth and, because they liked high pomps, the mass, coronations, pageants, tournaments, carols, attributed such activities *par excellence* to the translunary world. But remember that they thought it was the other way round. They thought that the ecclesiastical hierarchy and the social hierarchy on Earth were dim reproductions of the celestial hierarchies. The pageantry and ceremony which they indulged in to the utmost of their powers were their attempt to imitate the *modus operandi* of the universe; to live, in that sense, "according to nature." That is why so much medieval art and literature is concerned simply with asserting the nature of things. They liked to tell, and to be told again and again, about the universe I have been describing. Any poet in any poem is liable to start describing the angels, the spheres, the influences, the metals, and a hundred other things I have not had time for—gems, beasts, the Zodiac, the Seven Virtues, the Seven Sins, the Nine Worthies, the nature of winds, the divisions of the soul, herbs, flowers, what not. They wrote it, they sang it, painted it and carved it. Sometimes a whole poem or a whole building seems almost nothing but verbalized or petrified cosmology. In all this I have never found one trace of the savage idea that by representing the things on Earth you somehow helped them to happen in the universe. Their minds were not like that. It was rather the spontaneous desire of us "aliens outside the city wall" to participate as far as we can in the glory of the life of the city; like the Mothers' Union doing in the village hall the same play that was done in London—a legitimate, absurd attempt, and very good fun for all concerned.

Two points which may have caused some discomfort remain. Is it, imaginatively and emotionally, tolerable to have the Earth spatially central and, at the same time, in some other sense, a furlong outside the wall? And is it quite satisfactory to have an infinite space outside the highest heaven? It is, if we take their thought at its highest level. On that level it involves something of which no model could be drawn on a blackboard, nor even easily made in three dimensions.

Aristotle had said "Whatever is outside the highest Heaven is of such a sort that it needs no place, nor does time affect it." It is typically Aristotelian in its dry caution, typically pagan in its reverent timidity. Taken over by Christians, this of course turns into something much more positive and resounding. As one author says, all that heaven is *Deo plenum,* full of God. Or, as Dante says, it is *luce intellettual piena d'amore (Paradiso,* xxx, 40). In other words there isn't exactly any space beyond the cosmos. The Empyrean is the boundary of space, not in the absurd sense which would force us to put more space outside it but in the sense that it is the point at which the spatial mode of thought breaks down.

Dante makes this vivid to us by an astonishing *tour de force.* He cannot of course make the spaceless imaginable in the strict sense. What he does is to show us space turning inside out; that teaches us pretty effectively that spatial thinking, as we ordinarily know it, has broken down. First, to prepare us, he gives us this remarkable image. The Primum Mobile is described as the "vase" in which time has its roots—"look elsewhere for its leaves" *(Paradiso,* xxvii, 118-20). Time, of course, in the old philosophy, was generated by the movement of the Primum Mobile. But consider the image—a gigantic tree growing downwards through those 118 million miles, its roots in the stars, its leaves being the days and minutes we live through on Earth. I had almost said "the leaves of its *topmost* branches," for one cannot help thinking of them as topmost: what is down for us must be up for the tree, its sap must be coming up, its roots must be its lowest point. Thus he begins to turn the universe inside out. Then, later, in the Empyrean itself, he is shown a point of light round which nine lights are circling, the nearest to the center moving at the highest speed and the furthest out at the lowest. Of the center Beatrice says "Heaven and all nature hangs upon that point" *(Paradiso,* xxviii, 41–2); it is what Aristotle says in so many words of the Unmoved Mover. The point is an exposition of God; the nine (so to call them) planets are the nine angelic hierarchies and you see that this is our universe inside out. In our visible world the circumference, the Primum Mobile, moves quickest and is nearest to God; the Moon moves slowest and is nearest what we call the Center—i.e. the Earth. But the true nature of the universe is exactly the opposite. In the visible and spatial order Earth is center; in the dynamic, invisible order the Empyrean is center, and we are indeed "outside the city wall" at the end of all things. And the center of that Center, the center of Earth, is the edge, the very point at which all being and reality finally peter out. For in there (as we call it), out there (as we ought to call it) is Hell—the last outpost, the rim, the place where being is nearest to not-being, where positive unbeing (so to call it) asymptotically approaches that zero it can never quite reach.

Such was the medieval cosmos. It had of course one serious drawback. It wasn't—or a good deal of it wasn't—true. I have rather been inviting you to consider it as a work of art; perhaps, after all, the greatest work of art the Middle Ages produced. Of course it was not a mere fantasy. It was intended to cover, and up to a point did cover, the facts as they knew them. And perhaps in calling it untrue, we should all now mean something other than our grandfathers meant. They would have taken the Newtonian account as simply true and the medieval as simply wrong. It would be for them like the difference between a good map and a bad one. I suppose most people would now admit that no picture of the universe we can form is "true" in quite the sense our grandfathers hoped. We would rather speak of "models." And since all are only models, we should be prepared to find in each something of the nature of the artist as well as something of the object. From that point of view, too, a study of the various models has its interest. I think the medieval and Newtonian models—the one so ordered, so sublime, and so festive, the other so trackless, so incapable of form—reflect the older, more formal and intellectual world and the later enthusiastic, romantic world pretty well. What our own models—if you continue to allow us models—will reflect, posterity may judge.

Technology and Invention
in the Middle Ages

LYNN WHITE, JR.

THE HISTORY OF technology and invention, especially that of the earlier periods, has been left strangely uncultivated. Our vast technical institutes continue at an ever-accelerating pace to revolutionize the world we live in; yet small effort is being made to place our present technology in the time sequence, or to give to our technicians that sense of their social responsibility which can only come from an exact understanding of their historical function—one might almost say, of their apostolic succession. By permitting those who work in shops and laboratories to forget the past, we have impoverished the present and endangered the future. In the United States this neglect is the less excusable because we Americans boast of being the most technically progressive people of an inventive age. But when the historian of American technology tries to probe the medieval and Renaissance roots of his subject he runs into difficulties: the materials available to him are scanty and often questionable; for professional medievalists have left unmined this vein in the centuries on which they have staked their claim.

Broadly speaking, technology is the way people do things. (In a certain sense there is even a technology of prayer.) Yet it is startling to reflect that we have, as a rule, only the vaguest notion of how the men of the Middle Ages actually did things, and how, from time to time, they learned to do them better. In our museums we cherish medieval textiles; we recognize the crucial importance of the cloth industry in the growth of early capitalism. But what do we know of spinning and weaving, of fulling and dyeing, and of the improvements in quality and production which affected both the art and the

Reprinted by permission from *Speculum*, XV (1940) 2, 141–156. "A Note on the Sources" has been omitted here.

economics of the time?[1] We all know that St. Louis of
France went on crusades. But did he sail towards the Orient in
the same sort of ship[2] which Godfrey of Bouillon might have
used, had not this latter chosen, probably with good reason,
to journey by land? How had shipbuilding changed in the in-
tervening century and a half; under what influences had it
changed; and what could a ship of 1249 do which one of
1095 could not? And more particularly, what could a ship of
1492 accomplish in addition? Every textbook on American
history should begin with a discussion of those medieval improvements in shipbuilding and navigation without which the
exploration and settlement of the New World would have
been technically impossible. That chapter is lacking chiefly
because medievalists themselves have not studied these matters adequately.[3] To offer a final example: how is it that the

[1] For the western Middle Ages there is nothing comparable to N. A.
Reath and E. B. Sachs, *Persian Textiles and their Technique from the
Sixth to the Eighteenth Centuries* (New Haven, 1937), a history of cloth
not in the conventional terms of pattern, but rather in terms of the
methods of weaving, which so often underlie pattern. The very compe-
tent Emile Cherblanc is gradually publishing a technical *Histoire
général du tissu* (Paris, 1935–), but thus far has dealt only with ancient times. J. F. Flanagan, "The [Egyptian] origin of the drawloom
used in making early Byzantine silks," *Burlington Magazine,* xxxv
(1919), 167–172 and xxxvii (1920), 215, credits the Copts rather than
the Chinese with this basic invention; see also M. T. Schmitter, "Chine
ou Proche-Orient," *Revue archéologique,* 6th series, xiii (1939),
73–102. F. Orth, "Der Werdegang wichtiger Erfindungen auf dem Ge-
biete der Spinnerei und Weberei," *Beiträge zur Geschichte der Technik
und Industrie,* xii (1922), 61–108, xvii (1927), 89–105, is unsatisfactory for the earlier period. The technical aspects of G. Espinas's and
H. Pirenne's work on Flemish textiles are briefly summarized by A. L.
Gutmann, "Technical peculiarities of Flemish clothmaking and dyeing,"
Ciba Review, No. 14 (1938), 484–487. That the northern textile art
may be far more deeply rooted in history than has hitherto been suspected is indicated by W. von Stokar, *Spinnen und Weben bei den
Germanen* (Leipzig, 1938). E. K. Scott, "Early cloth fulling and its
machinery," *Transactions of the Newcomen Society,* xii (1931–32),
30–52, is less satisfactory than V. Geramb, "Ein Beitrag zur Geschichte
der Walkerei," *Wörter und Sachen,* xii (1929), 37–46. On the introduction of the spinning wheel, see *infra,* p. 75, n. 35.

[2] Cf. R. C. Anderson's comments in *Mariner's Mirror,* vi (1920),
18–20 on A. Jal, *Archéologie navale* (Paris, 1840, mémoire no. 7:
"Sur les vaisseaux ronds de St Louis."

[3] Despite the vast bibliography on the subject, it is evident that the
whole problem of the relations of hull-design, rig, and rudder demand
reëxamination. F. Moll, *Das Schiff in der bildenden Kunst* (Bonn,
1929) furnishes much of the raw material for such a study by publishing some 5000 pictures of ships from contemporary sources. Recent
discussion has centered on the rudder. Lefebvre des Noëttes, *De la marine antique à la marine moderne: la révolution du gouvernail* (Paris,
1935) attempts to show that the introduction of the hinged sternpost
or median rudder in place of the lateral steering-oar greatly increased
the size and efficiency of ships. G. La Roërie, "Les transformations du

importance of the late thirteenth-century Italian invention of spectacles [4] has not been more generally appreciated? Anyone familiar with the crescendo of intellectual life in the later Middle Ages would challenge that enthusiast who has ascribed the Renaissance to the discovery of eye-glasses; but surely no one in the bespectacled academic world will be sufficiently discourteous to doubt that this technical development does much to account for the improved standard of education and the almost feverish tempo of thought characteristic of the fourteenth and fifteenth centuries. People were able to read more, and to read in their maturer years.

If, then, we are to understand any one of the many "Middle Ages" (blessed be the pluralist bias of our tongue!) and their gradual metamorphosis into modern times, we must not neglect technology. Yet at present the laborers in this field are as few as the harvest is plenteous.

Perhaps the chief reason why scholars have been hesitant to explore the subject is the difficulty of delimiting its boundaries: technology knows neither chronological nor geographic frontiers.

The student of the history of invention soon discovers that he must smash the conventional barriers between Greek and

---

gouvernail." *Annales d'histoire économique et sociale,* VII (1935), 564–568, doubts the revolutionary importance of the sternpost rudder, but cannot deny that it quickly displaced the older form; cf. also the remarks of P. d'Hérouville, *Etudes classiques,* v (1936), 176–200, of L. Laurand, *Rev. de philologie,* LXIII (1937), 131–132, and H. de Sassure, *Revue archéologique,* 6th series, x (1937), 90–107. Unfortunately Lefebvre des Noëttes missed the earliest depiction of the modern rudder, found on a Belgian font of *ca* 1180 now in Winchester cathedral; cf. H. H. Brindley, "Mediaeval rudders," *Mariner's Mirror,* XII (1926), 211–216, 364, XIII (1927), 85–88, and R. and R. C. Anderson, *The Sailing Ship* (London, 1926), p. 86. Likewise he overlooks the vertical sterns of two clay models of boats, probably Saxon of the tenth century, now at Leyden; cf. D. Verwey, "An early median rudder and spritsail?," *Mariner's Mirror,* xx (1934), 230–231, 373. Van Nouhuys, "On early median rudders," *ibid.,* xxII (1936), 476, asserts that a Far Eastern document of 1124 describes such a rudder and that a Japanese monument of *ca* 1350 shows one. The whole history of the rudder is thrown into confusion by the discovery of a median rudder (published in *L'Illustration,* 3 Dec. 1938) in the famous Schefer manuscript in the Bibliothèque Nationale, illuminated in 1237 by Yahya, son of Mahmud; cf. E. Blochet, *Musulman Painting* (London, 1929), p. 21 and plates xxIV ff.

[4] I. del Lingo, "Le vincende di un' impostura erudita." *Archivio, storico italiano,* LXXVIII (1920), 5–53; G. Albertotti, "Lettra intorno all' invenzione degli occhiali," *Annali di oftalmologia e clinica oculistica,* L (1922), 85–104; M. von Rohr, "Aus der Geschichte der Brille," *Beiträge zur Geschichte der Technik,* XVII (1927), 30–50, XVIII (1928), 95–117; N. Scalinci, "A proposito di Alessandro della Spina e di storia della invenzione degli occhiali," *Rivista di storia delle scienze mediche e naturali,* xv (1933), 139–143.

barbarian, Roman and German, oriental and occidental. For medieval technology is found to consist not simply of the technical equipment inherited from the Roman-Hellenistic world[5] modified by the inventive ingenuity of the western peoples, but also of elements derived from three outside sources: the northern barbarians, the Byzantine and Moslem Near East, and the Far East.

The importance of the first of these, the barbarian influence, has been far too little understood even by those who have dabbled in the history of technology. Students of the fine arts have only recently led the way towards an appreciation of the essential unity and originality of that vast northern world of so-called "barbarians" which, in ancient times, had its focal point on the plains of Russia and of Western Siberia, but which extended from the Altai Mountains to Ireland: we are beginning to learn how profoundly it affected the aesthetic expressions of the Middle Ages. But even before the Germanic migrations, these barbarians had begun to influence Roman technology, and in later centuries they contributed many distinctive ingredients to medieval life:[6] trousers and the habit of wearing furs,[7] the easily-heated compact house as contrasted with the Mediterranean patio-house,[8] cloisonné jewelry,[9] feltmaking,[10] the ski,[11] the use of soap

[5] On ancient technology, see most recently A. Rehm, "Zur Rolle der Technik in der griechisch-römischen Antike," *Archiv für Kulturgeschichte*, XXVIII (1938), 135–162. A. Neuburger, *Technical Arts and Sciences of the Ancients* (New York, 1930) is comprehensive rather than accurate.

[6] See the judicious reflections of M. Bloch, "Les 'inventions' médiévales," *Annales d'histoire économique et sociale*, VII (1935), 638, and "Note sur un grand problème d'influences," *ibid.*, VIII (1936), 513–514. The mutual cultural relationships of the various barbarian peoples are still obscure, but see J. Peisker, "Die älteren Bezeihungen der Slawen zu Turkotataren und Germanen," *Vierteljahrschrift für Sozial- und Wirtschaftsgeschichte*, III (1905), 187–360, 465–533, and the criticisms of J. Janko in *Wörter und Sachen*, I (1909), 94–109, and of L. Niederle, *Revue des études slaves*, II (1922), 19–38.

[7] In 397 and 399 the wearing of trousers and boots (*bracae vel tzangae*) was strictly forbidden in the city of Rome, and in 416 long hair and fur garments (*indumenta pellium*) were likewise banned: an indication that the Romans were adopting the warmer German dress; cf. *Codex Theodosianus*, ed. T. Mommsen and P. M. Meyer (Berlin, 1905), XIV, 10, 2–4.

[8] M. Hehn, *Deutsche Wohnungswesen* (Leipzig, 1899), pp. 24–39. For a general consideration of the problems of domestic architecture, see R. Quenedey, "L'habitation urbain et son évolution," *Annales d'histoire économique et sociale*, VI (1934), 62–68, 138–147.

[9] M. Rostovtzeff, *Iranians and Greeks in South Russia* (Oxford, 1922), pp. 181–191; H. Rupp, *Die Herkunft der Zelleneinlage* (Bonn, 1937) suggests an Indian origin for this technique; E. Margulies,

for cleansing[12] and of butter in place of olive oil,[13] the making of barrels and tubs,[14] the cultivation of rye,[15] oats,[16] spelt,[17] and hops,[18] perhaps the sport of falconry[19] and certain elements of the number system.[20] Above all, the great plains invented the stirrup,[21] which made the horse etymologically responsible for chivalry, and, perhaps even more im-

---

"Cloisonné enamel," in *A Survey of Persian Art* (New York, 1938), I, 779–783, proposes an Iranian.

10 B. Laufer, "The early history of felt," *American Anthropologist*, XXXIII (1930), 1–18, points out that while the Greeks and Romans had some knowledge of felt, the word for it in all the Romanic tongues is derived from the Teutonic, indicating that the effective diffusion of this form of textile should be credited to the Germanic invasions.

11 O. Poulsen, *Skiing* (New York, 1924), pp. 170–177; A. Lunn, *History of Skiing* (New York, 1927), pp. 8–9; D. S. Davidson, "Snowshoes," *Memoirs of the American Philosophical Society*, VI (1937), 138–142; R. Lautier, "Sports d'hiver préhistoriques," *Revue archéologique*, 6th series, XIII (1939), 128–129. How profoundly even a simple technical improvement may modify the whole life of a community is illustrated by M. Lefournier, "La vie alpestre transformée par le ski," *Revue des deux mondes*, CV, VIII (1935), 879–891: a description of the social effects of the introduction of the ski into the French Alps in 1899.

12 F. M. Feldhaus, "Sapo, Lauge und Seife unserer Altvorderen," *Chemiker-Zeitung*, XXXII (1908), 837–838; F. W. Gibbs, "History of the manufacture of soap," *Annals of Science*, IV (1939), 169–190.

13 V. Hehn, *Kulturpflanzen und Hausthiere*, 7th ed. (Berlin, 1902), pp. 154–160.

14 F. M. Feldhaus, *Technik der Vorzeit, der geschichtlichen Zeit und der Naturvölker* (Leipzig, 1914), p. 285.

15 F. Netolitzky, "Unser Wissen von den alten Kulturpflanzen Mitteleuropas," *Deutsches Archäologisches Institut, Römisch-Germanische Kommission, 20. Bericht* (1930), pp. 39–41; E. Schiemann, *Entstehung der Kulturpflanzen* (Berlin, 1932), p. 174; F. Grube, "Cereal foods of the Anglo-Saxons," *Philological Quarterly*, XIII (1934), 143; B. Laufer, "Rye in the Far East and the Asiatic origin of our word series 'rye,'" *T'oung pao*, XXXI (1935), 237–273.

16 Schiemann, *op. cit.*, p. 184.

17 *Ibid.*, p. 147, supplemented by H. L. Warneck, "Zur Frage der Entstehungsmittelpunkt des Spelzbaues im deutschen Sprachgebiet Mitteleuropas," *Österreichische botanische Zeitschrift*, LXXXVII (1938), 62–68.

18 A. de Condolle, *Origin of Cultivated Plants* (New York, 1892), p. 163; Hehn, *op cit.*, pp. 473–480.

19 B. Laufer, *Chinese Pottery of the Han Dynasty* (Leyden, 1909), p. 231; O. Janse, "Notes sur les bractéates en or chez les Scandinaves," *Revue archéologique*, 5th ser., XIV (1921), 389–391; O. Schrader, *Reallexikon der indgerman. Altertumskunde*, 2nd ed. (Berlin, 1917–1923), pp. 280–284.

20 H. P. Lattin, "The origin of our present system of notation according to the theories of Nicholas Bubnov," *Isis*, XIX (1933), 185–186.

21 Lefebvre des Noëttes, "L'étrier à travers les âges," *Larousse mensuel*, VII (1926), 11–14; cf. R. Zschelle and R. Forrer, *Die Steigbügel in ihrer Formentwicklung* (Berlin, 1896), pp. 2–3, and Rostovtzeff, *op. cit.*, pp. 121, 130.

portant, the heavy plow which, as we shall see, is the technological basis of the typical medieval manor.

Naturally the problem of diffusion to and from the Greek
and Saracenic Orient constantly troubles the student of technology. Despite the laborious research which has been lavished on the Levant, each new wise man from the East com-
pels us to revise prevalent notions. First Lawrence of Arabia
challenges the long-accepted belief that the rapid development of western military architecture in the twelfth century
was based on the crusaders' observation of Moslem and Byzantine models;[21a] and now Arthur Upham Pope is bent on
proving that the basic principles of gothic construction were
derived from Iran.[22]

The various portions of this Oriental legacy can scarcely be
enumerated, if only because so few items of it have been satisfactorily established: even the distillation of alcohol, so
long thought to be an art borrowed from Islam, is now believed to be a western European invention.[23] Much work remains to be done—and done over! Let one illustration suffice: the fore-and-aft rig. Until such a rig was developed,
mariners were unable to tack effectively against the wind, and
oarsmen remained the only dependable nautical motive
power. Clearly the development of the fore-and-aft rig would
mark an epoch in the history of labor by eliminating the gal-

[21a] T. E. Lawrence, *Crusader Castles* (London, 1936). A new edition,
incorporating the latest materials, is being prepared by A. W. Lawrence, T. S. R. Boase, and Miss E. Jamison. A two-volume work is
announced by B. Ebhardt, *Der Wehrbau Europas im Mittelalter: eine
Gesamtdarstellung der Burgenkunde aller europäischen Länder.* The
necessity of studying castles in relation not simply to military technology but to geography and the social structure as well, is emphasized by
W. Knapp, "Zum Problem des Burgenbaus," *Zeitschrift des Deutschen
Vereins für Kunstwissenschaft,* I (1935), 322–325.

[22] *A Survey of Persian Art,* A. U. Pope, editor, 7 vols. (New York:
American Institute for Iranian Art and Archaeology, 1938–39). E. Lam-
bert, "Les voûtes nervées hispano-musulmanes du XIᵉ siècle et leur
influence possible sur l'art chrétien," *Hespéris,* VIII (1928), 147–175,
and "Les premières voûtes nervées françaises et les origines de la
croisée d'ogives," *Revue archéologique,* 6th series, II (1933), 235–244,
likewise emphasizes the Islamic roots of gothic engineering. Simultaneously with these discoveries, P. Abraham, *Viollet-le-Duc et le ration-
alisme médiéval* (Paris, 1934), has launched an attack on the theory
that gothic architecture is scholastic dialectic frozen in stone; cf. L.
Lecrocq, "Un procès de revision: le problème de la croisée d'ogives,"
Annales d'histoire économique et sociale, VII (1935), 644–646. The Section on Intellectual Coöperation of the League of Nations has undertaken a study of the origins of the gothic.

[23] A. J. V. Underwood, "The historical development of the distilling
plant," *Transactions of the Institution of Chemical Engineers,* XIII
(1936), 34–62, summarizes much of the earlier literature.

ley, it would cheapen sea transport by increasing the average speed of ships, and, by reducing the size of crews, it would vastly extend the range of ocean voyaging.[24] The earliest form of the fore-and-aft rig was the lateen sail. What is probably the most ancient picture of a lateen is found in a grafito on a ruined church at El-Auja in southern Palestine.[25] The church is pre-Moslem, but unfortunately the scratching cannot be dated. Lateen sails suddenly appear in Greek miniatures of the ninth century;[26] in the twelfth century they are found in objects of art produced at Venice, Amalfi, Benevento, and other Italian centers of Byzantine influence. Thence they spread to all the coasts of Europe and played a great part in speeding up commerce, in displacing rowers and in stimulating exploration.

But it is increasingly evident that Roman Catholic Europe drew technical novelties during the Middle Ages not only from Byzantium and Islam but perhaps in even greater measure from China. Nor were these borrowings always mediated by Greeks and Moslems, as paper was:[27] on the contrary, Europe got some things directly, by way of the caravan routes of Central Asia. Gunpowder,[28] the compass[29] and

[24] Slender evidence that under certain circumstances ancient mariners could tack is assembled by T. R. Holmes, "Could ancient ships work to windward?," *Classical Quarterly*, III (1909), 26–39, and D. Verwey in *Mariner's Mirror*, XXII (1936), 117.

[25] *Palestine Exploration Fund Quarterly* (1871), 28 and plate. Lateens may have been known in the sixth century: see J. Sottas, "An early lateen sail in the Mediterranean," *Mariner's Mirror*, XXV (1939), 229–230.

[26] The earliest clearly dated lateens are in Bibliothèque Nationale, *MS. grec 510*, fols 3ʳ and 367ʸ, painted in 886 A.D.; cf. H. H. Brindley, "Early pictures of lateen sails," *Mariner's Mirror*, XII (1926), 12–13. A. Jal, *Glossaire nautique* (Paris, 1848), p. 257, published a drawing of a lateen which he claimed was derived from *Bib. Nat. MS. grec 923*, fol. 266, of the ninth century. Neither H. Omont nor Brindley (cf. *loc. cit.*) could discover it there. Jal's drawing is, in fact, a composite of two lateen rigs of fol. 207ʳ of that manuscript; cf. also fol. 247ʸ for a smaller lateen. The Khludov Psalter, now in Moscow, likewise has a clear lateen rig on fol. 88ʳ. Brindley dates it twelfth century, but the Princeton Index of Christian Art places it in the ninth century. It may be added that something must be wrong with the current derivation of the word lateen from *Latin*: why should the Italians name a sail, which clearly they borrowed from the Greeks or Saracens, the *vela latina?* One suspects a false etymology.

[27] Cf. A. Blum. *On the Origin of Paper* (New York, 1934). May not the invention of paper have been the application to vegetable fibres of the idea of felting, so long practiced on animal hair by the nomads of Central Asia, as Laufer has shown?

[28] Cf. B. Rathgen, *Das Geschütz im Mittelalter* (Berlin, 1928), p. 665 ff.; E. O. von Lippmann, "Zur Geschichte des Schiesspulvers und des Salpeters," *Chemiker-Zeitung*, LII (1928), 2; C. Zenghelis, "Le feu

printing with cast movable type[30] were probably not derived from the Far East: the latest opinion credits them to Europe, whence they spread eastward into Islam. But what of church bells,[31] practically unknown in the Near East, but ap-

grégois et les armes à feu des Byzantins," *Byzantion*, VII (1932), 265–286; W. W. Arendt, "Zur Geschichte der Artillerie im Mittelalter." *Arkhiv istorii nauki i tekhniki*, VII (1935), 297–323, and "Das griechische Feuer," *ibid.*, IX (1936), 151–204; N. D. Cheronis, "Chemical warfare in the Middle Ages," *Journal of Chemical Education*, XIV (1937), 360–365.

[29] A. C. Moule, "The Chinese south-pointing carriage," *T'oung pao*, XXIII (1924), 83–97 showed that this was not a magnetic machine. The discussion was continued by R. Hennig, "Die Frühkenntnis der magnetischen Nordweisung," *Beiträge zur Geschichte der Technik*, XXI (1931–32), 25–42; E. O. von Lippmann, "Geschichte der Magnetnadel bis zur Erfindung des Kompasses (gegen 1300)," *Quellen und Studien zur Geschichte der Naturwissenschaften und Medizin*, III, i (1932), 44 pp.; and, best of all, by A. C. Mitchell's magnificently documented "Chapters in the history of terrestrial magnetism," *Terrestrial Magnetism and Atmospheric Electricity*, XXXVII (1932), 105–146, XLII (1937), 241–280, XLIV (1939), 77–80. Recent popular accounts are J. F. Kramer, "The early history of magnetism," *Transactions of the Newcomen Society*, XIV (1933–34), 183–200, H. Winter, "What is the present stage of research in regard to the use of the compass in Europe?," *Research and Progress*, II (1936), 225–233, also "Who invented the compass?," *Mariner's Mirror*, XXIII (1937), 95–102, and W. Ley, "The story of the lodestone," *Natural History* XLII (1938), 201–207.

[30] T. F. Carter, *The Invention of Printing in China and its Spread Westward* (New York, 1925), pp. 182–185; cf. J. Daland, "The evolution of modern printing and the discovery of movable metal type by the Chinese and Koreans in the fourteenth century," *Journal of the Franklin Institute*, CCXII (1931), 209–234. G. F. Hudson, *Europe and China: a survey of their relations from the earliest times to 1800* (London, 1931), pp. 165–168, disputes Carter's contention that the technique of casting movable type as developed *ca* 1440 in the Rhineland was unconnected with the similar, and earlier, Korean invention. However, admitting that contact between Europe and the Far East was not entirely broken by the collapse of the Mongol Empire, nevertheless that relation was maintained through a long chain of middle-men. It is therefore improbable that so intricate an art could have been carried from the Yellow to the North Sea without leaving intermediate traces. Recent students of the European invention have emphasized its antecedents in the casting process used by jewelers, the stamps of bookbinders and illuminators, and the printing of textiles. Articles in the *Gutenberg-Jahrbuch* (1926–) are especially valuable in this field; cf. also H. Guppy, "Stepping stones to the art of typography," *Bulletin of the John Rylands Library*, XII (1928), 83–121; M. Audin, "The mystery of the origins of typography," *Library Association Record*, 3rd series, I (1931), 153–162; K. Reinking, "Die Entwicklung der Technik des Handdruckes und die Beziehungen des Zeugdruckes zum Druck auf Papier," *Melliand Textilbericht*, XII (1931), 462–465.

[31] It is significant that the earliest large bells in the West, like those of the Far East, did not have clappers, but were struck from the outside; cf. L. Gougaud, "Clochettes celtiques," *Dictionnaire d'archéologie chrétienne et de liturgie*, III, ii (1914), 1983. These large bells, therefore, can hardly be mere enlargements of the Roman *tintinnabulum*, as H.Leclercq, "Cloche," *ibid.*, 1959, believes; for *tintinnabula* had clappers. On Chinese bells cf. A. C. Moule, "Chinese musical instruments," *Journal of the North China Branch of the Royal Asiatic Society*, XXXIX (1908), 35–46.

pearing at the two extremes of the Old World? Or the crossbow,[32] perhaps known in some form to the Romans, subsequently forgotten save in China, then introduced to Constantinople by the crusaders? Or the fiddle-bow,[33] which revolutionized western music; or the wheelbarrow,[34] which cut in half the number of laborers needed to haul small loads by substituting a wheel for the front man of the hand-barrow (we have been replacing men by wheels ever since!); or the spinning-wheel,[35] which speeded up the cloth industry; or the

[32] C. M. Wilbur, "History of the crossbow," *Annual Report of the Smithsonian Institution* (1936), p. 435; H. T. Horwitz, "Die Armbrust in Ostasien," *Zeitschrift für historische Waffenkunde*, VII (1916), 155–183, "Zur Entwicklungsgeschichte der Armbrust," *ibid.*, VIII (1920), 311–317, IX (1921), 73, 114, 139, and "Über die Konstruktion von Fallen und Selbstschüssen," *Beiträge zur Geschichte der Technik*, XIV (1924), 96–100. The only Roman representations of the crossbow are both, by a suspicious coincidence, in the museum of Le Puy! J. Hoops, "Die Armbrust im Frühmittelalter," *Wörter und Sachen*, III (1912), 65–68, maintains, by the interpretation of a highly ambiguous Anglo-Saxon riddle, that the crossbow continued in use during the Dark Ages. Certainly Anna Comnena, *Alexiad*, tr. E. A. S. Dawes (London, 1928), p. 255, considered the crossbow a Frankish novelty.

[33] H. G. Farmer, "The origin of the Arabian lute and rebec," *Journal of the Royal Asiatic Society* (1930), pp. 777–779 believes that the Arabs received the musical bow from the East and transmitted it to Europe. O. E. Anderson, *The Bowed Harp* (London, 1930) suggests a northern origin for the bow. The two theories are not mutually exclusive: the bow may have traveled from Central Asia or China to both Scandinavia and Islam. The history of bowed instruments in China is still obscure, cf. Moule, *op. cit.*, p. 130. It is, of course, possible that the bow may have reached China from the West, as did the organ: cf. A. C. Moule, "A Western organ in mediaeval [13th century] China," *Journal of the Royal Asiatic Society* (1926), 193–211, 726, and comments by H. G. Farmer, *ibid.*, 495–499. It may be remarked that the famous object held by King David in the Utrecht Psalter (*ca* 850) is neither a bow (supposedly the first) as K. Sachs, *Handbuch der Musikinstrumentenkunde* (Leipzig, 1920), pp. 170–171, thought, nor yet a long sword as K. Schlesinger, *Oxford History of Music, introductory volume* (Oxford, 1929), pp. 105–108, asserts, but rather a measuring rod: cf. *The Utrecht Psalter*, ed. by E. DeWald (Princeton, 1932), plate 99.

[34] Wheelbarrows appear in Western Europe at least by the later thirteenth century; cf. L. Baudry de Saunier, *Histoire de la locomotion terrestre* (Paris, 1936), p. 70. One cannot resist quoting Viollet-le-Duc, *Dictionnaire raisonnée du mobilier français* (Paris, 1874), II, 41: "Nous ne savons qui le premier a dit que la brouette avait été inventée par un sieur Dupin en 1669. . . . C'est un question d'ordre public, dans un certain monde, que tout, depuis l'art de penser jusqu'à la brouette inclusivement, date du regne de Louis XIV. Avouons cependant, pour ne rien exagérer, que les esprits larges admettraient peut-être que le XVIe siècle a été témoin d' un certain effort de l'esprit humain, et qu'alors, peut-être, la brouette aurait pu sortir du cerveau d'un des novateurs de cette époque. Mais remonter au delà, donner à la brouette une origine plus ancienne, est une de ces témerités qui tendent à rien moins que à nous faire rétrograder en pleine féodalité."

[35] There is no evidence to support the common assertion that the spinning-wheel came from India; but a correspondent who prefers to remain anonymous believes, from an examination of ancient textiles, that such a device was used in China very early. In 1298 guild-regu-

functional button[36] which, about 1300, started the greatest of revolutions in the history of costume? Above all, was that fundamental invention, the casting of iron,[37] which appears in Europe during the fourteenth century, an importation from the Far East where it was certainly practiced much earlier? Indeed, when even the *Enciclopedia italiana (s.v. pasta)* confesses that chow mein may well be the ancestral form of spaghetti, the whole of the Middle Ages seems to shrivel into a mere appendix to China!

But possibly more careful scrutiny will prove that some of these were gifts of Europe to China rather than the reverse. For the expansive vitality of the late-medieval technology of the West spread its influence round half the world, from Gardar to Cambaluc: at the very time when Norse settlers in Greenland were teaching the Eskimos to make coopered tubs, saws, and screws,[38] European engineers were delighting the

---

lations at Speyer permitted the use of yarn spun with a wheel in the woof of cloth, but not in the warp: cf. F. J. Mone, "Zunftorganization vom 13. bis 16. Jahrhundert," *Zeitschrift für die Geschichte des Oberrheins,* XV (1863), 281; H. T. Horwitz, "Zur Geschichte des Spinnrades," *Geschichtsblätter für Technik, Industrie und Gewerbe,* II (1915), 55.

[36] The thesis of A. Parent, *Le bouton à travers les âges* (Paris, 1935), that the button was not invented until the thirteenth century, is clearly in error: buttons were occasionally used in ancient times; cf. K. McK. Elderkin, "Buttons and their use on Greek garments," *American Journal of Archaeology,* XXXII (1928), 333–345, and for even earlier button-like fastenings, *ibid.,* XLI (1938), 563. However, the implications of the button for costume design were not realized until *ca* 1300. That Chinese styles influenced late medieval fashions is indicated by G. I. Bratianu, "Anciennes modes orientales à la fin du moyen âge," *Seminarium kondakovianum,* VII (1935), 165.

[37] Cf. especially T. T. Read, "The early casting of iron," *Geographical Review,* XXIV (1934), 544–554; "Largest and oldest iron-castings," *Iron Age,* CXXXVII (1936), 18–20; "Chinese iron, a puzzle," *Harvard Journal of Asiatic Studies,* II (1937), 398–407. Western developments are compactly presented by O. Johannsen, "Die Erfindung der Eisengusstechnik," *Stahl und Eisen,* XXXIX (1919), 1457–1466, resting on his "Die Quellen zur Geschichte des Eisengusses im Mittelalter und in der neueren Zeit bis zum Jahre 1530," *Archiv für die Geschichte der Naturwissenschaften und der Technik,* III (1912), 365–394, V (1915), 127–141, VIII (1918), 66–81; and cf. also his "Gab es in der Karolingerzeit schon Hochöfen?" *Stahl und Eisen,* LIII (1933), 1039–1040, which concludes that while fluid iron was sometimes produced in Europe as early as the eighth century, it was not cast in molds.

[38] E. B. Tylor, "Old Scandinavian civilization among the modern Esquimaux," *Journal of the Royal Anthropological Institute of Great Britain and Ireland,* XIII (1884), 348–357; B. Laufer, "The Eskimo screw as a culture-historical problem" *(sic), American Anthropologist,* new series, XVII (1915), 396–406; and especially T. Mathiassen, "Inugsuk, a mediaeval Eskimo settlement in Upernivik district, West Greenland," *Meddelelser om Grönland,* LXXVII (1930), 285–303, and "Contributions to the archaeology of Disko Bay," *ibid.,* XCIII, ii (1934), 116–118. For a discussion of plants introduced to Greenland by the Norse colonists, see M. P. Porsild, "Alien plants and apophytes in Greenland,"

Great Khan with new siege-engines of western design;[39] while shortly thereafter China received from Europe such diverse inventions as firearms[40] and eye-glasses,[41] and perhaps distilled liquors.[42] We may be sure that the merchants and missionaries who flocked to Cathay under the Yüan dynasty[43] went not devoid of technical skills. Perhaps when Far Eastern studies are more advanced, and particularly when the Harvard-Yenching Institute's historical dictionary of the Chinese language is completed, we may be able to deal with facts rather than with guesses.

The student of European technics, then, is compelled to follow his subject far beyond the usual geographical limits of medieval research. Similarly he finds that for his purposes the customary tripartite division of history into ancient, medieval and modern is completely arbitrary. In particular he finds no evidence of a break in the continuity of technological development following the decline of the Western Roman Empire.

The Dark Ages doubtless deserve their name: political disintegration, economic depression, the debasement of religion and the collapse of literature surely made the barbarian kingdoms in some ways unimaginably dismal. Yet because many

ibid., xcii, i (1932), 37–80. On possible Norse cultural influence upon Indians living south of Hudson's Bay see J. Löwenthal, "Irokesische Wirtschaftsaltertümer: ein Untersuchung zur Geschichte der ersten Entdeckung Amerikas, A.D. 1000," *Zeitschrift für Ethnologie*, lii (1921), 171–233; R. Hennig, "Normannen des 11. Jahrhundert in der Hudsonbai und an den Grossen Seen," *Petermanns geographische Mitteilungen*, lxxxv (1939), 58–60; C. T. Currelly, "Viking weapons found near Beardmore, Ontario," *Canadian Historical Review*, xx (1939), 4–7.

40 A. C. Moule and P. Pelliot, *Marco Polo: the Description of the World* (London, 1938), i, 318.

40 P. Pelliot, in *T'oung pao*, xxi (1922), 432–434, shows that while explosives were known in China as early as 1162, G. Schlegel, "On the invention and use of fire-arms and gunpowder in China prior to the arrival of Europeans," *ibid.*, 2nd series, iii (1902), 1–11, is wrong in believing that cannon were used in 1232. Cf. B. Rathgen, "Die Pulverwaffe in Indien," *Ostasiatische Zeitschrift*, xii (1925), 11–30, 196–217 and the comments of H. Goetz, *ibid.*, 226–229. T. T. Read, in *Geographical Review*, xxiv (1934), 548, pictures a Chinese cast-iron cannon dated 1377. A Chinese handgun dated 1421, now in the Berlin Museum für Völkerkunde, is amazingly like those manufactured at Nuremberg at that time; cf. W. Gohlke, "Das älteste datierte Gewehr," *Zeitschrift für historische Waffenkunde*, vii (1916), 205–206.

41 C. P. Rakusen, "History of Chinese spectacles," *Chinese Medical Journal*, liii (1938), 379–390, is inferior to K. Chiu, "The introduction of spectacles into China," *Harvard Journal of Asiatic Studies*, i (1936), 186–193.

42 R. P. Hommel, *China at Work* (Doylestown, Pa, 1937), p. 145.

43 Cf. most recently, I. V. Pouzyna, *La Chine, l'Italie et les débuts de la Renaissance* (Paris, 1935), and P. M. Sykes, *Quest for Cathay* (London, 1936).

aspects of civilization were in decay we should not assume too quickly that everything was backsliding. Even an apparent coarsening may indicate merely a shift of interest: in modern painting we recognize that Van Gogh's technical methods were not those of David; so, when we contrast a Hellenistic carved gem with a Merovingian enamel, our judgment should be cautious. Few will dispute that the Irish illumination and the Scandinavian jewelry of the seventh and eighth centuries stand among the supreme arts of all time; yet they are far from classical canons of taste, being rooted in an ancient, and quite separate, tradition of Northern art. So in the history of technology we must be discriminating. Changing tastes and conditions may lead to the degeneration of one technique while the technology of the age as a whole is advancing. The technology of torture, for example, which achieved such hair-raising perfection during the Renaissance,[44] is now happily in eclipse: viewed historically, our modern American "third degree" is barbaric only in its simplicity.

Indeed, a dark age may stimulate rather than hinder technology. Economic catastrophe in the United States during the past decade has done nothing to halt invention—quite the contrary; and it is a commonplace that war encourages technological advance. Confusion and depression, which bring havoc in so many areas of life, may have just the opposite effect on technics. And the chances of this are particularly good in a period of general migration, when peoples of diverse backgrounds and inheritances are mixing.

There is, in fact, no proof that any important skills of the Graeco-Roman world were lost during the Dark Ages even in the unenlightened West, much less in the flourishing Byzantine and Saracenic Orient. To be sure, the diminished wealth and power of the Germanic kings made engineering on the old Roman scale infrequent; yet the full technology of antiquity was available when required: the 276-ton monolith which crowns the tomb of Theodoric the Ostrogoth was brought to Ravenna from Istria; [45] while more than two centuries later Charlemagne transported not only sizable columns

44 F. Helbing, *Die Tortur* (Berlin, 1913), I, 269.

45 F. M. Feldhaus, "Die Ingenieure des Theoderich: die Hebe-Ösen am Grabmal des Theoderich," *Umschau*, XXXVIII (1934), 596–598. E. Feichter, "Die Lösung des Rätsels vom Theoderich-Grabmal in Ravenna," *Zeitschrift des deutschen Vereins für Kunstwissenschaft*, IV (1937), 1–15, interprets this remarkable structure as a Germanic chieftain's Hünengrab.

but even a great equestrian statue of Zeno from Ravenna across the Alps to Aachen.[46] Incidentally, we should do well to remember that the northern peoples from remote times were capable of managing great weights, as witness Stonehenge and the dolmens.

In military machines especially we might expect the barbarians to fall below the ancient standard; but at the siege of Paris in 886 we discover the Vikings, who presumably would be as untouched by Roman methods as any western people, using elaborate and powerful artillery; while the city itself was defended with catapults.[47] However, the Dark Ages do not seem to have improved on ancient artillery; the Roman level was not surpassed until the twelfth century when the trebuchet,[48] worked by counterweights, began to drive the less efficient tension and torsion engines from the field.

If the political and economic decay of the Dark Ages affected any technique adversely, it was that of road-building. Yet even here the case is not clear. For northern climates at least, the technical excellence of Roman roads has been exaggerated.[49] They had massive foundations, which sometimes survive to the present day; but the surface, consisting of slabs of masonry cemented together, made no provision for contraction or expansion. Heat made the slabs buckle and crack; water seeped under them and froze, separating them from the foundation. Repairs were difficult and expensive: no modern road-builder would consider imitating Roman

---

[46] Agnellus, *Liber pontificalis ecclesiae ravannatis*, c. 94, ed. O. Holder-Egger, in *Scriptores rerum langobardicarum et italicarum, saec. VI–IX* (Hanover, 1878), p. 338; Einhard, *Vita Karoli*, c. 26, ed. L. Halphen (Paris, 1923), p. 76.

[47] Abbo of St Germain, *De bello parisiaco*, ed. G. H. Pertz (Hanover, 1871), lines 156–157, 213–214, 360–366. The contention of E. Sander, "Der Verfall der römischen Belagerungskunst," *Historische Zeitschrift*, CXLIX (1934), 457–476, that the Romans did not transmit their siegecraft to the Middle Ages is refuted by F. Lammert, "Die antike Poliorketik and ihr Weiterwirken," *Klio*, XXXI (1938), 389–411.

[48] Rathgen, *Das Geschütz*, pp. 610–611; R. Payne-Gallway, *Projectile-throwing Engines of the Ancients* (London, 1907), p. 27.

[49] R. J. Forbes, *Notes on the History of Ancient Roads and their Construction* (Amsterdam, 1934), pp. 160–164, confirms the strictures of Ct Lefebvre des Noëttes, "La voie romaine et la route moderne," *Larousse mensuel*, VI (1925), 771–772. The date of the invention of the more flexible pavement is obscure; but a Flemish miniature assures us that *ca* 1450 it was being used to pave highways connecting cities: cf. J. W. Thompson and E. N. Johnson, *Introduction to the Middle Ages* (New York, 1937), p. 564, or the *Propyläen Weltgeschichte: Das Zeitalter der Gotik* (Berlin, 1932), p. 283. The most complete recent discussion of medieval roads is A. Birk, *Die Strasse: ihre verkehrs- und bautechnische Entwicklung im Rahmen der Menschheitsgeschichte* (Karlsbad-Drahowitz, 1934), pp. 149–282.

methods. It was the Middle Ages which developed the cheaper and more efficient method of laying cubes of stone in a loose bed of earth or sand which permitted expansion and made repairs easy: a type of paving still common.

Indeed, the technical skill of classical times was not simply maintained: it was considerably improved. Our view of history has been too top-lofty. We have been dazzled by aspects of civilization which are in every age the property of an élite, and in which the common man, with rare exceptions, has had little part. The so-called "higher" realms of culture might decay, government might fall into anarchy, and trade be reduced to a trickle, but through it all, in the face of turmoil and hard times, the peasant and artisan carried on, and even improved their lot. In technology, at least, the Dark Ages mark a steady and uninterrupted advance over the Roman Empire. Evidence is accumulating to show that a serf in the turbulent and insecure tenth century enjoyed a standard of living considerably higher than that of a proletarian in the reign of Augustus.

The basic occupation was, of course, agriculture. We have passed through at least two agricultural revolutions: that which began with "Turnip" Townshend and Jethro Tull in the early eighteenth century, and another, equally important, in the Dark Ages.

The problem of the development and diffusion of the northern wheeled plow, equipped with colter, horizontal share and moldboard, is too thorny to be discussed here.[50] Experts seem generally agreed: (1) that the new plow greatly increased production by making possible the tillage of rich, heavy, badly-drained river-bottom soils; (2) that it saved labor by making cross-plowing superfluous, and thus produced the typical northern strip-system of land division, as distinct from the older block-system dictated by the cross-plowing necessary with the lighter Mediterranean plow; (3) most important of all, that the heavy plow needed such

[50] E. C. Curwen, "Prehistoric agriculture in Britain," *Antiquity*, I, (1927), 261–289, maintains that the heavy plow was brought to England by the Anglo-Saxons. However, E. Barger's excellent "The present position of studies in English field-systems," *English Historical Review*, LIII (1938), 385–411, offers evidence indicating that the heavy plow and the strip-system were used in Britain and on both sides of the Roman-German frontier as early as the first century B.C. If this be true, then we must revise drastically our present notions both of the contrast between Roman Gaul and barbarian Germany and of the beginnings of the manorial system. Cf also H. Grosser, *Die Herkunft der französischen Gewannfluren* (Berlin, 1932), and M. Bloch, *Les caractères originaux de l'histoire rurale française* (Oslo, 1931), pp. 49–65.

power that peasants pooled their oxen and plowed together, thus laying the basis for the medieval cooperative agricultural community, the manor. But whatever may be the date and origin of the fully developed heavy plow, its effects were supplemented and greatly enhanced in the later eighth century by the invention of the three-field system, an improved rotation of crops and fallow which greatly increased the efficiency of agricultural labor.[51] For example, by switching 600 acres from the two-field to the three-field system, a com-

---

[51] Pliny, *Natural History*, XVIII, 20, tells how the people of Trier sowed wheat in March after their winter grain had been destroyed, and how they got good crops; but the incident is clearly exceptional. J. Hoops, *Reallexikon der germanischen Altertumskunde*, I (Strassburg, 1911), 24, finds no indication of the spring planting as a regular custom before documents of 765 and 771; thereafter it is frequently mentioned. The problems of medieval agricultural productivity have scarcely been formulated, much less solved. The question of increasing productivity per peasant (that is, the number of acres a peasant could till at any given period) has received no attention; a little work has been done on productivity per acre. Without improved use of fertilizer (about which, as Grosser, *op. cit.*, p. 22, remarks, we know practically nothing), presumably the yield per acre would decline as the soil became exhausted. The storminess of the climate after *ca* 1200 might also affect crops adversely (cf. C. E. P. Brooks, "Changes of climate in the old world during historic times," *Quarterly Journal of the Royal Meteorological Society*, LVII [1931], 23). Yet W. H. Beveridge, "Yield and price of corn in the Middle Ages," *Economic History*, I (1927), 160, and M. K. Bennett, "British wheat yield per acre for seven centuries," *ibid*, III (1935), 27–28, both find that there was great stability of yield from 1200 to 1450, and uphold the contention of R. Lennard, "The alleged exhaustion of the soil in medieval England," *Economic Journal*, XXXII (1922), 12–27, that the land was not depleted by long cultivation. In view of the adverse factors we may assume some slight improvement in agricultural methods after 1200, when our statistics begin, to account for this constancy of the food supply. Recently Lennard, "Statistics of corn yield in medieval England," *Economic History*, III (1936), 173–192, III (1937), 325–349 has pointed out that so many deductions of tithes, wages in kind, etc., were made before the yield was recorded that the official statistics do not represent the true productivity of the land. In general it has taken population several generations to rise to the optimum dictated by the resources made available by a new technique: cf. G. Bouthoul, "Population et progrès technique," *Revue international de sociologie*, XLIII (1935), 185–197. It may be suggested very tentatively that, although the medieval agricultural revolution which began in the Carolingian period was complete by 1200, the population continued to increase until its optimum was reached in the fourteenth century (cf. J. Beloch, "Die Bevölkerung Europas im Mittelalter," *Zeitschrift für Sozialwissenschaft*, III [1900], 405–423; J. C. Russell, "Medieval population," *Social Forces*, XV [1937], 503–511). It is too generally assumed that the population-plateau of the fourteenth to seventeenth centuries was caused by the Black Death and similar catastrophes. Technical changes in industry may improve the standard of living but cannot increase population, which until the recent diffusion of methods of birth control (cf. N. E. Himes, *Medical History of Contraception* [Baltimore, 1936], p. 168) was limited chiefly by the food supply. Only with the second agricultural revolution of the eighteenth century did population expand once more.

munity of peasants could plant 100 acres more in crops each year with 100 acres less of plowing. Since fallow land was plowed twice to keep down the weeds, the old plan required three acres of plowing for every acre in crops, whereas the new plan required only two acres of plowing for every productive acre.

In a society overwhelmingly agrarian, the result of such an innovation could be nothing less than revolutionary. Pirenne[52] is only the most recent of many historians to speculate as to why the reign of Charlemagne witnessed the shift of the center of European civilization, the change of the focus of history, from the Mediterranean to the plains of Northern Europe. The findings of agricultural history, it seems, have never been applied to this central problem in the study of the growth of the northern races. Since the spring sowing, which was the chief novelty of the three-field system, was unprofitable in the south because of the scarcity of summer rains, the three-field system did not spread below the Alps and the Loire.[53] For obvious reasons of climate the agricultural revolution of the eighth century was confined to Northern Europe.[54] It would appear, therefore, that it was this more efficient and productive use of land and labor which gave to the northern plains an economic advantage over the Mediterranean shores, and which, from Charlemagne's time onward, enabled the Northern Europeans in short order to surpass both in prosperity and in culture the peoples of an older inheritance.

In ways less immediately significant the Dark Ages likewise made ingenious improvements. One of the most important of these was a contribution to practical mechanics. There are two basic forms of motion: reciprocal and rotary. The normal device for connecting these—a device without which our machine civilization is inconceivable—is the crank. The crank is an invention second in importance only to the wheel itself; yet the crank was unknown to the Greeks and the Romans. It appears, even in rudimentary form, only after the

[52] H. Pirenne, *Mohammed and Charlemagne* (New York, 1939).

[53] Bloch, *Les caractères originaux*, pp. 31–35.

[54] J. Sion, "Quelques problèmes de transports dans l'antiquité: le point de vue d'un geographe méditerranéen," *Annales d'histoire économique et sociale*, VII (1935), 628–633, indicates a few of the geographical and climatic handicaps which prevented the Mediterranean lands from participating completely in the technological advances of the Middle Ages.

Invasions: first, perhaps, in hand-querns,[55] then on rotary grindstones.[56] The later Middle Ages developed its application to all sorts of machinery.[57]

Clearly there are nuggets in this stream for anyone to find. Perhaps the most successful amateur student of early medieval technology was the Commandant Lefebvre des Noëttes, who after his retirement from active service in the French cavalry, devoted himself to his hobby, the history of horses. He died in 1936 having made discoveries which must greatly modify our judgment of the Carolingian period.[58] From his investigations Lefebvre des Noëttes concluded that the use of animal power in antiquity was unbelievably inefficient. The ancients did not use nailed shoes on their animals,[59] and broken hooves often rendered beasts useless. Besides, they knew only the yoke-system of harness. While this was adequate for oxen, it was most unsatisfactory for the more rapid horse. The yoke rested on the withers of a team. From each end of the yoke ran two flexible straps: one a girth behind the forelegs, the other circling the horse's neck. As soon as the horse began to pull, the flexible front strap pressed on his windpipe, and the harder he pulled the closer he came to strangulation. Moreover the ancient harness was mechanically defective: the yoke was too high to permit the horse to exert his full force in pulling by flinging his body-weight into the task. Finally, the ancients were unable to harness one animal in front of another. Thus all great weights had to be drawn by gangs

[55] Cf. E. C. Curwen, "Querns," *Antiquity*, XI (1937), 133–151. On the development of the application of all forms of rotary motion, including the crank, cf. H. T. Horwitz, "Die Drehbewegung und ihre Bedeutung für die Entwicklung der materiellen Kultur," *Anthropos*, XXVIII (1933), 721–757, XXIX (1934), 99–125.

[56] E.g., in *The Utrecht Psalter* (ca 850), ed. DeWald, plate 58. It is probable that the diffusion of a simple device like the rotary grindstone (which is, after the spindle and potter's wheel, the earliest utilization of the flywheel principle) was far more influential in the development of practical mechanics than the complex water-clocks, automata, and organs emphasized by C. Koehne, "Zur Art der Verbreitung technische Fortschritte im früheren Mittelalter," *Geschichtsblätter für Technik, Industrie und Gewerbe*, III (1916), 275–280.

[57] Cf. T. Beck, *Beiträge zur Geschichte des Maschinenbaues* (Berlin, 1900), *passim*.

[58] *L'attelage et le cheval de selle à travers les âges* (Paris, 1931).

[59] This is one of the most disputed of Lefebvre des Noëttes' theses: cf. G. Méautis, "Les romains connaissaient-ils le fer à cheval?," *Revue des études anciennes*, XXXVI (1934), 88. J. Horn, *Über den ältesten Hufschutz des Pferdes: ein Beitrag zur Geschichte des Hufbeschlages* (Dresden, 1912), a very careful monograph, anticipated Lefebvre des Noëttes' negative conclusions.

of slaves, since animal power was not technically available in sufficient quantities.

According to Lefebvre des Noëttes this condition remained unchanged until the later ninth or early tenth century when, almost simultaneously, three major inventions appear: the modern horse-collar, the tandem harness, and the horseshoe. The modern harness, consisting of a rigid horse-collar resting on the shoulders of the beast, permitted him to breathe freely. This was connected to the load by lateral traces which enabled the horse to throw his whole body into pulling. It has been shown experimentally that this new apparatus so greatly increased the effective animal power that a team which can pull only about one thousand pounds with the antique yoke can pull three or four times that weight when equipped with the new harness. Equally important was the extension of the traces so that tandem harnessing was possible, thus providing an indefinite amount of animal power for the transport of great weights. Finally, the introduction of the nailed horse-shoe improved traction and greatly increased the endurance of the newly available animal power. Taken together these three inventions suddenly gave Europe a new supply of non-human power, at no increase of expense or labor. They did for the eleventh and twelfth centuries what the steam-engine did for the nineteenth. Lefebvre des Noëttes has therefore offered an unexpected and plausible solution for the most puzzling problem of the Middle Ages: the sudden upswing of European vitality after the year 1000.

However, Lefebvre des Noëttes failed to point out the relation between this access of energy and the contemporary agricultural revolution. He noted that the new harness made the horse available for agricultural labor: the first picture of a horse so engaged is found in the Bayeux Tapestry.[60] But while the horse is a rapid and efficient power-engine, it burns an expensive fuel—grain—as compared with the slower, but cheaper, hay-burning ox. Under the two-field system the peasant's margin of production was insufficient to support a work-horse; under the three-field system the horse gradually displaced the ox as the normal plow and draft animal of the northern plains. By the later Middle Ages there is a clear correlation on the one hand between the horse and the three-field system and on the other between the ox and the two-

60 *L'attelage*, fig. 146.

field system.[61] The contrast is essentially one between the standards of living and of labor-productivity of the northern and the southern peasantry: the ox saves food; the horse saves man-hours. The new agriculture, therefore, enabled the north to exploit the new power more effectively than the Mediterranean regions could, and thereby the northerners increased their prosperity still further.

Naturally Lefebvre des Noëttes made mistakes: only when his work receives the recognition it deserves will these be rectified. His use of the monuments is not impeccable; his almost exclusive concern with pictures led him to neglect the texts, particularly Pliny's assertion [62] that at times Italian peasants (presumably in the Po valley) plowed with several yokes of oxen; and he overlooks the complex question of the eight-ox plow-team as a basis for land division in pre-Carolingian times.[63] Moreover an etymologist has recently shown that the word for "horse-collar" in the Teutonic and Slavic tongues (English: hames) is derived from Central-Asiatic sources,[64] implying a diffusion of the modern harness westward from the nomadic steppe-culture. Doubtless criticism will eventually show that Lefebvre des Noëttes' three inventions developed rather more slowly than he thought. But that they grew and spread during the Dark Ages, and that they profoundly affected European society, seems already proved.

These discoveries regarding the utilization of animal power illustrate the novel results which may be expected from the study of medieval technology. No less profitable is Marc Bloch's brilliant and thoroughly documented investigation of the origin and spread of the water-driven mill.[65] His conclusion that, while it was invented in the first century before Christ, it did not become common until after the collapse of

[61] N. S. B. Gras, *History of Agriculture* (New York, 1925), pp. 234–235.

[62] *Natural History*, XVIII, 47–48.

[63] As suggested, for example, by F. Seebohm, *Customary Acres and their Historical Importance* (London, 1914).

[64] A. G. Handricourt, "De l'origine de l'attelage moderne," *Annales d'histoire économique et sociale*, VIII (1936), 515–522.

[65] M. Bloch, "Avènement et conquêtes du moulin à eau," *ibid.*, VII (1935), 538–563. Bloch misses the only Roman picture of an overshot water-wheel, reported in the *Nuovo bulletino di archeologia christiana* XXII (1917), 108; cf. also A. W. Parsons, "A Roman water-mill in the Athenian Agora," *Hesperia*, V (1936), 70–90. The ascription to the fourth or fifth century of the sophisticated turbine-like water-wheel preserved at the Conservatoire des Arts et Métiers in Paris is unwarranted: nothing is known of its provenience; cf. *Power*, LXXIV (1931), 502.

the Empire, confirms Lefebvre des Noëttes' contention that the technological position of the Dark Ages has been misunderstood.

The development of the windmill has not been so carefully sought out.[66] Windmills are found in tenth-century Persia, but rotating on a vertical rather than on a horizontal axis. The first authenticated windmill in Europe turns up in Normandy *ca* 1180.[67] Twelve years later Jocelin of Brakelond [68] mentions one near St. Edmundsbury and gives no indication that he considers it unusual. Within a generation this power-engine had become a typical part of the landscape on the plains of northwestern Europe.[69] In such a region it was a great boon; for the fall of rivers was so gradual that expensive dams and mill-ponds often had to be constructed to run water-driven mills; likewise these mill-ponds must often have flooded good agricultural land which the windmill freed for production. The spread of the windmill into the more mountainous southern regions, which were better equipped with rapid streams, was slow. The first Italian reference to a windmill seems to be Dante's description *(ante* 1321) of Satan threshing his arms like "un molin che il vento gira" *(Inferno,* xxxiv, 6). This southward and eastward diffusion, together with the horizontal axis of the western mill, probably indicates that the windmill was not an importation from Islam.

The cumulative effect of the newly available animal, water, and wind power upon the culture of Europe has not been

[66] The best recent discussion is H. T. Horwitz, "Über das Aufkommen, die erste Entwicklung, und die Verbreitung von Windrädern," *Technik Geschichte,* xxii (1933), 93–102. Cf. also H. P. Vowles, "An enquiry into the origins of the windmill." *Transactions of the Newcomen Society,* xi (1930–31), 1–14, and "Early evolution of power engineering," *Isis,* xvii (1932), 412–420.

[67] L. Delisle; *Études sur la condition de la classe agricole et l'état de l'agriculture en Normandie au moyen âge* (Paris, 1851), p. 514. The date 1105, so often presented even today, rests, as Delisle shows, on a forged charter. The third oldest European windmill appears at Dol in Brittany between 1191 and 1198: *Decretales Gregorii IX,* Lib. iii, Tit. 30, Cap. 23, in *Corpus juris canonici,* ed. E. Friedberg, ii (Leipzig, 1881), 563. Strangely, C. Visser, "De geschiedenis van den hollandschen windmolen," *Onze hollandsche molen: bijdragen tot de kennis en de geschiedenis van de windmolens in Nederland,* i (1926), 5–17, can discover none within the area of the modern Netherlands before 1299.

[68] *Memorials of St. Edmund's Abbey,* ed. T. Arnold (Rolls Series: London, 1890), i, 263.

[69] E.g., P. Boissonade, *Life and Work in Medieval Europe* (London, 1927), p. 186, notes that in the thirteenth century there were 120 windmills in the vicinity of Ypres; cf. also R. Bennett and J. Elton, *History of Corn Milling* (London, 1898), ii, 238.

carefully studied.[70] But from the twelfth and even from the eleventh, century there was a rapid replacement of human by non-human energy wherever great quantities of power were needed or where the required motion was so simple and monotonous that a man could be replaced by a mechanism. The chief glory of the later Middle Ages was not its cathedrals or its epics or its scholasticism: it was the building for the first time in history of a complex civilization which rested not on the backs of sweating slaves or coolies but primarily on non-human power.

The study of medieval technology is therefore far more than an aspect of economic history: it reveals a chapter in the conquest of freedom. More than that, it is a part of the history of religion. The humanitarian technology which our modern world has inherited from the Middle Ages was not rooted in economic necessity; for this "necessity" is inherent in every society, yet has found inventive expression only in the Occident, nurtured in the activist or voluntarist tradition of Western theology. It is ideas which make necessity conscious. The labor-saving power-machines of the later Middle Ages were produced by the implicit theological assumption of the infinite worth of even the most degraded human personality, by an instinctive repugnance towards subjecting any man to a monotonous drudgery which seems less than human in that it requires the exercise neither of intelligence nor of choice. It has often been remarked that the Latin Middle Ages first discovered the dignity and spiritual value of labor —that to labor is to pray. But the Middle Ages went further: they gradually and very slowly began to explore the practical implications of an essentially Christian paradox: that just as the Heavenly Jerusalem contains no temple, so the goal of labor is to end labor.

---

[70] O. Johannsen, "Die erste Anwendung der Wasserkraft im Hütten-wesen," *Stahl und Eisen,* XXXVI (1916), 1226–28, despite defects, illustrates what should be done.

Science in Medieval England

A. C. CROMBIE

. . .WITH THE APPEARANCE of [Robert] Grosseteste upon the scene, science in England took on an entirely new life and became, for a century and a half, for all practical purposes synonymous with science in Oxford. Grosseteste's influence was especially strong among the Franciscans, in whose house at Oxford he had taught, and who provided the most original scientific thinking of the period.

The achievements of English science in the thirteenth and fourteenth centuries can only be briefly indicated. The revolution introduced by Grosseteste was primarily one of method, and this made Oxford for a time the leading scientific center in the west; the study of mathematics, of physics, and of the logic of science came to be as characteristic of Oxford as were metaphysics and theology of Paris, and law and medicine of Bologna. Only in astronomy, dynamics, and magnetics could the Parisian science of the period match that of Oxford, though some of the best work was to be done neither in England nor in France, but in Germany (for example Jordanus Nemorarius's mechanics, Albertus Magnus's zoology and botany, and Theodoric of Freiberg's optics) and in Italy (for example Rufinus's botany, and medical studies at Bologna and Padua, whose medical schools were equalled in the west only by Montpellier).

By personality and position Grosseteste was well placed to exploit for their own good the historical circumstances in which he found the Oxford schools. In the twelfth century philosophers had learnt from Euclid's *Elements* and Aristotle's two *Analytics* the basic Greek conception of scientific explanation, according to which a phenomenon was explained when it could be deduced from general principles or a theory connecting it with other phenomena, just as the conclusions of Euclid's theorems were deduced from his axioms, postulates, and definitions, and the conclusions of previous theo-

"Science," pp. 584–604 in Vol. II of MEDIEVAL ENGLAND, new ed., ed. by Austin Lane Poole, 1958. Reprinted by permission of The Clarendon Press, Oxford.

rems. Aristotle had given a generalized account of the method, and shown that there were definite rules for selecting premises and for distinguishing between valid and invalid arguments. The first subjects to benefit from his new rational thinking were theology and law; its application to science at the end of the twelfth century was simply the last stage of a general intellectual movement, and by that time the formal structure of the new method had been filled in with material examples from the many specialized scientific writings translated from the Greek and the Arabic. Of these Grosseteste had a wide knowledge, and he saw that if science was to progress in his time, the primary problems to be investigated were those of method. His own scientific work, begun before 1209 and continuing even after he became bishop of Lincoln in 1235, made two major contributions.

First, in commentaries on Aristotle's *Posterior Analytics* and *Physics* he made a systematic application of logical methods of analysis, verification, and falsification to the problems of constructing and testing scientific theories by observation and experiment. His methods can best be described by means of a concrete example, the attempts made by himself and his chief disciple, Roger Bacon, to explain the rainbow. Grosseteste wrote several short treatises on optics, leading up to one on the rainbow; Roger Bacon's account of the problem appears in his *Opus Majus,* and follows the lines laid down by Grosseteste. Bacon in fact gave it as an example of the experimental method; his *Opus Majus, Opus Minus,* and *Opus Tertium,* all written in 1266–7, contained the chief thirteenth-century development of Grosseteste's conceptions of experimental and mathematical methods in science.

The basic problem in searching for an explanation of a phenomenon was, according to Grosseteste, to find the conditions necessary and sufficient to produce it. The inquiry began with a "resolution" of the phenomenon into its elements, and of this process Bacon gave an excellent example in describing how he collected instances of colors similar to those seen in the rainbow, so that the rainbow could be related to the general phenomenon of spectral colors. He examined the colors seen in rainbows, in spray made by mill-wheels and by squirting water from the mouth, in sunlight passed through a glass flask full of water or through a glass prism or hexagonal crystal on to a screen, and in different kinds of iridescent feathers. He concluded that an essential condition for the production of a rainbow was the presence of spherical water-drops in the atmosphere; he showed also, by means of an astrolabe, that the rainbow was always seen at an angle of about 42° from the incident light going from the sun to the drops.

The next stage was to find out how these conditions operated to produce a rainbow, and for this Grosseteste, Bacon, and their successors used the fruitful device of constructing a theoretical model. Grosseteste's model supposed that a cloud as a whole acted as a huge refracting lens, Bacon's that the effect was produced by the reflection of sunlight from the outer surfaces of individual raindrops. Neither will stand detailed examination, but, though they did not grasp their faults, both investigators did test the models they considered by subjecting consequences deduced from them to experiment. Later continental investigators, Albertus Magnus, Witelo, and Theodoric of Freiberg, all directly or indirectly influenced by the work of Grosseteste and Bacon, continued their work of searching for an adequate theoretical model; Theodoric, shortly before 1311, finally constructed a successful theory, based on the fundamental discovery that the sunlight entering each raindrop was not only refracted, and thus broken up into colors, but also reflected internally by the concave surface, which returned the colors to the eye of the observer. This same model was to be used by Descartes and Newton.

In using this process of experimental verification and falsification, Grosseteste assumed the principle of the uniformity of nature, and was guided in his choice of possible theories by the principle of economy. An important philosophical consequence of his logical analysis was his conclusion that scientific theories are at best probable, and not necessarily true. His understanding of these matters established the methods and interpretations of science developed by his successors both in Oxford and abroad.

Grosseteste's interest in optics was directly related to his second contribution to the scientific methods of his time. For two reasons, one methodological and the other metaphysical, he held that mathematics was essential for a scientific understanding of the physical world. The method by which he used mathematics for this purpose was Aristotle's principle of "subordination," according to which some physical sciences, for example optics and astronomy, were logically subordinate to a mathematical science, for example geometry, in the sense that they used particular cases of general mathematical laws. Grosseteste held that mathematics could be used to describe what happened, for example the reflection and refraction of light and the movements of the planets, but that the mathematical expressions did not reveal the physical cause of these optical and astronomical laws, which was to be sought in the nature of the substances involved. This distinction between mathematical and physical laws, analogous to the modern distinction between kinematics and dynamics, had been developed by Simplicius, from whom Grosseteste undoubtedly learnt it.

Grosseteste's conception of the nature of fundamental physical substance was a peculiar one which provided his second reason for holding that mathematics was essential for physical inquiry; he maintained that the fundamental physical substance was a fundamental "light" *(lux),* not identical with, but manifesting itself in, visible light. In a short treatise, *De Luce,* he described how in the beginning God created formless matter and a point of this fundamental light; this propagated itself in a sphere and produced the dimensions of space, and then, by a complicated series of changes and interactions, the heavenly spheres, the earth, and all the substances and creatures on it. This "cosmogony of light" was of Neoplatonic origin. Its importance in the history of science is, first, that it convinced Grosseteste himself that optics was the fundamental physical science; and secondly, because optics could not be studied without mathematics, that Grosseteste's influence committed a growing body of natural philosophers, both in Oxford and on the Continent, to the use of mathematical theories, not only in optics but also in all possible branches of science.

Grosseteste's own contributions to optics, apart from the study of the rainbow, consisted of a partially-correct explanation of the spherical lens and the suggestions that lenses could be used to aid weak sight, an unsuccessful attempt to formulate the law of refraction, and a most suggestive theory that light propagates itself in a series of pulses or waves. Other contributions were made by Grosseteste's followers. Roger Bacon, writing about 1266–7, developed his theory of propagation in the theory known as the "multiplication of species," designed to explain action at a distance, whether by light, heat, magnetism or gravity, extended his work on the rainbow and tried to explain the halo, gave a systematic classification of convex and concave lenses and discussed their use as aids to sight, and used his knowledge both of optics and of anatomy to try, with partial success, to understand the formation of an image in the eye. Bacon also discussed the reflecting properties of surfaces produced by rotating various conic sections about their axes, stimulated perhaps by the man whom, next to Grosseteste, he most admired, Petrus Peregrinus de Maricourt, a Frenchman who made a fundamental experimental study of the elementary properties of magnets; Bacon described experiments which he probably made himself with a floating magnet.

A follower of both Grosseteste and Bacon, the unknown author of the *Summa Philosophiae* formerly attributed to Grosseteste himself, seems to have been the first writer to point out that the colors produced by passing sunlight through a prism were refracted through different angles. The whole *Summa* is an excellent review of science about 1270, ranging from astronomy and cosmology through discussions of meteorology, optics, the magnet, chemistry, fossils, zoology, botany, and physiology. Later in the century, John Pecham wrote an admirable short textbook on optics, and in the first half of the fourteenth century John of Dumbleton, at different times a fellow of Merton and of Queen's Colleges at Oxford, tried to formulate the mathematical law relating intensity of light to distance from the source.

Throughout the Middle Ages meteorology formed a single, if heterogeneous, subject with optics, mainly because both were discussed in Aristotle's *Meteorology* and medieval scientists habitually published their original results in the form of commentaries on Aristotle and other authorities. Moreover, comets were regarded as meteorological phenomena, belonging to the region below the moon. Grosseteste seems to have observed "Halley's comet" in 1228, and he used his method of falsification in an interesting discussion of theories of comets. Roger Bacon also described a comet seen in July 1264, and attributed to its influence various distressing political consequences. Another meteorological phenomenon studied with interest in medieval as in modern England was the weather. A most remarkable series of records were kept during 1337–44 for the Oxford district by William Merlee, with a view of making predictions for farmers. He based forecasts partly on the state of the heavenly bodies, and partly on inferior signs of humidity; the moistening of salt, the carrying of sound from distant bells, and the increased activity of fleas.

Other physical problems discussed by Grosseteste in various special tracts were heat, which he regarded as a mode of motion of particles of matter, falling bodies, and astronomy; a mathematical problem that extended into his cosmogony was the summation of infinite aggregates; and a practical problem on which he wrote several treatises was the reform of the calendar. By the beginning of the thirteenth century the cumulative inaccuracy of the accepted Julian calendar had produced gross errors in the date of Easter, and, as Roger Bacon put it in his development, in the *Opus Majus,* of Grosseteste's proposals for reform, "every computer knows that the beginning of lunation is in error 3 or 4 days in these times, and every rustic is able to see this error in the sky." The recommendations made by Grosseteste and Bacon, based on determining accurately, from astronomical evidence, the exact length of the year and the relation between this and the mean lunar month, were used in attempts made to revise the calendar in the fourteenth and fifteenth centuries, but such is institutional and popular conservatism that nothing was achieved until the Gregorian reform of 1582, and this was not accepted in England until 1752.

In astronomy itself there was little advance in England during the fifteenth century. An English contemporary of Grosseteste, John Holywood or Sacrobosco, as he was called, working mainly in Paris, gave an account of the Ptolemaic system in his *De Sphaera,* an elementary textbook based on Arabic sources which remained standard for three centuries; an English translation was made for Prince Henry, son of King James I, and reading it as a schoolboy is said to have decided John Flamsteed (1646–1719), first astronomer royal, to devote himself to astronomy. Sacrobosco also wrote a treatise on the quadrant, an instrument for measuring angular altitudes. Roger Bacon observed the heavens with instruments and discussed astronomical theories at length in various writings; his emphasis on measurement seems to have helped to build up both the Parisian school of astronomy at the end of the thirteenth century and the school associated with Merton College, Oxford, in the fourteenth century.

Walter de Merton made his foundation, towards the end of the thirteenth century, expressly for the training of secular clergy, so that the learned professions and the civil service would be adequately supplied with men of sound education. The success of the college was immediate, and in science, especially in astronomy, mathematics, and medicine, it rapidly took over in England the leadership that had formerly belonged to the Franciscans. Practically every important English scientist of the fourteenth century was at some time in his career associated with Merton College, many of them as fellows.

The main achievements of the Merton school in astronomy were in the field of measurement and calculation. Basing themselves in the first place on the so-called Alfonsine Tables made at Toledo for King Alfonso X of Léon and Castile about 1272, men like John Maudith, William Rede, and Simon Bredon constructed astronomical almanacs for Oxford which gave this city something like the modern position of Greenwich. They have left manuscripts describing the construction of a variety of instruments, mainly for measuring and comparing altitudes and for representing planetary motions. Most striking are the instructions for making two such instruments, invented by himself, left by Richard of Wallingford, son of a blacksmith and eventually abbot of St. Albans; and at St. Albans he constructed, about 1320, an elaborate astronomical clock, showing the motions of the sun, moon, planets, and stars, and the ebb and flow of the tides. The excellent treatise on the astrolabe, a standard work on the subject in English, written later in the century by Chaucer, poet and busy administrator, is a product of this Oxford school. No less important than the work on measuring instruments were the improvements made by the Merton astronomers in mathematical technique, especially in trigonometry, of which John Maudith, Richard of Wallingford, and the contemporary Provençal Jew, Levi Ben Gerson may be considered the founders in its rigorous modern form. So important did astronomy become that William of Wykeham made special provision for two fellowships in the subject in the statutes of New College.

Another set of problems to which Merton mathematicians and other Oxford philosophers made fundamental contributions in the fourteenth century were those of dynamics and kinematics. In many respects these were the central problems of medieval physics, and in them can be seen most clearly that process of reformulation, leading to replacement, of originally Aristotelian conceptions and methods, which was the chief and essential medieval contribution to the revolution in physics completed in the seventeenth century.

Aristotle had conceived of the motion of a body from one place to another as a process requiring the continuous action of a motive agent, a conception precisely opposite to the seventeenth-century conception of inertia. So long as the external motive agent continued to operate, the Aristotelian theory held that velocity would be directly proportional to the motive power and inversely proportional to the resistance of the medium; remove the external agent, and the motion would stop. Many everyday phenomena supported these judgments, but three did not. First, according to this Aristotelian "law," there should be a finite velocity with any finite values of power and resistance, yet in fact if the power is smaller than the resistance it may fail to move the body at all. To escape this difficulty, Bradwardine used a modification of the "law" according to which velocity was proportional to the *excess* of power over resistance, and he tried to express by means of an algebraic function how *change* in velocity was related, as a dependent variable, to the independent variables, power and resistance.

Bradwardine's use of mathematical functions seems to have inspired the attempt made by the French physicist, Jean Buridan, to deal with the other two phenomena that provided difficulties for Aristotle's conception of motion, the motion of a projectile after leaving the projector, and the acceleration of a freely falling body. What was the motive power that kept the projectile going? This question had worried physicists since Aristotle himself. Buridan introduced a quantitative notion of *impetus,* analogous to Newton's *momentum,* imparted by the projector; this *impetus* maintained the projectile's velocity and enabled it to impart velocity to other bodies with which it collided. The acceleration of freely falling bodies Buridan attributed to successive increments of *impetus* added by gravity.

Work relevant to both problems was taken up again in Oxford. William of Ockham, in accordance with his general principles of inquiry, reduced motion to the fact that from instant to instant a body is observed to change its spatial relations with other bodies. He rejected Buridan's *impetus* as an unnecessary complication. Science, he declared in effect, should, in the interests of economy, confine itself to the description of changing relations between observable entities; "a plurality should not be postulated without necessity," as he expressed what came to be called Ockham's Razor; it was "futile" to postulate causes like *impetus*. Ockham's parsimony in hypotheses was here in some respects misplaced, for Buridan's *impetus* became the ancestor of Galileo's *impeto* or *momento*; but Ockham's general approach to scientific problems encouraged the view, to be used by Galileo and Newton in their negative criticism of contemporary physics, that the function of a scientific theory is in the first instance to correlate the observed data and not to reveal the essences of things.

In keeping with this view some contemporaries of Ockham developed some fruitful mathematical methods of describing changing relations between phenomena and rates of change. Bradwardine developed a kind of algebra in which letters of the alphabet were used for variable quantities while the operations of adding, dividing, &c., were described in words. John of Dumbleton described how to express relationship between two quantities by means of graphs, in which the lengths of vertical lines drawn at intervals perpendicular to a horizontal line represented, for example, velocity at successive intervals of time. Dumbleton and two other Mertonian mathematicians, William of Heytesbury and Richard Swineshead (the famous "Calculator"), proved algebraically, some time before 1335, the important rule, which may be called the Mertonian Rule, that the space traversed in a given time by a body moving with uniformly accelerated velocity was equal to the product of the total time of moving multiplied by the mean of the initial and final velocities. The French mathematician Nicole Oresme, later in the fourteenth century, proved this geometrically, and it gave Galileo the kinematic law of falling bodies, which he himself regarded as his profoundest discovery.

In none of the other sciences cultivated in the west in the Middle Ages did England achieve such profound and influential results as in the methodological and mathematical inquiries just considered, but some mention of them must be made to give a true picture of the scope of the medieval English interest in the problems of nature. Many of these problems were practical.

The long-characteristic English love of plants and animals is seen in the illustrations from nature in a bestiary and a herbal dating from the twelfth century, those in the latter, executed at Bury St. Edmunds, being especially good. A number of thirteenth-century English manuscripts contain excellent illustrations of animals of various kinds, especially of birds; Matthew Paris about 1250 described an immigration of crossbills, and illustrated the bird. Keen observation of nature by sculptors and carvers is shown in the capitals, bosses, and misericords of churches such as York, Ely, and Southwell. Books on falconry and fishing, especially the fifteenth-century *Treatyse of Fysshynge with an Angle* and *Boke of St. Albans,* and Walter of Henley's *Hosebondrie,* a standard treatise on agriculture from the thirteenth to the sixteenth century, are also the work of naturalists. Bartholomew the Englishman's popular work, *On the Properties of Things,* said to have been a source of Shakespeare's natural history, contains some good observation, for example his famous description of the domestic cat. The descriptions of plants in herbals improved generally in the fourteenth century, an English example being the herbal of the surgeon, John Arderne. At the same time commentaries on Aristotle's zoology, for instance those of Walter Burley and John Dymsdale, show an interest in theoretical biology.

The field of biology in which it was possible most easily to obtain some both practical and theoretical training was medicine. The *Anatomia Ricardi,* probably the work of an Englishman written in the late twelfth century, asserts that "a knowledge of anatomy is necessary to physicians in order that they may understand how the human body is constructed to perform different movements and operations." Some practical instruction in anatomy was probably required of the medical student at Oxford, as in continental medical schools, by the end of the thirteenth century; a manuscript of about that date illustrates a dissection, or post-mortem; but certainly the opportunities for dissection were necessarily meager and there is no evidence of research. The structure of the body was seen through the eyes of Galen and Avicenna, just as a modern medical student follows his textbook. But on going into practice the surgeon had perforce to rely on his own knowledge and skill, and the thirteenth and fourteenth centuries saw considerable improvements both in this art and in medicine in general, in which Englishmen played their part. In the mid-thirteenth century Gilbert the Englishman, who became chancellor of Montpellier, wrote a comprehensive work on medicine in which he described a number of diseases, including the local anaesthesia of the skin as a diagnostic symptom for leprosy, recognized for the first time that smallpox is contagious, advised operating for cancer, and recommended travelers to drink distilled water and sea-travelers to eat fruit. Early in the fourteenth century John of Gaddesden, the Oxford physician mentioned by Chaucer, gave, among much nonsense, good clinical descriptions of cases of ascites with obstructive jaundice, phthisis, leprosy, variola, smallpox, and other diseases; of operations for the stone and for hernia; of the reduction of dislocations; and described a new instrument for extracting teeth. Later in the century John Arderne served as army surgeon to two dukes of Lancaster, and saw the use of gunpowder; afterwards he practiced at Newark-upon-Trent and London. He was a surgeon of genius, describing his practice of cutting boldly, keeping the instruments clean, and using light dressings. He made a special study of fistula, describing and illustrating a new type of syringe and other instruments used in treatment; and he gave a good account of the Black Death in England. A medical encyclopedia written at the end of the fourteenth century by John Mirfeld, who seems to have been connected with the priory and hospital of St. Bartholomew, gives a good picture of medical knowledge and practice in London: at that time the number of hospitals, large and small, in the city ran into hundreds.

Another science to which both men of learning and unlettered craftsmen contributed in medieval England was chemistry. The learned were interested mainly in alchemy which, as Roger Bacon described in his *Opus Tertium,* both included a theory of matter and chemical change based on Aristotle's conception of elements and qualities, and as a practical subject "teaches how to make the noble metals and colors . . . not only can it yield wealth and very many other things for the public welfare, but it also teaches how to discover such things as are capable of prolonging human life. . . ."

Bacon regarded science as a whole as a means of obtaining power over nature, power that would not only increase wealth and health, but would also enable the military forces of Christendom to overcome the Tartars and Antichrist, whose advent he expected "from beyond the Caspian gates." Though no base metal was ever transformed into gold, no elixir found to prolong life, no powerful weapon invented to repel at a blow any possible invasion from the east, the pursuit of the objectives described by Bacon did achieve some valuable results for chemistry and for science in general. Alchemists learnt to use the balance, and discovered the properties of some metals, acids, and other substances. Bacon himself referred, without giving the recipe, to an explosive powder, and pointed out that its force would be increased by enclosing it in an instrument of solid material. Early in the fourteenth century Walter of Odington, a versatile mathematician who made astronomical observations at Oxford and wrote on optics and musical theory, composed a most interesting treatise on alchemy in which he attacked contemporary alchemists, with their gold-making, as humbugs, and tried to give mathematical precision to the whole subject. He described various chemical processes, calcination, solution, sublimation, congelation, and proposed a method of measuring the qualities of dryness, heat, and so on in degrees represented graphically by an adaptation of the procedures being worked out by his contemporaries at Merton.

The most striking results in industrial chemistry pursued in the Middle Ages in almost complete independence of learned interests, were achieved in metallurgy, and this, even more than alchemy, laid the foundations of quantitative chemistry, mainly through the processes used in assaying, which involved the use of the balance. Throughout the whole period the main advances, especially with the introduction of the blast furnace, were made in central Europe, but English metallurgy, centered mainly in the Weald of Kent and Sussex, was also active. The empirical control of processes to produce an accurate result is especially evident in the founding of bells of different pitch that would ring in tune. When firearms, apparently invented in China about the beginning of the thirteenth century, began to be made in the west in the fourteenth century, it was the bellfounders who turned out the guns. Cannons were introduced into England by Edward III, and the earliest-known illustration of a cannon occurs in an English work, by Walter de Milemete, dedicated to that monarch in 1327.

Cannons may have been used by the English at the siege of Berwick in 1319, and at Crécy in 1346; they were certainly used by them at Calais in 1347 and, according to Froissart, the English used 100 cannons, probably small mortars, at St. Malo in 1378. These were probably manufactured in Flanders or Germany, but by the end of the fourteenth century cannons were being made in England.

The same empirical control of processes and materials is found also in the arts of building and of constructing machinery. The overcoming of the many mechanical problems that culminated in the building of the great churches lies beyond the scope of this chapter; but achievements no less interesting were made in the medieval west in machinery: the watermill, the windmill, the use of geared wheels, the spinning wheel, the loom, the gigmill, the brace-and-bit, the lathe, the printing press, the mechanical clock all show the same restless inventiveness; nor must we forget the improvements in construction and rig, and the invention of the rudder, by means of which, at the end of the medieval period, western ships began to carry western arms, science, and manners to conquer the whole world.

In England, the use of machinery in the cloth industry, the staple of English trade from the twelfth century, is especially interesting. The number of water-mills had steadily increased in the west, regardless of political disturbances, since the fourth century, and, in the eleventh century, Domesday Book records some five thousand mills in England. In the twelfth century the undershot wheel on a horizontal axle was the common type; evidence for overshot wheels comes in the fourteenth century. Such mills were used for grinding corn and other purposes, but their most dramatic effect came at the end of the twelfth century with the introduction of the fulling-mill, in which trip-hammers were operated by a waterwheel. The cloth industry shifted wholesale from the cities of the plain like York, Lincoln, Winchester, and Oxford, into the hills of the West Riding, Cumberland, and the Cotswolds, where fast streams were available to drive the mills.

The first medieval machines were made of wood; this, in Mumford's phrase, "provided the finger exercises for the new industrialism." But machines of greater precision needed a material susceptible of more accurate shaping, and this was provided by the development of metallurgy. From the metallurgical, as well as the mathematical skill, first of Byzantium and the Arabic east and eventually, from the twelfth century, of the Latin west, came the earliest scientific instruments, the astrolabes and other devices requiring an accurate arrangement of parts, for measuring the movements of the heavenly bodies; refinements of metallurgy gave the surgeon the instruments to develop his art; and, at the end of the thirteenth or the beginning of the fourteenth centuries, the west produced, in the mechanical clock, the prototype of modern automatic machinery, with parts designed to produce a precisely controlled result.

The mechanical clock, driven by a falling weight which set in motion a train of geared wheels, was the latest of a series of time-keeping machines going back to the simple water-clocks of antiquity; its originality consisted in the complete mastery it showed of geared wheels and in the use of an oscillatory escapement mechanism which controlled the rate of motion. There are references to what may have been clocks of this kind in London, Canterbury, Paris, and other places at the end of the thirteenth century, and in Milan, St. Albans, Glastonbury, Avignon, and elsewhere in the early fourteenth century. But the earliest true clocks of which the mechanism is definitely known are the Dover castle clock, which is now in the Science Museum in London and used to be dated 1348 but is almost certainly later, and Henri de Vick's clock set up on the Palais Royal in Paris in 1370.

Clocks may be said to have introduced the ordinary man to the notion of mathematical time, divided into equal and indifferent intervals; mathematical space, extended into three dimensions in equal units of length, was made the measure of his world by the cartographer. As the natural and liturgical seasons gave way in the organization of time to a mechanical measure, so, alongside the hieratic maps, like the Hereford *Mappa mundi* of 1314, depicting the world divided into regions according to their spiritual relation with the holy city of Jerusalem, there were made maps by which travelers and mariners could find their way over the surface of the visible globe. Of the most accurate of these medieval maps, the *portolani* or compass-charts, made and used by mariners in conjunction with a compass, there are no known English examples; but two maps of England are pioneer ventures in mapping on land and show that progress was made. The first was drawn by Matthew Paris about 1250, and the second, the so-called "Gough map," was drawn by an unknown cartographer somewhat less than a century later. Both show roads and towns, but the second is much more accurate, and also indicates mileages, probably as estimated by travelers. Roger Bacon belongs also to the history of English cartography, not only for his recognition of the need for accurate astronomical measures of latitude and longitude, but also for a pregnant mistake. His belief that there was no great width of ocean between Europe and China became known to Columbus through the writings of Pierre D'Ailly and Aeneas Sylvius; it is said to have encouraged him to make the voyage by which he discovered the New World.

After the great advances of the thirteenth and fourteenth centuries, English science, and indeed that of almost the whole west outside Italy, showed little or no originality for over a hundred years. There were still astronomers at Oxford, and at Cambridge, but their writings mostly copied the work of their great predecessors; medicine was scarcely more alive. Thus it came about that when, in the sixteenth century, English scholars began once more to inquire vigorously into the problems of nature, they saw their work as a revival, and especially as a revival of the great days of Grosseteste, Roger Bacon, and Merton College. One of the most interesting figures in that revival, the mathematician Dr. John Dee, took pains to collect manuscripts of the mathematical and physical writings especially of Grosseteste, Roger Bacon, Pecham, and Bradwardine. Thomas Digges of University College, Oxford, describes how the pioneer work with telescopes done by his father, Leonard, "grew by the aide he had by one old written booke of the same *Bakons Experiments* . . ." The astronomer Robert Recorde, with Dee and the Diggeses among the first Englishmen to support the Copernican theory, wrote in recommending astronomical books: "Dyuers Englyshe menne

haue written right well in that argument: as Grostehed, Mich-
ell Scotte, Batecombe, Baconthorpe, and other dyuers . . ."
Later Sir Henry Savile, Warden of Merton, linked the great
past with the greater future of English science by founding at
Oxford the chairs in Geometry and Astronomy that bear his
name.

From the science of Bede to that of such a Savilian Professor as Sir Christopher Wren, to say nothing of Newton, is as
great a distance in achievement as it is in time. Far more
than was realized by the iconoclastic enthusiasts of the seventeenth century, that achievement was the measure of the
scientific vigor and originality of the medieval west; and, of
the western peoples, none entered with more enthusiasm than
the medieval English upon those inquiries that have made the
outlook of the modern world scientific, its arts industrial, and
its hopes material. But it has also been from early times a
virtue in the English to throw up, besides great and original
scientists, philosophers who have made the methods and implications of science their special study and have measured
these, with generosity and perception, against the whole
ambit of human knowledge and expectations. Many of the
problems of modern philosophers of science may be read in
the works of their medieval English predecessors. And if the
theme of continuity, which has been stressed in this chapter,
is true, we might expect to find in the habits of medieval
scientists something to remind us of the modern laboratory
student. Chaucer's description in the *Miller's Tale* of "hende"
Nicholas, a free-lance at Oxford, may perhaps be not unfamiliar.

> A chambre hadde he in that hostelrye
> Allone, with-outen any companye,
> Ful fetisly y-dight with herbes swote;
> And he him-self as swete as is the rote
> Of licorys, or any cetewale.
> His Almageste and bokes grete and smale,
> His astrelabie, longinge for his art,
> His augrim-stones layen faire a-part
> On shelves couched at his beddes heed.

WORKS FOR REFERENCE

The list includes only works in English. For a general history of medieval science see A. C. Crombie, *Augustine to
Galileo. The History of Science* A.D. *400–1640* (London,
1952), and for a more specialized study, *Robert Grosse-*

teste and the Origins of Experimental Science 1100–1700 (Oxford, 1953); both have extensive bibliographies. Basic works in this subject are C. H. Haskins, *Studies in the History of Mediaeval Science* (Cambridge, Mass., 1928), which deals with the translators; G. Sarton, *Introduction to the History of Science,* 3 vols. (Baltimore, 1927–47), a fundamental bibliographical study; and Lynn Thorndike, *A History of Magic and Experimental Science,* 6 vols. (New York, 1923–43).

Special studies of English medieval science and technology are:

Roger Bacon, Essays contributed by various Writers on the Occasion of the Commemoration of his Birth, ed. A. G. LITTLE (Oxford, 1914).

Bede: His Life, Times, and Writings, ed. A. HAMILTON THOMPSON (Oxford, 1935).

CROWLEY, T. *Roger Bacon, the Problem of the Soul in his philosophical Commentaries* (Louvain and Dublin, 1950).

EASTON, S. C. *Roger Bacon and his Search for a Universal Science* (Oxford, 1952).

GUNTHER, R. T. *Early Science in Oxford,* ii (Oxford, 1923).

JOHNSON, F. R. *Astronomical Thought in Renaissance England* (Baltimore, 1937).

McKEON, C. K. *A Study of the Summa Philosophiae of the Pseudo-Grosseteste* (New York, 1948).

MOODY, E. A. *The Logic of William of Ockham* (New York, 1935).

PAYNE, J. F. *English Medicine in the Anglo-Saxon Times* (Oxford, 1904).

Works containing studies of particular aspects of English science and technology are:

ALLBUTT, SIR T. C. *The Historical Relations of Medicine and Surgery to the End of the Sixteenth Century* (London, 1905).

SHERWOOD TAYLOR, F. *The Alchemists: Founders of Modern Chemistry* (London, 1952).

USHER, A. P. *A History of Mechanical Inventions,* 2nd edn. (New York, 1954).

WALSH, J. J. *Medieval Medicine* (London, 1920).

A basic reasoned bibliography is Lynn White's article, "Technology and Invention in the Middle Ages," *Speculum,* xv (1940), pp. 141 seqq. [reprinted above, pp. (67–87). ed.]

Marriage and AMOUR COURTOIS in Late Fourteenth-Century England

GERVASE MATHEW

ANY ATTEMPT TO analyze the relationship in late fourteenth-century England between the ideal of marriage and that of courtly love must begin with a recognition of the changing social structure of that time. For *l'amour courtois* was in its origins avowedly a class ideal, theoretically unattainable either by the vilain or the bourgeois: nor is there any evidence for its existence outside the limited, if fluid, knightly class and those who would wish to adopt its fashion.

At this period very little can be known of the unpropertied and the unprivileged, the peasants and farm servants in the countryside, the poorer artisans there or in the towns. We still possess some catchwords of the Peasants' Rising and a few rude paintings in some village churches; to them might be added the fragments of the ale-house songs in Rawlinson MS. D 913. But that is all. It may be possible to pierce through folk-song and folk custom to a medieval substratum and to find vestiges that suggest the late survival of much pre-Christian usage, notably in fertility cults; still the result would be inevitably hypothetic and only fitfully revealing. In late fourteenth-century England, as far as literary evidence can be assessed, the great mass of the people remain inarticulate.

But already there was a grouping throughout England that might be described as a middle class though its exact limits are difficult to determine. It might be said to include all those who possessed some property or some pride of status but who neither used nor aspired to use coat armor. For economic reasons it seems hardly to have been differentiated by the blurred distinction between town and country, except possibly in the north. To it would belong the guildsman in the town, many property-holders in the country, the reeve, the bailiff, the shipman, and the miller. This was a grouping that found its closest parallel in fourteenth-century Europe among the burgher class of the Hansa towns and Flanders. Partly this

Reprinted from ESSAYS PRESENTED TO CHARLES WILLIAMS, 1947, 128–135, by permission of Oxford University Press.

may have been the result of trade contacts and of the sustained predominance of East Anglia; the life of Margerie Kempe suggests how naturally King's Lynn was orientated to Lübeck, Dantzig, and Cologne. Primarily it was due to the presence of similar factors in a similar setting, the slow growth of a trading community consciously divorced from the ideals of a would-be international knightly class. It is suggestive that when the romance *Octovian* [1] was recast for a new audience in southeast England about 1350, the *courtois* elements, most of the love matter, and the introspection were replaced by a new emphasis on the shrewd triumphs of the butcher Clement and on the hero's skill in wrestling and in throwing the weight. Difficult as it is to ascribe its exact public to any medieval text it still seems possible to reconstruct some of the current ideals of this class from the great mass of literary evidence that remains.

In late fourteenth-century England medieval religion seems at its strongest within this grouping which provided not only the great preachers (and perhaps much of their audiences) but also the religious vitality of the Lollard movement. Margerie Kempe and the tailor Badsby were both born in this milieu. But it is curious how much of its didactic literature and of the popular gnomic wisdom turns avowedly upon a profit motive. Strong in the emphasis upon objective right and wrong it yet suggests a world very remote from that of Froissart's public. The ideal of marriage is neither cynical nor ignoble but completely un-*courtois*. The little treatise in Balliol MS. 354 "How the gode man taught hys sone" is late fourteenth century in its present form. The wise father tells his son to marry for love, to cherish his wife, and never to strike or curse her, to rule her gently, and to remember that though his servant she is also in some sense his companion. In the parallel piece preserved in Ashmole MS. 61 f7 the "gode Wyfe" instructs her daughter in what is in effect the *Hausfrau* ideal; a similar impression is conveyed by the Wycliffite tract "of weddid men and wifes" [2] and in the verses on a girl's upbringing in the "good Wyfe wold a Pylgremage." [3] It is an ideal quite compatible with the crude humors of the York guild-plays; the conception of the wife as a household shrew has always been the obverse to the ideal of the wife as a *Hausfrau*. It should be noted that though love is seen as a natural concomitant and perhaps as the cause of marriage it

[1] Ed. Weber, *Metrical Romances,* vol. iii, pp. 157 et seqq.
[2] Ed. Arnold, vol. iii, pp. 188 et seqq.
[3] Ed. E.E.T.S., E.S. (B).

is not love conceived in any *courtois* or even romantic sense; the love of man for woman referred to in Balliol MS. 354 is to be based on character, not looks.

Perhaps the attitude of all this grouping to the courtly love of the knightly romances is best conveyed by four fourteenth-century lines:

> Love is a selkud wodeness
> That the idel man ledeth by wildernesse
> That thurstes of wilfulnesse
> and drinket sorweness.[4]

A "selkud wodeness," a madness, an *insania mentis*.

Apart from an economic interpretation of history it would be difficult to discern any adequate reason for the patent difference in ideals between the trading and the knightly class in the reign of Richard II. It is improbable that at this period there was any race-distinction between them though it seems clear that some such distinction was believed in.[5] The knightly class can have been only a very small minority;[6] its cadre was formed by the new court, the magnates with the gentlemen of their households; the small groups[7] of knightly families in each shire who now controlled so much of the machinery of local administration; and the group of knightly families within Wales who raised the dues and levies for their absent lords. This is a cross-section adequately represented by the witnesses in the case of Scrope *v.* Grosvenor. Consciously it was a small minority linked together by the use of heraldry at a time when this was still restricted even among the larger landowners; it was welded by the acceptance of French knightly custom and in the case of many of its members by similar training in some great lord's household or by some experience of the wars. But an attempt to estimate the significance of its ideal of marriage for fourteenth-century England must take into account the fact that it possessed the prestige of fashion at a period when it was a commonplace of satirists that the soap-maker's son would wish to be knighted and the Franklin wished his son to be like the knight's. Sociologically it was long possible in England to combine the existence of

[4] Ed. P. Meyer (Rom. iv, p. 382).

[5] Cf. the evidence of Sir Robert Latom in the case of Scrope *v.* Grosvenor (ed. 1879, vol. i, p. 111). (Cf. ed. Nicholas, vol. i, p. 301.)

[6] For the beginning of this period cf. N. Denholm Young, "Feudal Society in the Thirteenth Century," *History,* September 1944.

[7] For the composition and political significance of this section cf. K. B. McFarlane, "Parliament and Bastard Feudalism," *R. Hist. S. Transactions,* 1944, pp. 53 et seqq.

clearly marked class distinctions with the fact that the classes flowed almost imperceptibly into one another. In the late fourteenth century, however great the value placed upon the possession of good blood, social status was in fact determined rather by training and by employment than by descent; Chaucer was to be unique as a poet, but in his official career he is a type. It was a society in which personal relationships held primary importance and in which the emotional content was provided by a romantic and perhaps adolescent conception of personal loyalty, friendship, and adventure.

At least within this milieu a conventional theory of marriage assumed that it was not only compatible with romantic love but ideally an expression of it. Owing to the conscious acceptance of French fashion such love was phrased in terms of that *amour courtois* first clearly formulated in twelfth-century France.

The place of *amour courtois* in medieval theory lies among the applications of the treatises *De Amicitia.* However deeply Ovid influenced its literary expression, its roots are with Cicero and Aristotle. Ultimately it seems based on the Ciceronian conception of friendship; the love of another for the other's sake. Because it is the love of another for the other's sake it finds its expression in giving and serving, not in getting, and is frustrated not when it fails to get but when it ceases to give. Therefore love service is the essential expression of *amour courtois.* In contrast to a blind and transient passion, *amour fol,* courtly love was conceived as *amour voulu,* an unchanging disposition of the individual will. It was the expression of an instinctive connaturality between two individuals and therefore could be conceived as part of the lover's nature. It was this that could provide a speculative basis for the emphasis on the vivid increase in all forms of sensibility which was held to follow from an experience that had affected the nature of the lover and for the emphasis on constancy as the test not so much of the sincerity as of the genuineness of a love. The "turtel" in Chaucer's *Parlement of Foules* reflects this cult of an unchanging loyalty:

> "Nay, God forbede a lover shulde chaunge!"
> The turtel seyde, and wex for shame al reed;
> "Thogh that his lady evermore be straunge,
> Yet let him serve hir ever, til he be deed." [8]

It is the same as the lesson that was first taught Troilus:

8 The *Parlement of Foules,* ll. 582–5.

Nay, nay, but ever in oon be fresh and grene
To serve and love his dere hertes queene;
And thenk it is a guerdon hir to serve
A thousandfold more than he can deserve.[9]

And as the refrain of the fifth of John Gower's *Cinkante Balades* "Pour tout le mond jeo ne la changeroie." [10]

A fourteenth-century Anglo-Norman allegory preserved in the Arundel MSS treats of the relationship between such love and marriage.[11] The imagery is influenced both by the *Romaunt of the Rose* and by Ovid. Love is a naked boy, yellow-haired and blind. He holds a dart and roses fly from him like sparks. His castle is raised on Loyalty and its keep is a loyal heart. His three enemies are Mistrust and Treason and their father Falsehood, while Jealousy is the mangonel with which they attempt to breach his castle wall. He who loves worthily must be loyal and have a loyal heart. He must have courtesy and always speak courteously. He must honor all women and always speak well of them. He must be able to keep his own counsel and to keep chaste and to keep his mind from *lecherie et ordure,* and if his love is answered he will know himself to be unworthy and will do all things to increase the pleasure and honor of her who has answered it. They will take each other in holy church. But being married they remain *amys et amye* and such good loving rightly used can please and serve God and bring them to a joy without end.

A similar union of a romantic love and marriage is assumed in the majority of the knightly romances that took their present form in late fourteenth-century England. Love is at first sight, there is much emphasis on the increase in the hero's prowess and in his emotional sensibility, on his love symptoms and elaborate courtesies; the love service and the love obedience come from him. The love of *Sir Degrevaunt*[12] and Melydor analyzed in detail in the northern dialect remains conventional *amour courtois*. But at the end Degrevaunt and Melydor live married for thirty years and have seven children.[13] *Sir Torrent of Portyngale* [14] at last marries

9 *Troilus and Criseyde,* ll. 816–19.

10 Ed. G. C. Macaulay, *French Works of John Gower,* p. 342.

11 Arundel MS. 14 (College of Arms). For the analysis of this allegory I am indebted to C. West, *Courtoisie in Anglo-Norman Literature,* pp. 144–50.

12 Ed. in Camden Society 30, pp. 177–256; cf. ll. 513–76.

13 Op. cit., ll. 1889–92.

14 Ed. E.E.T.S., E.S. 51

Desonal, *Sir Eglamour* Cristabelle,[15] *Sir Triamour*[16] the daughter of the King of Hungary; by 1400 the story of *Sir Otuel* has been altered[17] so that he can marry Belyssant.[18] A generation later the elaborate marriage plots in *Generydes*[19] illustrate how much the union of love and marriage has come to be assumed.

Again, probably as early as 1350, the romance of *William of Palerne*[20] took its present English form in the household of the Earl of Hereford.[21] It is essentially a *roman courtois*, with its conventional hero and well-lettered *courtoise* heroines. The love symptoms of William[22] and Melior[23] are those uniformly characteristic in French *courtoise* literature. Melior and William marry[24] and have sons. The elaborate composite romance of Partonope of Blois[25] may perhaps be dated soon after 1400. The plot centers on Partonope's disobedience to Melior and his eventual pardon:

> for in longe service it may happe that she
> wolde shew hyme of her benignyte.

Almost inevitably "knytte in wedloke to gedre thei be."[26] Between 1350 and 1400 there were three English redactions[27] of the Anglo-Norman love story of Ippomadon and La Fiere; La Fiere is again the typical heroine of a *roman courtois*, fair-haired, clear-eyed, self-controlled; Ippomadon makes himself her cup bearer and after the tournaments vows himself to be her servant always. They marry and have sons and after marriage are still described as lovers. The *Knight's Tale* expresses perfectly what had become the conventional and expected happy ending:

> and thus with alle blisse and melodye
> Hath Palamon y-wedded Emelye . . .

15 Ed. Camden Society 30; for the marriage, 1. 1297 et seq.; cf. ll. 145–80.

16 Ed. Halliwell. Percy Society.

17 In "Duke Rowlande and Sir Ottuel," ed. E.E.T.S., E.S. 35 (p. 53 et seq.).

18 Op. cit., 1. 1583 et seq.

19 E.E.T.S., 55.

20 E.E.T.S., E.S. (I).

21 l. 5529 et seq.

22 Op. cit., ll. 732–87 and 874–944.

23 Op. cit., ll. 433–579.

24 Op. cit., ll. 4832–5516.

25 Ed. Bödtker (E.E.T.S., E.S. 109).

26 Op. cit., 1. 12152; cf. ll. 1220–60, 1824; ll. 5212–56; 1. 10303 et seq.

27 Ed. Kölbing.

And Emelye him loveth so tendrely
And he hir serveth al so gentilly.[28]

"And he hir serveth al so gentilly." For the conception of a
constant love finding its expression in an unchanging love
service logically alters the ideal of marriage from that of the
husband's calm rule in the *Wyse Mans Advyse* into one of
mutual service, mutual obedience:

When Maistrie comth the God of love anon
Beteth hise winges, and farewel, he is gon! [29]

It finds its most explicit formulation in the *Frankeleyn's
Tale*.[30]

Thus hath she take hir servant and hir lord
Servant in love and lord in marriage;
Than was he bothe in lordship and servage;
Servage? Nay, but in lordshipe above,
Sith he hath bothe his lady and his love;
His lady, certes, and his wyf also
The which that lawe of love acordeth to.[31]

This is a conception paralleled more prosaically by John
Gower in his use of the symbol of a single heart in the
*Traitié selonc les auctours pour essampler les Amantz
Marietz*.[32]

Tout un soul coer eiont par tiel devis
Loiale amie avoec loials amis.[33]

It is suggestive that those of Gower's *Cinkante Balades* which
deal explicitly with marriage are phrased according to *amour
courtois* in its contemporary Paris mode.[34]

Tenetz ma foi, tenetz mes serementz;
Mon coer remaint toutditz en vostre grace.[35]

Although there is in contrast the massed literature of disil-

[28] *Knight's Tale*, ll. 2239–40, 2245–46.
[29] *Frankeleyn's Tale*, ll. 37–8.
[30] Cf. Arviragus's resolution when he marries Dorigen to:
       "hir obeye, and folwe hir wil in al
       As any lovere to his lady shal."
                          Ibid., ll. 21–2.
[31] Ibid. ll. 64–70.
[32] Ed. G. C. Macaulay, *French Works of John Gower*, pp. 379–92.
[33] Ibid., p. 381.
[34] Ibid., pp. 338–42.
[35] *Cinkante Balades*, I. 4. ll. 3–4.

lusionment and of irony, this also is perhaps a witness to the prevalence of the ideals from which it was the reaction.

There can never be sufficient evidence to determine the exact extent to which the ideal of love and marriage in the romances either influenced or reflected contemporary social custom. Though child betrothals and family alliances were clearly common enough in the knightly class neither were necessarily unaffected by it. It is significant that Richard II could conceive his marriage with Anne of Luxemburg in terms of a high-wrought and fantastic love, while the *Book of the Duchesse* shows that it was possible, and in fact fashionable, to describe the first marriage of John of Gaunt in phrases of pure *amour courtois*:

> In alle my youthe, in alle chaunce,
> She took me in hir governaunce.[36]

At least those who listened through the long-drawn chivalrous romances can never have forgotten the existence of an ideal of the relation between love and marriage. For it was a lesson almost monotonously inculcated by the barely individualized heroes and heroines as they flitted through plots formed by the tension of conflicting loyalties and surcharged with the fantastic adventures and the severances that are the tests of constancy.

[36] *Book of the Duchesse*, ll. 1285-6.

The Allegorical Interpretation of Medieval Literature

PAUL E. BEICHNER, C.S.C.

THE CONCENTRATION OF allegory in the air in the Middle Ages was heavy. Readers and hearers were exposed to it from various sources, and many probably followed simple allegories on the literal and on the figurative levels as naturally as we understand editorial cartoons.[1] An audience at a morality play followed the physical actions and the speeches of actors, knowing that the characters were personifications of virtues and vices, and other abstractions. No one expected such characters as Lechery, Pride, Gluttony, or Good Deeds, Goods, Kindred, and the like, to be rounded human beings. Homiletic allegories and spiritual and moral interpretations of scriptural texts were heard from the pulpit; no doubt, most of the congregation got the point. A deeper meaning than the literal sense on the surface was sought in poems which were true allegories, such as *The Romance of the Rose, Piers Plowman,* and *The Pilgrimage of the Life of Man*, and it was taken for granted that it would be found. The author usually made sure that his primary intention, the allegorical thrust of the work, was rather evident. Modern readers may interpret minor details or symbols in different ways, but there is seldom room for disagreement on main points.

My concern, however, is not with true allegories or moralities, those works in which the figurative sense is primary and the literal secondary—that is to say, those works in which the literal is the vehicle for the figurative or symbolic. I am concerned rather with allegoresis or allegorical exegesis—specifi-

Reprinted by permission of the Modern Language Association from *PMLA*, LXXXII (March, 1967), 33–38.

[1] The editorial cartoonist usually makes comments on current affairs by means of visual allegories. The one-to-one relationship between the symbols used and the objects signified is made certain by labeling the symbols with the names of the objects signified. The symbols count for nothing in themselves, whereas the things signified and the point or the message, which is sometimes stated or emphasized in a caption, are the important things.

cally, with the question of giving allegorical interpretations or moralizations to writings which are not primarily allegories. How far should a modern interpreter go? Is the methodology of medieval biblical exegetes or commentators to be followed in interpreting things which are not obviously biblical-religious poems or devotional writings?

At this point a brief word on the senses of Scripture will not be out of place, since space will not permit amplification with examples. Exegetes, believing Scripture to be divinely inspired, distinguished between two basic levels of meaning: first, the *sensus litteralis*, that is, the "human" or "natural" sense, sometimes called the "historical," the *prima facie* meaning of an account which would be couched in the language with the figures of speech of the writer, including any parables and short allegories which he might use; and second, the spiritual level, the *sensus spiritualis*, comprising (1) the allegorical or Christological and ecclesiological sense, (2) the tropological or moral sense, and (3) the anagogical or eschatological sense. These three planes of the spiritual sense were sometimes referred to collectively as the allegorical (or mystical) sense in contrast to the *sensus litteralis*.

The biblical exegete had a strong didactic purpose—to instruct in faith to be believed and in morals to be practiced. The purpose of the reader was to deepen his own faith or spiritual knowledge of God and neighbor, and also to increase his charity or love of God and neighbor by virtuous living. The reading of Scripture and the commentaries thus became a kind of meditation on texts and incidents in order to extract the spiritual juice from them. Petrus Riga says in the preface of his *Aurora* or *Biblia versificata* that he wishes to "elicit some allegories from the letter, as though the kernel from the nut, the grain from the chaff, the honey from the wax, the fire from the smoke, the meal from the barley, the wine from the grape." [2] When reading a piece of medieval literature which does not obviously seem to be an allegory should we apply this methodology and try to extract some spiritual, allegorical, or moral juice from it? Let us still leave the question unanswered at the moment.

Everyone who reads Chaucer's earthy, secular poem, the *Miller's Tale*, follows its literal or natural sense and probably

[2] *Aurora, Petri Rigae Biblia versificata: A Verse Commentary on the Bible,* ed. Paul E. Beichner, C.S.C., 2 vols. (Notre Dame, Ind., 1965: Pubs. in Mediaeval Studies, xix), I, 7: "studensque de ipsa littera aliquas allegorias elicere tanquam nucleum de testa, granum de palea, mel de cera, ignem de fumo, medullam de hordeo, uinum de acino."

becomes increasingly aware of the poetic justice in it. It is the story of an old carpenter, his young wife, "hende" Nicholas, and Absolon; and it involves three motifs, "the flood," "the misdirected kiss," and "the branding." Now let me give it an allegorical interpretation, specifically, a *moralitas* or *significatio*. To invent one is fun, even an edifying exercise, but I would not claim that it is Chaucer. A person is still free to read the *Miller's Tale* as a sheer *fabliau*. I think the *moralitas* should go like this:

> The foolish old carpenter is man, with good intentions but rather stupid. His young wife is the soul to whom he is united, and she is hard to manage, watch over, or constrain. "Hende" Nicholas is the flesh, always on hand, an attractive nuisance. Absolon is the vanity of the world. Things happen when man is deceived and the flesh and the vanity of the world try to possess his soul. But at the end of life there is judgment and retribution.

This *moralitas* or *significatio* is quite stylized. You can expand it or make up another sometime at your leisure. And it is easy to learn the system. One needs only to read some tales and their moralizations in the *Gesta Romanorum* [3] in order to moralize other tales in similar fashion. It does help, of course, if one first decides who are the "good guys" and who are the "bad guys." It is quite obvious that such a *moralitas* for the *Miller's Tale* is something I have tacked onto the story. It is not essential, whereas poetic justice and the morals of the characters are essential to the story because the author Chaucer put them there. I do not disagree with Professor

[3] *Gesta Romanorum,* ed. Hermann Oesterley (Berlin, 1872); photo-offset reprint, Georg Olms Verlagsbuchhandlung (Hildesheim, 1963). *Gesta Romanorum,* translated by Charles Swan, with a preface by E. A Baker (Broadway Translations, 1924). Swan's edition of 1824 was revised and corrected by Wynnard Hooper (Bohn's Antiquarian Library, 1877; paperbound repr., Dover Books, 1959). *The Early English Versions of the Gesta Romanorum,* ed. S. J. H. Herrtage, EETS, E.S., XXXIII (1879).
Some collections of tales, however, were intended to supply *exempla* or illustrations for points which a preacher himself wished to make. Such a collection of stories without significations and moralities is *An Alphabet of Tales: An English 13th Century Translation of the Alphabetum Narrationum Once Attributed to Étienne de Besançon,* ed. Mrs. M. M. Banks, EETS, CXXVI, CXXVII (1904, 1905). The alphabetical arrangement of the tales according to topics to be illustrated—from "I. Abbas non debet esse nimis rigidus." to "DCCCI. Ypocrisis. Ypocrita a demone deuoratur."—would have precluded the moralization of the tales from the intention of the compiler and probably from the intention of the busy preacher who consulted the work.

Olson when he says: "The ending of the tale is just, in that its punishments are exactly suited to the moral paradigms of the characters punished." [4] His concern with the poetic justice of the story belongs to the level of the *sensus litteralis,* whereas I have concocted a tropological sense or a morality for the *Miller's Tale.*

Incidentally, recourse to the *sensus spiritualis,* allegorical or moral, enabled many an exegete to find edification in some episodes recorded in the Bible which would scarcely be edifying on the level of the historical sense. A good example of this is the allegory for the affair of Juda and Thamar in the *Aurora* of Petrus Riga,[5] which he took from earlier commentators, either Isidore of Seville or Rabanus Maurus.

To return to Chaucer and the question of a superimposed allegory. Jankyn, the fifth husband of the Wife of Bath, read to his spouse a series of *exempla* or "tales of wicked wives." Among them is the anecdote of the man who confided to a friend that a tree grew in his garden on which his three wives had hanged themselves, and the friend eagerly begged him for a shoot of that "blissed tree" to plant in his own garden (*CT,* III [D], 757–764). The same story or one like it appeared in various places before Chaucer used it. That in the *Gesta Romanorum* has this application or *significatio:* "My beloved, the tree is the cross of Christ. The man's three wives are pride, lusts of the heart, and lusts of the eyes, which ought to be thus suspended and destroyed. He who solicited a part of the tree is any good Christian." [6] It is doubtful that

4 Paul A. Olson, "Poetic Justice in the *Miller's Tale,*" *MLQ,* XXIV (1963), 230. The article analyzes the characters from a moral point of view, but they are still Chaucer's characters; they do not signify abstractions or other things as a *moralitas* would require.

5 *Aurora, Lib. Gen.,* ll. 1265–88 (*De coitu Iude cum Thamar*), ll. 1289–1314 (*Allegoria*).

6 Swan, Tale XXXIII, Application. Oesterley, cap. 33 (p. 331): "Carissimi, hec arbor est sancta crux, in qua perpendit Christus. Hec arbor debet poni in orto hominis, dum anima habet jugem memoriam de passione Christi. In ista arbore tres uxores hominis suspenduntur, scilicet superbia vite, concupiscencia carnis et concupiscencia oculorum. Homo enim datus mundo tres uxores ducit: una est filia carnis, que vocatur voluptas, alia filia mundi, que vocatur cupiditas, tercia filia diaboli, que vocatur superbia. Sed cum peccator gracia dei adheret penitencie, iste uxores voluntarie suas non habentes se suspendunt. Cupiditas se suspendit fune elemosyne, superbia fune humilitatis, voluptas se suspendit fune jejunii et castitatis. Iste, qui quesivit surculos, est bonus Christianus, qui toto conamine hoc debet appetere et querere, non tantum pro se, sed pro aliis vicinis. Ille, qui flevit, est miser homo, qui magis diligit carnem et ea que carnis sunt, quam ea que sunt spiritus sancti. Tamen sepius talis ad informacionem boni viri ad rectam viam poterit duci, et sic vitam eternam obtinebit."

the writer had to stretch very hard to invent that application; he was used to stretching. But Chaucer's Jankyn tells the story as one of many calculated to exasperate the Wife of Bath, scarcely a spiritual or noble purpose. To superimpose a moralization like that in the *Gesta* on top of the anecdote as related by Jankyn destroys its purpose.

The first appearance in writing of the story of Leir and his three daughters is in Geoffrey of Monmouth's *Historia Regum Britanniae* (lib. II, cap. 11–14). Since Geoffrey was concerned with writing pseudo-history, he made his folk tale sound like history. To give it an aura of truth, early in his account he made Leir the founder of Leicester, a city Leir named for himself. This would not make it an allegory, and neither would the interpretation of the name Cordeilla *corde illa,* to mean "she from the heart" or "she with a heart" to fit her father.[7] Geoffrey told a story which found its way into many chronicles and translations, into the *Gesta Romanorum* and *The Faerie Queene,* and which became the plot of Shakespeare's *King Lear.* In one English version of the *Gesta Romanorum* the Leir story is so modified that only the plot remains, while Leir becomes Theodosius, an emperor of Rome, and his three daughters are unnamed; but it does have a *moralitas.*[8] In the second English version of the *Gesta* the story is rather close to that of Geoffrey of Monmouth. It does not end with a *moralitas* but with a paragraph pointing out the obvious, as though the story had been told as an *exemplum* to illustrate flattery and truth.[9] It seems to me that only readers of the *Gesta Romanorum* or those medieval readers with a strong desire to have a morality for every

[7] J. S. P. Tatlock, *The Legendary History of Britain* (Berkeley and Los Angeles, Calif., 1950), p. 382: "As to Leir's daughters, whatever any earlier form of Cordeilla's name, the good Latinist author must have meant Cor-de-illa to fit her loyal love."

[8] Herrtage, p. 53 (from *MS. Harl.* 7333): "Moralite. Derè Frendis, this Emperour may be callid ech worldly man, the which hath thre doughters. The first doughter þat seith, 'I loue my fadir more þan my self,' is þe worlde, whom a man lovith so wele, þat he expendith all his lif aboute hit; but what tyme he shalbe in nede of dethe, scarsly if þe world woll for all his love yeve him five knyghtes, scil. v. bordis, for a cofre to ley his body ynne, in þe sepulcre ..." For the Latin, see Oesterley, p. 673: *"Moraliter.* Karissimi, iste imperator protest dici quilibet homo mundanus qui habet tres filias ..."

[9] Herrtage, p. 53 (from *MS. Addit.* 9066): "Here may men se what fayre flaterynge wordes done, that vntrewly fullfillen the be-heste that they make; and here also mony men may here, what comys to hem that sayen the truthe, as Cordell did: For it is written, they that glosen the, and praysen the, dysseyuen the, and they that tellen þe truthe and the sothe, they louen the, and are thy good Frendes, &c."

story of good and evil would have wanted one superimposed on the Leir story. Most readers would have wanted an author's telling of the story to accomplish its effect in its own natural way. Even the author of the second English version of the *Gesta* seemed to feel that the usual type of *moralitas* would be injurious to the Leir story.[10]

Dame Siriz is an early *fabliau* without poetic justice and without a moralization.[11] One will recall how Dame Siriz, a crude and colorful old procuress, by using the "weeping dog" trick induced a virtuous young wife to receive a lover. The old hag first doctored up her little female dog with mustard and pepper to make it weep and then persuaded the young lady that the dog was her daughter who had been transformed because she had rejected the advances of a young man. Needless to say, the client of Dame Siriz got what he wanted. The author of the *fabliau* seemed to be concerned with dialogue and the gradual disclosure of the character of Dame Siriz and not with morals. However, the same story may be found in the *Gesta Romanorum* with this application:

> My beloved, the soldier (the husband) is Christ; the wife is the soul, to which God gave free will. It is invited to the feast of carnal pleasures, where a youth, that is, the vanity of the world, becomes enamoured of it. The old woman is the devil; the dog, the hope of a long life, and the presumptuous belief of God's clemency, which lead us to deceive and soothe the soul. But Christ will come during the night, and condemn the sinner to death.[12]

10 Perhaps it should be noted here that the "bond story" and the "story of the three caskets" had been told and retold by others before Shakespeare used them in the *Merchant of Venice*. In the *Gesta Romanorum* they are supplied with a morality. For that of the "bond story" see Herrtage, pp. 164–165, and for that of "the three caskets" see pp. 304–306; see also the Notes, pp. 475 and 491, for other occurrences of these stories.

11 In *Middle English Humorous Tales in Verse*, ed. George H. McKnight (Boston, 1913), pp. 1–20. See also the Introduction, pp. xxi–xliii.

12 Swan, Tale xxviii, Application. In his translation Swan changed the conclusion of the tale by adding that the husband returned unexpectedly "and put the whole party to a shameful death." He also supplied the last sentence of the application above. This interpolation, he thought, "afforded a better moral." See also the rather detailed Latin moralization of the story in Oesterley (p. 327): "Carissimi, iste miles est Christus, uxor casta et decora anima per baptismum lota, cui dedit deus liberum arbitrium et sue voluntati tradidit, quando de hoc mundo ad patrem ascendit . . ."

What I am stressing, I suppose, is that tales or anecdotes have been composed and then diffused throughout space and time without the author or the transmitters having been the least bit concerned with an allegorization or moralization of them. The fact that somewhere sometime a person imbued with the didactic spirit gave a story such an interpretation is no reason for assuming that everyone did, or must, interpret it in the same way then or thereafter. How a writing is read by a reader, or used by an author, or a pedagogue, or a preacher, depends upon the person and his purpose.[13]

It is well known, of course, that allegorical interpretation of the classics was practiced for one reason or another during the Middle Ages. Long after fears of contamination with pagan religion had been laid to rest and the gods were thought of as allegorical personifications which could be used in new poems as symbols, the dubious morality of some of the human beings remained a problem. The wisdom of the ancients, however, was thought to be contained in great poems, in the *Aeneid* for example, and it could be extracted through allegoresis and moralization. Fulgentius in the sixth century gave impetus to interpreting the *Aeneid* allegorically, and Bernardus Silvestris, the twelfth-century poet of the

---

[13] Thomas Hoccleve's purpose in translating two stories, including their moralizations, from the *Gesta Romanorum* was to make them available in English: "The Tale of Jereslaus's Wife and Her False Brother-in-Law" (*Hoccleve's Works. I. The Minor Poems*, ed. Frederick J. Furnivall [EETS, E.S., LXI, 1892], pp. 140–178), and "The Tale of Jonathas, His Magic Ring, Brooch, and Cloth, and His Deceitful Concubine Fellicula" (pp. 215–242). See Herrtage, pp. 311–322 and 180–196, and also Oesterley, cap. 249, pp. 648–654 and cap. 120, pp. 466–470.

Having translated the story of Jereslaus's wife in verse, Hoccleve showed his work to his friend.

> "Thomas, it is wel vn-to my lykyng;
> But is ther aght þat thow purposist seye
> More on this tale?" "Nay, my freend/no thyng."
> "Thomas/heere is a greet substance aweye:
> Where is the moralizynge . . . ?" (*Works*, I, 174; ll. 8–12)

Since no *moralizacio* was in the copy of the *Gesta* which Hoccleve had been using, his friend went home and brought his copy.

> And to this moralyzynge I me spedde,
> In prose wrytynge it / hoomly and pleyn,
> ffor he conseillid me / do so / certeyn. (ll. 24-26)

Hence, it would appear that Hoccleve realized the tale could stand without a moralization, but if it was publicized as a translation from the *Gesta Romanorum*, the moralization had better be translated too. However, he had the good judgment not to use verse. The moralization of the second tale is also in prose.

school of Chartres, gave the public his allegorical interpretation of the *Aeneid*,[14] although he is better known for *De universitate mundi*, his allegorical work in verse and prose like *De consolatione philosophiae* of Boethius. Pedagogues and teachers of Latin to young students could resort to allegorical interpretations or moralizations of the classics in delicate situations, or they could use Christian works, as was often recommended, for example in the thirteenth century by Vincent of Beauvais and Jacques de Vitry.[15]

Nevertheless the reading of the Latin classics for themselves, for the *sensus litteralis* as distinguished from an allegorical interpretation, continued. This was the usual way that literary men read them while at the same time they treated the doings of the gods as myths and fables. With every appearance of a quotation or use of classical material in a Middle English poem, I do not believe we are justified in assuming that the author wished the reader to become involved in allegoresis of the classical material. Thus, I do not believe that Chaucer intended that a reader of his summary of the *Aeneid* in the first book of *The House of Fame* should even be distracted by remembering that allegorical interpretations of the *Aeneid* had ever been written. But he does tell the reader, if he wants more information concerning the death of Dido, to "Rede Virgile in Eneydos/Or the Epistle of Ovyde" (*HF*, ll. 378–379). This does not mean the allegorical commentary on the *Aeneid* of Bernardus Silvestris or the Old French *Ovide moralisé*.

Bestiary materials should not be excluded from a consideration of allegoresis. The first bestiary or *Physiologus* was developed in the early period of the Church, probably among the Christians of Alexandria, where the practice of interpreting the Bible according to the *sensus spiritualis* was very

[14] *Commentum Bernardi Silvestris super sex libros Eneidos Virgilii*, ed. Guilielmus Riedel (Gryphiswald, 1924). Bernardus says (p. 3) that the poet, inasmuch as he is a philosopher, writes of the nature of human life and his method is to describe under a covering (*sub integumento*) what the human spirit placed temporarily in the human body does or suffers. This covering is a kind of description wrapping the understanding of truth beneath a fictional narrative. Bernardus proposes to remove the covering or wrapper. He is careful to distinguish this kind of interpretation from the learning of virtue or prudence from the good example or the bad example of the characters: "Verbi gratia: ex laboribus Eneae tolerantiae exemplum habemus, ex affectu eius in Anchisem et Aschanium pietatis, ex veneratione quam diis exhibebat . . . ex votis et precibus quas fundebat quodammodo ad religionem invitamur. Per immoderatum vero Didonis amorem ab illicitorum appetitu revocamur" (pp. 2–3).

[15] See *Aurora*, Vol. I, pp. xxxii–xxxiii.

strong. If God could speak to men by means of the words and events recorded in the Bible, as Creator He could also speak to men by means of the book of nature, for all creation was intended for man's instruction as well as his use. Hence the natures, habits, or qualities of animals could be expounded in such a way as to present lessons in religious doctrine or moral instruction. The natural history of the animals, of course, was unnatural and quaint to say the least, but the significations were important. Like the animals themselves after creation, the first bestiary materials increased and multiplied and spread over the literary world.

Significations for birds were worked out in similar fashion. For example, the *Aurora* (*Lev.*, ll. 635–742) gave the natures and significations of the twenty birds named in Leviticus xi.13–19. Because these birds were considered unclean, they signified evil things. Thus, a translation of the two distichs on the mythical griffin: "The griffin, a winged animal with four feet, snatches men and terrifies horses: signified by it is the cruel crime of the mighty who drink the deaths of men with ferocity." [16] The vulture quite aptly signifies the war profiteer. "It is the nature of the vulture to rejoice at conflict, to wish for corpses, and to follow the armed camp to seek food: those men are similar who wish for war, who follow the camp, who gape for spoils, and who hunger for gain." [17] Gower appropriated and used the accounts, in whole or in part, of eleven of these birds in his *Vox clamantis*.[18]

The understanding of significations of birds and beasts, which were made common through allegorical interpretations of biblical material and through the bestiaries, led rapidly to the use of these creatures as symbols by medieval and renais-

[16] *Aurora, Lev.*, ll. 639–642:

> Pennatum gryphes animal pedibusque quaternis
> Innitens homines carpit, abhorret equos:
> Designatur in hoc facinus crudele potentum
> Qui mortes hominum cum feritate bibunt.

[17] *Aurora, Lev.*, ll. 655–658:

> Vulturis est rixis gaudere, cadauera uelle,
> Vt cibus occurrat, bellica castra sequi:
> Sunt similes qui bella uolunt, qui castra sequuntur,
> Qui spoliis inhiant esuriuntque lucrum.

[18] The eagle and the griffin, *Aurora, Lev.*, 635—642—*V.C.*, VI, 985–992; the kite, 647–648—VI, 101–102; the vulture, 655–658—V, 537–540; the crow, 659–660, 663–666—IV, 305–310; the ostrich, 667–672—IV, 1059–64; the owl, 673–676—VI, 95–98; the hawk, 683–686 —VI, 719–722; the screech-owl, 687–694—III, 1693–1700; the cormorant, 695–698—III, 1587–90; the bat, 735–740—VI, 89–94.

sance artists and writers. A convenient illustration of the use of such animal symbolism is the miniature representing "The Car of Avarice" in the *Hortus deliciarum* of Herrade de Landsberg.[19] Although it is one of a series of miniatures based on the battle of virtues and vices or *Psychomachia* of Prudentius, if it is considered alone, it might aptly be titled "The Animal Faces of Avarice." Placed in the center of a circular design and representing the devil, Avarice ("Avaricia, id est, diabolus") sits in her car, holding coins in one hand and a three-pronged hook in the other, for according to the inscription "Avarice lives evilly in soiled garments and holds a trident in her hand because of her rapacity." The car is drawn by the fox and the lion, holding in their mouths the ends of a scroll which reads: "Avarice says: 'I lick with the fraud and cunning as it were of a fox, or pursuing wealth by force I gnaw like the cruel lion'." Statements at the circumference indicate that the fox symbolizes fraud ("Fraus est vulpes") and the lion symbolizes ambition ("Ambitio est leo"). Six other vices associated with Avarice or employed by her are designed as draped human busts with animal heads. Each holds an identifying scroll, and four point a finger at Avarice. That at the top of the circle is the pig: "Filthiness is the pig" ("Sordiditas est sus"). Continuing clockwise with a translation of the scrolls: "Tenacity barking like a dog.— Hunger for acquiring is an ox.—Rapacity is a wolf.—Violence is a bear.—Love of money, that is, an inordinate appetite for acquiring, is a vulture." Appropriate statements fill the spaces above their heads: for example, above the vulture: "Avarice rejoices over the death of a kinsman"; above the bear: "Avarice terrifies by clamor and threats"; above the ox: "Avarice devours the hay of the world, i.e., wealth, like the ox."

The interpretation of names was sometimes practiced by medieval writers. Very many of the lives of the saints in the *Legenda aurea* begin with an interpretation of the name of the saint worked out in such a way as to symbolize or direct attention to his virtues, which are held up for our admiration

[19] See *Hortus deliciarum*, Pl. LIbis (Supplément), in Herrade de Landsberg, *Hortus deliciarum*, publié aux frais de la Société pour la Conservation des Monuments Historiques d'Alsace; texte explicatif par A. Straub et G. Keller (Strasbourg, 1901). Unfortunately the original, late twelfth-century manuscript was burnt on 24 or 25 August 1870 at Strasbourg in the conflagration ignited by the bombardment of the city. Tracings of approximately two-thirds of the miniatures, however pale by comparison with the brilliant originals, had been made on earlier occasions for various purposes and were dispersed. These were collected and the best were published.

if not for our exact imitation. Readers of Chaucer are familiar with such an interpretation of the name *Cecilia* in the Prologue of the *Second Nun's Tale* (*CT*, VIII [G], 85–119). But one is not thereby justified in "etymologizing" the names of persons in other kinds of tales by borrowing and adapting, or creating *ex nichilo*. For example, it could be done very easily for the name *Nicholas,* but the clerk in the *Miller's Tale* is as unlike St. Nicholas as a saint's life is different from a *fabliau*. The result would be a parody of the *Legenda aurea*[20] applied to Chaucer's "hende" Nicholas. If Chaucer had intended the reader to think of such an interpretation, he would have given it. However, one must still recognize the significance of names of some characters chosen by an author for other reasons, particularly the names of characters who are personifications in allegories, or who are partial or *quasi* personifications such as January and May, and Justinus and Placebo in the *Merchant's Tale*.

My view regarding the allegorical interpretation of non-allegorical types of literature has been gradually emerging. I do not favor the invention, by the reader, of a *moralitas* or *significatio* for tales, anecdotes, and *fabliaux*; neither do I think that a romance portraying the ups and downs of a hero should be interpreted as an allegory of the life of man; and I do not think that a search for a *sensus spiritualis* in secular literature similar to that sought by exegetes in the Bible can be more than a pious exercise of ingenuity. To interpret non-allegorical literature in these ways is like looking for faces or pictures in the clouds; anyone with a vigorous imagination can see what he wishes. No one will deny a reader the right to meditate on his reading in this fashion, but if he presents his interpretations for others to read, he is engaging in creative writing.

On the other hand, if I may be permitted a figure of my own, much of the intellectual coin and medium of intellectual exchange in the Middle Ages had become radioactive by coming in contact with the spiritual interpretation of the Bible and by repeated use in allegories. Besides their literal sense some words carried non-literal allegorical meanings or

---

20 Jacobus a Voragine, *Legenda aurea,* ed. Th. Graesse, 3rd ed., 1890: photo-offset reprint, Otto Zeller (Osnabrück, 1965), p. 22: "Nicolaus dicitur a nicos, quod est victoria, et laos, quod est populus, id est Nicolaus, quasi victoria populi i.e. viciorum quae et popularia et vilia sunt; vel victoria proprie, quia multos populos vita et doctrina docuit vitia et peccata vincere. Vel Nicolaus dicitur a nicos, quod est victoria, et laus, quasi victoriosa laus; vel a nitor et laos, quod est populus, quasi nitor populi . . ."

connotations, as *Jerusalem*, meaning "the Church" or "heaven." Animals and other things often used as symbols did not easily shake off all symbolism when they escaped from bestiaries and allegories. Famous people, including biblical personages, were likely to be considered as types of some thing, which the use of the name by a writer would recall, for example, Samson and strength, Absalom and rather effeminate beauty and long hair. And just as some truly allegorical works contained non-allegorical matter and statements to be understood literally and univocally, for example, the advice of the God of Love to the Lover in *The Romaunt of the Rose* (ll. 2280–84) to wash his hands, clean his teeth, comb his hair, and remove dirt from under his nails, so too non-allegorical works sometimes contained some allegorical items and details of symbolic significance.

How can such things be determined in a work which is not an allegory? The only way, I suppose, is for a person to read enough allegories and allegorical commentaries on the Bible to acquire a feeling for tropes, types, clichés, personifications, and symbols, as well as the biblical things for which an allegorical sense was common. When miscellaneous things of this nature are found in a work which is not an allegory, some items will be understood immediately as bits of allegory, particularly the passages involving personifications, but the reader will still have to use his good judgment and determine from the context whether or not an allegorical sense or symbolic value is to be attached to some things or passages in addition to the literal sense which is absolutely necessary. Not every lion encountered in a story represents either Christ, or St. Mark the Evangelist, or the devil, or a vice; some lions represent only themselves.

PART III

Chaucer and His Works

In and Out of Dreams

BERTRAND H. BRONSON

WHAT, WE ARE now to ask, did Chaucer make of that world of perpetual wonder and miracle into which every one of us passes, not once or twice in a lifetime, but for some hours of every twenty-four: the world of dreams? What for him is its credit? What are its properties and proprieties? And how may its reservoirs be drawn upon for the needs of literature?

As to credit, Chaucer perhaps never made up his mind. That dreams can be prophetic he is not prepared to deny. That they may have physiological causes he is quite ready to grant. That they may sometimes be a figurative commentary or obscure interpretation of events he can well conceive. Certainly, that they may contain divine revelations he must, as a good Christian, implicitly believe, though assurance in particular cases is nowadays most difficult to attain. He appears to have read widely on the whole subject, and to have acquired a very respectable familiarity with the theory and content of medieval dream-lore. The Boethian vision, Macrobius on Cicero, and the vaster scheme of Dante were formative influences on his thought, and the impress of *The Romance of the Rose* on his poetry was lifelong.

In practice, however, he *uses* dreams always dramatically, making them fit his context; or leaving the basic questions open, with a frank confession of his inability to decide. In *The House of Fame* he professes himself put to a stand by the whole problem. But, in the *Nun's Priest's Tale,* Pertelote will give a positive physiological reading, while Chauntecler will be equally certain that he is being forewarned. Criseyde, falling in love, dreams prophetically of an exchange of hearts with her eagle; Troilus, in jealous apprehension, dreams with equal truth of his lady kissing the tuskèd boar that Cassandra identifies as Diomed. Pandarus, whatever his deeper senti-

Reprinted from Chapter 2, IN SEARCH OF CHAUCER by Bertrand H. Bronson, by permission of the University of Toronto Press.

ments, professes utter scepticism: "A straw for alle swevenes signifiaunce!" he cries. . . .

When we study Chaucer's dream-visions, we are struck by his characteristic use of reading as a device to launch his poems. This has frequently been mentioned as a stock convention of the *genre,* but I believe it to be much more integral, more dynamic, and more individually employed in Chaucer's dream-poems than in those of earlier poets. The French poems from which Chaucer levies tribute do not present the dreamer as a reader. To Chaucer, reading seems to be a natural gateway from the active life to the contemplative, from waking to dreaming; and probably he thought of himself as unusual in this regard. Relatively few laymen in his time, we may be fairly sure, had developed the singularly unconvivial habit of solitary reading for pleasure. Manuscripts primarily literary could not have been common, and they were customarily read in company, aloud. Very noteworthy, then, is Chaucer's repeated calling of attention to this personal trait of his. In *The Book of the Duchess,* he takes a romance to help him pass a sleepless night, considering it better amusement than backgammon or chess. In the *Parliament,* he again emphasizes his inveterate habit of reading for private profit or delight: the whole day passes unobserved in this manner. And no one can forget the eagle's mingled scorn and commiseration in *The House of Fame* for Geoffrey, who, for recreation after his day's work, shuts himself up like a hermit and sits dumb as a stone over his books until he's quite dazed— though we allow him for companionship spiced cakes and a chirping glass from the royal pitcher! Thus early we find Chaucer setting himself apart from his fellows as a *reading* man; and throughout his work he never lets us forget the fact.

What we notice first in the dream-visions is the importance of books in the structure of the poems. The sequence made familiar by *The Book of the Duchess* and *The Parliament of Fowls* is from sense-impressions to the pleasures of reading, and then to that heightened state of excitement in which the poem reaches what is at least its overt *raison d'être.* But it may be noticed that the timing differs in all four works. In *The House of Fame,* the reading is set inside the vision, where the poet traces the *Aeneid* scene by scene on the walls of Venus' temple, in a blend of picture and incised writing that had been briefly anticipated in the Duchess poem, where the dreamer's chamber walls and windows were similarly enriched with the Troy story and the Romance of the Rose—indeed, a kingly kind of illuminated manuscript. Dido's story is recounted in *The House of Fame* as if simultaneously read, seen, and heard; but the poet's interjected moral reflections on the action belong outside the dream, to the re-telling. Neither prologue to *The Legend of Good Women* contains any account of specific reading. Instead, there is, before the dream, a good deal about the value of books both old and new. The main use of reading in this work comes, of course, at the end of the dream, in the series of legends all drawn from books.

These shifts of temporal sequence affect the organic connection between book and dream and give rise to questions of causal and logical relationship. Theoretically, the contents of the book and the dream do not need to be connected. The possible relations could extend from that extreme all the way to exact parallelism. The last might be insipid, however, and the first would be pointless. We may naturally assume that some sort of significantly calculated relation will subsist in the author's intention, whatever our estimate of the artistic merit, cunning, or success of his strategy. But it is for him to determine whether that relation shall be close or remote, obvious or subtle, direct or indirect: whether the book's connection with the dream shall be straightforward, oblique, or contradictory. . . .

What came first to the creator's mind would naturally be, not the book, but the dream. The object or goal of the poem as a whole lay in the dream which was to be its artistic culmination. In the dream, therefore, lay implicit the determinative suggestion of the suitable kind or use of reading—the kind that might serve as an appropriate bridge to that other country, to the vision which was the poem's *raison d'être*. From this point of view, the relation, taken generally, is one of cause and effect in reverse order: the choice of reading is the effect of the dream-content, of which the book should appear to be the plausible but topsy-turvy cause. If we have faith in Chaucer's art, we must believe that this relation *was* predetermined, and should attribute to our own lack of insight, or to some historical accident, any failure to discern the point of the connection. We must not join Sypherd in subscribing to the pretty apology of Alceste:

> And eke, peraunter, for this man ys nyce,
> He myghte doon yt, gessyng no malice,

> But for he useth thynges for to make:
> Hym rekketh noght of what matere he take!
>
> (F, 362–365)

The poet who could invent that delightful excuse could hardly be guilty of the offence. Medieval writers, we are told, set no such store by the principle of "organic unity" as we do today. It might be safer to say that their delight in the incongruous, as many an ancient cathedral seems to testify in its details, was a good deal livelier than ours. But they were also worshippers of rational order and great builders of systems. Few readers would maintain that theme as a structural element was foreign to the mind of the poet who assembled the main blocks of *The Canterbury Tales,* or that the creator of *Troilus and Criseyde* was devoid of a sense of artistic unity. Where Chaucer expatiates unduly, as to our sense he sometimes does, it is because things crowd in upon him by association, not because he has to beat the bushes for matter to stuff a shapeless sack. We have more frequent occasion to complain of his impatience, in truth, than of his irrelevant prolixity. His common refrain is: "But it would take too long to go into it now!" And where he seems to be unsure of his purpose, it is safer for us to suspend judgment pending further enlightenment.

When, therefore, Chaucer chooses to open *The Book of the Duchess* with the tale of Ceyx and Alcyone, we may assume that he does so in the conviction that the tale strikes a note, and makes a pronouncement, and sets up vibrations, that are deeply consonant with the import of his poem. He has considered that his reponsibility is to find a story harmonious with Gaunt's recent bereavement. The Ovidian narrative fulfills this requirement: it establishes the mood, gently elegiac, adumbrated at the poem's commencement; and its reverberations echo in the sequel whenever the black knight breaks the course of his reminiscent narrative to complain of his loss and give voice to his despair and longing for death. It allows the humble friend, the poet, to express to the bereaved noble, indirectly, such consolation as one can offer in the presence of deep personal loss, the comfort of commiserating sympathy:

> Awake! let be your sorwful lyf!
> For in your sorwe there lyth no red. . . .
> To lytel while oure blysse lasteth!   (202–211)

It sheds the dignity of classical example, a poignant but statuesque and generalized beauty, muted with distance, over the shock and clamor of present anguish.

The Parliament of Fowls, whether or not it was prompted by current events, is a love-vision surprisingly unorthodox. The perplexities of love are the subject announced in the opening stanzas; love and its complexities are the subject of the birds' debate. This debate is the patent reason for the poem's existence: it is climax and end, and must in some form have been in Chaucer's mind from the start. Obviously, he wished to show love from various points of view, masculine and feminine, high and low; to exhibit the refined idealism of courtly love, and its unreality and egoism; the natural reactions of simple creatures incapable of such exaltation, and their useful but also self-centered motivation. To bring these all together was a practical difficulty. Courtly love is secret as to its particular object. Moreover, mere vulgarity is not necessarily amusing. There was also the realistic obstacle that the lower orders may not freely criticize their betters to their faces. Allegory, therefore, was essential. The inherent difficulties might be circumvented at one happy stroke by personifying all these conflicting points of view as types of birds. A vision would liberate from the inconveniences of verisimilitude and would give the ironic imagination much freer, and probably safer, play. Vision, moreover, would carry the question to levels of ultimate importance by showing these human contrasts in a vaster perspective of universal powers, the elemental forces of love and nature that influence heaven and earth. For presiding deity of so diverse a scene, he might take his cue from Alain's majestic conception of the goddess of Nature, all-embracing and fructifying, "vicar of the almighty Lord"; and from the same source a hint of that arbitrary and self-willed divinity, the Venus whose confining temple walls signified exclusive dedication to her sole worship, and whose service was a consuming flame. The contrast between the large and life-giving bounty of the one and the anti-social inwardness of the other could be further developed by drawing upon Boccaccio's convenient and engaging account of the artifice of the Garden and Temple of Venus.

Obviously, the debate was pre-ordained to show love as a cause of dissension, not of accord. Granting a kind of idealism in the self-abnegation of courtly love, it was still a private and restrictive virtue, and "tid thereof as often harm as prow." There were other, and perhaps better, kinds of idealism that refined spirits all too easily forgot: in particular, the disinterested habit of, not the private, but the honest public, servant, who spent himself for the common weal. Such was the lofty ideal that Cicero of old had raised for emulation; and it was a gauge by which to measure the worth of that finely spun sentiment upon which courtly lovers set such a premium. Why not invoke the promise of Africanus in Scipio's Dream, where he declared:

> What man, lered other lewed
> That lovede commune profyt, wel ithewed,
> He shulde into a blysful place wende,
> There as joye is that last withouten ende. . . .
>
> (46–49)

It would be interesting to note the response to such a shock of an audience expecting the conventional celebration of love in a courtly poem for St. Valentine's Day.

By some such train of thought, we may fancy, Chaucer might arrive at the rationale of his poem. He promises a love-vision, but even at the start there is a hint in his not referring to Love as a god but only as a feudal lord, and in his insistence on his personal detachment: he will say only, "God save swich a Lord!" He knows nothing of him at first hand, but what he reads of his tyranny is almost dumbfounding. He is very fond of reading—it is his idiosyncrasy—and recently he was hot in pursuit of some information in an antique volume and read on eagerly the whole day long. What it was he was seeking, he quite deliberately refrains from saying. Obviously, had he wished us to know, he would have told us. Not telling, under the circumstances, is concealing. But our curiosity is whetted, and naturally everyone expects him to produce documentary evidence, from his reading, of Love's "myrakles and his crewel yre"—something to bear out his speechless amazement. Instead, he proceeds to outline the Dream of Scipio, chapter by chapter: a work as far as possible from the track on which he had set our train of thought. Could any effect be more certainly calculated for surprise? For what do you think Africanus says, in Tully? He says that our present mode of existence is only a kind of death but, for the good, a dying into immortal bliss. And who are the good? They are those who find no delight in the life of the senses but exert their utmost efforts for the commonwealth. Lawbreakers and sensualists, on the contrary, when they die, shall age after age whirl painfully about the earth until they have atoned for their wickedness. Four times Africanus points his namesake the way into "that blysful place," "that hevene blisse," "that place deere" reserved for the "soules cleere"; and when he appears in turn to the poet that night, to lead him into that blissful place, the paradisal garden of love, it would seem that the ironic point could hardly escape the most inattentive of Chaucer's listeners.

As the poet dropped his book and prepared for bed, he was troubled, both because he had what (he says) he didn't want, and did not have what he wanted. The phrase was caught from Boethius' *Consolatio,* and it occurs where Philosophy is instructing her pupil that however great the abundance of earthly goods, man's needs and desires are not sufficed. This has a very present bearing on African's downright injunction, "That he ne shulde him in the world delyte"; and Chaucer, by his outline of Scipio's dream, has already set all earthly circumstance in a context that inevitably belittles the temporal in comparison with things eternal, both in quantity and quality. That this was his deliberate intention, who can doubt?

Indeed, in a variety of ways, Chaucer tacitly declares, over and over, that in so far as his poem is a vision of terrestrial love it is written against the grain. At its conclusion, he blandly apologizes, saying that another time, with luckier reading, he hopes to meet with a more auspicious dream. This parting testimony to the poet's implicit assumption of a connection between book and dream, the implied allusion here to the reading that had so wryly conditioned this particular vision, has been very oddly ignored as an evidence of the poem's intended unity and deliberate *ordonnance.*

The work, then, has moral depth and responsibility, a sound and coherent structure. But it has also unabashed lightness of heart; and in its own kind is a sort of Valentine's Day equivalent of a Midsummer Night's Dream. It is too nimble for criticism, which hops always behind. When we try to do justice to its serious implications, we lumber into travesty and all but extinguish its spirit of mocking gaiety. And when we try to appreciate its fun, we heavily explain or weakly paraphrase and quote, and fall short of its deeper meaning. Critical writing on this single poem is almost a paradigm of all the elucidatory inflections that have been tried on Chaucer's work through its whole extent. We have buried it under a mountain of commentary, both gravel and granite, only to find that, like Eulenspiegel, it was elsewhere during the obsequies.

A few further remarks about the parliament (im)proper will provide demonstration of what has just been asserted. Among the bird-folk who take part in the debate, the social distinction of the principals inevitably involves the others in a relative rating; and though their seating in Nature's "house" does not rank them, Chaucer's classification into seed-fowl,

water-fowl, and worm-fowl more than invites us to attach
general labels to each from analogous human society. The
simplest solution, in such a context, is surely the most acceptable. The purpose of Chaucer's allegory is not the propounding
of riddles. The "fowles of ravyne," as all readers agree, correspond to the nobility great and lesser, whose proper business
in feudal times was mainly to hunt, and to make love and war.
The water-fowl are big and aggressive birds and they are the
first of the commoners to come forward with a verdict. They
have two spokesmen, the goose and the duck, one female and
one almost certainly male, one chosen and one self-appointed,
but both speaking to the same end. Their advice is strictly
practical: to arrive at a working agreement, to get a return for
the investment on both sides. It's as easy to fall in love "ther
profyt sholde aryse" as to love where nothing can be gained.
They would understand Tennyson's northern farmer: "Doän't
thou marry for munny, but goä wheer munny is!" These clues,
in a satirical reference, are consistent with the mercantile
class, and there are no indications to the contrary. The seed-
fowl are next to give their verdict, in the person of the turtle-
dove. They are clearly gentlefolk, and their point of view,
while not martial, is fairly close to that of the nobility. They
are country-dwellers, and they have the country conservatism
and some idealism. They can appreciate the idea of fidelity
without thought of reward, and loyalty even unto death is an
ideal to which they respond. They are contemptuous of the
materialism of the water-birds. Though modest, they are happily a numerous company and cover the greensward. Their
elected spokesman, the turtle-dove, declares modestly that love
is an ever-fixed mark, that bends not with the remover to
remove.

Then comes the turn of the worm-fowl, folk of a nondescript
way of life, pickers-up of scraps. Their idea of the "comune
spede," it develops, is not even so lofty as the *quid pro quo* of
the water-fowl: it is every bird for himself. "Only give me *my*
mate," says the cuckoo, speaking for them all, "and you're
welcome to go on disputing forever. If those others can't
agree, let each live solitary all his life long!" The merlin, with
heavy irony, bestows the fitting comment on this position. "Of
course:—when the glutton has stuffed *his* paunch, how can
anyone else be discontented?" It is evident that the worm-fowl
are a miscellaneous lot, with neither a definable mode of living nor a code based on principle. In a pre-industrial society,
the Masses lack a proper name.

When we look back from the dream-debate to the book, we

can discern a sufficient latent motivation for the political coloring. As a Valentine's Day poet, Chaucer had apparently—but deliberately—started off on the wrong foot. Cicero's political theory was no very orthodox springboard for a love-vision. But Chaucer, as royal ambassador in marriage negotiations, had seen love being made the specious pretext and nominal goal of the most cold-blooded bargaining for material and diplomatic advantage: "Though his fair daughter's self, as I avowed/At starting, is my object!" So that, in an unexpected and ironic way, politics was an entirely appropriate leading-note for a love-vision. The poet had not ostensibly found what he had been looking for, but perhaps he had achieved something even more valuable—a surer basis for sound counsel. "For out of olde feeldes . . . Cometh al this newe corn from yer to yere." With continued study, he might on some lucky day attain his ideal: the felicity of a perfect coincidence between the wisdom acquired and the occasion to use it. On that day, the double sense of the word *rede,* a word upon which in his last stanza he lays such purposive stress by fourfold repetition, will be fused in perfect accord. Reading and counseling will be united in the harmonious function of the scholar-diplomat. Tully, in fact, had pointed the way, and in his own person had realized the wished-for fusion.

Resuming, now, our comparative search for the rationale of these poems, we find ourselves, in *The House of Fame,* precluded from approaching the reading by way of the poem's climax because we lack certain knowledge of what the latter was, or was to have been. We assume that the climax was the original idea from which the rest of the work germinated, and that therefore in Chaucer's conception the story of Dido was appropriate anticipatory matter. The necessary conditions would have been met if in the conclusion the crowd pressing towards the man of great authority had parted to disclose a man and a woman (i.e., their simulacra) in altercation before him, complaint being preferred by the woman in a narrative sufficient to carry the scene effectively. For a knowing audience, there would have been clues to individual identities, short of positive certainty:

> For though I telle noght his propre name,
> Men shal wel knowe that it is the same,
> By signes, and by othere circumstances.

(Canterbury Tales, VI, 417–419)

As a love-vision, the poem would appear to have been planned as a kind of palinode, somewhat disproportioned by

Chaucer's imagination having been overstimulated by his two inventions, the eagle and the goddess Fame. The moral of the whole might have been, to adopt the words of Pandarus:

> O tonge, allas! so often here-byforn
> Hath mad ful many a lady bright of hewe
> Seyd "weilaway, the day that I was born!"
> And many a maydes sorwe for to newe.
> And for the more part, al is untrewe
> That men of yelpe, and it were broughte to preve.
> Of kynde non avauntour is to leve. (III, 302–308)

Boasting and lying and infidelity go together, and the poet probably came back to earth a sadder, wiser, and even more disillusioned man than when the eagle carried him away. The poem, obviously, would lose point were there not some topical allusion concealed at the end. For then, the conclusion, more than merely harmonious, would be made out of the same classical or legendary stuff as the beginning, which would be too savorless. And it was, we recall, to hear "tidings" that Geoffrey was transported from his books. He was to "pause awhile from learning, to be wise!" But the truncated ending taken together with the Ernulphian curse at the opening against those who "mysdemen" the poem through malice, presumption, hate, scorn, envy, despite, jest, or villainy, more than suggests that he felt he was running special risks of giving offence, and that perhaps it was wisest of all to suppress what he had learned.

We might have expected *The Legend of Good Women* to commence—as it does *not*—in the following way:

> The poet thinks about the power of love, and about its precariousness: especially about the sad lot of women who yield their hearts and fortunes with entire trust, only to be betrayed and abandoned. Not that he has any first-hand evidence to bring forward. But in the course of his reading, he has come upon many instances of such unhappiness. He accepts such stories as truth. He is generally inclined to give faith and reverence to books for preserving the history of former generations. One has, of course, to take many things on trust, considering that the possibilities of knowledge through personal observation are so very limited.
>
> He was reading, of late, in an ancient book in which he came upon the story of a lady once Queen of Thrace. This noble woman, he learned, chose to give up her own life and go down to Hades that her husband might live. She did so, and was later rescued by Hercules, who

brought her back to the land of the living. The poet thought he had never heard of greater unselfishness and sacrifice. While he was meditating upon her story, he fell asleep and began to dream.

The dream into which he lapsed was, as it developed, much on the order of that which forms the substance of the Prologue we now have in version G of the extant work.

It is fairly easy to guess why Chaucer did not follow the foregoing routine in the present case. Looking back over the finished course, one understands at once why it would not have done. The object, here, is to establish a frame for a series of time-honored stories about women true in love. If the poet put the best one of all in the form of introductory reading, the climax would have been reached before the vision occurred. Or, supposing that he had merely told a story of this kind, recounting it at the outset as introductory reading, the effect of the subsequent dream could only be that of an injunction to wake up and get on with his reading and consequent versifying. The dream would be an ineffectual interruption. If the purpose of the vision was to motivate the writing of stories of faithful women, none of these, obviously, could be allowed precedence of the vision. And if one hoped to pay special tribute to a living lady figuratively represented as one of the story-heroines, the artistic way would not be to tell her history at the very beginning. One might, on the contrary, save that history for the end of the series, to pay her climactic honor; but people may die before ambitious poems are completed, and the tribute was in order now, at once. Honor, therefore, must be paid in the prologue itself.

Still looking at the problem as if before composition, we have found that an acceptable way of opening such a poem as this is to talk of reading. Tribute to written authority will make weight eventually by reinforcing the credibility of the "cases" to be cited out of old authors, and will sound a harmonious prelude. But mere *talk* of books makes an awkward pathway to dream. Chaucer acknowledges the fact in *The Legend of Good Women,* and pleads for our patience:

> But wherfore that I spak, to yive credence
> To olde stories and doon hem reverence,
> And that men mosten more thyng beleve
> Then men may seen at eye, or elles preve,—
> That shal I seyn, whanne that I see my tyme;
> I may not al at-ones speke in ryme. (F, 97–102)

How, then, to get to the dream itself without recounting a particular tale?

As we now know, the answer is, to let the description of actual nature for once anticipate the landscape of dream. Let the real scene be concentrated upon with intentness, as though it were a delightful book—the Book of Nature, as Curtius has noted, was already a familiar metaphor—and let the dream steal upon the poet engaged in this delightful study. Then the dream may properly reflect the waking pleasure:

> The wery huntere, slepynge in his bed,
> To wode ayeyn his mynde goth anon.
>
> (*Parliament of Fowls,* 99–100)

The daisy upon which the poet has been brooding with passionate intensity may thereupon, in his dream, be transfigured into the beautiful queen who comes to intercede for him with the God of Love. The parallel here with the *Parliament* is undeniably close. As Scipio passes over from the book into the dream, altering his role yet remaining recognizable, linking the two states of awareness, so here the daisy, by apotheosis, becomes the connecting link between the real and the dream-world. But now the device is handled with far greater finesse. Scipio discharges his office and at once disappears, whereas Alceste becomes the controlling figure of the whole vision, integrating the work and justifying all that follows.

The differences between the two prologues are so important that distinct poems are the result. The change in temperature from F (the earlier version) to G is from *caldo* to *freddo,* and cannot but strike every reader sensitive to climatic conditions. In F, the poet appears to display a continuous and intense personal involvement. In G, on the contrary, the tone of everything that is revised or now first introduced is invariably soberer, more detached, more suited to advancing years. It would be a welcome task to trace the details, but time forbids. One instance may be given, a new couplet in G, spoken by Alceste:

> Whil he [Chaucer] was yong, he kepte youre [Love's]
> estat;
> I not where he be now a renegat. (400–401)

The striking differences center round the treatment of the daisy and its double personification. F presents the flower, the daisy, as a feminine singular; G, as plural or neuter: the change is from "this flour" to "these floures," from "she" to "it." The lyric outburst in F, beginning in the third person and passing at once to direct address, is cancelled in G. This is the passage in F:

> *She* is the clernesse and the verray lyght
> That in this derke world me wynt and ledeth.
> The hert in-with my sorwfull brest *yow* dredeth
> And loveth so sore that *ye* ben verrayly
> The maistresse of my wit, and nothing I. . . .
> Be *ye* my gide and lady sovereyne! (84–94)

Thus, F makes little or no secret of the fact that the flower all the while is the poet's earthly goddess. When he sees her in the dream, it is only continuing his adoration, to offer the ballade in her praise as his private tribute (not the tribute, as in G, of the carolling ladies):

> For as the sonne wole the fyr disteyne,
> So passeth al my lady sovereyne,
> That ys so good, so faire, so debonayre. (F, 274–276)

The inference is unforced, therefore, that in the glow of his first inspiration the poet did not wish to conceal the fact that he was paying a personal tribute, justifying thereby the extravagance of his devotion to the Marguerite, and of course maintained throughout her reincarnation as Alceste. Revising, he felt constrained to eliminate the evidence of this private involvement, actual or assumed. It might be a sign of actuality that in F he had neglected, or did not care, to divide the dream from its consequences by mentioning an awakening.

> And with that word my bokes gan I take,
> And right thus on my Legende gan I make.
>
>   (F, 578–579)

It may readily be granted that the changes of G produce an effect of better organization, greater unity, simpler relation of parts, surer control, and a generally tidier poem. But they also rob it of the appealing urgency of the more complex and psychologically more fascinating original version.

More than one scholar has conjectured that Alceste in the *Legend* prologue is allegorically meant for Queen Anne, who in 1386 (a likely date for F) had been four years married to Richard, had reached the age of twenty, and who but six years later was to die of the pestilence. Skeat and a series of distinguished Germans regarded the identification as virtually certain, but there are famous names in the opposition, and we must side with the latter. To pose doubts and objections is easier by far than to produce convincing proof of personal identities from internal evidence. Yet, since rashness is the assumed prerogative of those who will not stay for an answer, let us now put questions. Can the following queries be met in such a way as to leave the hypothesis intact?

Would Chaucer have felt it appropriate to associate the daisy, with its French name and French associations, and Richard's Queen, with her Bohemian origins and quite different name? And if the marguerite was already connected with the Queen in some social and literary cult, is it likely that no trace of the fact would have survived?

Would Chaucer have thought it appropriate to pay his devotions to Her Majesty in the glowing terms employed by a courtly lover addressing his mistress, even at times laying aside the decorum of figurative statement? Would he have dared? Temperamentally, could he have found it possible?

Would Chaucer have been so graceless as to equate the Queen with the tragic, self-sacrificial figure of Alcestis, who died that her husband's life might be prolonged? And would he, if he chose to pay her that compliment, immediately then cancel it out by causing Alceste herself to refer to the Queen as a third person?—

> And whan this book ys maad, yive it the Quene,
> On my [Alceste's] byhalf, at Eltham or at Sheene.
>   (F, 496–497)

Revising the poem after the Queen's death, would Chaucer then feel obliged to remove all those more passionate expressions of personal devotion which in her lifetime would certainly have been the height of presumption but which perhaps now might have a chance to pass into history as an idealizing memorial tribute? Would he choose such a time to expunge them, supposing him to have been motivated by any genuine sentiment? Would consideration for Richard have prompted such action rather than suppressing the poem? Was he going to read it again at court? And if the expressions, sincere as they seem, were merely artificial, why should he now be concerned to rub and scrape?

With the identification of Alceste as Queen Anne has gone a parallel identification of the God of Love as King Richard. This assumption raises considerations broader than might seem to be suggested by a simple equation. We have to look at the matter from two directions; for if the God of Love stands in the poem for Richard, Richard stands likewise for the God of Love. Of course, we ought not to handle gossamer as if it were buckram; but psychological effects have natural causes. Now Richard, looked at as the God of Love, carries to our sense an air of flim-flam. To require this role of him is not to honor or exalt him but to reduce his actual dignity to the level of amateur theatricals and puerile make-believe:

>   And in his hand me thoghte I saugh him holde
>   Twoo firy dartes, as the gledes rede,
>   And aungelyke hys wynges saugh I sprede.

(F, 234–236)

For Richard, this role was not important, whatever its meaning for his foreign envoy and trusted man of affairs. When this king speaks, it is to accuse the poet of being his foe, recreant both in work and in deed, one who has renounced his law and hindered others from loving, by writing *Troilus and Criseyde* and translating the *Rose*. The king (Richard?) threatens the poet with cruel pains for these heresies. He then, however, graciously forgives him at the intercession of Alceste (Anne?), who on her part engages that Chaucer will spend the most of his time henceforth in composing a glorious legend of faithful women and false men (rather than in the performance of his further duties as Clerk of the King's Works). If the poet will do this, says Richard *qua* Cupid, he is content to let him go free. But he must be sure to introduce the Queen's own story (Alceste's) and it will be best to begin his book with the legend of Cleopatra. He may choose his own meters and he will be wise to summarize and abridge where possible, lest his *Te Deum* turn to simple tedium.

If somewhat of this sort is what happens to Richard impersonating the God of Love, the effect on the God of Love is equally, or more, disastrous when he plays Richard. Love as a personified abstraction has, to give his ideal image authority and power over our imagination, the tributary joys and sorrows of a hundred generations of humankind. There is no doubt (in our hearts) of the reality "of his myrakles and his crewel yre." What the poet has to say of him in description as he moves over the meadow of dream, a youthful figure of unearthly brightness and fresh beauty, awe-inspiring, subtracts nothing from his divine idea. He is angel-like, a paradisal being: his garments woven in an air of glory, his golden hair crowned with a sun, his face almost too radiant for mortal eyes. The supreme compliment of his leading by the hand the Queen Alceste, flower-like in green, pearl-white, and gold, exalts her, too, into the realm of the ideal—

>   So womanly, so benigne, and so meke,
>   That in this world, thogh that men wolde seke,
>   Half hire beaute shulde men nat fynde
>   In creature that formed ys by kynde. (F, 243–246)

The measure of her ideality, and the height of the compliment that Chaucer may be paying to an earthly creature whom she partly symbolizes, are clearly established by the ethereality of the God of Love. If the latter be not inviolate, the other sinks likewise to favor and to prettiness. And that transcendence cannot be preserved while we think of an earthly figure in the god's borrowed graces. It is essential for the full effect of the poem that the image of Love be kept free from every personal human equation.

Questions thus arise as to the effective limits of such allegorical personifications. Here is a figure, Marguerite–Alceste, of whom we feel that, if we could name her counterpart in Chaucer's waking life, our intimate appreciation of the poem would be enhanced and enriched. There is another, the God of Love, who can only be debased by the imposition of human features, to the detriment of the work of art as a whole.

The mind appears to be extremely sensitive in estimating the balance between its ideas of persons and their symbolic representation for a particular purpose or a selective emphasis. If the emphasis goes one way, the result is caricature; if the other, glorification. If the symbol chosen is too vast, too exalted, too inhuman, or simply too definitely alien, the imagination balks at the substitute. We have no difficulty in accepting the Lady Blanche and the Man in Black, in *The Book of the Duchess,* as the courtly images of the Duke and Duchess of Gaunt, however much idealized. But Fortune in that poem is unthinkable as surrogate for any human creature; as are, in the other dream-visions, Venus, Nature, Fame; and here, the God of Love. In *The House of Fame,* the eagle, to be sure, is human enough, but his superhuman function as celestial flying-machine makes absurd any possible human reference —though he can simulate a familiar voice. Had he simply said "Come!" and had the poet thereupon found himself moving through space or already arriving at Fame's palace, knowing not how, the eagle might have been allegorically serviceable; but then wings too would have been unnecessary for this kind of zodiacal trapeze-work, as previously they had been in Scipio's dream. But, on the contrary, the earthbound eagles in the *Parliament of Fowls* cause us no trouble as potential representatives of elevated personages. Here, no use is made of their avian character except to impart an aura of ironic fantasy. They are birds altogether human, even to their blushes. But, for the sake of comedy, the baser fowl, though also human, act and chatter like birds. We are guarded against thought of the diet of the formel eagle and her suitors; but we are often reminded of the lower orders' less disgusting fare: the latter becomes a means of definition. Precisely the same sort of ironic picture is drawn, with greater fullness and humorous complexity, of Chauntecler and Pertelote in double exposure, where the personification and the natural interact with mutual entertainment, so that we can hardly decide which is the personification and which the actuality, which sense and which symbol: whether birds are being personified as man and wife, or humanity gallinized as cock and hen.

The proper naming is, of course, an essential part of the technique; and by his choice the Nun's Priest, even as he commences, intends to leave no doubt from which side we are to take our bearings. Human proper names in this case, however appropriate, would have significantly altered the point of view. But the birds in the dream-visions have to get on as best they may with their generic appellatives alone. Further distinctions would only have encumbered them in their function as class-representatives; and even the principals benefit from their anonymity. True names here would have destroyed the fantasy; classical names would have been ridiculous; royal names would have been dangerous; courtly names would have been insipid; Christian names would have been humiliating.

All that has been said is but a narrow review of these endlessly fascinating poems, which exhibit so many individual beauties and such swift advances in mastery of convention and freedom of invention and imagination. They display, besides, many signs of Chaucer's growing concern about his status as a poet: so much so that reputation comes to seem almost more central, more truly the subject of *The House of Fame* and the *Legend*, with its built-in bibliography, than the dream-vision itself. . . .

Troilus and Criseyde

G. T. SHEPHERD

TROILUS AND CRISEYDE is a story of love and war—a story about sex in an aggressive society. It is well to see the story plain. It is the stuff of romance in every sense of the word. When we begin the poem, we are immediately aware of the type of treatment to expect. Quickly too we become conscious of the weight and scale of the poem and of the grand ambition of the poet. We know that this was intended to be, that it was and remains a major piece of European writing. We can recall that this is the work which for three centuries at least was Chaucer's best known work, the work most closely associated with a recognition of his genius.

Yet nowadays it is easy to feel a sense of inadequacy in the reading and in a re-reading of the poem. We are like modern visitors in an old cathedral, aware in a general way of what cathedrals of this sort are about, and immediately sensible of the size, majesty and complexity of the structure, but troubled by a sense that what we see is the product of a piety different from our own, and by the suspicion that there are coherences and intentions which are no longer obvious. Frequently our notions of an antique grandeur are focused by memorable images of trivia. Rather mournfully we have to admit that a baffled astonishment and a superficial analysis may have furnished us with respectfully patronizing phrases to last us all our lives.

Entry to poems, as to English cathedrals, is free. Anyone can look at what he likes and linger by what he pleases. Life is short and this poem is long. We can come and go and make all sorts of abstractions from it. And we can usually go back once more to the poem and show by book and verse that most of these abstractions are incomplete or wrong. We might, for instance, sharpen our modernity on the poem and read it as if it were a tale of inverted sentimentality about a tearful bully-

From CHAUCER AND CHAUCERIANS, ed. D. S. Brewer. Copyright © 1966 by University of Alabama Press. Reprinted by permission of the University of Alabama Press.

boy who could sit and watch Pandarus laying the long string of traps to catch a provocative Criseyde as deftly as poachers catch rabbits, and yet himself lacked the resolution to make a clean appropriation of the victim: and yet if we submit to the poem, we are bound to acknowledge eventually that however unattractive Troilus may appear, however little we approve of his role in the action, the poem presents him unequivocally as the dominant figure, quite wholeheartedly and admiringly as its hero. And similarly we shall subdue at length any tendency to read Pandarus into prominence as the one figure of sense and sanity in what, were the story a mere scheme of incidents, might be taken as an ironic exposure of social hypocrisy. For in the poem itself, in the Fifth Book Pandarus shrivels to complete insignificance.

The readiest temptation perhaps is to read the whole as another Romeo and Juliet story, as if the two young lovers stood out stereoscopically against a hostile world. But here again we shall observe that the ethic of the lovers is never at odds with the ethic of their society, that neither Troilus nor Criseyde fundamentally opposes the moral decisions towards which society drives them. Troilus falling in love as a young man should, becomes thereby, so we are told explicitly, more militarily useful, more socially acceptable. The pair of lovers discussing the line of action to be taken when Criseyde must leave Troy, reject all but the obvious course of separation, obedient to their social duties. Criseyde's conventional behavior is never meant to trouble us. Rather it is her one act of apparent spontaneity, her one lapse in decorum—the giving of Troilus's brooch to Diomed—that is received as the confirmation, almost as a sacramental sign of her treachery.

If we emphasize the determinism of the story and see human endeavor completely blocked and thwarted by a Fate enforcing a pattern of its own on to the sequence of events, the text obliges us to acknowledge that much of the narrative is given up to describing the ingenious contrivances by its actors which presumably bring about events exactly as the course of Fate requires. Crises may be ordained by the stars in their courses, as the poet allows; the rainstorm which brings the lovers together was marked for this purpose by the conjunction of the planets. But Pandarus had already noted that the night was likely to be wet and planned accordingly. In a careful and engrossed reading Pandarus must appear quite as active as Fate in the development of the affair.

When the end is reached, could we really think of the story

primarily as a cautionary tale for these young folk, who allow themselves to be seduced by false goods and transient pleasures? But in casting backwards from the final dazzlement of the poem, it is plain that in the Third Book the love of Troilus and Criseyde was treated as a real good, and that throughout the poem Troilus again is a figure not merely of potential, but of realized worth and *trouthe*. What was done earlier was done gloriously, and is not undone by a nobler end.

Interpretations multiply. Maybe one or other reading of the poem can satisfy at some time or other: but not all the time. A sense of inadequacy will reassert itself, and it is not simply that virtuous sense of inadequacy in response that afflicts any sensible person confronting a masterpiece, but in the case of this medieval poem a suspicion of miscomprehension.

Most of our ready abstractions indeed rest quietly upon the assumption that the poem is a lengthy working out in words of one or other of our own moral prejudices in situations and action like those we believe we observe directly in life. This is a situation, affecting the critical judgment, which it is difficult for a modern reader, especially a modern English reader fed on novels, to escape from, for several reasons. In the first place and obviously enough, because *Troilus and Criseyde* was written in the fourteenth century, the conventions that control the moral values in the poem are sufficiently different from our own to invalidate some of our tacit requirements.

The poem is about love and war but not about modern love and war. No doubt every age struggles consciously or unconsciously to set the instincts of sex and aggression loose from old outworn convention and to discover new patterns to which current expressions of sex and aggression can be worked so that they seem tolerable and socially decent. There is plenty of evidence that fourteenth-century English society sought to emancipate itself from some earlier medieval conventions by which sex and aggression had been socialized. But in the outcome, men at this time managed these things in a fashion very different from our own, and their writing (which is one of the most powerful ways of establishing and of expressing these social conventions) embodies their different attitudes.

Nowadays we usually assume that we have excluded sex and war from the approved routine of patterned behavior and have relegated them to the unconventionalized areas of social life. War remains perhaps an intermittent dread but it is dreaded as alien to our life, an extra-human event, something that breaks in from outside. Ordinary life is not controlled by unquestioned assumptions that business as usual means war. But in fourteenth-century England war was a normal state of affairs. Mars ruled and men kissed the rod. Year after year they shipped out to France the armies, the elaborate munitions and provisions of war. War was strenuous day-to-day drudgery for kings and courts and commons.

Troilus and Criseyde reflects and accepts this tedious insistence. The background of war is much more prominent in Chaucer's telling of the story than in Boccaccio's. The confrontation of the nations, the everlasting state of siege, the daily skirmishes and the truces, the councils of state and the debates on policy, these constitute a great stable pattern to the life imaged in the story. It is the world of the commissariat and general headquarters, where war is routine business. There is no real and lasting escape possible for the lovers out of this grim world to some soft paradise of love. Exchanging Criseyde for Antenor is plain political good sense on both sides. Criseyde indeed throughout the story is vulnerable, because she is always politically expendable. The story of the lovers is not a private story: its occasions and crises rise from the public war. Their struggle for secrecy emphasizes rather than obliterates the intrusiveness of the society.

We do not take war like this and refuse to let our storytellers present it with these conventions, except perhaps in cowboy stories, part of whose charm no doubt resides in the recall of ancient behavior patterns of European aggressiveness. But normally we reject an image of life enclosed in conventions of war. Even the modern cult of violence in fiction is, somewhat paradoxically, part of this rejection, for violence offers opportunities for exciting incursions by the extraordinary into the accepted normality of life which is now essentially pacifist. There is no interest at all in violence in *Troilus and Criseyde*. Permanent war swallows Troilus very quietly in the end. In fourteenth-century England war was too ordinary for noisy demonstrations.

We also struggle nowadays less successfully to deconventionalize sex, by alleging in our fictions that sexual relations are most ideal when all formal bonds, whether exercised by society, inheritance, or rationality, are as loose as possible. Sex is treated as an exercise in freedom, in which the spark of personality should be least restrained, most emergent and most sensitive. There is of course a subtle continuity and modification over generations in ideas of this sort, but there is little evidence to suggest that men and women of the fourteenth century regarded love in this way. In its most developed manifestations love between the sexes was concerned with conquest and service, not with freedom. Love was treated as a state of dependence existing between unequals. In some aspects the man was the inferior; in others, the woman. Always many social obligations and questions of honor were directly involved—and honor has always a public face. Indeed what we may tend to think of as barriers to union or the external superfluities of true love, these earlier people regarded as the prerequisites of a love that could be esteemed. The observance of convention was what made love human and noble and distinguished it from careless instinctive sexuality—with which the Middle Ages were very familiar. No doubt hypocrites could flourish as well in the fourteenth century as in our own times. No doubt also that our own assumptions about sexual love will look as queer and arbitrary and inconsistent after a few centuries as fourteenth-century attitudes look to us,

That age then did not think of war as an avoidable evil, or of sex as an unmitigated good. Often enough it seems scarcely to have distinguished the underlying instincts at all and to have acted as if it regarded the manifestations of sex and war as the indifferent marks of general personal assertiveness. This is one reason why chivalry often strikes us as such an amorphous, inconsistent ideal. In the history of the time war often has the appearance of an extension of sexuality by other means. This was the very character of the Trojan War:

> And in diverse wise and oon entente,
> The ravysshyng to wreken of Eleyne,
> By Paris don, they wroughten al hir peyne.
>
> (I, 61–3)

A singularly squalid and dishonorable occasion we may think for a great war. Yet Troilus uses the same precedent (IV, 547–50) as a compelling reason for preserving Criseyde's honor. Hector and Deiphebus too are willing to accept Criseyde as part of the cause for which they fight. The appreciation of the values of sex may be noble, it is certainly not tender. Troilus and Criseyde are not two gentle hearts bound in an equal love. Love stirs in Criseyde as she sees Troilus when

His helm to-hewen was in twenty places:
(II, 638)
she has a keen prevision of what her surrender will be like:

How that an egle, fethered whyt as boon,
Under hir brest his longe clawes sette
And out hir herte he rente.
(II, 926–8)

These are both victor-victims. Their careers focus the values which the story assumes.

With some effort it is perhaps possible even at this distance of time to discern a configuration of these values. But there is a more subtle difficulty in reading *Troilus and Criseyde*. Normally, a modern novel exemplifies and embodies certain moral prejudices as well as a certain view of them. This may be some traditional European view of unembarrassed acceptance, or more likely now it will be an avowedly progressive, or plain anarchic view of social behavior. Whatever it is, it will be implicit, recognizable and in a successful novel sufficiently consistent. Once we have made the backward leap through conventions this is also what we should find in reading most medieval romances. Usually a romance writer takes over his matter from some other story and then gives it his own *sens,* the particular coloring of sentiment and moral appeal which unconsciously and consciously he has decided is appropriate to the story. With a moderately practiced storyteller each telling will have its own consistency, and once the story is under way the audience will have selected and fitted for reception the right emotional filter and can respond to the story directly without constant reference to this distinction between matter and *sens.*

But this is not possible with *Troilus and Criseyde.* Although the story is told in terms of historical conventions about love and war which can perhaps be broadly identified, the *sens* of this poem was never simple and consistent, to be absorbed unconsciously in large measure. The view we are required to take of the *sens* as well as of the matter is being constantly altered and manipulated. The telling demands that we change our filter repeatedly and the changes seem to be quite deliberately devised. In the poem the signals of change are given by the Narrator. In the original telling of the poem they were probably actually worked by the reciter of the poem.

It could be claimed that the Narrator is the only fully-developed character in the poem—he is certainly the only figure who reacts and changes with the sequence of the events narrated. The Narrator is an I, a mask worn by the person who speaks the script. This public apparition of an I is not, of course, Chaucer the man, not even Chaucer the poet: it is the mask made by Chaucer, originally perhaps, as the frontispiece to the Corpus *Troilus* Manuscript suggests, for Chaucer the performer to wear as he delivered the poem to a court audience. The I is not then the voice of the "second author," as this apparition is sometimes called in dealing with a modern novel: it is rather the voice of a "third speaker." As long as a printed text is thought of as the standard form of a story, the recession of speakers is difficult to grasp. Chaucer certainly aspired to give *Troilus and Criseyde* a fixed text and said so quite plainly at the end of the poem. But the norm of composition for a vernacular poet was still the actual speaking of the story, the *narratio.* In composing *Troilus and Criseyde* before delivery, Chaucer was doing what an established comedian of stage or screen who is his own scriptwriter does in preparing one of his entertainments. He has to subdue his selected matter to his own technique of delivery, to exploit the reputation he has already acquired and the responses he should be able to anticipate from a particular and fairly familiar audience. He has to make a script which shall suit his story, his public appearance and the audience. He knows that the recognized features of the mask he is to wear will modify and be modified by the story. For the mask mediates the story. The entertainer is the manipulator and also part of the story he is presenting.

Similarly, the Narrator in *Troilus and Criseyde* is both inside and outside the story. Introducing the poem the Narrator speaks about himself. Later, at points of the story he will act the part of Troilus or Pandarus or Criseyde, and project to his audience a degree of identification. Sometimes he will speak as if he were the unobtrusive and rapid recorder of events. Sometimes, the Narrator delivers, in his own assumed first person as *auctor,* appropriate didactic comment. Sometimes he is on intimate and knowledgeable terms with the audience, and distances his story material. He exhibits a whole range of devices by which he guides or participates in the audience's reactions, devices familiar to medieval storytellers, but rarely given the artistic coherence in a finished text independent of actual performance. In *Troilus and Criseyde* Chaucer has convincingly stylized in permanent form the ephemeralness of a living entertainment and the mobility of actual delivery.

Yet the purpose of Chaucer as "second author," if we may judge it from the development of the poem, as well as from its total effect, is surprisingly serious. He is handling a venerable story with dignity and with strong and deep moral and philosophical implications. His original audience we may assume was not expecting to take the performance quite so seriously as on reflection afterwards they would discover Chaucer had intended them to. The depth and range of the poem, announced with a disingenuous simplicity at the beginning, hinted at more confidently in the openings of the successive books, is only gradually disclosed in the narration, and only fully revealed at the very end. Chaucer is not competing with his contemporaries, the "makers" of vernacular romance:

> But litel book, no makyng thow n'envie,
> But subgit be to alle poesye;
> And kis the steppes, where as thow seest pace
> Virgile, Ovide, Omer, Lucan, and Stace.
>   (V, 1789–92)

And *poesye* is the title of honor Chaucer reserved for the work of the great poets of antiquity and Italy, whose achievements in this poem he emulates.

Thus as a composition the poem moves along two distinct lines. The *narratio* is visible enough. It is concerned with the story material Chaucer took out of Boccaccio. It is with the telling of this story that the Narrator is kept busy. But there is in the poem a concern to describe a line of causality and destiny, which shall show the events of the story at a higher degree of generality. To recognize this line is not to abstract from the poem, not to disentangle a meaning or a message, for the line runs throughout the poem. The poet himself, not the Narrator, is in charge of this line. This is what the old rhetoricians called the *argumentum* of a piece of writing. Commentators on Boethius' *Topics* called it the *vis sententiae*. It is the theme of a work in the actual process of evolving, the line of force along which the *narratio* is directed.

From the beginning of the poem we are conscious that the whole action is under the grip of a larger control. On the surface the Narrator presents it as "the lawe of kynde" we are advised to follow. But the counterweight comes early, "O blinde world, O blynde entencioun," a somber murmur which gathers strength. The naïve Narrator is another blind man leading blind men to their fates. We are acknowledging the *argumentum* when we realize the illusion implicit in the *narratio*. All the ways of the world, all the solemn dealings with sex and war which seem so compulsive and yet so uncontrollable, are neither one nor the other. As guides by themselves they work confusion, as values they are a vanity. The fixed and familiar courses down which men seek to outrun and outwit their fellows lead nowhere any man wishes to be. The world with its seemingly hard and inescapable conventions imaged in the poem is illusion, a necessary illusion, which exacts from us a disillusionment. Hope lies in another realm, scarcely related to the iron necessities of human society. The *argumentum* of the poem depends upon a melancholy, unsensationalized view of life, compounded out of a Christian quietism and a faintly sentimental stoicism. It reflects a mood of many Englishmen in the late fourteenth century.

In public Chaucer was no more than a minor functionary and his appearance in court would depend upon a reputation as a sophisticated entertainer, not as a speculative moralist or an interpreter of his times. The *narratio* must carry the *argumentum* very lightly. To the secret hearts and thoughts of men in high places he remained a stranger. What went on in public he could learn only by humble and deferential observation. He could earn a little license for solemnity as well as for jest if he were sufficiently entertaining.

The poet's intention and the anticipated responses of this court audience control the strategy: which in brief was to introduce the story with a touch of disengaging flippancy, to develop it swiftly, brightly but elaborately, to let the passions and the responses of the audience run and gather head, and then to make his purpose plain when the emotional effects are irresistible. There is much jocularity and irony in the detail of the telling. But it is often mock-jocularity and the irony of enhancement. Chaucer talks a thing down in order to build it up.

The use of this sort of device indicates the delicacy of the whole task. Perhaps we can assume that a medieval audience, even the most sophisticated, was pretty inflammable. Most of the way the poet cannot go too far or too fast in evoking participation with the story and identification with its characters. The audience must not find its conventional values openly mocked by unrelieved catastrophe. So the Narrator must maintain throughout something of that initial naïveté, lest he be held responsible for the calamity. The poet cannot make a moral too emphatically, so the Narrator cannot be seen to identify himself too steadily with the logic of the destinies involved, or pass too magisterial a judgment on the actors who suffer them. The poet has to satisfy a whole range of worldliness which appreciates display, luxury, leisure and the solid reassurance of wealth and power and rank. So the Narrator presents, quite simplemindedly, sequences of fashionable behavior, moments of worldly triumph and success, counsels of conventional wisdom. Throughout the poem there is sufficient humor to placate the unsentimental, enough undiscussed absolutes to win the idealist, some unwounding cynicism to disarm the disillusioned. By using the Narrator the poet can recall the audience from an excessive engrossment in certain aspects of the story. The Narrator can be used to lighten the ominous, to anticipate and therefore blunt the distracting keenness of the miseries, and still, by exhibiting the degree of his own involvement, inject expectancy into a story of what is already foreseen.

In the practical management of his Narrator Chaucer had of course a duty towards himself. He had to write—probably this came easily enough to a writer of his experience—a part which would suit his own delivery, his own powers of expressiveness of voice, gesture and elocution. More important, the poet in putting the poem together had to maintain his own morale, to remain confident that what he was doing was worth doing, to refuse to lose his own way in the story, and to ensure that in working out his intention he should achieve what every author aims at in a major work, a continuing fallout of meaning, which should sift slowly down into the memory and modify understanding. The *argumentum* must shine clear even though it may seem to annul in part the *narratio* that carries it forward.

Problems of narration at this degree of complexity and skill fascinated Chaucer. He was to devise new and more complicated problems for himself in *The Canterbury Tales,* which represent the ultimate achievement in medieval storytelling, when the mobile recession of the narrating voices is often as puzzling and ingenious as the construction of a Chinese box. Fortunately *Troilus and Criseyde* is easier to follow. It is all one story and its narrative advancing through the complexities of presentation is strong and clear.

Perhaps we marvel more at the construction of the poem than Chaucer's contemporaries would have done. For he was practicing, albeit with the greatest skill and success, what the schools and handbooks had taught Europeans about composition for nearly two millennia. Usually in the arts of rhetoric, instruction on how to develop a *narratio* is included in the teaching on the presentation of a case in a court of law, but even in the earlier handbooks some attention is given to the presentation of fictional material, whether drawn from legend or history or the contemporary scene. It was recognized that such fictions required a highly flexible method of treatment. Style and delivery were expected to follow the variety of incident and the reactions of the persons involved, so that the audience should become directly concerned in affairs as they were being presented. Even a perfunctory reading of, for instance, the pseudo-Ciceronian treatise *Ad Herennium* will illuminate Chaucer's methods in composition and elocution in *Troilus and Criseyde.*

But the practical and slightly mechanical exposition of rhetorical teaching in *Ad Herennium* does not deal with the subtler but overriding need in all effective discourse for a narrator to carry his audience with him all the time. This is what more sophisticated theory knew as *ethos*. It is the witness a speaker bears, in telling his tale, to his own integrity and to the credibility of his matter, thereby exhibiting these qualities to the audience as instruments of persuasion. It creates a milieu satisfactory and attractive to the audience and propitious to the speaker's cause. *Ethos* is properly employed, Quintilian observed, when it is applied throughout the whole discourse and thus builds up a slow but ineradicable conviction in the audience.

Ethos then will assume the employment of certain artistic principles. It is never easy to discern the standards of taste and the canons of excellence that a poet is implicitly accepting in his composition. If we judge a work successful then we rationalize our judgment, usually by invoking criteria taken over from our own critical inheritance and training. These have no absolute value, and most of our attempts to make them more precise even to ourselves will distort them. To seek for the artistic principles behind the composition of *Troilus and Criseyde* is as difficult as to evaluate the moral world of its story. But once again we can be comforted that Chaucer's own professions of faith in art are likely to have been nearly as ill-defined, semi-consciously indeterminate and arbitrarily traditional as our own but, quite certainly, different. If we are to assess his ideas about his art, and his works of art, these differences require very delicate and modest exploration which must always remain mindful that every clear discrimination carries with it the seed of an exaggeration.

In modern poetry, as was pointed out by Cecil Day Lewis, we look for marks of originality of thought and expression, intensity in emotional effect and evocative power in the use of words. No medieval poet sought to display these virtues. It is true that in some medieval poems (including *Troilus and Criseyde*) we sometimes think that we can observe them, but no medieval poet and no medieval audience seems to have attached any particular value to these instances, and as often as not, it may be suspected that we deceive ourselves when we believe we have observed them displayed. It is wiser to turn to another triad of artistic virtues, to the Dionysian triad of integrity, harmony and clarity, for guidance in assessing the aspirations of a medieval artist. And although in formulations of medieval thought this triad was associated with the contemplation of the Divine Beauty itself, there can be little doubt that, over centuries, secularized versions of these ideals conditioned the construction and qualified the assessment of human artifacts. In some such terms as integrity, harmony and clarity we can best sum up Chaucer's aesthetic.

Integrity expounded in literary terms implies full and complete development—the wholeness of perfection, grandeur and size. The *formosus,* the pretty, is beautiful, but with an impairment in magnitude. Perfection suggests a controlled prodigality, a plenitude in utterance. Thus we can appreciate in part the medieval poet's quest for *amplificatio. Troilus and Criseyde* has this fullness.

Every story has to be given adequate setting and sufficient motivation. Most modern storytellers, however, select from a much narrower field than Chaucer thought necessary. There is a mass of particularity in the poem far in excess of what Chaucer found in his source. His method of narration in this poem requires that he should maintain throughout a total relevance. All Pandarus's guileful persuasions, Criseyde's wavering calculations and Troilus's Boethian speeches are needed. Though he abhorred prolixity and condemned it as the vice of his age in its writing, he did not mark the boundaries of relevance where later writers would. In Book Five, for example, when Troilus wishes to know the truth about Criseyde's delay among the Greeks and to learn the meaning of his dreams of the boar, he consults his sister, the prophetess Cassandra (V, 1450–1533):

> She gan first smyle and seyde "O brother deere
> If thow a soth of this desirest knowe
> Thow most a fewe of olde stories heere . . ."

And she begins far back with the story of Diana's punishment of Greeks and how the war of Thebes began and summarizes all twelve books of Statius's epic:

> And so descendeth down from gestes olde
> To Diomede and thus spak and tolde.

coming at length to an exposition of the dream. In such a proceeding sudden intensity is never achieved and evocation is dispersed. But there is another power to replace the delightful mysteriousness of supposing more than one is told. We are exposed to more than we want to comprehend, and excess squeezed into a narrow space can have a genuine artistic function. Again the comparison with the multitudinous decorative effect of a great cathedral can be invoked. Prodigality is impressive, so is the open suggestion of endless involution of destiny.

The same principles are at work in Chaucer's presentation of character. The plot is central. But the story, as Chaucer tells it in its wholeness and fullness, generates the characters it needs. If we insist on assessing the individuality and psychology of these characters we do it from outside the poem. They needed not to be psychologically coherent as long as their presentation sustains and gives substance to the *narratio*. That we can reassemble them and interpret them as portraits of potentially real people is an astonishing testimony to the integrity and consonance of Chaucer's art, but should not be taken as a guide to his method.

This method is seen most simply in the treatment of Troilus. If we read his character from the action in which he is involved we see him as a prince, as a hopeful, successful, then despairing lover, as a bitter fighter. We are told he is handsome, young, fresh, strong, resolute in action and successful in war. We watch him behave in love as a pattern of amorous gallantry should behave. He suffers "this wondrous maladie" to perfection. He swoons, he weeps, he languishes. He is properly passionate, both masterful and humble in the consummation of his love. He becomes jealous and desperate and angry. He is indeed the ideal young male character, quick, proud, active, passionate, easily cast down, resolute when his course is clear, delighted by success, impatient of delay—psycho-biologically, the perfect specimen, or as Chaucer puts it,

Oon of the beste entecched creature
That is, or shal, whil that the world may dure.
(V, 832–3)

Accordingly, readers find him the least satisfying of the
major characters of the poem, somewhat flat and character-
less; and properly so. He refuses to come out of the poem.
There, he serves as one of the poles where the forces con-
verge in this story about sex and war. He is what the story
needs him to be. His function is obvious, simple and directly
comprehensible.

Criseyde's function is not much more elaborate. Though
her appearances in the poem are covered with a continuous
sheen of sentiment and charm so that at the slightest encour-
agement we are willing to lead her out of the poem as if she
were a particular woman whom we delight to know, yet she
is the familiar, if never commonplace figure of every English
romance, of every woman's magazine, another Emily or Fe-
lice, the passive pole in this story of a struggle for possession.
She is presented as the type of the unlucky beloved. When
she is described in Book Five, the Narrator speaks of her, as
he speaks of Troilus, as an example of the general. She is set
alongside Nature's mean, she embodies the virtues that all
heroines of romance exemplify, the beauty of figure, face and
hair; discretion, fairspokenness, kindness in word and
thought, a dignity, liveliness and gentility, sentimentality and
fearlessness. These are characteristics that had been tabulated
centuries before Chaucer's time, for example by Hugh of St.
Victor in his *Summa Sententiarum*, VII, I, as the moral and
social gifts in a woman that draw men's love. Even in describing her, the Narrator disassociates himself from any
knowledge of Criseyde as a person. He knows her only in the
story. He can do no more than report of her what "they wri-
ten that hir syen." "Trewely I can not telle hir age," nor
whether she had any children.

The effect of this last device is, it must be allowed, equivo-
cal. Chaucer's refusal to let the Narrator know these things
can indeed reinforce the sense of verisimilitude by inviting the
imagination to supply the illimitable reality of a completely
individuated character. No doubt Chaucer knew as well as
we do what was won by withholding. But it is an aspect of
his management of the Narrator, not of his characterization.
He is controlling the audience's responses of pity and moral
bewilderment. Criseyde is only the part she plays. She is presented whole and without development. Her faithlessness is

imprinted on "hir browes joyneden y-fere." She is throughout her final reputation. Again and again in the last book the Narrator tells us that these things fall and can fall no otherwise than as "the story telleth us." Criseyde, like Troilus, is a function of the plot.

Pandarus may make a somewhat different impression from the two main characters but the method of presentation is similar. He is established in an extraordinarily rich and complex fashion through word and deed; so much is given that we are willing to take more, and ensconce him beside Falstaff or Polonius, Pickwick or Micawber. Let no one deny Chaucer the achievement and the triumph. Yet Chaucer uses him as a trigger mechanism to the action, as a support to the main figures, and is as merciless in dispatching him when he is superfluous to the action as ever King Henry was to Falstaff. In the story he is the fluid element between the two static presentations of the exemplary figures, the princely lover and the unlucky beloved. He appears rich and complex because, in himself less important, he promotes and takes part in their interaction.

To incorporate a static exemplary figure into an action, especially to show reciprocal interaction between two figures of this kind, is a difficult task. It was a difficulty encountered by many medieval storytellers and certainly rarely solved by them to our satisfaction. Often the difficulty is bypassed by the use of arbitrary incidents such as the giving of love potions, or magic girdles, by casual hunts, or dreams, by supernatural events, or by the use of the equally arbitrary but formal device of allegory. In such ways the narrative can be jerked forward in the desired direction. For though *Troilus and Criseyde* is a much more complicated piece of writing than the ordinary romance or saint's life, it does not escape from similar problems in narration. Troilus is so completely a prince in love, constrained by honor and truth, Criseyde so plainly a desirable young woman, protected by "danger," that they cannot so transform themselves out of character to take part in the story without an intermediary.

Pandarus's role then is what by the sixteenth century all readers knew it to be, that of pander. He embodies society's acceptance of the ways in which lust and aggressiveness can get to work, the element in which the lovers move towards each other, the means by which the two predetermined characters are interlocked in the action of the poem. Once again characterization is dependent upon the story. In Book Three (ll. 241ff.) the Narrator indulging the irony has Pandarus confessing to be exactly what the action of the story will make of him.

A realization of the wholeness and integrity of a poem of this size comes slowly. But we can often on reflection discern aspects of it as we proceed. For example, we might take note of a response we make to the last book. The book seems to go on for a very long time. It is certainly not that the story loses its power here, nor that the telling of it flags. This last book is perhaps the most compelling part of the whole poem. But this is the book of Troilus's woe, a record of the interminable ache. I suppose that it offends our modern moral sense. We know from the beginning of the poem that the end is Criseyde's unfaithfulness. But Chaucer has his Narrator disclose it as steadily and carefully as he began the story of Troilus's joy, omitting nothing, no single anguish, conducting his hero through ever-diminishing circles of hope to the central black despair. The unprotesting objectivity about this even-paced narration is almost inhuman. It has an integrity which we sentimental moderns find difficult to face.

Our response to the last book and its effectiveness in preparing for the end serve as indications of the careful structural composition of the poem and the harmony and consonance of its parts. The five books of *Troilus and Criseyde* recall the five-act structure of the Elizabethan play. But Chaucer employs the structure differently. Though *Troilus and Criseyde* is "litel myn tragedye," he does not produce in it the line of the Shakespearian tragic plot, where we expect and usually find a rise in emotional tension through the first four acts to a climax towards the end of the fifth: a line of asymmetrical development. *Troilus and Criseyde* shows nothing of this unidirectional development in mounting intensity. The feeling that the Fifth Book goes on for a very long time is in part prompted by finding the conventional expectancy disappointed. The narrative climax of the poem occurs undoubtedly in the Third Book, where the lovers come to their felicity. This is the pivot about which the poem swings. The end is announced at the beginning. The climax of the action stands almost plump, even by arithmetic, in the middle of the whole. It is the story of double woe, the misery of longing leading through joy to the anguish of losing. The trajectory is circular rather than ballistic. The end of the poem is a deliberate anticlimax.

The effect of the whole construction is curious. Whereas in

modern writing the structure seems usually to be related to a psychological development, many medieval works seem to rely upon purely formal or mathematical relationships. We expect the form of a work to follow and to imitate and to reinforce the psychological curve of the narration. And perhaps insofar as this identification of form and content has been mastered as a technique of composition, modern literary practice has effected a real advance on that of earlier times. It is difficult to see how at any time the simple cyclical effects of some of the alliterative poems or even the formal triptych arrangement of seduction and hunting scenes in *Sir Gawain and the Green Knight,* or the careful numerical arithmetic in compositions of some French and German poets can have contributed to the strictly literary power of these works. These formal devices are usually neither audible, nor visible nor legible. They require a spatial apprehension and suggest that a poem was assumed to be a flat material object, an inscription on some extended surface. We can allow that *Troilus and Criseyde* has a hard, marmoreal elegance and symmetry. But Chaucer turns all things to advantage. The actual form of the poem encompasses the intention of the story. The circular and spatially symmetrical arrangement of his *narratio* is perfectly suited to his *argumentum* of the disillusioning power of necessity. The narrative line by the end has described the wheel of fortune. In this medieval poem at least, a curious spatial form is used to identify the psychological curve of the story.

Many details in the poem reveal this consonance and harmony of construction. Songs and letters and dreams are introduced symmetrically and significantly. Recurrent themes such as the Procne legend, and images such as that of blindness and fire knot strands of the narrative together. Incident after incident ironically answers back one to another. The twelfth-century *Arts of Poetry* had compared a poem with the human body, beautifully proportioned and articulated, designed in detail for complex activity directed to a single end. Chaucer had learned his lesson well.

But the greatest lesson English poets in the last medieval centuries learned from the *Arts of Poetry* was elegance—a graceful clarity comparable with that which shines in stone from the sculptures of the Northern cathedrals. They taught English writers a New Poetry. The poetry of the Anglo-Saxons had great resources of force, economy, allusiveness, and resonance—a concrete splendor which we readily appreciate nowadays. In the progress of English poesy the first poem that can be put beside *Beowulf* for artistic achievement is *Troilus and Criseyde,* and it marks in English the triumphant fulfilment of those ideals of clarity, brightness and sequaciousness which the twelfth-century *Arts of Poetry* promulgated and which were extraordinarily difficult for English vernacular poets to make their own. In *Troilus and Criseyde* elegance, brightness and clarity are at once functional and decorative. In verbal style the poem is rich, varied, highly ornamented, making use of all those devices recommended by the rhetoricians and named appropriately enough colors.

Imagery of light carries much of the meaning of the poem, most obviously in Book Three, which opens with the invocation drawn from Dante. With our modern training in symbol reading we can readily submit to the power of the recurring opposition of light and dark, day and night, which often marks changes in gradient of the narration. The accounts of vigils and daybreaks, of Pandarus first setting out on his mission while the small birds sing in a May sunrise, of the midnight darkness when the lovers come together and Pandarus withdraws the little lamp, of Troilus watching at the city gate till daylight has completely gone, owe a great part of their effectiveness to the unobtrusive use of highly affective symbols. Criseyde's grace and beauty are invariably presented in terms of light.

But the clarity Chaucer achieves in the poem is more than decorative and more than symbolic. There is a light which gives form and definition to the whole, casting on the *narratio* and the *argumentum* the illumination of an intellectual light which sharpens indeed the complexity, but banishes obscurity. And this is perhaps part of the abiding impression of the poem as a whole. It is hard and vast and also luminous. It is this *lumen siccum* which penetrates through the story to the mind and then to the conscience of the reader. It has made the whole complicated story as plain as daylight and yet is able to reveal it as a fiction. The clear-eyed detachment in the telling should have prepared us against the moral weariness we encounter in the last book if we were reading it too simply and too sentimentally. In the foreknowledge indicated throughout, in the premonitions, in the melancholy infused into the joy, in the constantly flickering ironies, in the comic and tender handling of detail, in the juxtaposition and succession of incommensurate standards, the Narrator has warned the audience throughout. The end has been prepared for. It is, after all, only a made-up story, just pretense.

Nowadays we want novels to claim something more, to claim to be an illusion of life complete and unbroken. Yet here in *Troilus and Criseyde* we find Chaucer constructing a whole long complex narration of human behavior, presenting, albeit in poetic mode, a realistic account of life, holding the outcome firmly in mind throughout, and yet when he comes to the end admitting that it is only a tale. As a general rule most modern readers, following Flaubert, would deny that any author could get away with this somersault. It is of course a device of alienation, but a device available only to writers of fairy stories. And yet this conclusion which at first sight, and perhaps always to a thoroughly secularized eye, looks like a petering out of purpose is a product of the illumination that shines through the poem, the manifestation of the *argumentum* which the *narratio* has been secretly harboring. It gives an image of truth and order to the poem which the fictional story itself does not possess.

In the epilogue to the poem the variable accents of the Narrator seem to be lost in the voice of Chaucer the poet (still not of Chaucer the man). How often does an entertainer at the end of his piece add, "But all you people here, seriously now, I want to say a few special words in conclusion . . ." The device itself is not puzzling. It is the direct appeal recommended for the peroration. We can, if we choose, believe that Chaucer the man believed his own words here. Indeed he would have been a very peculiar medieval person if he had not. But the technique of detachment that the Narrator has employed in the last book, the quiet and unemphatic dismissal of the characters, allows him to take up this new posture from which he makes a final withdrawal from his audience with no sense of discontinuity or surprise. It is the most affecting, the most beautiful ending to any work in English. It is holy and mysterious, repelling tumult and applause. It retrospectively realigns the whole work it concludes.

Yet it cannot be denied that taken as a statement of substance this epilogue contradicts and annuls what the story was about. The Narrator has at many stages cast a glow of joy and glory upon sex and war. Troilus is a figure of manly virtue, of honor and good faith; Criseyde is eternally desirable; their love is a human good. Their parting, Troilus's misery and Criseyde's weakness, these are evil. Artistically the poem is triumphantly successful, but at the level of moral abstraction the story falls apart.

Behind the story is the double standard of the times. It is difficult to recognize that the secular culture of Plantagenet England with all its brilliance, wit and elegance, and its social and administrative complexity, its achievements in peace and war, was only a subculture. It rested on no firm, comprehensive frame of its own, but relied for its intellectual cohesion upon the postulates of ecclesiastical thinking and the standards of monastic morality. These were still so powerful and ingrained in the habits of thought and expression that they were able to control the wills of men and the habits of a society which could be embarrassed by them. New paths of virtue, new forms of moral perfection, had still no firm identity. Even glimpses of them could look too readily to be no more than illusions produced by feebleness of will or ignorance of truth or perversity of judgment. In the fourteenth century any rival morality still lacked the intellectual substructures needed to give it plausibility and conviction. Men of that time extracted the sting out of cries of faith and reason by an honest acceptance of a complete divorce between them. They lived as awkwardly or easily with fundamental inconsistencies as we do now. Late medieval society had to wait another century or so before their old problems of faith and morality were stabilized again. Literature in England waited still longer, before another amorous prince, Spenser's Red Cross Knight, could seek and find his love and heaven together in the pursuit of Holiness. But from the inherent contradictions in his own society Chaucer in *Troilus and Criseyde* makes a huge coherent success. Indeed Chaucer's work can always serve as a triumphant denial of that idle and fashionable truism that a chaotic and muddled age deserves a chaotic and fragmentary art.

But *Troilus and Criseyde* is not an heroic poem exemplifying ideal conduct. It is a romance in a tragic mode, the fullest and most explicit working out in English of the mood of doom and fatality which overhangs the best of the medieval stories. No explanation of Beowulf's death satisfies. It is not easy to accept that Roland died at Roncesvalles simply because he broke a blood vessel. We cannot readily discern what brings about the disaster that overlays all the second part of the alliterative *Morte d'Arthur*. All that lies between the actions of such heroes and their lamentable deaths is an impenetrable and gathering gloom. We sense in these tragic stories an inexorable process, we cannot see it at work. This would be true also of *Troilus and Criseyde,* if the conclusion of the poem with its backward extension in significance did not illuminate the process. The leap into transcendence here shows this medieval manner of tragic storytelling aware at last of its own law and intention and purpose. All these medieval stories involve in their telling an encounter with the limits beyond which human will or human passion or human virtue cannot pass. But these stories are told so that the audience is aware, vaguely perhaps, that at these boundaries there *is* something beyond. The fiery breath of the dragon is not the only cause of the tragic death. What else it is, we cannot see; the story points to the unexpressed, to what we may often conveniently but inexpressively call Fate, but it is unconditioned even by a name, for it exists at the limits of interpretation even, a featureless, unimaginable power which is felt to encompass the whole life of man and society. This is indeed the *apeiron,* the unlimited, of the old Greek philosopher Anaximander. Out of the *apeiron* a cosmos is built up by the mingling of opposites. Back into the *apeiron* the cosmos crumbles at length by the unavoidable conflict of these opposites. This is the world of medieval tragic action. The forces that begin life are the forces that destroy life. They are the forces of self-assertion working in the forms of love or war or both. The tragedy itself, the pitiful event, is not very significant. A fall from prosperity to adversity is ordinary enough. What is significant is the illumination that tragedy should bring of another order. What Troilus sees looking down from beyond the seventh sphere is the truth of this sort of tragedy, an apprehension of what is "Uncircumscript, and al maist circumscrive."

This is not the mode of Shakespearian tragedy, nor of the Greek, nor of Romantic tragedy. It is not a kind of tragedy that justifies or enhances the moral statures of its actors, or works a moral purification in the consciences of its audience. In this more intellectual mode the actors are absorbed into the tragic story, and it is the full and completed story that instructs the audience of the inadequacy of the action displayed.

The Prologue to
the Canterbury Tales

NEVILL COGHILL

This happy breed of men, this little world. . . .
Richard II

EVERY POEM OF Chaucer's that we have considered derived from some work or works in other tongues, though
each had touches of a kind of novelty that we have learnt to
call "Chaucerian." As his work matured these touches became more frequent and pervasive. His way of looking at
things changed the things he looked at more and more, and
every change seemed to lift them and the poem, for a moment at least, into what still seems a present actuality and
away from literary convention. We have come, in the course
of time, to value the flavor of actuality above almost all
flavors in our reading, and it is for this reason that Chaucer
seems so "modern."

Yet if none of these poems could be called wholly "modern" in that some of their poetical pleasures depend upon our
power to recognize and enjoy a host of medieval ways of
thought, *The Prologue* to *The Canterbury Tales* needs no
spiritual glossary. It at once fills the imagination with the
simple clarities of daily fact. Chaucer's astounding originality
had at last taken the lead in its long and loving partnership
with tradition, his trust in what he saw and heard in the
world about him had lovingly invaded and conquered the do-
main of poetry. Experience had wedded Authority, and perhaps achieved sovereignty in the marriage.

The result was a new sort of poetical truth, the creation of
a poetry of fact by a wise, sure-eyed, and sensitive selection
of daily detail, mellowed and harmonized by a humane and
often an amused approval, qualified wherever approval was

Reprinted by permission from THE POET CHAUCER by Nevill
Coghill, published by Oxford University Press.

withdrawn by an ironical wit. It was a new way of looking at people.

This kind of vision that we have seen so gradually maturing came to sudden fullness towards the year 1386 and brought with it a number of enormous ideas that, once embodied, seem the simplest possible; but how or why or in what order they came to him we do not know.

Nothing forbids us to believe that the Canterbury Pilgrimage idea sprang upon him in an instant with all its inner logic intuitively complete. Or it may have dawned gradually. He has not told us. My guess would be that it came, or began to come, to him as he was tidying up his papers for the move from his house in Aldgate. He had time on his hands, dismissed as he had been from his comptrollerships, time to wonder what could be made of a miscellaneous heap of manuscripts such as his tale of Palamon and Arcite, his Life of St. Cecilia, his little clutch of "tragedies," his story of Griselda. They must in some moods have seemed a job lot. Was there no way in which their differing qualities could be bound into the unifying strength of a single work? And could anything be done with "Melibee"?

There were many collections of stories in existence, some of which cannot but have been known to Chaucer. Boccaccio had written no less than three, the *Ameto,* the *Filocolo* and the *Decameron.* John Gower, co-dedicatee of *Troilus and Criseyde,* was even then at work on the *Confessio Amantis,* a collection strung together, not to say hamstrung, by their single preposterous theme of Courtly Passion jacketed in the Seven Deadly Sins, each tale an example of some sin or sub-sin, as if Cupid had borrowed Christianity to sermonize his incompatible cult. Chaucer himself had attempted, in *The Legend of Good Women,* to rope a set of tales together on the very cord that ultimately strangled them, the constancy of women.

Yet it could not be denied that a collection of stories gained something from a unifying principle, something dear to Chaucer with his concern for poetical form. But it was gained at the risk of monotony and restriction. It leaned towards the ridiculous and the literary and seemed to exclude actuality altogether.

Chaucer now found a solution to this problem so obvious that everyone else had missed it. It was to unite the diversity of his tales by allotting them to a diversity of tellers joined in some likely common purpose. This, analytically speaking, is the root principle of *The Canterbury Tales*.

He found his diversity of creatures in the circumstantial world about him, God's world, his own world, the world of the Port of London, the world of England itself. There lay the right raw material for all his special gifts. And so a second organizing principle or idea becomes discernible in the huge conception, namely to paint a National Portrait Gallery.[1]

He did not underline this idea. It is simply there, for every reader to infer. In all our literature there is not such another picture of a whole society, and Chaucer contrived it in some two-and-thirty characters and 860 lines.

It was second nature with him that his sense of actuality should mingle with his sense of hierarchy. He presented his characters in the jumble and haphazardry of life, with a mild apology for his neglect of rank. All was to seem fortuitous, and yet all the ranks and vocations, the trades and the professions were there. What Shakespeare would have called "degree" was omnipresent, though in a deliberately disordered chain, and the historian can rebuild out of *The Prologue* the twin ladders of Church and State as they then were, with scarcely a rung missing.

A high kind of gentle blood is seen in the Knight and his son, a lesser somewhat emulous gentry in the land-owning Franklin. The learned professions appear in the Serjeant-at-Law and the Doctor. The Merchant stands for the upper reaches of commerce, for the new class of wool exporters and exchange manipulators, beginners in capitalism, while the Haberdasher and his associates represent the slightly smaller fry of London traders, though each

> Was shaply for to been an alderman.

The Wife of Bath, a provincial and a woman, was a clothmaker, an expert in the newest and most important of England's industries at the time. Another provincial, this time a sea-dog, was the Shipman, owner and master mariner. All these were of some rank. They would have servants at home, they would exact and enjoy a high local prestige. Next below them were the churl-folk, of whom the Miller was the grandest, his own master, with the coveted right to work a mill, a

---

[1] But this of course did not prevent him from touching up some of his portraits with bits out of his favorite books. The table manners of the Prioress, for instance, are taken from the *Roman de la Rose*.

man to give himself airs. The swaggering Simkin of *The Reve's Tale* was such another, with a wife

> as digne as water in a dich.

Then came the servant class: upper servants like the Manciple and the Reve, lower servants like the Yeoman and the Cook, each pair representing Town and Country between them. At the absolute bottom of the social scale came the country Ploughman, and bottom though he was, he was nearest among these lay-folk to the Knight in generous Christianity. They were both *animae naturaliter christianae*.

The Church was hardly less exactly represented. The Monk from his monastery, the Prioress from her convent, her attendant Priests, the village Parson, and the roaming Friar, sufficiently covered the more usual religious categories. The courtly pretensions of the Prioress and the humble origins of the Parson (he was the Ploughman's brother) showed the comparative unimportance of personal rank in the religious life. Somewhere between laity and ecclesiastics came the Clerk of Oxford to represent the Universities, a poor scholar who as yet had got no benefice. At an infinite moral and social depth below all these came the Pardoner and the Summoner. It is true that the Pardoner might enjoy a certain prestige founded on superstition, but his natural level was with the Summoner, "his freend and his compeer." Both were laymen, hangers-on of the Church, and hated.

For all the methodical selection and artistic ingenuity that must have gone to the presenting of these characters, it was an almost greater triumph to have made them seem so gloriously haphazard in their congregation. This was partly contrived by the stroke of genius that could imagine the only two places in England where they would all be likely to meet on equal terms, an Inn and a Cathedral, and the circumstance, a pilgrimage, that could credibly unite them in a common purpose. The journey between the two would be the occasion for their diverse tales. Chaucer himself could be on such a pilgrimage; once again he could place himself inconspicuously at the heart of his poem. He had found a form absolutely perfect for his special talents.

But there is something deeper than either form or talent in *The Prologue* to *The Canterbury Tales*. That deeper thing was his attitude to the created world. The devices of craftsmanship and ingenuity, and the happy thoughts that embellish a large design are only the servants or children of such vision. It took a Chaucer not only to hit upon them, but to handle them, and that handling-power seems to me centered in the Chaucer who had written in *The House of Fame,* so many years before,

> "O God!" quod y, "that made Adam,
>   Moche ys thy myght and thy noblesse!"

He had always taken joy in the created world, a joy tinged with quizzical wonder. The simplicity of his delight in things for being what they were was qualified by an acute and questioning intelligence, and this in turn qualified by a gravely comic personal humility. So bland, so unselfconscious, so mild a spectator of God's plenty could be simple without naïveté, romantic without foolishness, ironical without cruelty. He seems omnivorous and yet a dainty feeder. The freshness of his gaze is like that of a man who can see what is familiar to him without losing the vividness of a child's vision. Nothing is blurred, every color is as true as in heraldry or in a primitive painting. His eye, "gilding the object whereupon it gazeth," at the same time perceives with a perfectly mature intelligence, deeply pleased, amused, and upon occasion touched. The perfect good manners of his observation, and of his observations, has a Christian courtliness derived from the poetry of dream and a robustness derived from his gradual awakening into a sunlit actuality. It was the April of the world, to him no cruel month. Such a vision, crisped by wit, now centered itself on men and women. He proceeded to invent a way of describing them.

He had already invented one way in *Troilus and Criseyde,* where the characters grow into action from within. Pandarus creates himself out of conversation and that inner wiliness of his. But this way of presenting character is a slow one, suited only to a few protagonists engaged at deep levels of feeling. It would not suit a group of pilgrims casually met. Chaucer now hit upon another way of presentation, the selection and adding up of outward detail into the prime number that makes a human being, as he appears objectively, with no more inner life (and no less) than men and women seem to have when we meet and talk to them fortuitously and are struck by their personalities.

As in our own lives, at some gathering, we are variously struck by one or another, so Chaucer. He varied his presentation from the full-length portrait to the thumbnail sketch. Of some, their appearance, personal history, likes, dislikes, qualities, and aptitudes are described in detail, sometimes with a snatch of conversation, such as we have learned to expect from him. "And I seyde his opinion was good," was his comment on the opinions of the Monk. Apparently grave, it rings across the centuries in Chaucer's accent of sardonic innocence.

As the casual is an ingredient of the actual, he has a trick in some descriptions of pointing observation by a series of footnotes or afterthoughts; thus ends the description of the Monk, for instance:

> He was nat pale as a forpyned goost.[2]
> A fat swan loved he best of any roost.
> His palfrey was as broun as is a berye.

Only one character is presented by the technique of *Troilus and Criseyde,* and that one of the most important, Harry Bailey the Host. Like Pandarus he is built up out of what he does and says rather than what he looks like. The same miracle of clarity and fullness is achieved.

There is some reason for thinking Harry Bailey and one or two others were portraits taken from actual men, well known in London at the time. The Subsidy Rolls of Southwark record what might be called the "black market" practices of one "Henri Bayliff, ostyler" in 1375–6, and he may well have sat unconsciously for Chaucer's portrait. Thomas Pynchbeck, Serjeant-at-Law in 1376 and Baron of the Exchequer in 1388, may be the original of Chaucer's Man of Law:

> Ther koude no wight *pynche* at his writyng.[3]

If so, this is Chaucer's only plain pun.[4] Proust tells us that a book is a great cemetery in which, for the most part, the names on the tombstones have been effaced. It is a paradox that Henri Bayliff and Thomas Pynchbeck are ghosts, and their portraits, if portraits they were, flesh and blood. But it is possible to hunt too far in factual record to trace what are essentially imaginations. To search the registers of Bath for a woman named Alison five times married is to look for the bones of Pharaoh's lean kine.

The spiritual power of a zest for actual life shows itself not only in the plenty and variety of his pilgrims, but especially

---

[2] Tormented soul.

[3] No one could find fault with what he wrote. (Italics are mine.)

[4] Except perhaps
> So whan this Calkas knew by calkulynge.
>
> (*Troilus and Criseyde*, I, 71.)

in their normality. He did not exaggerate or look for freaks, he delighted in the world as he found it. Incapable of stale vision, he also had the perennial happiness of touch described by Dryden as belonging only to a master, "to draw a full face, and to make the nose and cheeks stand out, and yet not employ any depth of shading. This is the mystery of that noble trade, which yet no master can teach his apprentice." Zest in experience and clarity in language are the unflagging qualities of *The Prologue*. "Execution," said Blake, "is the chariot of Genius."

Chaucer's delight in normality is what chiefly differentiates him from Dickens, with whom he has so often been compared. Dickens is a master of the eccentric. When we think of him a wonderful host of fabulously erratic figures comes to mind, adorable grotesques, monsters of iniquity, paragons of pathos, of optimism, cunning, meanness, benevolence. Everything is in untameable, romantic excess. Micawbers, Mantalinis, Fagins, Pickwicks, Pecksniffs, and a hundred other giants of comic or terrible eccentricity are spawned by his unflagging imagination. The very waiters at wayside inns, the tramps on the road, have their violent idiosyncrasies. But Chaucer's world is almost freak-free, his characters perfectly life-size. Only the Wife of Bath seems larger and louder than life. But she is a special case.

The frame of the poem into which ambled Chaucer's characters from the normal world was circular. Ever since the *Book of the Duchess* Chaucer had favored a poetry that circled back to its starting point, one that ended in its beginnings. Now, in late life, he planned another boomerang poem, with a trajectory from London to Canterbury and back. This, he supposed, would allow him room for 120 tales. It is a measure of the confidence he felt in his great idea and in his power to complete it. Thirty pilgrims, including himself, two stories from each on the way out, two on the way back, and a dinner for the best. It was a wide elbow-room.

Chaucer never completed his circle. He left nine great arcs of it, gapped and imperfectly joined. If the cavalcade reached Canterbury in the pilgrim mood prepared by *The Parson's Tale,* nine of his tellers had been crowded out altogether with no chance of a victorious dinner, and only Chaucer himself had been allowed two tales, one interrupted.

Others had been interrupted too; *The Monk's Tale* had been brought to a timely, the Cook's and the Squire's to an untimely end. All these interruptions, save that of the Cook, were a part of Chaucer's artistry in the actual. Simpleton-Chaucer could be rudely told to stop by Harry Bailey:

"Thy drasty rymyng is nat worth a toord!"

But the Monk, having asserted his dignity by a show of serious learning, needed no less a person than the Knight to check his tediousness. The Squire, gathering himself for an almost endless recital,

> First wol I telle yow of Cambyuskan . . .
> And after wol I speke of Algarsif, . . .
> And after wol I speke of Cambalo . . .
> And ther I lefte I wol ayeyn bigynne. . . .

is choked by the praises of the Franklin, the only person present, except his proud Father, fit to interrupt him. Human endurance and the decencies of hierarchy were in this way both respected. The truncation of *The Cook's Tale,* however, remains unexplained, and I for one regret it more than the interruption of the Squire, deplored by Milton. The greatest interruption of all, however, was not to a tale but to the cavalcade itself. Actuality sweeps in at a gallop with the Canon and his Yeoman. It is almost the finest comic surprise in the poem, a rushing in of the outer world into the world of imagination, life breaking in upon plan haphazardly with the bit between its teeth.

But the poem was never completed. Had it been so, perhaps every tale would have suited its teller. As things are there are a few anomalies. Yet for the most part they fit so well that one might say the tales grow out of the characters and the characters grow out of the tales. And both grow out of *The Prologue* and the linking colloquies between tales.

Within this living framework of an English actuality are placed the no less living fantasies of Europe; for if *The Prologue* is a cross-section of fourteenth-century English life, the *Tales* are a cross-section of fourteenth-century imagination through Christendom.

Romance-Epic in the High Style as in *The Knight's Tale,* and in the Low, as in *Sir Thopas,* scurrilous *fabliaux,* saints' lives, tragic anecdotes, Aesopian fable, Arthurian tale, themes from the classics and from folklore, oriental tales, sermons with *exempla* and without, and the huge and perennial discussion in *Melibee* on the merits of violence and nonviolence, so familiar to us all, make up a wide catch of home and foreign fish in Chaucer's English net. If it is a rough truth that the Middle Ages were interested in narrative, and the Renaissance in character, here in *The Canterbury Tales* was the first meeting-place of those two epochs. It was a work that held the past and looked forward into the future.

The poetical qualities of *The Prologue* and the links between tales differ from those of the tales themselves in many ways, though not in all, nor at all times. But in general the latter are dominated by fantasy and speculation and are as much (but no more) removed from *The Prologue* as a man's imagination is removed from his appearance. Together they body forth the civilization of the fourteenth century as seen in sunlight and domesticity. That it could be seen in other ways, as Langland saw it for instance, was no concern of Chaucer's. He chose to measure the world by its smiling self rather than by the Kingdom of Heaven. More than this, his yardstick was in a sense homely and private. Although a courtier at the geographical center of politics, he found no material for poetry in the major national events of his times. Plague, schism, the Peasants' Revolt, and the clashes between Richard II and his nobility, that were to end in deposition and regicide, have no place in his poem of England. Jack Straw's massacre of the Flemings in 1381 was poetically no more to Chaucer than the flurry in a farmyard roused by the rape of Chanticleer.

This homeliness is apparent in his imagery. It is the imagery of common sight and sense, achieving the poetry of fact. He has a steady, effortless power of making what seem to be prose statements gleam and glow as they never do in prose. His similes are for the most part the obvious ones of common conversation, though none the less charming for that:

> Whit was his berd as is the dayesye . . .

> His eyen twynkled in his heed aryght,
> As doon the sterres in the frosty nyght . . .

> As hoot he was and lecherous as a sparwe . . .

> As leene was his hors as is a rake . . .

But imagery as we know it in Shakespeare, Donne, Milton, or Keats, the imagery of broken opalescences, halftones, imprecise suggestion, sudden wonder, extended learning, remote allusion and, above all, the imagery of metaphor that shows one thing instantly in terms of another with a flash of revelation, is nowhere to be found in *The Prologue,* and rarely if ever in the rest of Chaucer's work.

Yet, in a more primitive sense of the word, *The Prologue* is nothing but a series of images, pictures of things directly present to the senses. Shape and color reach us sharply and immediately, as if from some bright and clearly defined object in life, say a geranium. These bright natural images move to a dance of syllables and to a turn of meaning on the rhyme that give a sudden sharpness of definition, as when the sun comes out on a garden. There is an ever-present liquidness of movement in his language, now unrecapturable in poetry because those gliding terminations that he knew so well how to use have vanished from our language. We can no longer make the music of such a line as

> And smalë fowelës maken melodyë

We can make other music, but this kind is lost to us for ever.

A quizzical but affirmative delight in the created world, an eye for the immediate image and an ear for the natural music of speech gathered their forces in Chaucer to express in *The Prologue* his long experience of the daily dealings of men and women. The greatness of his work lies not only in the pleasure of so sharp and happy-hearted a sight of times past, but also in the power it imparts to us to see men and women, our own contemporaries, with a like vision, a like sympathy and amusement, a like intelligence, in their individual actuality. Every reader of *The Prologue* feels he has learnt to open a Chaucerian eye upon the world.

Idiom of Popular Poetry
in the Miller's Tale

E. T. DONALDSON

A POET WHO abandons the poetic idiom of his time and nation and devises one entirely new in its place creates for the would-be critic of his language a difficult problem. Criticism of the language of poetry can exist only through comparison with contemporary and earlier writings, and when, as sometimes happens, the critic cannot find between these and the work of the innovator enough similarity even to reflect the differences, he has to resort, in lieu of criticism, to merely quoting the innovator admiringly. With Chaucer the problem is even greater than with Milton, Shakespeare, Wordsworth, or Eliot. For while we may at least be sure that they were brought up in an English literary tradition from which they more or less consciously revolted, the disquieting suspicion always arises that Chaucer, bred if not born in a culture predominantly continental, may not have been very much aware of the literary tradition from which he was presumably in revolt; and this means that anyone who, in search of comparisons with Chaucer's diction, goes to the most prolific of the vernacular literary traditions, the romance, or to the closely related lyric, must consider himself to be in danger of wasting his time.[1]

But Chaucer did, after all, write in English, however continental his background may have been, and it stands to reason that diligent search will reveal at least a few correspondences with the popular English poetic diction of his day. Complete analysis of his own vocabulary is now—and has been for

Reprinted from ENGLISH INSTITUTE ESSAYS 1950 (1951), 116–140, by permission of Columbia University Press.

[1] The researches of Laura H. Loomis in recent years have, however, done much to justify such comparison by demonstrating Chaucer's familiarity with the native romance tradition. See "Chaucer and the Auchinleck MS. . .," in *Essays and Studies in Honor of Carleton Brown* (New York, 1940), pp. 111–28; "Chaucer and the Breton Lays of the Auchinleck MS," *SP*, XXXVIII (1941), 14–33; and her study of "Sir Thopas" in *Sources and Analogues . . .* (Chicago, 1941), pp. 486–559.

some time—possible through use of the Chaucer *Concordance;* [2] in this one can study all the contexts of every word he ever used, and hence can try to determine the values he placed upon the words he appropriated from the conventional vocabulary of popular poetry. It is the evaluation of these borrowings that I have undertaken; but since the job is a tricky one at best, I have thought it advisable to begin with those words which, while common in contemporary romance and lyric, occur only a very few times in Chaucer and are therefore to be suspected of carrying a rather special sort of weight. Only by such drastic limitation of the subject can it be treated at all in the time allotted.

In approaching the problem of evaluation there are two subordinate poems that I have found to be of some help. The first is Fragment A of the Middle English translation of the *Roman de la Rose.* That this is really Chaucer's work cannot be entirely proved. Most scholars think it is, [3] and I have little doubt that it is. But even if it is not, it is at least the sort of poem we should suppose him to have written in his poetic immaturity. For while it is not nearly so free as Chaucer's mature works are from that conventional diction—those clichés—by which the whole vernacular tradition was infected, [4] it nevertheless frequently has that quality, common to all Chaucer's indisputable works, of uniting perfectly simple English words with extraordinary ease into genuinely poetic language of a kind that makes the phrase "poetic diction" seem entirely too high-flown to be apt. Whether it is by Chaucer or not, its diction, occasionally but not consistently conventional, seems to represent a half-way point between popular English poetry and the *Canterbury Tales.* I find it critically illuminating, therefore, in comparing the Fragment with the *Canterbury Tales,* to observe how the mature Chaucer places in new and sometimes startling contexts words which a poet of somewhat less refined taste (probably the young Chaucer) had used flatly in time-honored contexts.

Rather firmer help is offered by Chaucer's *Sir Thopas.* For

---

[2] Ed. by Tatlock and Kennedy (Washington, 1927).

[3] For a summary of scholarly opinions on the authorship of the Fragment see Joseph Mersand, *Chaucer's Romance Vocabulary* (New York, 1939), p. 60, n. 7.

[4] See, for instance, the old poetic word, "swire" (neck); and the conventional alliterative phrases *styf in stour* and *byrde in bour.* To conserve space, location of lines from Chaucer and the *Roman* will not be given: they may be readily found with the help of the *Concordance.* Quotations from Chaucer are from F. N. Robinson's edition [Boston, 1933].

this parody, while a criticism of vernacular conventions of
every sort, is above all a criticism of standard English poetic
diction. Therefore, if we find—as we do—words that Chaucer makes fun of in *Sir Thopas* showing up in seemingly innocent contexts elsewhere in his work, we shall have at least
a small area in which to exercise criticism of Chaucer's
idiom. Let me confess at once that the total critical yield
from the words of this sort that I have noticed is not great
and that it makes possible, not a wider appreciation of Chaucer's more serious poetry, but of some of his comic effects. In
this paper I shall deal largely with the effect upon the *Miller's
Tale* of certain words introduced from the vernacular poetic
tradition. It goes almost without saying that this effect is ironical and that more irony is not the sole product I should have
wished to achieve from my investigation. Still, this is only a
beginning, and "after this I hope ther cometh moore"—if not
from me, from better critics. The following is therefore presented as an example of a technique by which it may be possible to arrive at a better understanding of Chaucer's poetic
idiom.

Since in the *Miller's Tale* I shall be dealing with ironical
context, I shall start with an illustration of an ironical use of
conventional idiom that is, thanks to the brilliant work of
Professor Lowes, known to every Chaucerian. Lowes has
demonstrated that the key to the portrait of the Prioress is in
the second line, which, in describing her smiling as "ful sym-
ple and coy," endows her with a pair of qualities that were
also those of innumerable heroines of Old French romance.[5]
It is, incidentally, a measure of Chaucer's gallicization, as
well as of his tact with a lady who likes to speak at least a
sort of French, that these conventional words, along with
most of the others in her characterization, are not commonly
applied to ladies in Middle English romance. Furthermore,
Lowes shows that in describing her person—gray eyes, delicate soft red mouth, fair forehead, nose *tretys*—Chaucer borrows from stock French descriptions of ladies details that
were full of courtly reminiscences for the cultivated reader of
the time, though with impeccable taste he foregoes the complete physical catalogue that an Old French heroine would
feel herself entitled to. If Lowes had wished to reinforce his
point, whose delicacy needs no reinforcement, he could have
gone on to examine Chaucer's own works for the reappear-

[5] J. L. Lowes, "Simple and Coy . . . ," *Anglia*, XXXIII (1910),
440–51.

ance of the words used to describe the Prioress. He would have found, for instance, that "coy" is used of no other woman in Chaucer, though it appears in the stereotype "as coy as a maid," used only of men. "Simple," as Lowes does observe, is also the attribute of Blanche the Duchess—Chaucer's most serious conventional portrait; but it is applied further to three romantic ladies in the first fragment of the *Roman,* and, in Chaucer's mature work, it is used twice of Criseide, perhaps in a delicate attempt to be suggestive about her manner without being communicative about her character. It is worthy of note that the Prioress' nose *tretys* is foreshadowed by the face *tretys* of Lady Beauty in the English *Roman;* but the word is otherwise non-Chaucerian. Further, while ladies' noses receive full treatment in the translation of the *Roman,* elsewhere the only female nose mentioned in the stubby one that the miller's daughter inherited from her father in the *Reeve's Tale*—"With kamus nose, and eyen greye as glas," an interesting mutation, incidentally, on the Prioress, "Hir nose tretys, hir eyen greye as glas." And of all the women in Chaucer, only the Prioress and Alison, heroine of the *Miller's Tale,* have mouths or foreheads worthy of note: a case, perhaps, of the Colonel's Lady and Judy O'Grady. Finally, if one had time one might, I think, profitably investigate the words "fetys" and "fetisly," both used in describing the Prioress, but elsewhere appearing only in contexts which render highly suspect the particular sort of elegance they suggest.[6] In any case, the Prioress' portrait is a masterpiece of idiomatic irony, though the idiom is that of French poetry rather than of English.

With this much preliminary let us turn to the *Miller's Tale.* Upon this, Chaucer's worst ribaldry, it is generally agreed that he lavished his greatest skill, and in particular upon his description of the three principal characters—Alison, Absolon, and *hende* Nicholas, and upon their dialogue with one another. One of the devices he used most skillfully was that of sprinkling these characterizations and conversations with clichés borrowed from the vernacular versions of the code of courtly love—phrases of the sort we are accustomed to meet, on the one hand, in Middle English minstrel romances and, on the other, in secular lyrics such as those preserved in Harley MS 2253—but phrases that are not encountered else-

---

[6] Aside from Fragment A of the *Roman,* where the words are common they are normally used only by lower-class speakers; the only exceptions are in the portraits of the Prioress and the Merchant.

where in the serious works of Geoffrey Chaucer. The comic
effect of this imported courtly diction will, I hope, be understood as we go along. At the start it is necessary to bear in
mind only that by the fourteenth century at least, the aim
and end of courtly love was sexual consummation, however
idealized it may have been made to appear, and that of the
various factors upon which the *ars honeste amandi* depended
for its idealization the conventional language associated with
it was not the least important.

The key to the matter, as one might expect, is in the constant epithet applied to the hero of the *Miller's Tale*—that is,
in hende Nicholas' almost inseparable *hende*. Any one who
has done even cursory reading in popular English poetry of
Chaucer's time—and before and after—will heartily agree
with the *Oxford Dictionary's* statement that "hende" is "a
conventional epithet of praise, very frequent in Middle English poetry." Originally it seems to have meant no more than
"handy, at hand"; but it gradually extended its area of signifi-
cation to include the ideas of "skillful, clever" and of "pleasant, courteous, gracious" (or "nice," as the *Oxford Dictionary* says with what I take to be exasperated quotation
marks); and it simultaneously extended its area of reference
to include, under the general sense "nice," almost every hero
and heroine, as well as most of the rest of the characters sid-
ing with the angels, in Middle English popular poetry. Thus,
the right of the Squire of Low Degree to the hand of the
King's Daughter of Hungary is established by the minstrel
poet's exclamation:

> The squir was curteous and hend,
> Ech man him loved and was his frend.

And another poet boasts of Sir Isumbras,

> Alle hym loffede, that hym seghe:
> Se hende a man was hee! [7]

Such examples could be multiplied indefinitely. Indeed, the
average popular poet could no more do without "hende" than
he could do without the lovers whose endless misadventures
gave him his plots, since unless a lover was "hende," he or
she was no proper exponent of courtly love. We should,

---

[7] *Squyr of Lowe Degre*, ed. by Mead, ll. 3–4; *Sir Ysumbras*, ed. by
Schleich, ll. 17–18; for examples of many of the characteristics dis-
cussed here, see W. C. Curry, *The Middle English Ideal of Personal
Beauty* (Baltimore, 1916).

therefore, have a right to expect the adjective to modify such Chaucerian characters as Troilus and Criseide, Arveragus and Dorigen, Palamon, Arcite, and Emily. But in Chaucer's indisputable works the word, while it is used eleven times with Nicholas, appears only twice elsewhere, and it is applied to none of the more serious characters, such as those just mentioned. The translator of Fragment A of the *Roman* had, to be sure, used it twice to describe amiable folk associated with the garden of the Rose; but thereafter it is spoken only by the Host, that distinguished exponent of bourgeois good manners, when he calls upon the Friar to be "hende" to the Summoner; and by Alice of Bath, who expresses with it the charm possessed by her fifth-husband-to-be, jolly Jankin, who is a spiritual sibling of Nicholas' if there ever was one. It is clear from these usages, as well as from the even more eloquent lack of its use in any genuinely courtly context, that for Chaucer "hende" had become so déclassé and shopworn as to be ineligible for employment in serious poetry.

But by the same token it was highly eligible for employment in the *Miller's Tale*. Nicholas is, after all, a hero of sorts, and he deserved to be as "hende" as any other self-respecting hero-lover. But in the present context the word mocks the broad meaning "nice" that is apparent in non-Chaucerian contexts. Indeed, its constant association with Nicholas encourages one to feel that here "hende" does not so much define Nicholas as he defines it. Furthermore, he defines it in a way that is surprisingly true to the less usual senses of the word, for Nicholas turns out to be a good deal less romantically "nice" than he is realistically "clever, skillful." He even represents the earliest meaning of the word, "at hand, handy"; for the Miller, analyzing his love-triangle in proverbial terms, remarks that always the "nye slye" (the sly dog at hand, Nicholas) displaces the "ferre leeve" (the distant charmer, Absolon). But most important, in Nicholas as in other heroes, the quality of being "hende" is the cause of his success in love. In the quotations given above we learn that it was because they were "hende" that Sir Isumbras and the Squire of Low Degree were generally beloved. Nicholas is also lovable, but his lovableness is of the rather special sort that would appeal to a woman of Alison's tastes and morals. In short, the coupling of word and character suggests in Nicholas nothing more than a large measure of physical charm that is skillful at recognizing its opportunities and putting itself to practical sexual use; and this is a sorry degradation for an adjective that had been accustomed to modify some of the nicest people in popular poetry, who now, as a result of Nicholas, begin to suffer from guilt by association.

A somewhat similar aspect of Nicholas' character is reflected in the line that tells us,

> Of deerne love he koude and of solas.

For his aptitude at *derne love,* "secret love," Nicholas must have been the envy of a good many young men in contemporary English poetry. For instance, in the Harley MS we meet several swains whose unsuccessful involvement in secret love affairs is their chief source of poetic woe.

> Lutel wot hit any mon
> hou derne loue may stonde,

grumbles one of these before going on to explain with what agonies and ecstasies it is attended.[8] Such lyricists were probably apt to pretend to themselves that the secretive line of conduct suggested by the phrase "derne love," while it may have made things difficult, was nevertheless one of the ennobling conditions imposed upon them by the courtly code. Chaucer, however, seems to have felt otherwise, for while many of his heroes experience "secree love," none besides Nicholas is very "derne" about it. Elsewhere Chaucer does not even use the common adjective to modify other nouns besides "love," apparently feeling that its reputation had been ruined by the company it had kept so long. Even in Old English, of course, the word was ambiguous, reflecting sometimes justified secrecy and sometimes secret sin; and among the moral lyrics of the Harley MS there is one whose author makes it clear that for him "derne dedes" are dirty deeds.[9] From his avoidance of the adjective it appears that Chaucer also subscribed to such an opinion. Moreover, the modern reader of the Harley love lyrics will probably sympathize with him, for it sometimes seems that, whatever the lovers pretend, they respected the principle of "derne love" more because of its value in protecting them from outraged husbands or fathers than from any courtly ideal of preserving their lady's good name.[10] Thus, long before Chaucer's time "derne love" was

[8] See *The Harley Lyrics,* ed. by G. L. Brook (University of Manchester, 1948), 32.1–2; also 3.36 and 9.43 (references are to poem and line numbers.)

[9] See *OED,* "dern," and Brook, 2.5–11.

[10] See Brook, 24.17–20.

already in potentiality what it becomes in actuality in Nicholas, a device for getting away with adultery, if not really a sort of excuse for indulging in it. Therefore Nicholas' aptitude parodies an ideal already devalued through misuse in the vernacular; and since even at its most exalted the courtly code of secrecy might be described as crassly practical, his aptitude also parodies that of more genuinely courtly lovers than the Harley lyricists.

Turning to Nicholas' rival, jolly Absolon, one may find further instances of this technique of Chaucer's. What Absolon lacks in the way of Nicholas' "hende-ness" he tries to make up with his own "joly-ness." The epithet "joly" is not as consistently used with Absolon as "hende" is with Nicholas, and since it has a wide variety of meanings and is common in Chaucer, it may not be so readily classified. Suffice it to say that it is generally in the mouths of bourgeois characters and that in the senses "handsome" and "pretty" it modifies men or women with equal frequency. But it is, perhaps, the secret of Absolon's ill-success that all his jollification makes rather for prettiness than for masculine effectiveness. One recalls that Sir Thopas, though a sturdy hero, possesses some of the charms of a typical medieval heroine, and the Miller seems to suggest by several of the terms in his portrait of Absolon that the latter had somehow or other fallen across the fine line which in medieval poetry separated feminine beauty from that of beardless youths. For in his description he uses words that a minstrel poet would normally apply to a pretty girl. For instance,

His rode was reed, his eyen greye as goos,

and the gray eyes will remind us of the Prioress, as well as of countless other medieval heroines and, it must be granted, a number of heroes, though not in Chaucer, who reserves gray eyes for ladies. But in possessing a "rode"—that is, a peaches-and-cream complexion recommended by fourteenth-century Elizabeth Ardens, Absolon places himself in the almost exclusive company of Middle English damsels.[11] The complexion of truly manly males of the time was, after all, generally obscured by a good deal of beard, and hence apt to remain unsung. It is significant that the only other "rode" in all Chaucer belongs to Sir Thopas, a feminine feature that con-

---

[11] For examples see Curry, pp. 92–94. In contexts not concerned with romantic love or lovers this word, as well as others discussed here, was commonly employed without regard to gender.

trasts startlingly with the saffron beard of that curiously constituted creature. Absolon further distinguishes himself (from
his sex, I fear) by being the only character in Chaucer to be
associated with the adjective "lovely," which is applied to the
looks he casts upon the ladies of the parish and to no other
thing Chaucerian, though to hundreds of things, especially
things feminine, in popular poetry.[12]

Readers of the latter would naturally expect the flesh of
this pretty fellow to be

> As whit as is the blosme upon the rys,

and it comes as a surprise that it is not Absolon's flesh, but
his surplice, that is described in these terms. But the line, either in much the same form or, if one wants pink flesh, with
the variation "as reed as rose on ris," is one of the clichés
found almost inevitably in descriptions of women.[13] For instance, the variant form is applied to Lady Beauty's flesh in
the *Roman* fragment. But in what we are sure is Chaucer's
work there is elsewhere no such phrase—indeed, there is elsewhere no such thing as a "ris," "spray," at all. When he
quietly transfers the conventional descriptive phrase from the
body to the clothing that covers it—in this case Absolon's
surplice—Chaucer is, of course, creating the humor of surprise; but more important, the trick enables him to evoke for
the reader the hackneyed context, with all its associations, in
which the phrase usually appears, while at the same time the
poet can make literal use of the phrase's meaning in his own
more realistic description. There is an even more effective example of this economy in the portrait of Alison, to which I
shall now turn.

The pretty heroine of the tale exemplifies most brilliantly
Chaucer's reduction of the worn-out ideal, expressed by the
worn-out phrase, to its lowest common denominator of sexuality.

> Fair was his yonge wyf, and therwithal
> As any wezele hir body gent and smal.

Now the weasel, as Lowes had observed,[14] is Chaucer's own
fresh image, and its effectiveness is obvious. But the fact that
Alison's body is "gent and smal"—shapely and delicate—

[12] For an example see Brook, 14.32. *OED*, "lovely," records the word
at *Anel* 142, but Skeat and Robinson read "lowly."

[13] Curry, p. 94; also Brook, 3.11, 5.32.

[14] *Geoffrey Chaucer* (Oxford, 1934), p. 177.

makes her the sister of every contemporary vernacular heroine who is worthy of having a lover.[15] Lady Beauty, paragon of embraceable women in the *Roman,* is in a similar way shapely—

> Gente, and in hir myddill small—

and it is natural that Sir Thopas should be "fair and gent." Possibly with Sir Thopas "gent" has its non-physical sense of "high-born, noble," but in view of the fact that the poet later commends his "sydes smale"—an item of female beauty— one may detect in the word at least a suggestion of ambiguity. On the other hand, while many lovely women in Chaucer's known works are "gentil," none besides Alison is "gent." His third and last use of the adjective is in the *Parliament of Fowls,* where it describes, appropriately enough, the "facounde gent," the "noble" eloquence, of the down-to-earth goose (a sort of female Miller in feathers) who speaks so uncourtly of the tercel eagles' love dilemma. Thus, in applying the stale adjective "gent" to Alison's body the Miller seems to be regarding her from a point of view less ideal and aesthetic than realistic and pragmatic.

As in the case of the Prioress, Chaucer's restraint (I suspect that here it is only a teasing sort of restraint) prevents him from listing—except for one startling detail—the other conventional charms of Alison's body. We might expect from the Miller that our heroine would be—as Lowes has said— "anatomized in good set similes as inescapable as death," as, for instance, is Annot of the Harley lyric "Annot and John." [16] But the reader who wants this is doomed to disappointment, for what he gets is less of Alison's body than of her wardrobe. Several of the conventional terms, however, that one expects to meet in corporeal catalogues are still present, even though they are applied only to her clothing. Her sides, to be sure, are not like the Harley Fair Maid of Ribblesdale's,

> Whittore then the moren-mylk,[17]

but her apron is, a quality it shares in Chaucer only with the silk purse of the pink-and-white fleshed Franklin. This same apron lies, moreover,

> Upon hir lendes, ful of many a goore.

15 Curry, p. 102.
16 See Lowes, *Geoffrey Chaucer, loc. cit.;* Brook, 3.11—20.
17 Brook, 7.77; also Curry, p. 81.

Now "gore," which meant originally a triangular piece of land and later (as here) a triangular strip of cloth, hence by synecdoche a skirt or apron, is obviously a technical word, and the fact that Chaucer used it only twice may not be significant. But when one recalls the number of vernacular ladies—including Alison's namesake in the Harley lyrics—who were "geynest vnder gore," or "glad vnder gore," [18] one may, perhaps, become suspicious. To be sure, scholars assure us that these phrases, along with such variants as "worthy under wede," "lovesome under line," "semely under serk," are merely stereotyped superlatives and presumably have no sexual connotation. [19] But in their literal meanings they could have such a connotation, and in their origin they probably did have. For instance, the poet of *Gawain and the Green Knight* speaks of the lady of the castle as "lufsum vnder lyne" only when Gawain is being subjected by her to the most powerful sexual temptation. And inasmuch as Chaucer, violating his self-imposed restraint, takes pains to mention the "lendes" (the loins), a word that appears a little later in frankly sexual context [20]—that are hidden beneath the "gores" of Alison's apron, it is possible that his employment of the word "gore" is evocative as well as technical; that he is, indeed, by providing a sort of realistic paraphrase of the conventional expression, insinuating what the lover of the Harley Alison really had in mind when he called his mistress "geynest vnder gore." This is only a possibility, and I should not want to insist upon it. But the possibility becomes stronger when we recall Chaucer's other use of the word [21]—in Sir Thopas' dream,

> An elf-queene shal my lemman be
> And slepe under my goore.

Whatever "gore" means here—presumably cloak—its context is unmistakable.

Nowhere does Chaucer's idiom devaluate with more devastating effect the conventional ideal to the level of flat reality than in two sentences occurring near the end of Alison's portrait. Like many a lyric and romance poet the Miller discovers that he is not clever enough to describe the total effect his

[18] Brook, 4.37, 3.16.

[19] See *OED*, "gore," *sb.* 2, 2: *Sir Gawain and the Green Knight*, ed. by Tolkien and Gordon (rev. ed.: Oxford, 1930), note on l. 1814.

[20] "And (Nicholas) thakked hire aboute the lendes weel."

[21] In MS Harley 7334, A3322 reads: "Schapen with goores in the newe get," which Tatlock regarded as a possible Chaucerian revision: see Robinson's textual note on the line.

lady produces—indeed, he doubts that any one is clever enough. The poet of the *Life of Ipomedon* was later to remark of a lady,

> In all this world is non so wyse
> That hir goodnesse kan devyse,

while the Harley Alison's lover had already asserted,

> In world nis non so wyter mon
> That al hire bounte telle con.[22]

True to the convention, the Miller exclaims of his Alison,

> In al this world, to seken up and doun,
> There nys no man so wys that koude thenche
> So gay a popelote, or swich a wenche.

But the Miller's mind is not on the "bounte" (excellence) or "goodnesse" of Alison; and his crashing anticlimax, ending with the word "wenche," which, in Chaucer, when it does not mean servant-girl means a slut,[23] is a triumph of the whole process we have been examining. Another occurs a little later. Once more the Miller is following convention, this time comparing Alison to a flower. John had said of Annot in the Harley lyric,

> the primerole he passeth, the peruenke of pris,[24]

and the Miller also begins his comparison with the cowslip, the "primerole":

> She was a prymerole, a piggesnye.

But the accompanying item is no longer a "pervenke of pris," an excellent periwinkle, but a "piggesneye," something which, while it may be also a flower (perhaps, appropriately enough, a cuckoo flower),[25] remains, unmistakably, a pig's eye. Beneath the Miller's remorseless criticism the Blanchefleurs and even the Emilys of Middle English romance degenerate into the complacent targets of a lewd whistle.

[22] *Lyfe of Ipomydon,* ed. Koelbing, ll. 123–24; Brook, 4.26–27.

[23] In his thorough study of the dialect of the *Reeve's Tale* in *Transactions of the Philological Society* (London) for 1934, p. 52, Tolkien observes that "wench" "'was still a respectable and literary word for 'girl' in Chaucer's time, and was probably in pretty general use all over the country." But it was not a respectable word in Chaucer's eyes (except in the sense "servant-girl"), as a study of his uses will quickly reveal; see the Manciple's definition, H211–22.

[24] Brooke, 3.13; cf. 14.51–53.

[25] See Manly's note, citing an *EDD* definition for Essex, in his edition of *CT* (New York, 1928), p. 560.

In their conversation with Alison the two clerks talk like a couple of Harley lyricists.[26] But Absolon, fated to accomplish more words that deeds, naturally has the richer opportunity to speak in the vernacular of love—or rather, to quote Absolon, of love-longing.

> Ywis, lemman, I have swich love-longynge,
> That lik a turtel trewe is my moornynge,

he laments outside her window. Love-longing was, of course, a common complaint, positively epidemic in the Middle Ages, and most of Chaucer's lovers have at least occasional attacks of it. But as with certain modern diseases, its name seems to have varied with the social status of its victim, and in Chaucer only Absolon and Sir Thopas are afflicted with it under that name. They are therefore in a tradition that includes knights as illustrious as Sir Tristram, not to mention those rustics the Harley lovers,[27] but fails to include Aurelius, Arcite, Troilus, or even the less admirable Damian. The inference is that for Chaucer the phrase "love-longing" implied a desire of the flesh irreconcilable with courtly idealism, though fine for Absolon. Absolon is also following popular tradition when he introduces the figure of the legendarily amorous turtle-dove into his declaration: "like a turtle true in my mourning." Ordinarily, however, it is the lady who is the dove, a "trewe tortle in a tour" [28]—faithful and remote in her tower, but curiously inarticulate, considering that she is a dove and that doves are rarely silent. Thus, the conventional image is reset in a context that is more natural and in this case more genuinely poetic. Another simile of Absolon's for conveying his distress—

> I moorne as dooth a lamb after the tete—

[26] One is frequently tempted to suggest that Chaucer had the Harley lyrics in mind when he was composing *MT*, but in view of the poor conditions that existed for the preservation of secular lyrics, to associate Chaucer with a few survivals seems too large an economy. Particularly close correspondences may be noted with the lyric "De Clerico et Puella" (Brook, 24), a dramatic dialogue in which a maiden initially repulses a clerk's plea of secret love: notice especially the third stanza, where she rebukes him ("Do wey, thou clerc, thou art a fol") and warns him of the consequences if he should be caught in her bower, and compare Alison's initial resistance ("Do wey youre handes") and her warning (A3294–7); further, the Harley lyric's window where the two had kissed "fyfty sythe" (1. 23), and the carpenter's shot window. But the situation is, of course, a very old one (see *Dame Sirith*), and the Harley lyric may go back remotely to the same source from which Chaucer's immediate source stems.

[27] See Brook, 4.5; *Sir Tristrem,* ed. by Koelbing, l. 1860.

[28] Brook, 3.22; cf. 9.3.

is the Miller's own audacious contribution to the language of love, and demonstrates the ease with which Chaucer, employing a sort of merciless logic, can move from a wholly conventional image involving animals to one wholly original and wholly devastating.

Elsewhere, Absolon keeps closer to what we should expect. Alison, for instance, is his 'swete brĭd" or "brīd"—that is, his sweet bird, bride, or possibly even "burd" (maiden): as in the romances and love lyrics it is often difficult to tell which of the three the lover means, or whether he is himself altogether sure.[29] In the other works of Chaucer birds are clearly birds, brides clearly brides, and "burd" does not occur except once of a lady in the *Roman*. Perhaps, however, it is only fair to observe that Chaucer's avoidance elsewhere of this trite form of endearment results in a use of "dear heart" and of the substantive "swete" so excessive as to amount to a triteness of Chaucer's own devising.

Continuing in the lyrical tradition even after the shame of his debacle, Absolon calls Alison his "deerelyng"—the only instance in Chaucer of this indestructible term.[30] But Absolon's lyricism reaches its highest point, naturally, before his disillusionment when, close to what he mistakes for the Promised Land—in this case the shot-window of the carpenter's bower—he begs for Alison's favors—that is, for her "ore" (mercy), as lyric poets usually expressed it. A Harley poet describing a similar crisis in his relations with his mistress reports,

> Adoun y fel to hire anon
> Ant cri[d]e, "Ledy, thyn ore!" [31]

And much earlier, according to Giraldus Cambrensis, a priest of Worcestershire had so far forgotten himself at the altar as to displace the liturgical response "Dominus vobiscum" with the lyrical refrain "Swete lamman, dhin are." [32] Thus, Absolon was conforming to a very old tradition when, about to receive his kiss, he

---

[29] The Harley lyrics have "burde," maiden (Brook, 3.1, 5.36), "brudes," maidens (6.39), "brid," maiden? (14.17), and "brid," bird for maiden (6.40). In the *King's Quair*, stanza 65, "bridis" rhymes with "bydis" (abides), but clearly means "birds."

[30] See, for instance, *William of Palerne*, ed. by Skeat, l. 1538.

[31] Brook, 32.16–17.

[32] *Opera*, ed. by J. S. Brewer, II (London, 1862), 120.

> doun sette hym on his knees,
> And seyde, "I am a lord at alle degrees;
> For after this I hope ther cometh moore:
> Lemman, thy grace, and sweete bryd, thyn oore!"

"Ore," the venerable word that is so often in the mouths of love-sick swains in Middle English, occurs in Chaucer only here. And the immediate similarity but impending difference between Absolon's situation and the situation of the average lyric lover epitomizes the technique we have been examining.

One final illustration of Chaucer's use—or abuse—of conventional idiom will suffice. Every reader of medieval romance knows that sooner or later the poet is going to describe a feast, if not a literal feast of food, at least a metaphorical one of love; and readers of English romances, including, in this case, Chaucer's own, can anticipate with some accuracy the terms in which the feast is going to be described—all the mirth and minstrelsy, or mirth and solace, or bliss and solace, or bliss and revelry, or revelry and melody by which the occasion will be distinguished. In the *Miller's Tale* the feast is, of course, of the metaphorical kind, consisting in the consummation of an adulterous love; and the obscene Miller, with his vast talent for realism, adapts the hackneyed old phrases most aptly to the situation. The carpenter, snug if uncomfortable in his kneading trough on high, is alternating groans with snores—"for his head mislay"—while Alison and Nicholas are in his bed below.

> Ther was the revel and the melodye;
> And thus lith Alison and Nicholas
> In bisynesse of myrthe and of solas.

At this feast the carpenter's snores furnish the "melodye," while his wife and her lover experience the "solas"—that seemingly innocent word for delight which here receives the full force of Chaucer's genius for devaluation—the completion of a logical process that began when we first heard it said of "hende" Nicholas that

> Of deerne love he koude and of solas.

It is, of course, true that the idiom I have been examining is just what we should expect of the Miller's cultural background—and of that of his characters [33]—and it would be

---

[33] According to L. A. Haselmayer, "The Portraits in Chaucer's Fabliaux," *RES*, XIV (1938), 310–14, conventionalized portraits existed—

possible to dispose of it by simply labeling it "verisimilitude." But verisimilitude seems to me among the least important of artistic criteria, and I refuse to believe that the courtly idiom in the *Miller's Tale* accomplishes nothing more than that. Perhaps I should have made a larger effort than I have to distinguish the Miller from Chaucer, and my interchanging of their names must have grated on some ears. But as I see it, much of Chaucer's irony in the *Canterbury Tales* becomes operative in the no man's land that exists between the poet Chaucer—who if he read his poems aloud must have been a very personal fact to his own audience—and the assigned teller of the tale, whether the Miller, the Knight, or, in *Sir Thopas*, Chaucer the pilgrim. The irony produced by the use of popular poetic idiom in the *Miller's Tale* becomes operative in this no man's land and operates in several directions. First, the idiom tends to make of the tale a parody of the popular romance, rather like *Sir Thopas* in effect, though less exclusively literary. Then, too, it reinforces the connection between the *Miller's Tale* and the Knight's truly courtly romance that the *Miller's Tale* is intended to "quite" (to repay); for it emphasizes the parallelism between the two different, though somehow similar, love-rivalries, one involving two young knights in remote Athens, the other two young clerks in contemporary Oxford. And in so far as it does this, it tends to turn the tale into a parody of all courtly romance, the ideals of which are subjected to the harshly naturalistic criticism of the fabliau. But finally, while doing its bit in the accomplishment of these things, the idiom Chaucer borrows from popular poetry contributes to the directly humorous effect of the *Miller's Tale,* and that is probably its chief function.[34]

---

though in only a vestigial form—in the French fabliaux with which Chaucer was acquainted. It was perhaps from these that Chaucer got the idea of using conventional poetic idiom in ironic contexts.

[34] Since this was written, Fr. Paul E. Beichner has in a delightful paper fully demonstrated the effeminacy of Absolon and its traditional nature; see "Absolon's Hair," *Mediaeval Studies,* XII (1950), 222–33.

Chaucer's Shipman's Tale

WILLIAM WITHERLE LAWRENCE

I

WHILE NOT, PERHAPS, in Chaucer's most genial vein, the tale told by the Sea-Captain is, as we all know, a brilliant piece of work, deserving very careful study. Moreover, it raises critical questions of considerable interest and importance, in regard to which further investigation seems desirable.

First of all it may be noted that of the six fabliau tales in the Canterbury collection, those of the Miller and the Reeve, the Friar and the Summoner, the Shipman and the Merchant (not counting the fragmentary *Cook's Tale*),[1] the one which is closest to the French type is that of the Shipman. For it displays with special clearness the characteristic technique of the jongleurs. In using this term I do not forget that authorship of the fabliaux was not confined to profes-

Reprinted by permission from *Speculum,* XXXIII (1958), 56–68.

[1] This classification is of course not my own. Arrangement of Chaucer's tales in mutually exclusive categories is impossible; there is frequent overlapping, and in some cases different views as to the preponderance of any one type are possible. In an excellent monograph to which I shall have occasion more than once to refer, Spargo classifies "under flexible definition" as Chaucer's fabliau tales those of the Miller, Reeve, Pardoner, Wife of Bath, Summoner, Merchant and Manciple (John Webster Spargo, *Chaucer's Shipman's Tale; the Lover's Gift Regained,* FF Communications, No. 91 [Helsinki, 1930]). Attention should also be called to Spargo's treatment of the tale, and reprinting in full of the Italian analogues by Boccaccio and Sercambi, in *Sources and Analogues of Chaucer's Canterbury Tales,* ed. W. F. Bryan and Germaine Dempster (Chicago, 1941), pp. 439–446. Tales with a moral emphasis are perhaps best classified as exempla, though such emphasis is sometimes added to pieces better listed otherwise. Bédier, *Les Fabliaux* (Paris, 1898, etc.), warns us that "les fabliaux ne sont point des dits moraux" (p. 34). The tale of the Wife of Bath, with its Arthurian setting, the queen presiding over an assembly resembling the Courts of Love, seems to depart from the fabliau. The *Manciple's Tale* may perhaps be placed in the "pourquoi" type—why all crows are black—but with strong influence of the *Ovid Moralisé,* etc. The *Friar's Tale,* with its hits at summoners, and its neat little plot, should, I believe, belong with the fabliaux.

These, however, are matters for individual judgment. Anyone who writes about the *Shipman's Tale* will be much indebted to Spargo's work.

sional minstrels. In all probability Chaucer followed the out-
lines of his source pretty closely. Professor Spargo observed
"There is no *a priori* reason why the *Shipman's Tale* should
not have been taken over almost verbatim from an Old
French *fabliau.*" [2] Perhaps some reservations are here necessary. Of course Chaucer the storyteller habitually proceeded
with far greater freedom than Chaucer the translator of didactic material, and in the *Shipman's Tale* we constantly hear
his voice, not that of the typical fabliau maker. Moreover, we
shall presently find reasons for believing that in some respects
the poet altered his source. [3]

Although the general characteristics of the fabliau are
familiar, [4] two or three of the main points of resemblance to
Chaucer's literary treatment in the *Shipman's Tale* may be
briefly summarized. The jongleurs were chiefly concerned to
make the points of the story rapidly and strikingly, often with
a surprise at the end, and never to lose the attention of the
audience. In the tale before us the favorite plot of the deceived husband, the faithless wife, and the demanding lover
(here, as often, a cleric), moves swiftly to its climax, not
impeded, as elsewhere in Chaucer's fabliau tales, by digressions, by citation of learned authorities, or by illustrative example. We get farthest from the type in the *Merchant's Tale,*
with its leisurely progress, its highly personal tone, its references to biblical characters, the long comments of the Merchant's friends Justinus and Placebo, and the discussion between Pluto and Proserpine. Particularly to be noted in the
Shipman's Tale is the large amount of dialogue, which gives
vividness and dramatic quality—out of four hundred and
thirty-four lines, more than half, two hundred and thirty-
seven, are in this form. Here again we are close to the
French technique.

[2] In the monograph cited in the preceding note, p. 56.

[3] Spargo treated Chaucer's indebtedness somewhat differently in his
essay in *Sources and Analogues,* p. 439. Tatlock, in his posthumously
published *The Mind and Art of Chaucer* (Syracuse, N. Y., 1950), p. 91,
remarked that "in . . . the *Shipman's Tale* Chaucer may have used no
other version than that in the *Decameron,* VIII, 1." R. A. Pratt, *MLN,*
LV (1940), 142–145, shows that in some features of the tale Chaucer
was closer to Sercambi than to Boccaccio, though "there is no proof
that . . . Chaucer was retelling Sercambi's *novella*" (p. 143). It seems
likely that all three worked from a fabliau now lost, versions of which
may have varied. Chaucer's localization of the tale "at Seint Denys,"
and possibly the phrase "Quy la?" (214) may indicate a French original.

[4] J. Bédier, *Les Fabliaux,* especially pp. 28 ff.; and 289 ff.; W. M. Hart,
in *Kittredge Anniversary Papers* (Boston and London, 1913), pp. 209 ff.

Like the fabliaux, the *Shipman's Tale* has little set, formal description of the personages, such as, for example, that of the wife in the *Miller's Tale* ("Fair was this yonge wyf," etc. A 3233 ff.), which runs to thirty-eight lines. The rich characterization of the wife of the merchant of Seint Denys is conveyed mainly through dialogue and incidents in the action. All that we learn of her in the opening lines is that she was "of excellent beautee," and "compaignable and revelous"— then the poet turns to other matters than description. As to the husband, we have been told in an interesting article that "Chaucer gives us an extraordinarily full portrait of a substantial citizen, a merchant," [5] but it will be noticed that the emphasis on the merchant's wealth supports the plot, since he must be a man of means, able to accommodate the lover with a loan, and that this emphasis is conveyed chiefly through the dialogue. The case is similar with the monk. His appearance is not formally summed up, in a single passage, but his affability and generosity are stressed, also aiding the plot, since the wife must think him an obliging person, willing to lend her a hundred franks. There are, indeed, bits of personal description of the monk tucked away in the narrative here and there (25 ff., 62 ff., 398 ff.). But this is a very different procedure from the single vivid portrait of "deynous Symkyn" in the *Reeve's Tale* (A 3925 ff.), with his round face, flat nose, and bald head, his arsenal of weapons, his quarrelsome disposition, his thievery, and his strutting about like a peacock; or the twenty-seven lines (A 3312 ff.) in which the parish clerk Absolon rises up before us in the *Miller's Tale*.

In one striking respect, however, the *Shipman's Tale* differs from the fabliaux. They are, as Hart puts it, "absolutely impersonal in style, technique, and subject matter." [6] They do not indulge in personal generalizations. The satirical element, which Bédier thinks exaggerated by the critics, is usually to be inferred from the words and action. The spirit of the fabliaux, he says, "est sans arrièreplans, sans profondeur; il manque de métaphysique. . . . Il est la malice, le bon sens joyeux, l'ironie un peu grosse, précise pourtant, et juste." [7] But the teller of our tale can hardly wait to philos-

---

[5] Gardiner Stillwell, "Chaucer's 'Sad' Merchant," *Review of English Studies*, xx (1944), 1–18. The quotations in the present discussion follow the text in F. N. Robinson's edition of the *Complete Works* (Boston and New York, 1933). I hope that I shall not be accused of discourtesy in generally omitting academic titles in citations.

[6] Hart (see note 4 above), p. 209.

[7] Bédier, p. 317.

ophize. "Women's love of having a good time causes more expenditure of money than the attention given them on festive occasions is worth, but all this passes like a shadow on the wall; the one who has to pay for it is the wretched (sely) husband—he has to clothe and array us, and if he doesn't then someone else has to pay, or lend us money, which is a dangerous thing." This is clearly the utterance of an individual pilgrim. It has long been recognized, though it has also been sharply questioned, that the original teller of the story must have been a woman, as the pronouns indicate, and that this must have been the Wife of Bath, since the other female pilgrims are members of a religious order. The discrepancy in the pronouns was not removed by Chaucer when he transferred the tale to the Shipman. The immediate introduction of the philosophizing vein reminds us strongly of the Wife's prologue; the remark that the attention bestowed on women passes like a shadow on the wall accords with her lament for her lost youth. Moreover, as has often been observed, we seem to hear Dame Alison speaking when the merchant's wife tells the monk about the six things which women desire in marriage (B 1363 ff.). Tatlock summed up the matter, emphasizing that "the *Shipman's Tale* was certainly written not for the Shipman but for a woman . . . thare cannot be the smallest doubt that the woman is the Wife of Bath. . . . The Shipman no doubt had his faults, but muliebrity was not one of them. Nor is the subject, drawn from trivial social life, appropriate to him." [8]

It looks, then, very much as if Chaucer deliberately altered his fabliau or fabliau-like source to fit the Wife of Bath. This is confirmed when we examine the probable alterations in the plot and the suppression of material unfavorable to the wife in the story—points which seem hitherto to have escaped the attention of critics, though in the mass of comment on the *Tales* one can never be sure. When these matters are carefully considered, they will, I believe, go far to settling the old question whether the Shipman or the Wife was the original teller of the tale, if indeed they do not settle it completely.

[8] J. S. P. Tatlock, *The Development and Chronology of Chaucer's Works,* Chaucer Society, Second Series, No. 37 (London, 1907), pp. 205 ff.; see also G. L. Kittredge, *Chaucer and His Poetry* (Cambridge, Mass., 1915), p. 170; Robinson, *Complete Works,* p. 837; Manly and Rickert, *Text of the Canterbury Tales* (Chicago, 1940), II, 350; R. K. Root, *Poetry of Chaucer* (Boston, etc., 1906, 1921), p. 189. Many others who have believed that the tale first belonged to the Wife of Bath might be cited.

Of course, the fabliau which was probably Chaucer's immediate source has been lost, but we are fortunate in being able to form a very good idea of it from the analogues in Boccaccio and Sercambi, and from the general type of tale, familiar to students of popular literature.[9] The ingenious little plot, of the kind dear to the jongleurs, appears to be, reduced to its lowest terms, as follows. A lover obtains the last favors from the wife of a rich man, in return for a sum of money, which he borrows from the husband. The lover later tells him that he has returned it to the lady, who is thus obliged to give it back to her husband. So the lover obtains his desires for nothing, and the wife is tricked. This is the situation in the Italian analogues. In Boccaccio: "Gulfardo [the lover] partitosi, e la donna rimasa scornata, diede al marito il disonesto prezzo della sua cattività: e così il sagace amante senza costo godè della sua avara donna." So in Sercambi: "Madonna Soffia, vedendosi così esser beffata, pensò di non cadere in tal fallo mai con persona che per quel modo riabia quello che dato l'avesse; e così oservò poi." [10]

But when we turn to Chaucer, what do we find? The story ends in very different fashion; the wife, with ready wit, tells her husband that she has spent the money on the adornment of her person, to his honor, and that she will readily discharge the debt—in bed. To this he assents. The whole closes, then, with the lady's triumph, not her discomfiture (B² 1590 ff.):

> This wyf was nat afered nor affrayed,
> But boldely she seyde, and that anon;
> "Marie, I deffie the false monk, daun John!
> I kepe nat of his tokenes never a deel;
> He took me certeyn gold, that woot I weel,—
> What! yvel thedam on his monkes snowte!
> For, God it woot, I wende, withouten doute,
> That he hadde yeve it me bycause of yow,
> To doon therwith my honour and my prow.

---

[9] The basic tale was classified by Johannes Bolte as one type of the general class "The Lover's Gift Regained." (See Spargo in the discussions cited above in Note 1.) The illustrations of this type (C) are (disregarding those later than Chaucer) the stories in the *Decameron*, VIII, 1 and 2, and the *Shipman's Tale*. In attempting to reconstruct the general lines of the lost fabliau it seems entirely legitimate to end with the wife's discomfiture, since that is the case in the Italian, and since the fabliau makers were always glad to take a fling at unfaithful wives.

[10] The text of both quotations follows that in *Sources and Analogues*, pp. 441 ff.

The inference is inescapable; Chaucer made this striking alteration in the plot when he assigned the tale to the Wife of Bath.[11]

Moreover, there are in Chaucer's lines none of the direct condemnations of the French wife's character or conduct which appear in the Italian analogues. In Boccaccio's version, Neifile, the teller, observes in her opening remarks that a woman who sells her virtue for a price deserves to be burnt, and in the tale itself the lover is shocked at the woman's greed, so that his love turns to hate, and he plans to trick her, though he exacts her part of the bargain. ("Gulfardo, udendo la'ngordigia di costei, sdegnato per la viltà di lei, la quale egli credeva che fosse una valente donna, quasi in odio transmutò il fervente amore, e pensò di doverla beffare.") In Sercambi the wife is accustomed to sell her favors for money, and his tale is headed "De Avaritia et Luzuria." But nothing of all this appears in Chaucer's story. Of course the lady is far from virtuous, but so was the Wife of Bath, who was not averse to illicit sexual intercourse (D 611 ff.).

> Venus me yaf my lust, my likerousnesse,
> And Mars yaf me my sturdy hardynesse;
> Myn ascendent was Taur, and Mars therinne.
> Allas! allas! that evere love was synne!
> I folwed ay my inclinacioun
> By vertu of my constellacioun;
> That made me I koude noght withdrawe
> My chambre of Venus from a good felawe.[12]

In Boccaccio the wife's reason for desiring the money is not explained ("ella avesse per alcuna sua cosa bisogno di fiorini dugento d'oro"), but in Chaucer she must have a hundred franks by the coming Sunday to pay the dressmaker's bill, "or ellis I am lorn" (180 f.). Her bargain with the monk, then, depends on more than mere lust or greed. Apparently, as far as the story informs us, she was telling her husband the truth when she said that she had spent the money on herself,

[11] A convenient table in R. A. Pratt's article, *MLN*, LV (1940), 142–145, indicates briefly in parallel columns the treatment by Sercambi, Chaucer, and Boccaccio of the principal episodes in the tale.

[12] The astral influences governing the Wife's temperament are analyzed by W. C. Curry, *Chaucer and the Mediaeval Sciences* (New York, 1926), pp. 91 ff. Curry very properly emphasizes, however, that the portrait of the Wife is a study in human personality, not a mosaic of astrological data (p. 117). The importance of this interesting book has not, I think, been fully realized.

though of course deceiving him as to the way in which it was obtained.[13]

In view of the preceding considerations, added to the strong evidence of the pronouns in the opening lines, I do not see how we can continue to question that Chaucer first gave the *Shipman's Tale* to the Wife of Bath.[14] But dissents to this conclusion must now be considered.

II

In his two-volume edition (1894), surely one of the pleasantest ways to read the *Tales,* A. W. Pollard enclosed the passage in the *Shipman's Tale* which clearly makes the speaker a woman in quotation marks, as he did also in his portion of the well-known Globe Edition (1898, etc.) Many years later this procedure was defended, and the argument that the story originally belonged to the Shipman elaborated, in a detailed and important article by Frederick Tupper.[15] Although his theories have not always won acceptance (as that the tales are built up on the framework of the Seven Deadly Sins), Tupper was a very able scholar, whose comments must have careful consideration. They contain, I think, all the important points which have thus far been advanced in dissenting from the view that the Wife of Bath was the original teller

[13] R. M. Lumiansky, in his entertaining review of the pilgrimage, *Of Sondry Folk: the Dramatic Principle in the Canterbury Tales* (Austin, Texas, 1955), p. 76, thinks that the Wife of Bath was the original teller of our story, but that "since her prologue presumably was written after the Shipman's Tale, we are not justified in using passages from that prologue in an argument which assumes that she is the teller of the Shipman's Tale." On the contrary, I think that we are justified; that the long prologue to her present tale represents a more detailed description of her character, not a different conception of it. Such would be entirely in keeping with Chaucer's procedure with other pilgrims—the Squire, the Pardoner, and the Merchant, for example. The little portraits in the *General Prologue* agree, in general, remarkably well with what we are told later; they are not contradicted. In what way is the elaborate account of the Wife's character and conduct in her prologue inconsistent with the earlier sketch? That sketch is chiefly concerned with her personal appearance, but we are told she is bold and hearty, well able to keep the jokes going round, though she knows all about the art of love. But as to this, her relations with her five husbands, and other acquaintances in youth—Chaucer is keeping it all for a later occasion ("therof nedeth nat to speke as nowthe").

[14] This conclusion has the authority of Kittredge (*Chaucer and his Poetry,* p. 170): "The Shipman's Tale was originally intended for a woman; for the Wife of Bath, beyond a doubt. It accords with her character both in style and sentiment . . . And there are many expressions in the story which were clearly written for her and for her alone."

[15] Frederick Tupper, "The Bearings of the Shipman's Prologue," *JEGP,* XXXIII (1934), pp. 352–372, esp. 356 ff.

of our tale, and, so far as my knowledge extends, his arguments have never been adequately met. I therefore take them as a basis for analysis.

Tupper maintained that the Wife of Bath "surely never at any stage of her development gave advantage to the masculine enemy by such a flagrant betrayal of the cause of womanhood as in her supposed version of the Shipman's story, where the merchant's faithless wife is no less a butt than the merchant himself," and quoted the Host's comment (B 1630 f.) that the monk deceived both husband and wife. Since "material similar to that in [the Wife's] story and perhaps once intended for her" is introduced into the tale, "Chaucer may have carelessly borrowed from his own stores without the necessary change of pronouns. . . . [Putting the passage in quotation marks] becomes a conscious artistic touch, not an oversight. A recitation of the opening section, with due regard of the voice for the sudden transition . . . from a man's stern criticism of 'revelous' women to his clever mimicry of a gaily bedecked wife's taunting chant of triumph over the purse of husband or lover makes delighted assurance doubly sure." . . . The Shipman's story is not "dictated by deep antagonism to chapmen, but at the worst by a good-natured contempt, at the best by a half-regard for members of a class which, in his own intimate experience and hearsay, was easily victimized by rascally designs upon its wares and its women." [16]

The contention that the *Shipman's Tale* is unsuited to Dame Alison seems to me to rest on a forgetfulness of her

[16] Much of the same line of argument will be found in a brief article by R. W. Chapman, "The *Shipman's Tale* Was Meant for the Shipman," *MLN*, LXXI (1956), 4–5, who cites suggestions by Von Düring and Raymond Preston (notes 3 and 4) favoring his view. He emphasizes the supposed change of voice in the opening lines, indicating, he thinks, not only a woman but a man; the suggestion that there is a connection between the treatment of the merchant of Seint Denys and of the Shipman in the *General Prologue;* and the contention that the story is not well suited to the Wife of Bath. He believes that since the Shipman is called "a good felawe" in that prologue (395), that is, he says, "an excellent companion on the way," the Sea-Captain "can tell an entertaining story with some flair, even with touches of mimicry," in "a rueful basso" and "a piping falsetto."

Since the positive tone of the article may perhaps lead some readers to consider the question settled, and since I am mentioned among others as favoring the generally accepted view, I have made a brief rejoinder, "The Wife of Bath and the Shipman," *MLN*, LXXII (1957), 87 f. I pointed out that the phrase "good felawe" in the *General Prologue* (395) clearly means "rascal," as the lines following and usage elsewhere indicate; see Manly, *Canterbury Tales by Geoffrey Chaucer* (New York, 1928), p. 534, and Robinson's note, *Complete Works*, p. 762. Hence it is no argument for the Shipman's supposed ability in mimicry. Moreover, it is a convention that all the pilgrims are good storytellers.

frank revelations in addressing the pilgrims, of her expressed conviction in regard to the relations of the sexes, particularly as illustrated by her own experiences. She is concerned to defend women and their full enjoyment of feminine privileges, but she is unsparing in portraying their frailties—a complexity in her character which must not be judged by the crude gibes at women in the fabliaux. One of the marks of Chaucer's greatness as a poet is his recognition of the fact that men and women cannot be characterized, after the fashion of most medieval poets, in the light of a single predominating quality. The discrepancy between the true characters of the pilgrims and what they would like to be thought to be is suggested again and again in the little vignettes of the *General Prologue*. Contradictions in personality are analyzed in detail in the full-length portraits of the Wife of Bath, the Pardoner and the Merchant. Before we maintain that the *Shipman's Tale* would be "a flagrant betrayal of the cause of womanhood" we ought to read the Wife of Bath's prologue, one of the most acid pictures of the weaknesses of women in medieval literature. In what way is the tale before us inconsistent with the character of Dame Alison? Because the heroine deceives her husband and commits adultery? Well, the five times married Wife constantly and cruelly tricked her husbands ("O Lord! the peyne I dide hem and the wo!" D 384), and, as we have just seen, she unblushingly confesses that she would sin sexually with any rascal if she chose (D 615 ff.). Deception, indeed, is one of women's regular weapons.

> For half so boldely kan ther no man
> Swere and lyen, as a womman kan.   (D 227 f.)
> Deceite, wepyng, spynnyng God hath yive
> to wommen kyndely.   (D 401 f.)

It really does not seem necessary to emphasize all this by further quotations.

There is, I believe, no contradiction in the opening lines of the *Shipman's Tale*, no need to assume another voice at line 11, no break in the continuity of thought.

> Swich salutaciouns and contenaunces
> Passen as dooth a shadwe upon the wal;
> But wo is hym that payen moot for al!
> The sely housbonde, algate he moot paye,   11
> He moot us clothe, and he moot us arraye.

If we assume that the tale was written for the Shipman, but

that he suddenly shifted to a female point of view, how were readers to know this? The scribes did not have the benefit of quotation marks. Listeners, we are told, were informed by a change of voice, but what evidence is there of any such change? It was not Chaucer's habit to leave such matters in the dark; he is one of the least obscure of poets. Again, it does not seem legitimate to argue, as Tupper did, that in the passages in the tale not in accordance with his theory Chaucer may have "carelessly" introduced into it material once intended for the Wife of Bath. How can a piece of carelessness become "a conscious artistic touch"? Another point deserves attention. The unflattering portrait of the merchant of Seint Denys has often been connected with the statement in the *General Prologue* that the Sea-Captain stole the chapmen's wine, and so presumably had no love for them, and was glad to take shot at one of them.[17] But we do not have to fly to the wine-stealing to explain why the husband is not treated too tenderly; the cuckold was a common butt of medieval merriment. Again, it must be emphasized immediately that Chaucer was not original in making the husband a merchant; this is in the Italian analogues. In Boccaccio the husband is a "ricco mercatante," and in Sercambi "banchieri e merchadante." There is every reason to suppose that this was the case in the lost fabliau. It is, of course, conceivable that both Chaucer and the fabliau writer hit on this touch independently, since it helps the plot to have the husband a well-to-do man, a merchant, able to lend the monk the money. But it does not seem likely, in view of the Italian parallels; probably Chaucer had the rich merchant right before him. It is just possible, however, that in shifting the story from the Wife of Bath to the Shipman he was influenced by the captain's cheating of the chapmen, for whom that worthy had no special affection.

In one respect Tupper had an apparently valid argument: that the tale is unsuited to the Wife because the lady is tricked by the monk. Would Alison have selected this anecdote as her first contribution to the pilgrimage? Yes, I think she might have done so. For, as we have seen, Chaucer altered the story in various ways to give a more favorable picture of the wife of Seint Denys, particularly by omitting any

[17] This has been connected with the Shipman as the original teller by Tupper and Chapman, in the articles just cited, and by Tatlock and Lumiansky in the transference of the story to that pilgrim. (Tatlock, *Development and Chronology*, pp. 206 ff.; Lumiansky, *Of Sondry Folk*, p. 77.)

reference at the end to the deception practiced on her, and
introducing the episode, which has no parallel in the Italian,
in which the wife, by her ready wit, persuades her husband to
forgive the debt, so that she comes out ahead in the game.
That the Host gleefully exclaims that she, as well as her husband, was tricked, is no argument that the tale cannot have
first belonged to the Wife, since the Host's words are not addressed to her as teller, but to the Shipman. There was now
no need for playing down the fact that the French wife had
been deceived by the clever monk. Harry Bailly, as usual,
draws his own moral; he is interested, as an innkeeper, in
seeing that undesirable characters do not lodge in his hos-
telry. The dignified Monk cannot have relished this, but
Harry restores the balance between lay and religious by calling next on the Prioress.

The whole situation will be clearer, perhaps, if we try to
follow Chaucer's probable procedure in working with this
material.

III

The Wife of Bath obviously interested the poet very deeply
from the beginning, as her ample portrait in the *General Prologue* suggests. And when he first put together the Canterbury
collection he was especially attracted to the fabliaux,[18] here
contriving, after starting with the long and dignified *Knight's
Tale*, to have such stories told by the Miller, the Reeve, and
the Cook, ostensibly as a result of the bickerings and urgings of
those pilgrims. To all this the tale of the Man of Law, no
matter whether that worthy related the woes of Melibeus or
of Constance, was no doubt a designed contrast. In order to
restore the gaiety of the journey Chaucer then planned, after

18 As I have suggested (*Chaucer and the Canterbury Tales*, p. 17 f. *et
passim*). I further suggested that Chaucer may even on that account
have been somewhat influenced to choose a pilgrimage as a framework,
since he could then attribute the telling of vulgar tales to the common
folk, and not appear himself, as an aristocratic poet, responsible for
them. As I anticipated, this has aroused some dissent. But consider the
evidence. Look at the poet's apologies (*General Prologue*, 725 ff.; *Miller's Prologue*, 3167 ff.). Notice that of the first half-dozen tales four are of
the fabliau type, those of the Miller, Reeve, Cook (fragmentary), and
Shipman (earlier given to the Wife of Bath). The *Knight's Tale*, a story
written earlier and utilized as a dignified beginning for the series, does
not indicate any present absorption in romance. Chaucer did not even
trouble to remove its striking inconsistencies when he used it for narrative on the highroad—its prefaced Latin quotation, and the statement
that the story is being *written* (A 1201).

the usual sparring as to who should be the next speaker, to give the Wife a fabliau. But later on he changed his mind, deciding to assign to her a central place in the Marriage Discussion, and to analyze her character more fully, as in her present prologue. He also gave her a new story, that of the Loathly Lady and the knight of Arthur's court, a striking illustration of female "maistrye," so heavily emphasized in that prologue. This meant giving her former tale to someone else, and the Shipman was selected for this honor. It also meant some alterations in previous work, some changes both in the story itself and in the connecting material. But these changes were never fully carried out.

The present *Shipman's Tale* was, indeed, far less suited to the hardy captain than to Dame Alison. Whether a given story is appropriate to its teller is not determined by ability in narration; "it is a convention that such a company, gathered by chance, should all be expert storytellers; that a drunken miller can tell a tale full of brilliant characterization and nicely balanced action, or a bluff soldier like the Knight weave a romance with all the art of a seasoned minstrel." [19] The question is whether the subject matter is such as might appeal to a person of the social station and character of the narrator. Thus the Miller might well have relished a bawdy anecdote of thievery and "swyving," the Knight a narrative of chivalric devotion. So the Wife of Bath, none too refined a figure, though with some social pretensions (she could not bear to have any woman precede her at the offering in church), might have been given a tale of monkish trickery and female deception but ultimate triumph, set in the bourgeois society with which she was familiar. But we should expect something different from the skipper of the Maudelayne, who had led a rough life on the high seas.

Reconstruction of Chaucer's shifts and alterations is a ticklish business, and I have already expressed in print the opinion that in considering the *Tales* as a piece of literature it is best to work from what the poet has left us. But in the present instance the reader is, I think, entitled to ask how Chaucer may have proceeded if he first gave the Wife of Bath the present *Shipman's Tale*, and to have an answer, without being asked to believe that this answer is correct in every detail. Fortunately we have some pretty plain evidence to guide us as to the poet's general method of work.

19 Lawrence, *loc. cit.*, p. 42.

I here assume that Chaucer's final design for the arrangement of the tales, so far as we can follow it, is best revealed by allusions in them and in the linking material to time, place, etc., and not by the obscure and dubious evidence of sequence in the manuscripts. So the Ellesmere order, which brings the Wife of Bath's prologue and her tale of the Loathly Lady after the Man of Law, must be abandoned in favor of that in the Oxford Chaucer, earlier advocated by Bradshaw and Furnivall, in which the Shipman follows the Man of Law. In recent years this has found increasing favor, and indeed Manly, who earlier placed great reliance on manuscript evidence in determining Chaucer's intentions, and was chiefly responsible for the vogue of the Ellesmere sequence, changed his mind. The one exception to the Oxford order would be the placing of the Physician and Pardoner (Group C) after the Franklin, which makes the Nun's Priest directly precede the Wife of Bath. This sharpens the dramatic interplay in the Discussion of Marriage, and has been advocated by various scholars. It does not, however, affect the question now in hand.[20]

It is, of course, very clear that in adding to the tales, and in revising them, Chaucer often failed to remove resulting contradictions and inaccuracies. The instances in which this is the case when he inserted in the collection material originally intended for another purpose are very familiar, but must be mentioned once more. The *Knight's Tale* begins with a Latin quotation quite unsuited to the teller and to wayside narrative, and in line A 1201 we read "But of that storie list me nat to write." Again, it is very improbable that the Second

---

[20] The best sequence to adopt has recently been discussed in detail and convincingly by Robert A. Pratt, "The Order of the *Canterbury Tales*," *PMLA*, LXVI (1951), 1141–1167. I had reviewed the whole matter in the book just cited, suggesting the place for the Shipman which he advocates, and others had expressed a preference for it. On the whole, then, the sequence which seems best to represent Chaucer's tentative design at the time of his death, is A B¹ B² D E F C G H I. This is the order in the Oxford and Globe editions, except for the shift of that troublesome bedfellow Group C, in which there is no evidence of location.

The attempt by S. B. Greenfield, *Modern Language Review,* XLVIII (1953), 51 f., to explain away the Rochester-Sittingbourne contradiction and vindicate the Ellesmere order is not convincing. We cannot dismiss "we been almoost at towne" (D 2294) as a mere tag, and after the Summoner's earlier promise that he will tell two or three tales about friars "er I come to Sidyngborne" (D 845 ff.), it seems entirely natural to refer the later phrase (D 2294) to that town. That the Summoner tells only one tale, instead of the two or three that he has promised, is of no consequence. In the angry exchange of words he is going the Friar one better in his promised revenge.

Nun, whose prologue and tale are "with the highest probability" [21] early work, should speak of herself as an "unworthy sone of Eve" (G 62), no matter what ecclesiastical usage lay behind the phrase. The only evidence for placing the tale lies in the first line of the prologue of the Canon's Yeoman following. So it is also with the shifting of a story; the prologue and epilogue of the Man of Law contain pretty decisive indications that Chaucer originally gave to him the story of Melibeus, but later took this over for himself as teller, thus making the "maistrye" of Dame Prudence the beginning of the Discussion of Marriage. [22] He did not, however, bother to correct the Man of Law's statement in his prologue that he would speak in prose, or in his epilogue the hits at legal phraseology in the tale preceding.

The question which speaker should follow the Man of Law has, of course, long been a bone of contention. I forbear to summarize conflicting arguments, but will say immediately that I believe too little attention has been given to the suggestion by R. F. Jones that the Wife of Bath was first the speaker at the end of the Man of Law's epilogue. [23] Jones assumes that in Chaucer's first arrangement she told the tale later given to the Shipman. Perhaps his theory that she originally was also introduced in the epilogue has escaped notice to some extent, since it was put forth in connection with other arguments which need not here be discussed. It may be well to have the relevant lines before us. The Host has just called on the Parson to preach to the company.

> "Nay, by my fader soule, that schal he nat!"
> Seyde the . . . ; "heer schal he nat preche;
> He schal no gospel glosen here ne teche.   1180
> We leven alle in the grete God," quod . . . ;
> "He wolde sowen som difficulte,
> Or springen cokkel in oure clene corn.
> And therefore, Hoost, I warne thee biforn,
> My joly body schal a tale telle,   1185

[21] Robinson, *Complete Works*, p. 862.

[22] See Germaine Dempster, "A Period in the Development of the *Canterbury Tales* Marriage Group and Blocks B2 and C," *PMLA*, LXVIII (1953), 1142–1159. Mrs. Dempster's views in regard to the *Tales* should always have careful consideration. Earlier conjectures by Skeat, Miss Hammond, Tatlock and others are noted by Robinson, p. 800. See also Pratt, note 20, above.

[23] Richard F. Jones, "A Conjecture on the Wife of Bath's Prologue," *JEGP*, XXIV (1925), 512–547, especially 521 ff.

> And I schal clynken you so mery a belle,
> That I shal waken al this compaignie.
> But it schal not ben of philosophie,
> Ne phislyas, ne termes queinte of lawe.   1190
> There is but litel Latyn in my mawe!"

Jones pointed out that "my joly body" is entirely appropriate for a woman; the wife of the merchant of Seint Denys in the tale following, whose utterances sometimes recall those of Dame Alison, uses it of herself (B² 1613).

> "Ye shal my joly body have to wedde;
> By God, I wol nat paye yow but abedde!"

The phrase does not seem right for the rough Shipman. If it be objected that Jones's contention that the Wife of Bath was originally the speaker in this epilogue is supported by no manuscript, it may be well to remember that the reading "Shipman" (1179) is found only in a manuscript which Manly and Rickert describe as "merely a bad 15 C edition of no textual authority," and that if manuscript evidence is to be followed either the Squire or the Summoner would have to be the speaker.[24] But each of these pilgrims has a genuine prologue of his own, and the characterization in the epilogue fits neither the romantic Squire nor the hypocritical Pardoner, whose sermon would be just what the speaker is trying to avoid. The Wife fits perfectly—a jolly soul ("in felaweshipe wel koude she laughe and carpe"). It looks, then, as if Chaucer did not revise this epilogue when he shifted the following tale from the Wife to the Shipman. Such negligence would be quite in accord with his usual practice.

But with the epilogue to the French story Chaucer's procedure had to be quite different. For it is obvious that this epilogue, as we have it, is not the result of altering a word or two; it is expressly designed to fit the Shipman (B 435 ff.).

> "Wel seyd, by *corpus dominus,*" quod oure Hoost,
> "Now longe moote thou saille by the cost,

---

[24] Jones suggested that B 1179 originally read "Seyde the Wyf of Bathe; 'he shal nat preche' " (p. 524, note 29). In line 1181 "he" would have been originally "sche." His supporting arguments for such changes should be noted. This whole matter is discussed in detail by R. A. Pratt, *PMLA,* LXVI (1951), 1154 ff., who accepts Jones's contention that the Wife of Bath was originally the speaker in the Epilogue to the tale of the Man of Law, and adds new confirmatory evidence. We must remember that Chaucer may conceivably have sacrificed material now lost.

Sire gentil maister, gentil maryneer!
God yeve the monk a thousand last quade yeer!
A ha! felawes! beth ware of swich a jape!
The monk putte in the mannes hood an ape,
And in his wyves eek, by Seint Austyn!
Draweth no monkes moore unto youre in."

There was now, as has already been observed, no reason why the deception practiced by the monk on the merchant's wife should not be brought out, since the Wife of Bath was no longer the teller of the tale.

In some such fashion we may reconstruct Chaucer's probable procedure. But as to the details—just what he deleted, just what he added, and just what he left, partly for later alteration, nobody can dogmatize. It is a constant temptation, in analyzing his work, to attempt to reach certainties which the available evidence will not support.

IV

If the suggestions in the preceding pages are correct, a few general conclusions may be in order, at the risk of some repetition. The *Shipman's Tale* is noteworthy, as being, of all Chaucer's fabliau stories, closest to the French type, though bearing unmistakably the poet's own seal and superscription; a little masterpiece of lively narrative and brilliant characterization conveyed chiefly through action and dialogue, and not impeded, as frequently elsewhere, by digressions, exempla, and learned citations. Much of the credit for its narrative excellence must go to the unknown author of the lost fabliau which in all probability served as the direct source for Chaucer's work, as well as, perhaps in varied form, for the analogue in the *Decameron* and for the tale of Sercambi, who imitated that collection. The final integration of the story into the narrative of the pilgrimage was less successful, however, as was also that of the *Man of Law's Tale* preceding, since Chaucer obviously altered his original plan, which had given the story of the monk and the wife of Seint Denys to the Wife of Bath. We may cautiously conclude that the resulting inconsistencies in the text were due to the fact that his full interest was not engaged when he made his shift. He seems to have worked at times a good deal on the spur of the moment, not bothering much about details, perhaps realizing that contradictions would not greatly disturb his readers or listeners, who were chiefly intent on a good story, and thinking that later on he would set things in order in satisfactory fashion. For the moment there was too much joyous writing still to be done, and too many business distractions. In the last ten years of his life he was much occupied with the royal affairs, perhaps residing for a part of the time elsewhere than in London. The Canterbury pilgrimage was the solace of his leisure hours. At the time when he changed the assignments of the Man of Law and the Wife of Bath he was apparently in the midst of enthusiasm for the Discussion of Marriage and the ampler psychological development of the Wife in her prologue, in connection with which he had found a better illustration of "maistrye" in the tale of the Loathly Lady and the knight of King Arthur's court. That the present *Shipman's Tale* was far more appropriate to Dame Alison than to the hardy mariner apparently did not greatly disturb him—even the pronouns, which clearly point to a woman as teller, were left for future correction. We have constantly to realize, I think, that with all its marvelous qualities, the Canterbury collection is after all only a fragment of the projected work, in part unrevised and unretouched. There is no use in trying to explain away obvious imperfections. *Quandoque bonus dormitat Homerus.*

The Tale of Melibeus

WILLIAM WITHERLE LAWRENCE

IN THE BRILLIANT sisterhood of the stories of Canterbury the *Tale of Melibeus* is certainly the neglected stepchild. Today we seldom glance at her, and, if we do, it is with pity and disdain. The appreciative critics will have none of her. The late Mr. Chesterton and Mr. H. D. Sedgwick, for example, have not so much as mentioned the *Melibee* in their substantial volumes. Even the specialists are frequently condemnatory. Professor R. D. French, in his excellent *Chaucer Handbook,* speaks of the translation as "Chaucer's literary sin." The late Professor W. P. Ker, whose sagacity need not be emphasized, has told us that "the *Tale of Melibeus* is perhaps the worst example that could be found of all the intellectual and literary vices of the Middle Ages—bathos, forced allegory, spiritless and interminable moralizing . . . beyond rivalry for its enjoyment of the rankest commonplaces. There is glow and unction about its mediocrity; the intolerable arguments of Dame Prudence are a masterpiece, as though written in an orgy and enthusiasm of flatness and insipidity." [1]

To the question why Chaucer should have busied himself with this sort of thing the answers have been varied. No doubt the sudden drop from verse, which the poet employed with such mastery, to prose, which was even in his hands awkward and undistinguished, accounts in part for our feeling that the *Melibeus* is dull, though I do not recall having seen this emphasized. Professor Hotson's theory that "the *Melibeus* is a political tract, designed to dissuade John of Gaunt from launching on the invasion of Castile, in 1386," must certainly be rejected. To conclude that John of Gaunt would have been moved by a close translation of a popular

Reprinted by permission of the New York University Press from ESSAYS AND STUDIES IN HONOR OF CARLETON BROWN (1940), 100–110.

[1] G. K. Chesterton, *Chaucer* (New York, 1932); H. D. Sedgwick, *Dan Chaucer* (New York, 1934). The *Melibeus* is not listed in the index to either volume. R. D. French, *A Chaucer Handbook* (New York, 1929), p. 246. W. P. Ker, in *English Prose Selections,* ed. Henry Craik (London, 1893), I, 42 ff.

and well-known work, written in the preceding century, and containing nothing pointing directly to the invasion of Castile, is to attribute to that robust hero a supernormal sensitiveness. The suggestion has been made that the tale is revenge upon the Host for interrupting *Sir Thopas;* and Professor Ker even toyed with the idea, which his good sense rejected, that it is a satire on heavy moral writing, as the piece preceding is on the doggerel romances. Certainly the poet was not punishing his readers for the sins of the Host, and he knew that a travesty is best if short. Ker went on, however, to put the matter in its true light: the *Melibeus* was dull neither to Chaucer nor to his contemporaries. "The peculiarity of Chaucer is that with all this progress in his art he kept close to the general sense of his age, and had always, in some corner of his being, the average mind of the fourteenth century. To that part of him belong all his prose works. The *Tale of Melibeus* is representative of the ideas and tastes of millions of good souls. Being representative, it could not be alien from Chaucer." The interest of the tale for the Middle Ages has also been emphasized by another distinguished scholar. Indeed, if this story is a Cinderella, Professor Tatlock may almost be called her fairy godmother, who discerns her true virtues beneath her russet dress, transforms her before our eyes, and sends her off to the ball to dance in company with her gayer sisters.[2]

The truth is that just those qualities in this long piece which we find tedious were highly esteemed in the Middle Ages. If we imagine it freed from all that bores us, there would not be much left. But, since it affected our forefathers so differently, it offers an unrivaled opportunity for studying changes in literary taste, for contrasting medieval and modern conceptions of what makes profitable reading. To this even the elementary student and the "general reader" should give some attention today. They cannot be expected to plow through the whole of the *Melibeus,* but they should be reminded that they must read not only what diverts them, but what does not, if they really wish to know Chaucer and to understand the significance of his work for the days in which it was written.

[2] J. Leslie Hotson, "The *Tale of Melibeus* and John of Gaunt," *SP,* XVIII (1921), 429–452. F. J. Mather, edition of Chaucer's *Prologue,* etc. (Riverside Literature Series, Boston, etc., 1899), p. xxxi. I have endeavored to show the fallacy of the theory that *Sir Thopas* is a satire on the Flemings, *PMLA,* L (1935), 81–91. W. P. Ker, *loc. cit.,* 42 f. J. S. P. Tatlock, *Development and Chronology of Chaucer's Works* (Chaucer Society, London, 1907), pp. 188–197.

The very fact that the *Melibeus* lacks interest should stimulate interest to find out why this is so.

This pursuit would be more entertaining, though less instructive, if Chaucer had put something of himself into the tale. His version is a close translation of a French condensation of the *Liber Consolationis et Consilii* of Albertanus of Brescia, written in 1246, but he was also familiar with the Latin. How highly the work was esteemed is shown by its translations into Italian, German, and Dutch, and its inclusion in the *Ménagier de Paris,* a fourteenth-century manual of domestic economy, and in the sixteenth century in a French treatise on chess, and an edition of the *Livre du Chevalier de la Tour Landry.* Chaucer's rendering was no task of his salad days; as Professor Robinson remarks, "all the literary associations favor an assignment to the Canterbury period." He knew two other works by Albertanus, and there is every reason to suppose that he valued the *Melibeus* not merely because it would appeal to his readers, but for its own sake, and that it was mainly on this latter account that he gave himself the very considerable labor of translating it.[3]

Much of the fascination which the *Melibeus* held for medieval readers lay, of course, in its pervading didacticism, and its wise saws drawn from past authorities and from current tradition. Times have changed; sustained moralizing is repellent to us today. We are absorbed in concrete issues; we believe that we enjoy an advanced civilization, and yet that the world is changing so rapidly that the past is no guide for its problems. The Middle Ages, as every one knows, felt otherwise. Where we look forward to new ideologies, new "deals," new principles of government and justice, they looked backward in the confident trust that earlier and happier times could best teach them how to live. They were conscious of being in a world not yet reduced to order, and were eager to get it arranged according to the most approved moral principles. In criticizing the *Melibeus,* Professor Tatlock has emphasized their "perpetual relish in the gnomic style," and pointed out how frequently Chaucer employed it and how much he obviously enjoyed it. Furthermore, "the interest of

[3] For the details of Chaucer's relationship to his sources, and the popularity of the *Melibeus,* see F. N. Robinson, *Complete Works of Geoffrey Chaucer* (Cambridge, Mass., The Riverside Press, 1933), pp. 846 ff.; Tatlock, *loc. cit.;* Thor Sundby, *Albertani Brixiensis Liber Consolationis et Consilii* (Chaucer Society, Copenhagen, 1873), valuable as an edition and for its excellent introduction; W. W. Skeat, *Complete Works of Geoffrey Chaucer* (Oxford, 1894), III, 426–427.

the earlier Middle Ages in creative literature had been chiefly for lyric feeling and for action; they had produced little analysis of human motive and shown little knowledge of the human heart. At a certain stage in the intellectual development of a people, these become intelligible and attractive; witness the rise of literary allegory into popularity in the thirteenth century. Now *Melibeus* offers both; strange as the statement may seem at first, *Melibeus* really shows insight." [4] With this I am quite in agreement, and I wish that Professor Tatlock had further developed this point. But I think that another and more important feature of the tale has been strangely neglected—its repeated and earnest pleading for peace rather than war, for mediation and law rather than private revenge. Compared with this, its moral lessons, its psychologizing, and its elegant extracts seem of secondary significance.

First of all it is well to understand clearly the course of the story. For the *Melibeus* is a story, thus contrasting sharply with the *Parson's Tale*. The Parson does not give his hearers narrative, but a typical medieval sermon, into which has been inserted a tract on the Seven Deadly Sins. Omitting the loquacities of Dame Prudence as far as possible, the outline of the action and the discussion may run something as follows.

There was a young man named Melibeus, rich and powerful, who had a wife Prudence and a daughter Sophie. In his absence, three enemies entered his house and beat his wife, and inflicted five wounds on his daughter, leaving her for dead. Upon his return he gave himself over to grief, but his wife advised him to have patience, to call his friends and relatives together, and to ask their advice. This he did. Many thought it best for him to take vengeance on his foes, but the wiser ones counseled caution. Melibeus determined upon revenge, but Dame Prudence admonished him not to be overhasty. He answered that he would not be guided by her, especially on account of the dangers in following the counsels of women. Prudence replied at length, defending her sex, and finally persuaded him to be governed by her. She also bade him heed the precepts of God, not to give himself over to anger, to keep his own counsel, and to distinguish between good and bad advisers. Melibeus asserted that vengeance is right, but she rejoined that one wrong does not cure another, that the strongest defence a man may have is to be beloved by his friends and neighbors, that vengeance is a mistake, that he had sinned against the Lord, and that the judge who had jurisdiction over his enemies should punish them. These points she argued in detail, also warning him not to put dependence upon his wealth, or to give himself over to his passions. Melibeus promised to follow her counsels absolutely. Thereupon she sent for his enemies, pointed out to them the evils of war and the blessings of peace, and converted them so that they promised to make amends. Her action was confirmed by her kinsmen and friends. The enemies of Melibeus came to him, and promised to give him such satisfaction as he thought best. At first he was minded to deprive them of their goods, and send them into exile, but was dissuaded by Prudence, so that he forgave them completely, as God forgives sinners.[5]

As narrative, this is thin stuff, stiff and conventional, poor in description, lacking in suspense, and too obviously a mere vehicle for moralizing. The chief characters have no life or individuality, save Dame Prudence, who is a canny soul, knowing how to manage a husband, letting him weep to relieve his feelings, soothing his vanity, and making "semblant of wratthe" when necessary. There is interminable talk, and little action. But the shortcomings of the story as a story bothered the Middle Ages very little. The important thing for them was that it was allegory, from which they could draw valuable moral lessons. This form of literature charmed them like a wizard's spell, and its influence was never more potent than in the thirteenth and fourteenth centuries. Even when in prose, it had something of the emotional stimulus of poetry. As Henry Osborn Taylor remarks, "allegory became the chief field for the medieval imagination."[6] Modern times have ceased completely to feel its fascination. As a living force in literature it is dead today, surviving only when the story has become the main interest, as in *Gulliver's Travels,* or when it commands attention for the perfection of its artistry, as in the *Divine Comedy*, or as a social document, in *Piers Plowman.*

What is the chief message of the *Melibeus?* At first sight, the tale seems to be that of a man sorely tried under adversity and at length, by the exercise of virtue, restored to happi-

---

[5] Robinson, pp. 201–224.
[6] *A Historian's Creed* (Cambridge, Mass., 1939), p. 126.

ness, like Job. Indeed, there is reason to suppose that the Book of Job may have influenced the invention of the simple plot. The author quotes from it; the question why God allows man to suffer cruel affliction is touched upon, and the symposium of the friends of Melibeus reminds us of the discourses of Eliphaz the Temanite and Bildad the Shuhite and Zophar the Naamathite. The Book of Job had of course been a favorite allegory in the Middle Ages ever since Pope Gregory the Great wrote his famous commentary. But Melibeus is not, like Job, a good man tested by the Lord (and Satan); [7] he is a man who has sinned. The allegory is clumsy enough, but its significance is clear from the words of Dame Prudence, who is at once an actor in the tale, and its expositor. Melibeus is the "honey-drinker" who has tasted so much of temporal riches and delights that he is drunken; he has forgotten Christ, against whom he has sinned, so that the three enemies of man, the world, the flesh, and the devil, have wounded his soul (his daughter Sophie) in five places, that is, through the five senses (Robinson, 213-214). So Dame Prudence says "I conseille yow . . . aboven alle thynges, that ye make pees bitwene God and yow; and beth reconsiled unto hym and to his grace" (221). The allegory creaks a good deal at the end, when the good wife sends for the three enemies and converts them to such sweet reasonableness that they are willing to make humble amends, and submit themselves to Melibeus. That is not the way the world, the flesh, and the devil usually treat a sinner, no matter how much prudence and wisdom he may display. However, the medieval man was not censorious; he took allegory as he found it, and thanked God for what it taught him.

Much more striking than the significance of the *Melibeus* as an allegory of sin and God's forgiveness is its constant insistence that peace is better than war, and composition or legal punishment better than private vengeance. This, I believe, interested Albertanus chiefly, which was perhaps the reason why his allegory stumbled at the end. At first, Melibeus is all for violent measures: "it semed that in herte he baar a crueel ire, redy to doon vengeaunce upon his foes, and sodeynly desired that the werre sholde bigynne" (Robinson, 202). Then follows the best scene in the story, vividly set forth, and not

---

[7] I do not forget that the motivation of the underlying folk tale has been much obscured by the processes of growth in the Book of Job. See Morris Jastrow, Jr., *The Book of Job; its Origin, Growth and Interpretation* (Philadelphia and London, 1920).

overloaded with quotations until Dame Prudence begins to speak. Were it in verse, I venture to think that it would have been admired; as it is, real conviction and eloquence occasionally break through the crabbed prose. Melibeus has called together his friends, and asked their counsel. The physicians advise vengeance, and so do envious neighbors and feigned friends and flatterers. But "an advocat that was wys" reminds them that to begin war and execute vengeance is not lightly to be undertaken. But most of those present, especially the young folk, cried out "War! War!"

> Up roos tho oon of thise olde wise, and with his hand made contenaunce that men sholde holden hem stille and yeven hym audience. "Lordynges," quod he, "ther is ful many a man that crieth 'Werre! werre!' that woot ful litel what werre amounteth. Werre at his bigynnyng hath so greet an entryng and so large, that every wight may entre whan hym liketh, and lightly fynde werre; but certes, what ende that shal therof bifalle, it is nat light to knowe. For soothly, whan that werre is ones bigonne, ther is ful many a child unborn of his mooder that shal sterve yong by cause of thilke werre, or elles lyve in sorwe and dye in wrecchednesse. And therfore, er that any werre bigynne, men moste have greet conseil and greet deliberacion." (Robinson, 203)

It is plain that Melibeus, even after a long discourse from Dame Prudence, still stands for the principle of an eye for an eye and a tooth for a tooth.

> "Certes," quod Melibeus, "I understonde it in this wise: that right as they han doon me a contrarie, right so sholde I doon hem another. For right as they han venged hem on me and doon me wrong, right so shal I venge me upon hem and doon hem wrong; and thanne have I cured oon contrarie by another." (Robinson, 210)

But after much more eloquence from his spouse he is converted to a better way of thinking, so that at the end he is reconciled to his enemies and they to him, and he gives up all thought of vengeance. The importance of this general point was clearly seen by Sundby, in his excellent edition of the Latin text. He noted that Albertanus "safely leads his readers to the goal he had proposed: condemnation of feuds and wilful wars, and submission to law. *This is the principal tend-*

ency of his book, and very remarkable for the time when it was written." [8] It is a pity that Sundby did not develop this further, and that its significance has not been seen by those who have endeavored to explain the English *Melibeus.* In order to understand it fully we must consider the contemporary administration of justice, and the career of Albertanus.

Precisely the conflict which we trace in the *Melibeus* between private revenge and organized justice marks the development of law in the later Middle Ages. The earlier centuries had striven chiefly for the regulation of private vengeance, the systematization of penalties, and the termination of long-standing feuds. As time went on, and the power of the state increased, and the practical features of Roman law were better understood, the old Germanic concept of vengeance as the recognized method of inflicting punishment and gaining redress was gradually abandoned. The influence of the Church was particularly important; specifically through the "Peace of God," which exempted certain parts of the community from warfare, and the "Truce of God," which restricted times and seasons when war might be waged. In the thirteenth century, especially in the reign of Louis IX in France, these humanizing and liberalizing tendencies were marked in lay authority in the so-called *asseurement,* or suspension of hostilities by mutual consent of the contending parties, and in the *quarantaine du roi,* which set up a truce of forty days, and protected relatives not directly concerned in the original criminal action. Religion, ethics, and law are mingled in the arguments of Dame Prudence, as they were in medieval attempts to organize justice by Christian teaching in the administration of a man of the deep and sincere piety of St. Louis. He was far more powerful than many of his predecessors—he was really King of France, not merely an important noble among other contentious nobles. His influence and example spread far beyond the boundaries of his own kingdom. In 1258 he endeavored to interdict private warfare altogether in France, but without complete success. The old custom of private vengeance was not to be abolished so quickly. Not until well into the fourteenth century was it effectively replaced by punishment at the hands of duly constituted au-

8 Sundby, p. xvii. Italics mine. I did not notice Sundby's remarks until after the first draft of this article was written. How they have escaped the attention of readers of the English text for so long I do not see. Possibly they have received attention in criticism which I have overlooked.

thorities. Justice was often administered in a strange way, alternating between cruel severity and complete forgiveness—as we may observe in the closing pages of the *Melibeus*.[9]

That Albertanus of Brescia was fully aware of these changes and greatly interested in them there is every reason to suppose. He was a judge, and consequently forced to face the practical realities of punishment. Some of the best advice against hasty vengeance in the *Melibeus* is put into the mouth of "an advocat that was wys" (Robinson, 202). Though the exact dates of his birth and death are not known, Albertanus was certainly a contemporary of Louis IX, and he must have been affected by what was going on in jurisprudence in France, a country which was then in so many ways exercising a predominating influence in Western Europe. His home was in Northern Italy, where such influence might be expected. He was a bookish man, familiar with a wide range of authors, including writers on law. Besides five extant Latin *sermones* and the *Melibeus* allegory, he wrote two Latin treatises, *De Amore et Dilectione Dei* and *De Arte Loquendi et Tacendi*. Furthermore, he was active in public affairs. It is noticeable in the *Melibeus* that little distinction is made between "werre" and "vengeaunce," and indeed in those days they were much alike. Of what we should call "war" today he had ample experience in the struggles between the North Italian cities and the Holy Roman Emperor; he appears at a conference as a delegate from a Brescian borough, and in 1238 commanded the castle of Gavarno. His *De Amore* was composed in prison.[10]

Viewed against this background, the *Melibeus* takes on, I think, a new significance. To men wearied of continual strife, in countries exhausted by internal struggle and foreign invasion, this parable, written by no monkish idealist but by an active citizen, judge, and military leader, expressed the hope of something better and finer in the administration of justice and the settlement of wars. We may recoil at its prolixity, we may yawn at its trite aphorisms, we may smile at its crude allegory, but we cannot deny that it shows a wisdom and a vision of which the thirteenth century stood sadly in need. It was no less timely in the age of Chaucer. The exhaustion and

[9] For the legal situation in medieval France, and its reflection in imaginative literature, see F. Carl Riedel, *Crime and Punishment in the Old French Romances* (New York, 1938), esp. 11–43.

[10] For biographical details in regard to Albertanus, see Sundby's Introduction.

depression in England in the reign of Richard II are too familiar to need emphasis. How deeply the evils of war and the perversion of justice impressed Gower and Langland we know; can they have been absent from Chaucer's mind when he translated the *Melibeus?* May they not, indeed, have been one of the chief reasons why he made the translation? The allegory was popular for other reasons, of course, but we may well doubt whether it would have attained such vogue had it been merely, like thousands of other works, a Christian manual or a didactic floralegium.

Whether the *Melibeus* was translated expressly for the *Canterbury Tales* it is impossible to say. I believe that Chaucer valued it mainly for its own sake, not because it would fit a given situation. With it and the *Tale of Sir Thopas,* however, he solved very neatly the problem of not seeming to compete himself for the dinner given at the common cost at the end of the journey. Obviously, the prize could be awarded neither to a parody nor to a piece so little of a real "tale" as the *Melibeus.* With it, moreover, Chaucer secured that happy mingling of the grave and gay which is so clear a part of his design. No serious comment follows it; on the contrary, the Host seizes on a minor feature—the submission of Melibeus to Dame Prudence—and gloomily compares her patience with the tantrums of his own helpmeet. In the emphasis on the "maistrye" which Melibeus allows his wife eventually, though of a different mind in the beginning ("certes, if I governed me by thy conseil, it sholde seme that I hadde yeve to thee over me the maistrye," Robinson, 204), lies the germ of the later discussion of supremacy in marriage among the pilgrims. This rankles in the breast of the Nun's Priest, who is subject to petticoat rule, and whose tale is a curious parallel to the *Melibeus,* with the roles of husband and wife reversed. The cock "tok his conseil of his wyf, with sorwe" and would have lost his life but for his own adroitness; he could quote authorities far more copiously than she, whereas Prudence snows Melibeus quite under with her citations; the "Mulier est hominis confusio" and "Wommennes conseils been ful ofte colde" are the direct opposite of the exaltation of woman and her help in trouble in the *Melibeus.* All this leads on, in turn, to the Wife of Bath's prologue ("He yaf me al the bridel in myn hond") and tale ("Thanne have I gete of yow maistrye") and so to the later discussions and tales. We shall be clearer in our minds about the sequence in which it is best to read the tales after the publication of Professor Manly's forthcoming studies, and the discussion which will no doubt ensue. It seems plain, however, that the order in the Ellesmere MS is not satisfactory, and that much is to be said for reading the tales in the sequence determined by internal evidence of time, stages of the journey, etc., of the sort employed by Furnivall and followed by Skeat in the Oxford Chaucer.

Upon the position of the *Melibeus* in the drama of the pilgrimage I do not wish to dwell, especially as I have discussed this fully elsewhere,[11] but rather to point out that it is primarily a humanitarian document, very much in the taste of its own time, and for that very reason more powerful in its appeal than an argument in more modern terms would have been. A good deal in the preceding pages will be familiar to specialists in the medieval field, but it has been set down in the hope that it will help those less familiar with that field to see clearly why the *Melibeus* was reckoned, in its own day, an integral and important part of the "sentence and solas" of the *Canterbury Tales*.

[11] "The Marriage Group in the *Canterbury Tales*," *MP*, XI (1913), 247–258.

The Pastons and Chaucer[1]

VIRGINIA WOOLF

THE TOWER OF Caister Castle still rises ninety feet into the air, and the arch still stands from which Sir John Fastolf's barges sailed out to fetch stone for the building of the great castle. But now jackdaws nest on the tower, and of the castle, which once covered six acres of ground, only ruined walls remain, pierced by loopholes and surmounted by battlements, though there are neither archers within nor cannon without. As for the "seven religious men" and the "seven poor folk" who should, at this very moment, be praying for the souls of Sir John and his parents, there is no sign of them nor sound of their prayers. The place is a ruin. Antiquaries speculate and differ.

Not so very far off lie more ruins—the ruins of Bromholm Priory, where John Paston was buried, naturally enough, since his house was only a mile or so away, lying on low ground by the sea, twenty miles north of Norwich. The coast is dangerous, and the land, even in our time, inaccessible. Nevertheless the little bit of wood at Bromholm, the fragment of the true Cross, brought pilgrims incessantly to the Priory, and sent them away with eyes opened and limbs straightened. But some of them with their newly-opened eyes saw a sight which shocked them—the grave of John Paston in Bromholm Priory without a tombstone. The news spread over the countryside. The Pastons had fallen; they that had been so powerful could no longer afford a stone to put above John Paston's head. Margaret, his widow, could not pay her debts; the eldest son, Sir John, wasted his property upon women and tournaments, while the younger, John also, though a man of greater parts, thought more of his hawks than of his harvests.

The pilgrims of course were liars, as people whose eyes have just been opened by a piece of the true Cross have

[1] *The Paston Letters*, edited by Dr. James Gairdner (1904), 4 vols.

every right to be; but their news, none the less, was welcome. The Pastons had risen in the world. People said even that they had been bondmen not so very long ago. At any rate, men still living could remember John's grandfather Clement tilling his own land, a hard-working peasant; and William, Clement's son, becoming a judge and buying land; and John, William's son, marrying well and buying more land and quite lately inheriting the vast new castle at Caister, and all Sir John's lands in Norfolk and Suffolk. People said that he had forged the old knight's will. What wonder, then, that he lacked a tombstone? But, if we consider the character of Sir John Paston, John's eldest son, and his upbringing and his surroundings, and the relations between himself and his father as the family letters reveal them, we shall see how difficult it was, and how likely to be neglected—this business of making his father's tombstone.

For let us imagine, in the most desolate part of England known to us at the present moment, a raw, new-built house, without telephone, bathroom, or drains, armchairs or newspapers, and one shelf perhaps of books, unwieldy to hold, expensive to come by. The windows look out upon a few cultivated fields and a dozen hovels, and beyond them there is the sea on one side, on the other a vast fen. A single road crosses the fen, but there is a hole in it, which, one of the farm hands reports, is big enough to swallow a carriage. And, the man adds, Tom Topcroft, the mad bricklayer, has broken loose again and ranges the country half-naked, threatening to kill any one who approaches him. That is what they talk about at dinner in the desolate house, while the chimney smokes horribly, and the draught lifts the carpets on the floor. Orders are given to lock all gates at sunset, and, when the long dismal evening has worn itself away, simply and solemnly, girt about with dangers as they are, these isolated men and women fall upon their knees in prayer.

In the fifteenth century, however, the wild landscape was broken suddenly and very strangely by vast piles of brand-new masonry. There rose out of the sandhills and heaths of the Norfolk coast a huge bulk of stone, like a modern hotel in a watering-place; but there was no parade, no lodging houses, and no pier at Yarmouth then, and this gigantic building on the outskirts of the town was built to house one solitary old gentleman without any children—Sir John Fastolf, who had fought at Agincourt and acquired great wealth. He had fought at Agincourt and got but little reward. No one took his advice. Men spoke ill of him behind his back. He was well aware of it; his temper was none the sweeter for it. He was a hot-tempered old man, powerful, embittered by a sense of grievance. But whether on the battlefield or at court he thought perpetually of Caister, and how, when his duties allowed, he would settle down on his father's land and live in a great house of his own building.

The gigantic structure of Caister Castle was in progress not so many miles away when the little Pastons were children. John Paston, the father, had charge of some part of the business, and the children listened, as soon as they could listen at all, to talk of stone and building, of barges gone to London and not yet returned, of the twenty-six private chambers, of the hall and chapel; of foundations, measurements, and rascally work-people. Later, in 1454, when the work was finished and Sir John had come to spend his last years at Caister, they may have seen for themselves the mass of treasure that was stored there; the tables laden with gold and silver plate; the wardrobes stuffed with gowns of velvet and satin and cloth of gold, with hoods and tippets and beaver hats and leather jackets and velvet doublets; and how the very pillow-cases on the beds were of green and purple silk. There were tapestries everywhere. The beds were laid and the bedrooms hung with tapestries representing sieges, hunting and hawking, men fishing, archers shooting, ladies playing on their harps, dallying with ducks, or a giant "bearing the leg of a bear in his hand." Such were the fruits of a well-spent life. To buy land, to build great houses, to stuff these houses full of gold and silver plate (though the privy might well be in the bedroom), was the proper aim of mankind. Mr. and Mrs. Paston spent the greater part of their energies in the same exhausting occupation. For since the passion to acquire was universal, one could never rest secure in one's possessions for long. The outlying parts of one's property were in perpetual jeopardy. The Duke of Norfolk might covet this manor, the Duke of Suffolk that. Some trumped-up excuse, as for instance that the Pastons were bondmen, gave them the right to seize the house and batter down the lodges in the owner's absence. And how could the owner of Paston and Mauteby and Drayton and Gresham be in five or six places at once, especially now that Caister Castle was his, and he must be in London trying to get his rights recognised by the king? The king was mad too, they said; did not know his own child they said; or the king was in flight; or there was civil war in the land. Norfolk was always the most distressed of counties and its country gentlemen the most quarrelsome of mankind. Indeed, had Mrs. Paston chosen, she could have told her children how when she was a young woman a thousand men with bows and arrows and pans of burning fire had marched upon Gresham and broken the gates and mined the walls of the room where she sat alone. But much worse things than that had happened to women. She neither bewailed her lot nor thought herself a heroine. The long, long letters which she wrote so laboriously in her clear cramped hand to her husband who was (as usual) away, make no mention of herself. The sheep had wasted the hay. Heyden's and Tuddenham's men were out. A dike had been broken and a bullock stolen. They needed treacle badly, and really she must have stuff for a dress.

But Mrs. Paston did not talk about herself.

Thus the little Pastons would see their mother writing or dictating page after page, hour after hour, long, long letters, but to interrupt a parent who writes so laboriously of such important matters would have been a sin. The prattle of children, the lore of the nursery or schoolroom, did not find its way into these elaborate communications. For the most part her letters are the letters of an honest bailiff to his master, explaining, asking advice, giving news, rendering accounts. There was robbery and manslaughter; it was difficult to get in the rents; Richard Calle had gathered but little money; and what with one thing and another Margaret had not had time to make out, as she should have done, the inventory of the goods which her husband desired. Well might old Agnes, surveying her son's affairs rather grimly from a distance, counsel him to contrive it so that "ye may have less to do in the world; your father said, In little business lieth much rest. This world is but a thoroughfare, and full of woe; and when we depart therefrom, right nought bear with us but our good deeds and ill."

The thought of death would thus come upon them in a clap. Old Fastolf, cumbered with wealth and property, had his vision at the end of Hell fire, and shrieked aloud to his executors to distribute alms, and see that prayers were said "in perpetuum," so that his soul might escape the agonies of purgatory. William Paston, the judge, was urgent too that the monks of Norwich should be retained to pray for his soul "for ever." The soul was no wisp of air, but a solid body capable of eternal suffering, and the fire that destroyed it was as fierce as any that burnt on mortal grates. For ever there would be monks and the town of Norwich, and for ever the Chapel of Our Lady in the town of Norwich. There was something matter-of-fact, positive, and enduring in their conception both of life and of death.

With the plan of existence so vigorously marked out, children of course were well beaten, and boys and girls taught to know their places. They must acquire land; but they must obey their parents. A mother would clout her daughter's head three times a week and break the skin if she did not conform to the laws of behavior. Agnes Paston, a lady of birth and breeding, beat her daughter Elizabeth. Margaret Paston, a softer-hearted woman turned her daughter out of the house for loving the honest bailiff Richard Calle. Brothers would not suffer their sisters to marry beneath them, and "sell candle and mustard in Framlingham." The fathers quarrelled with the sons, and the mothers, fonder of their boys than of their girls, yet bound by all law and custom to obey their husbands, were torn asunder in their efforts to keep the peace. With all her pains, Margaret failed to prevent rash acts on the part of her eldest son John, or the bitter words with which his father denounced him. He was a "drone among bees," the father burst out, "which labour for gathering honey in the fields, and the drone doth naught but taketh his part of it." He treated his parents with insolence, and yet was fit for no charge of responsibility abroad.

But the quarrel was ended, very shortly, by the death (22nd May 1466) of John Paston, the father, in London. The body was brought down to Bromholm to be buried. Twelve poor men trudged all the way bearing torches beside it. Alms were distributed; masses and dirges were said. Bells were rung. Great quantities of fowls, sheep, pigs, eggs, bread, and cream were devoured, ale and wine drunk, and candles burnt. Two panes were taken from the church windows to let out the reek of the torches. Black cloth was distributed, and a light set burning on the grave. But John Paston, the heir, delayed to make his father's tombstone.

He was a young man, something over twenty-four years of age. The discipline and the drudgery of a country life bored him. When he ran away from home, it was, apparently, to attempt to enter the King's household. Whatever doubts, indeed, might be cast by their enemies on the blood of the Pastons, Sir John was unmistakably a gentleman. He had inherited his lands; the honey was his that the bees had gathered with so much labour. He had the instincts of enjoyment rather than of acquisition, and with his mother's parsimony was strangely mixed something of his father's ambition. Yet his own indolent and luxurious temperament took the edge from both. He was attractive to women, liked society and tournaments, and court life and making bets, and sometimes, even, reading books. And so life, now that John Paston was buried, started afresh upon rather a different foundation. There could be little outward change indeed. Margaret still ruled the house. She still ordered the lives of the younger children as she had ordered the lives of the elder. The boys still needed to be beaten into book-learning by their tutors, the girls still loved the wrong men and must be married to the right. Rents had to be collected; the interminable lawsuit for the Fastolf property dragged on. Battles were fought; the roses of York and Lancaster alternately faded and flourished. Norfolk was full of poor people seeking redress for their grievances, and Margaret worked for her son as she had worked for her husband, with this significant change only, that now, instead of confiding in her husband, she took the advice of her priest.

But inwardly there was a change. It seems at last as if the hard outer shell had served its purpose and something sensitive, appreciative, and pleasure-loving had formed within. At any rate Sir John, writing to his brother John at home, strayed sometimes from the business on hand to crack a joke, to send a piece of gossip, or to instruct him, knowingly and even subtly, upon the conduct of a love affair. Be "as lowly to the mother as ye list, but to the maid not too lowly, nor that ye be too glad to speed, nor too sorry to fail. And I shall always be your herald both here, if she come hither, and at home, when I come home, which I hope hastily within XI. days at the furtherest." And then a hawk was to be bought, a hat, or new silk laces sent down to John in Norfolk, prosecuting his suit, flying his hawks, and attending with considerable energy and not too nice a sense of honesty to the affairs of the Paston estates.

The lights had long since burnt out on John Paston's grave. But still Sir John delayed; no tomb replaced them. He had his excuses; what with the business of the lawsuit, and his duties at Court, and the disturbance of the civil wars, his time was occupied and his money spent. But perhaps something strange had happened to Sir John himself, and not only to Sir John dallying in London, but to his sister Margery falling in love with the bailiff, and to Walter making Latin verses at

Eton, and to John flying his hawks at Paston. Life was a little more various in its pleasures. They were not quite so sure as the elder generation had been of the rights of man and of the dues of God, of the horrors of death, and of the importance of tombstones. Poor Margaret Paston scented the change and sought uneasily, with the pen which had marched so stiffly through so many pages, to lay bare the root of her troubles. It was not that the lawsuit saddened her; she was ready to defend Caister with her own hands if need be, "though I cannot well guide nor rule soldiers"; but there was something wrong with the family since the death of her husband and master. Perhaps her son had failed in his service to God; he had been too proud or too lavish in his expenditure; or perhaps he had shown too little mercy to the poor. Whatever the fault might be, she only knew that Sir John spent twice as much money as his father for less result; that they could scarcely pay their debts without selling land, wood, or household stuff ("It is a death to me to think of it"); while every day people spoke ill of them in the country because they left John Paston to lie without a tombstone. The money that might have bought it, or more land, and more goblets and more tapestry, was spent by Sir John on clocks and trinkets, and upon paying a clerk to copy out treatises upon knighthood and other such stuff. There they stood at Paston— eleven volumes, with the poems of Lydgate and Chaucer among them, diffusing a strange air into the gaunt, comfortless house, inviting men to indolence and vanity, distracting their thoughts from business, and leading them not only to neglect their own profit but to think lightly of the secured dues of the dead.

For sometimes, instead of riding off on his horse to inspect his crops or bargain with his tenants, Sir John would sit, in broad daylight, reading. There, on the hard chair in the comfortless room with the wind lifting the carpet and the smoke stinging his eyes, he would sit reading Chaucer, wasting his time, dreaming—or what strange intoxication was it that he drew from books? Life was rough, cheerless, and disappointing. A whole year of days would pass fruitlessly in dreary business, like dashes of rain on the window pane. There was no reason in it as there had been for his father; no imperative need to establish a family and acquire an important position for children who were not born, or if born, had no right to bear their father's name. But Lydgate's poems or Chaucer's, like a mirror in which figures move brightly, silently, and compactly, showed him the very skies, fields, and people whom he knew, but rounded and complete. Instead of waiting listlessly for news from London or piecing out from his mother's gossip some country tragedy of love and jealousy, here, in a few pages, the whole story was laid before him. And then as he rode or sat at table he would remember some description or saying which bore upon the present moment and fixed it, or some string of words would charm him, and putting aside the pressure of the moment, he would hasten home to sit in his chair and learn the end of the story.

To learn the end of the story—Chaucer can still make us wish to do that. He has pre-eminently that storyteller's gift, which is almost the rarest gift among writers at the present day. Nothing happens to us as it did to our ancestors; events are seldom important; if we recount them, we do not really believe in them; we have perhaps things of greater interest to say, and for these reasons natural story-tellers like Mr. Garnett, whom we must distinguish from self-conscious storytellers like Mr. Masefield, have become rare. For the story-teller, besides his indescribable zest for fact, must tell his story craftily, without undue stress or excitement, or we shall swallow it whole and jumble the parts together; he must let us stop, give us time to think and look about us, yet always be persuading us to move on. Chaucer was helped to this to some extent by the time of his birth; and in addition he had another advantage over the moderns which will never come the way of English poets again. England was an unspoilt country. His eyes rested on a virgin land, all unbroken grass and wood except for the small towns and an occasional castle in the building. No villa roofs peered through Kentish treetops; no factory chimney smoked on the hillside. The state of the country, considering how poets go to Nature, how they use her for their images and their contrasts even when they do not describe her directly, is a matter of some importance. Her cultivation or her savagery influences the poet far more profoundly than the prose writer. To the modern poet, with Birmingham, Manchester, and London the size they are, the country is the sanctuary of moral excellence in contrast with the town which is the sink of vice. It is a retreat, the haunt of modesty and virtue, where men go to hide and moralise. There is something morbid, as if shrinking from human contact, in the nature worship of Wordsworth, still more in the microscopic devotion which Tennyson lavished upon the petals of roses and the buds of lime trees. But these were great poets. In their hands, the country was no mere jeweller's shop, or museum of curious objects to be described, even more curiously, in words. Poets of smaller gift, since the view is so much spoilt, and the garden or the meadow must replace the barren heath and the precipitous mountainside, are now confined to little landscapes, to birds' nests, to acorns with every wrinkle drawn to the life. The wider landscape is lost.

But to Chaucer the country was too large and too wild to be altogether agreeable. He turned instinctively, as if he had painful experience of their nature, from tempests and rocks to the bright May day and the jocund landscape, from the harsh and mysterious to the gay and definite. Without possessing a tithe of the virtuosity in word-painting which is the modern inheritance, he could give, in a few words, or even, when we come to look, without a single word of direct description, the sense of the open air.

> And se the fresshe floures how they sprynge

—that is enough.

Nature, uncompromising, untamed, was no looking-glass for happy faces, or confessor of unhappy souls. She was herself; sometimes, therefore, disagreeable enough and plain, but always in Chaucer's pages with the hardness and the freshness of an actual presence. Soon, however, we notice something of greater importance than the gay and picturesque appearance of the mediaeval world—the solidity which plumps it out, the conviction which animates the characters. There is immense variety in the *Canterbury Tales,* and yet, persisting underneath, one consistent type. Chaucer has his world; he has his young men; he has his young women. If one met them straying in Shakespeare's world one would know them to be Chaucer's, not Shakespeare's. He wants to describe a girl, and this is what she looks like:

> Ful semely hir wimpel pinched was,
> Hir nose tretys; hir eyen greye as glas;
> Hir mouth ful smal, and ther-to soft and reed;
> But sikerly she hadde a fair foreheed;
> It was almost a spanne brood, I trowe;
> For, hardily, she was nat undergrowe.

Then he goes on to develop her; she was a girl, a virgin, cold in her virginity:

I am, thou woost, yet of thy companye,
A mayde, and love hunting and venerye,
And for to walken in the wodes wilde,
And nought to been a wyf and be with childe.

Next he bethinks him how

Discreet she was in answering alway;
And though she had been as wise as Pallas
No countrefeted termes hadde she
To seme wys; but after hir degree
She spak, and alle hir wordes more and lesse
Souninge in vertu and in gentillesse.

Each of these quotations, in fact, comes from a different
Tale, but they are parts, one feels, of the same personage,
whom he had in mind, perhaps unconsciously, when he
thought of a young girl, and for this reason, as she goes in
and out of the *Canterbury Tales* bearing different names, she
has a stability which is only to be found where the poet has
made up his mind about young women, of course, but also
about the world they live in, its end, its nature, and his own
craft and technique, so that his mind is free to apply its force
fully to its object. It does not occur to him that his Griselda
might be improved or altered. There is no blur about her, no
hesitation; she proves nothing; she is content to be herself.
Upon her, therefore, the mind can rest with that unconscious
ease which allows it, from hints and suggestions, to endow
her with many more qualities than are actually referred to.
Such is the power of conviction, a rare gift, a gift shared in
our day by Joseph Conrad in his earlier novels, and a gift of
supreme importance, for upon it the whole weight of the
building depends. Once believe in Chaucer's young men and
women and we have no need of preaching or protest. We
know what he finds good, what evil; the less said the better.
Let him get on with his story, paint knights and squires, good
women and bad, cooks, shipmen, priests, and we will supply
the landscape, give his society its belief, its standing towards
life and death, and make of the journey to Canterbury a spiritual pilgrimage.

This simple faithfulness to his own conceptions was easier
then than how in one respect at least, for Chaucer could
write frankly where we must either say nothing or say it
slyly. He could sound every note in the language instead of
finding a great many of the best gone dumb from disuse, and

thus, when struck by daring fingers, giving off a loud discordant jangle out of keeping with the rest. Much of Chaucer—a few lines perhaps in each of the Tales—is improper and gives us as we read it the strange sensation of being naked to the air after being muffled in old clothing. And, as a certain kind of humor depends upon being able to speak without self-consciousness of the parts and functions of the body, so with the advent of decency literature lost the use of one of its limbs. It lost its power to create the Wife of Bath, Juliet's nurse, and their recognisable though already colourless relation, Moll Flanders. Sterne, from fear of coarseness, is forced into indecency. He must be witty, not humourous. He must hint instead of speaking outright. Nor can we believe, with Mr. Joyce's *Ulysses* before us, that laughter of the old kind will ever be heard again.

> But, lord Christ! When that it remembreth me
> Up-on my yowthe, and on my Iolitee,
> It tikleth me aboute myn herte rote.
> Unto this day it doth myn herte bote
> That I have had my world as in my tyme.

The sound of that old woman's voice is still.

But there is another and more important reason for the surprising brightness, the still effective merriment of the *Canterbury Tales*. Chaucer was a poet; but he never flinched from the life that was being lived at the moment before his eyes. A farmyard, with its straw, its dung, its cocks and its hens is not (we have come to think) a poetic subject; poets seem either to rule out the farmyard entirely or to require that it shall be a farmyard in Thessaly and its pigs of mythological origin. But Chaucer says outright:

> Three large sowes hadde she, and namo,
> Three kyn, and eek a sheep that highte Malle;

or again,

> A yard she hadde, enclosed al aboute
> With stikkes, and a drye ditch with-oute.

He is unabashed and unafraid. He will always get close up to his object—an old man's chin—

> With thikke bristles of his berde unsofte,
> Lyk to the skin of houndfish, sharp as brere;

or an old man's neck—

> The slakke skin aboute his nekke shaketh
> Whyl that he sang;

and he will tell you what his characters wore, how they looked, what they ate and drank, as if poetry could handle the common facts of this very moment of Tuesday, the sixteenth day of April, 1387, without dirtying her hands. If he withdraws to the time of the Greeks or the Romans, it is only that his story leads him there. He has no desire to wrap himself round in antiquity, to take refuge in age, or to shirk the associations of common grocer's English.

Therefore when we say that we know the end of the journey, it is hard to quote the particular lines from which we take our knowledge. He fixed his eyes upon the road before him, not upon the world to come. He was little given to abstract contemplation. He deprecated, with peculiar archness, any competition with the scholars and divines:

> The answere of this I lete to divynis,
> But wel I woot, that in this world gret pyne is.

> What is this world? What asketh men to have?
> Now with his love, now in the colde grave
> Allone, withouten any companye,

he asks, or ponders

>   O cruel goddes, that governe
> This world with binding of your worde eterne,
> And wryten in the table of athamaunt
> Your parlement, and your eterne graunt,
> What is mankinde more un-to yow holde
> Than is the sheepe, that rouketh in the folde?

Questions press upon him; he asks questions, but he is too true a poet to answer them; he leaves them unsolved, uncramped by the solution of the moment, thus fresh for the generations that come after him. In his life, too, it would be impossible to write him down a man of this party or of that, a democrat or an aristocrat. He was a staunch churchman, but he laughed at priests. He was an able public servant and a courtier, but his views upon sexual morality were extremely lax. He sympathised with poverty, but did nothing to improve the lot of the poor. It is safe to say that not a single law has been framed or one stone set upon another because of anything that Chaucer said or wrote; and yet, as we read him, we are of course absorbing morality at every pore. For among writers there are two kinds: there are the priests who take you by the hand and lead you straight up to the mystery; there are the laymen who imbed their doctrines in flesh and blood and make a complete model of the world without excluding the bad or laying stress upon the good. Wordsworth, Coleridge, and Shelley are among the priests; they give us text after text to be hung upon the wall, saying after saying to be laid upon the heart like an amulet against disaster—

> Farewell, farewell, the heart that lives alone

> He prayeth best that loveth best
> All things both great and small

—such lines of exhortation and command spring to memory instantly. But Chaucer lets us go our ways doing the ordinary things with the ordinary people. His morality lies in the way men and women behave to each other. We see them eating, drinking, laughing, and making love, and come to feel without a word being said what their standards are and so are steeped through and through with their morality. There can be no more forcible preaching than this where all actions and passions are represented, and instead of being solemnly exhorted we are left to stray and stare and make out a meaning for ourselves. It is the morality of ordinary intercourse, the morality of the novel, which parents and librarians rightly judge to be far more persuasive than the morality of poetry.

And so, when we shut Chaucer, we feel that without a word being said the criticism is complete; what we are saying, thinking, reading, doing has been commented upon. Nor are we left merely with the sense, powerful though that is, of having been in good company and got used to the ways of good society. For as we have jogged through the real, the unadorned countryside, with first one good fellow cracking his joke or singing his song and then another, we know that though this world resembles, it is not in fact our daily world. It is the world of poetry. Everything happens here more quickly and more intensely, and with better order than in life or in prose; there is a formal elevated dullness which is part of the incantation of poetry; there are lines speaking half a second in advance what we were about to say, as if we read our thoughts before words cumbered them; and lines which we go back to read again with that heightened quality, that enchantment which keeps them glittering in the mind long afterwards. And the whole is held in its place, and its variety and divagations ordered by the power which is among the most impressive of all—the shaping power, the architect's power. It is the peculiarity of Chaucer, however, that though we feel at once this quickening, this enchantment, we cannot prove it by quotation. From most poets quotation is easy and obvious; some metaphor suddenly flowers; some passage breaks off from the rest. But Chaucer is very equal, very even-paced, very unmetaphorical. If we take six or seven lines in the hope that the quality will be contained in them it has escaped.

> My lord, ye woot that in my fadres place,
> Ye dede me strepe out of my povre wede,
> And richely me cladden, of your grace
> To yow broghte I noght elles, out of drede,
> But feyth and nakedness and maydenhede.

In its place that seemed not only memorable and moving but fit to set beside striking beauties. Cut out and taken separately it appears ordinary and quiet. Chaucer, it seems, has some art by which the most ordinary words and the simplest feelings when laid side by side make each other shine; when separated lose their lustre. Thus the pleasure he gives us is different from the pleasure that other poets give us, because it is more closely connected with what we have ourselves felt or observed. Eating, drinking and fine weather, the May, cocks and hens, millers, old peasant women, flowers—there is a special stimulus in seeing all these common things so arranged that they affect us as poetry affects us, and are yet bright, sober, precise as we see them out of doors. There is a pungency in this unfigurative language; a stately and memorable beauty in the undraped sentences which follow each other like women so slightly veiled that you see the lines of their bodies as they go—

> And she set down hir water pot anon
> Biside the threshold in an oxe's stall.

And then, as the procession takes its way, tranquilly, beautifully, out from behind peeps the face of Chaucer, grinning, malicious, in league with all foxes, donkeys, and hens, to mock the pomp and ceremonies of life—witty, intellectual, French, at the same time based upon a broad bottom of English humour.

So Sir John read his Chaucer in the comfortless room with the wind blowing and the smoke stinging, and left his father's tombstone unmade. But no book, no tomb, had power to hold him long. He was one of those ambiguous characters who haunt the boundary line where one age merges in another and are not able to inhabit either. At one moment he was all for buying books cheap; next he was off to France and told his mother, "My mind is now not most upon books." In his own house, where his mother Margaret was perpetually making out inventories or confiding in Gloys the priest, he had no peace or comfort. There was always reason on her side; she was a brave woman, for whose sake one must put up with the priest's insolence and choke down one's rage when the grumbling broke into open abuse, and "Thou proud priest" and "Thou proud Squire" were bandied angrily about the room. All this, with the discomforts of life and the weakness of his own character, drove him to loiter in pleasanter places, to put off coming, to put off writing, to put off, year after year, the making of his father's tombstone.

Yet John Paston had now lain for twelve years under the bare ground. The prior of Bromholm sent word that the grave cloth was in tatters, and he had tried to patch it himself. Worse still, for a proud woman like Margaret Paston, the country people murmured at the Pastons' lack of piety, and other families she heard, of no greater standing than theirs, spent money in pious restoration in the very church where her husband lay unremembered. At last, turning from tournaments and Chaucer and Mistress Anne Hault, Sir John bethought him of a piece of cloth of gold which had been used to cover his father's hearse and might now be sold to defray the expenses of his tomb. Margaret had it in safekeeping; she has hoarded it and cared for it, and spent twenty marks on its repair. She grudged it; but there was no help for it. She sent it him, still distrusting his intentions or his power to put them into effect. "If you sell it to any other use," she wrote, "by my troth I shall never trust you while I live."

But this final act, like so many that Sir John had undertaken in the course of his life, was left undone. A dispute with the Duke of Suffolk in the year 1479 made it necessary for him to visit London in spite of the epidemic of sickness that was abroad; and there, in dirty lodgings, alone, busy to the end with quarrels, clamorous to the end for money, Sir John died and was buried at Whitefriars in London. He left a natural daughter; he left a considerable number of books; but his father's tomb was still unmade.

The four thick volumes of the Paston letters, however, swallow up this frustrated man as the sea absorbs a raindrop. For, like all collections of letters, they seem to hint that we need not care overmuch for the fortunes of individuals. The family will go on whether Sir John lives or dies. It is their method to heap up in mounds of insignificant and often dismal dust the innumerable trivialities of daily life, as it grinds itself out, year after year. And then suddenly they blaze up; the day shines out, complete, alive, before our eyes. It is early morning and strange men have been whispering among the women as they milk. It is evening, and there in the churchyard Warne's wife bursts out against old Agnes Paston: "All the devils of Hell draw her soul to Hell." Now it is the autumn in Norfolk and Cecily Dawne comes whining to Sir John for clothing. "Moreover, Sir, liketh it your mastership to understand that winter and cold weather draweth nigh and I have few clothes but of your gift." There is the ancient day, spread out before us, hour by hour.

But in all this there is no writing for writing's sake; no use of the pen to convey pleasure or amusement or any of the million shades of endearment and intimacy which have filled so many English letters since. Only occasionally, under stress of anger for the most part, does Margaret Paston quicken into some shrewd saw or solemn curse. "Men cut large thongs here out of other men's leather. . . . We beat the brushes and other men have the birds. . . . Haste reweth . . . which is to my heart a very spear." That is her eloquence and that her anguish. Her sons, it is true, bend their pens more easily to their will. They jest rather stiffly; they hint rather clumsily; they make a little scene like a rough puppet show of the old priest's anger and give a phrase or two directly as they were spoken in person. But when Chaucer lived he must have heard this very language, matter of fact, unmetaphorical, far better fitted for narrative than for analysis, capable of religious solemnity or of broad humour, but very stiff material to put on the lips of men and women accosting each other face to face. In short it is easy to see, from the Paston letters, why Chaucer wrote not *Lear* or *Romeo and Juliet,* but the *Canterbury Tales.*

Sir John was buried; and John the younger brother succeeded in his turn. The Paston letters go on; life at Paston continues much the same as before. Over it all broods a sense of discomfort and nakedness; of unwashed limbs thrust into splendid clothing; of tapestry blowing on the draughty walls; of the bedroom with its privy; of winds sweeping straight over land unmitigated by hedge or town; of Caister Castle covering with solid stone six acres of ground, and of the plain-faced Pastons indefatigably accumulating wealth, treading out the roads of Norfolk, and persisting with an obstinate courage which does them infinite credit in furnishing the bareness of England.

PART IV

The Other Major Poets

God's Wenches and the
Light That Spoke

NEVILL COGHILL

(Some notes on Langland's kind of poetry)

I

IT WAS YMAGYNATYF who first recognized that Langland
wrote poetry and he rebuked him for it. "Thow medlest the
with makynges," he said, "and mightest go sey thi sauter." [1]
One may take this as the stricture upon himself of a reli-
giously minded man, looking back over five and forty winters
of a life he judged to have been largely wasted, "for there ar
bokes ynowe to telle men what Dowel is, Dobet and Dobest
bothe." He had let himself play about with poetry, only to
form an incurable and time-consuming habit that led nowhere. He might have been better employed.

And indeed there were books enough about the good life
and the way of salvation. What was unique in Langland's was
the way it was "made." There had been dream-visions, allegories, pilgrimages, delineations of the Seven Sins, discussions
of the Three Lives, satires and complaints before: nor was
the rumbling grumble of alliteration anything new: in fact
there had been almost everything that seems to make his
poem. Yet it is unmatched because of the quite peculiar
workings of his mind—the workings of *Ymagynatyf*, if by
that phantom we may designate Langland's modes of
memory,[2] association of ideas and images, sense of perspective, and feeling for words.

He had many of the gifts that great poets commonly have:

Reprinted from ENGLISH AND MEDIEVAL STUDIES PRESENTED TO
J. R. R. TOLKIEN, ed. N. Davis and C. L. Wrenn (1962), 200–218,
by permission of George Allen and Unwin Ltd.

[1] B Text, Passus XII, 16–18.

[2] Cf. H. S. V. Jones, "Imaginatif in Piers Plowman," *J.E.G.P.*, xiii
(1914), 583–8.

magnitude of design, passion, intuitions of things natural and supernatural, moral intensity, an instinctive ease in seeing one thing in terms of another, luck if not cunning in language, an obsessive theme. There are passages when his genius seems to fail him, as he flounders in the troublesome debates in which his quest involves him: but that is neither here nor there. What matters is that he has a great poet's stunning-power, and there are elements in it that I seem to meet nowhere but in him. They are not easy to account for, or even to describe, for this very reason; he breaks all convention and cannot readily be accommodated by the accepted language of criticism.

First among his unique creative gifts is a huge fluidity: *Piers Plowman* flows with powerful ease, up and down through Time and Space, with sudden tides that take unforeseeable directions without a word of warning: they carry the reader, sometimes protesting, from inner to outer worlds, natural and supernatural, with the arbitrary energies of a dream that has its secret purposes and destinations. In the end a reader perceives something of their organic shape, though no map that he can make of them is entirely satisfactory. To give example of the mobility of which I am speaking, the poem opens with the world at work in a field, moves swiftly to Westminster and back, undertakes a pilgrimage, but pauses to plow what is said to be a half-acre but seems to be another image for the working world. The Dreamer then awakes in the Malvern Hills, and turns inward into the life of the mind, moves once more to the life of London, then to the life of Nature in this middle-earth, and after many encounters in other places for the most part nameless, finds himself between Jericho and Jerusalem, stands at Calvary, descends into Hell, and returns thence to his cottage in Cornhill in time for Easter Mass. Beyond that it moves into an indeterminate Christendom, centered by implication in Rome, but yet is soon without a center of any sort and is seen as a devastated area with no other confines than the world itself. In the course of this astonishing pilgrimage of his in space, the Dreamer is present at the coronation of Richard II, confers with Abraham and Moses, is an eye-witness of the Crucifixion, and of the Harrowing of Hell, and after watching the building of Holy Church, sees it torn down by Antichrist. Present, Past, and Future are as instantly present to him as are the varied regions of his search, and though there is no logical pattern in these swift movements, there is a cogency in each as it happens. The fluidity and freedom of these shifting tides of dream result in a total form which could only come from a poet of archetypal or myth-creating power. However we analyze the detail of its structure, it has organic shape— the shape is a spiritual hunger of search for some great epiphany that will show us what we are seeking, in a dream: the epiphany is granted and the Dreamer stumbles upon glory: but when it has been given into his hands to hold for ever, it is taken from him by an enemy and he is left in desolation and awake, with all his journey still to do. This is surely the shape of a universal experience.

Piers Plowman is often described as an allegory, even as the greatest of English allegories,[3] and that will do well enough for ordinary purposes: no one will be greatly misled. But the poem is so exceptional in its modes of vision that when we look at it closely we are forced to revise this general account of it and consult our definitions. The most trenchant and authoritative description of allegory I know is that of C. S. Lewis, where he is speaking of the equivalences or correspondences, perceived by a poetic mind, between material and immaterial things:

> This fundamental equivalence between the immaterial and the material may be used by the mind in two ways. . . . On the one hand you can start with an immaterial fact, such as the passions which you actually experience, and can then invent *visibilia* to express them. If you are hesitating between an angry retort and a soft answer, you can express your state of mind by inventing a person called *Ira* with a torch and letting her contend with another invented person called *Patientia*. This is allegory. . . . But there is another way of using the equivalence, which is almost the opposite of allegory, and which I would call sacramentalism or symbolism. If our passions, being immaterial, can be copied by material inventions, then it is possible that our material world in its turn is the copy of an invisible world. . . . The attempt . . . to see the archetype in the copy, is what I mean by symbolism or sacramentalism.[4]

Pure allegory of this kind is nowhere better seen than in the *Psychomachia* of Prudentius, which Lewis instances. It must be among the finest of the mechanical operations of the

3 C. S. Lewis, *The Allegory of Love* (Oxford, 1936), p. 158.
4 Ibid., pp. 44–45.

spirit. As it is all of a piece throughout, a single quotation will suit my present purpose: it is from the passage that describes the battle between *Pudicitia* and *Sodomita Libido*.[5]

> And now, at hand, next on the grassy field,
> Steps Virgin Chastity with shining shield,
> Whom Sodom-Lust, with home-grown torches girt,
> Assaults with flaming sulphur, pitch and dirt,
> And at the Maid's chaste eyes she seeks to poke
> Her flaming pine, to blast them with foul smoke.
> Yet with a stone the Virgin's fearless hand
> Strikes down the She-wolf's arm and furious brand.
> Thus from her sacred face the flames she smote,
> Then with a sword she cut the Harlot's throat.

Piers Plowman is a world and an age away from the *Psychomachia*. Gone are the modish rhetoric and the august Virgilian background, gone the notion of the soul as an orderly battlefield for the passions, where decisive victories in epic style smash, rather than probe, its problems. Who now can feel the manifold of moral tensions in any sort of temptation, sexual or other, in terms of a straight fight between two strapping amazons, whose sex is predetermined by purely grammatical considerations?

Perhaps Prudentius and his early readers felt it so, but for us these equivalences no longer suffice: imagination must make some wider cast, like that of Flaubert's who, in bodying forth the temptations of St. Antony, [6] anticipated those of Gide.[7]

> J'ai repoussé le monstrueux anachorète qui m'offrait, en riant, des petits pains chauds, le centaure qui tâchait de me prendre sur sa croupe,—et cet enfant noir apparu

---

[5] Prudentius, *Psychomachia*, lines 40–50:
> enim gramineo in campo concurrere prompta
> virgo Pudicitia speciosis fulget in armis,
> quam patrias succincta faces Sodomita Libido
> adgreditur piceamque ardenti sulpure pinum
> ingerit in faciem pudibundaque lumina flammis
> adpetit, et taetro temptat subfundere fumo.
> sed dextram furiae flagrantis et ignea dirae
> tela lupae saxo ferit inperterrita virgo,
> excussasque sacro taedas depellit ab ore.
> tunc exarmatae iugulum meretricis adacto
> transfigit gladio.
>
> (Loeb edn (Cambridge, Mass., 1949), i. 282.)

[6] *La Tentation de Saint Antoine* (Paris, 1954), p. 14.

[7] *Si le grain ne meurt* (Paris, 1928), p. 345.

au milieu des sables, qui était très beau, et qui m'a dit
s'appeler l'esprit de fornication.

Prudentius, however, was more concerned to tell us that Lust
was bad than to tell us what it was like, and consequently the
more his "equivalence" is elaborated, the more it disappears.
And this is true of his whole poem. With sturdy Latin steps
he follows the *ignis fatuus* of a literary formula, little thinking that it is the poet's business to show us the forms of
things unknown, and rakes round the shelf-access of his mind
for images already invented. As all are known, so all are pre-
dictable, and we watch the outcome of their battles with that
yawning expectation commonly accorded to a *bombe surprise*: it is cold, tasteless, and inevitable.

Langland's personified figures are of a different kind and,
at their best, give no sense of having been fabricated: *Glutton* sounds as if he had been seen not once but many times in
some Colwall pub, and *Coveytise* at any Winchester fair:

And thanne cam Coueytise, can I hym noughte descryue,
So hungriliche and holwe sire Heruy hym loked.
He was bitelbrowed and baberlipped also,
With two blered eyghen, as a blynde hagge:
And as a letheren purs lolled his chekes,
Wel sydder than his chyn: thei chiueled for elde:
And as a bondman of his bacoun his berde was bidraueled.

(B v. 188–94)

and, later,

"Repentedestow the eure," quod Repentance, "ne res-
titucioun madest?"
"Yus, ones I was herberwed," quod he, "with an hep
of chapmen,
I roos whan thei were arest, and yrifled here males."
"That was no restitucioun," quod Repentance, "but
a robberes thefte,
Thou haddest be better worthy be hanged therfore
Than for al that that thow hast here shewed."
"I wende ryflynge were restitucioun," quod he, "for I
lerned neuere rede on boke,
And I can no Frenche in feith, but of the ferthest
ende of Norfolke."

(B v. 232–9)

Where did Langland hear this enchanting joke? Could he

have invented it? It has the ring of natural authenticity. And
who was *Sir Hervy* that looked so hungrily and hollow that
he gave Langland an idea of covetousness? Skeat notes that
by Skelton's time the name had become traditional for a
picklock, and quotes *"Haruy* Hafter, that wel coude picke a
male."[8] But perhaps Skelton found the name in Langland,
and Langland found it in life: Sir Hervy might have been
some famished, covetous priest he knew, for Proust tells us
that a creative writer uses all his acquaintance in imagining a
character:

> . . . il n'est pas un geste de ses personnages, un tic, un
> accent, qui n'ait été apporté à son inspiration par sa
> mémoire, il n'est pas un nom de personnage inventé sous
> lequel il ne puisse mettre soixante noms de personnages
> vus, dont l'un a posé pour la grimace, l'autre pour le
> monocle, tel pour la colère, tel pour le mouvement avan-
> tageux du bras, etc.[9]

Yet if we doubt the historicity of Sir Hervy, there is always
Lady Meed. Nowhere is she called Alice Perrers in the poem,
but it is hardly possible that this woman did not sit (in Langland's mind) for her portrait as the *Radix Malorum,* married
to a fiend and feoffed with the Seven Sins. For Langland she
symbolized Graft.

Whether we call *Lady Meed* an allegorical or a symbolic
character, she is, as imagery, simple enough, such as another
poet, even a Prudentius, might have "invented." But unique
in Langland's "making" of personified abstractions is the
character of Piers himself. The equivalences are kept shadowy and changeable: *Piers* is not a plain label like *Pudicitia.*

Only gradually do we become aware of the significances
the name includes and it is worth remarking that those who
know the poem best differ among themselves over shades of
meaning in him—a sure sign (since no one attributes this to
incompetence in Langland) that Piers is a living character
that can be argued over like Falstaff, and not an unmistakable abstraction like *Sodomita Libido,* whose nature is not in
doubt, in spite of her grammatical sex. The meanings in Piers
are the central meanings of the entire poem and we see them
dissolve into one another at every fresh epiphany, with accu-

[8] W. W. Skeat, *The Vision of William concerning Piers the Plowman*
(Oxford, 1886), ii. 81, note to C VII. 197.

[9] *Le Temps retrouvé* (Paris, 1927), pp. 54–55.

mulated and ascending richness. The solid, simple farmer, honest worker, faithful son of the Church, who alone knows the way to Truth, returns long after as the Good Samaritan, a figure for Charity, and is seen at last in Christ, or Christ in him: into these meanings we must also pour others which Langland found in the gloss and adumbrated in his retelling of this parable: the man who fell among thieves is Fallen Man himself. The Priest and the Levite that passed by on the other side are the Patriarchs. The Good Samaritan is Christ in his humanity. To this gloss, Langland added identifica- tions: the *patres antiqui* of Hugh of St. Victor [10] were to Langland Abraham and Moses, emblems of Faith and Hope: what else then could the Good Samaritan be but an emblem of Charity? All these meanings pass into Piers when we hear of the entry of Jesus into Jerusalem, to joust in Piers' arms, *humana natura,* and when Christ rises in triumph out of Hell, he still has some touch of Piers about him:

"Is this Iesus the Iuster?" quod I, "that Iuwes did to deth?
Or is it Pieres the Plowman? . . ."

(B xix. 10–11)

Later still we are told that Jesus, while on earth, lived the lives of Dowel, Dobet, and Dobest: [11] so these meanings, which are the quest-meanings of the whole poem, also pass into Piers and we are brought to realize that he has stood for them throughout and is their human custodian, the builder of Christ's church and house of unity. If we are to "lerne to

[10] See the passage from *Allegoriae in novum testamentum* quoted by D. W. Robertson and B. F. Huppé, *Piers Plowman and Scriptural Tradition* (Princeton, 1951), pp. 207–8.

[11] See B xix. 104–85:

> In his iuuente this Iesus atte Iuwen feste
> Water into wyn tourned, as holy writ telleth,
> And there bigan God of his grace to Dowel.
> For wyn is lykned to lawe and lyf of holynesse. . . .

[Cf. Walafridus Strabus on John ii. 7: "Christus . . . maluit de aqua vinum facere, ut doceret se non solvere legem, sed implere, nec in E- vangelio alia facere vel docere quam quae prophetia praedixit." (Migne, *Patr. Lat.,* cxiv. 363.)]

> And whan he was woxen more, in his moder absence, . . .
> . . . he conforted carful, & caughte a gretter name,
> The whiche was Dobet, where that he went. . . .
> . . . "And blessed mote thei alle be, in body & in soule,
> That neuere shal se me in sighte, as thow doste nouthe . . .
>   *Beati qui non viderunt, et crediderunt, etc."*
> And whan this dede was done, Dobest he taughte,
> And yaf Pieres power and pardoun he graunted
> To alle manere men mercy & foryyfnes. . . .

loue and leue of alle othre," which is the last advice of Kynde,[12] and sums the whole moral content of the poem, and of Christianity, we must seek Piers. No wonder, where so many significances crowd in, if critics differ in their emphasis when they interpret it! What I would at present stress, however, is not the *meaning* but the *"making"* of Piers: we recognize in him at first an allegorical figure, a visible, invented personification for an abstraction that we may call "Dowel." Next, an abstraction still personified, he teaches the Dreamer about the tree of charity. Then we see him identified with the Good Samaritan who is a figure from parable, not allegory, and in company with Abraham and Moses, who are neither abstractions nor fictions but historic people, used as symbols of Faith and Hope. Then he is Christ's humanity, visible and historical; and the sum of Charity seen in person. When we look to our definitions, we see that all that is finest and most central in this figure is "made" by a coalescence or fusion of allegory, parable, and symbol, and that is the poetic fact that volts it with imaginative power, unmatched in its own region of discourse. Langland is a visionary poet trying to discern the shape and meaning in our mortal predicament, through whatever kind of imagery rises to and is accepted by his mind, not an allegorical versifier at work upon a tidy little scheme, according to known rules.

We can see this same principle (the fusion of allegory and symbol) giving vigor to his sense of landscape, and even of action. To consider landscape first, the poem opens with one of the most memorable in English poetry: it was once believed to be an allegorical scene, invented to suit the poet's didactic intention. To the east, on high, a Tower of Truth. Below and to westward, a Dungeon of Care: in between, a fair field, full of folk. In these every reader can recognize an allegory of Heaven, Earth, and Hell, a fabricated theatrical set. But now it chances that this landscape has been identified and is as visible and as visitable as it ever was, in the Malvern Hills.[13] There stands the Herefordshire Beacon, high to the east; below it lies the dungeon-site of Old Castle, a little to the west: in between them the rolling fields of Colwall parish. These were the *visibilia* which came, for Langland, to symbolize our human situation and the choice between one or other of the eternities before us: many a church in Lang-

---

[12] B xx. 207.
[13] A. S. Bright, *New Light on Piers Plowman* (London, 1928), p. 45.

land's time had a like image of Doom over its chancel arch:
but Langland saw it in his native countryside. Yet from this
symbolizing mountain in his poem there descends to the
Dreamer a Lady, "in lynene yclothid," who is an allegory, a
figure invented to stand for Holy Church. An allegory has is-
sued from a symbol.

This same mixture of kinds can be seen in actions as well
as in people and places. Another of the memorable moments
in the poem is the action of Kynde when he "comes out of
the planets" at the call of Conscience to protect the House of
Unity, attacked by Antichrist and the Seven Sins. It is hardly
possible to imagine an occasion that could sound more obviously allegorical: this is the action taken by Kynde:

> Kynde Conscience tho herde, and cam out of the planetes,
> And sent forth his foreioures, feures, & fluxes,
> Coughes, and cardiacles, crampes, and tothaches,
> Rewmes, and radegoundes, and roynouse scalles,
> Byles, and bocches and brennyng agues:
> Frenesyes, and foule yueles, forageres of kynde,
> Hadde yprikked and prayed polles of peple,
> That largelich a legioun lese her lyf sone.
> There was—"harrow and help!, here cometh Kynde
> With Deth that is dredful, to vndone vs alle!"
>
> (B xx. 79–88)

Skeat in fact believed this to be an allegory, invented to
show how Nature will fail man and may even prove his
enemy in his hour of need:

> Conscience supposes that Nature, for love of Piers the
> Plowman, will assist men against spiritual foes. But the
> result is represented as being very different; for Nature
> also becomes man's enemy, afflicting him with various
> bodily diseases. . . . Yet Nature is, at last, man's true
> friend: see line 109.[14]

When we take up this reference, we find line 109 to be as
follows:

> And Kynde cessede tho to seon the peuple amende.
>   (C xxiii. 109: B xx. 108)

But Skeat's interpretation is mistaken. Langland was not

14 Ed. cit., ii. 277, note on C xxiii. 80.

inventing an allegory to show the caprices of Nature, but showing how Nature serves God by putting the fear of death into man, if he cannot be brought to repent by any other means. Langland believed that he had witnessed a similar occasion in his own lifetime—in January 1362, to be precise [15] —and had no need to invent an allegory: he recorded a fact and interpreted it as a symbol, *"in tokenynge of drede,* That dedly synne at *domesday* shal fordon hem alle":

> He preued that thise pestilences were for pure synne,
> And the southwest wynde on Saterday at euene
> Was pertliche for pure pryde, and for no poynt elles.
> Piries and plomtrees were puffed to the erthe,
> In ensample, ye segges, ye shulden do the bettere.
> Beches and brode okes were blowen to the grounde,
> Torned vpward her tailles in tokenynge of drede,
> That dedly synne at domesday shal fordon hem alle.
>
> (B v. 13–20)

Kynde, an allegorical figure, performs a symbolic action: he is coming to man's rescue on the Day of Antichrist by warning him of death. When he sees that the warning has been effective, he relents.

II

If I have labored this matter of allegory and symbolism, it is not to deny the dichotomy, but to show that Langland, at his most Langlandian, and at the top of his powers as a poet, obtains his effects by blending or fusing them in his imagery: he may not have done this on purpose, but it was the way his mind worked. This is one of the things that distinguishes his poem from a merely allegorical work, like *Sawles Warde, The Abbey of the Holy Ghost, La Voie du Paradis, The Castle of Love,* and so on. As it seems certain that Langland read and used this last-mentioned poem in one of its many versions, it is of interest to notice the things in it that attracted him and what he did to turn them into poetry.

The Castle of Love is like something pinned out on a board, a blueprint for a poem of piety. It begins with a versified account of the Creation and the Fall of Man and ends with the Incarnation and Passion of Christ, the Harrowing of Hell, the Resurrection and the Ascension. Inserted in this

[15] Ed. cit., p. 64, note on C vi. 117.

cosmic story, after the account of Adam's expulsion from
Eden, there comes the parable of the King who had a Thrall
that did amiss, and was put in prison: the King has four
daughters who are concerned at this: two of them, Mercy
and Peace, plead for the Thrall's release: their sterner sisters,
Righteousness and Truth, demand his continued detention.
The King, however, also had a son, and he, by offering to
take the Thrall's place, promises to pay the needed ransom:

> I sal take the clething of that wretchid prison
> And priuily for him sal I paye ransoun:
> Of his kynde wil I become
> And for him wil y take dome. . . .
> On this maner sothfastnes and mercy
> Sal sone be made gode frendes verraly:
> Also pece and rightwisnes
> Thai sal kis with gret swetnes.[16]

This parable, which is much in the manner of those in the
Gesta Romanorum, is glossed in the expected way, and the
poem makes, as it were, a fresh start and proceeds to the invention from which it takes its name, by plunging into allegory. A Castle is prepared for the King's Son and we are told
it is the body of the Virgin Mary:

> This is the Maydenes bodi so freo;
> Ther neuer nas non bote heo
> That with so fele thewes iwarned wes
> So that swete mayden Marie was.[17]

The Castle is built on a rock—two versions go so far as to
call it a "cragg" grey and hard,[18] which is the Virgin's heart!
Here indeed is a call upon us for the suspension of our disbe-
lief. The Castle has four crenellated turrets (the Four Cardinal Virtues), three baileys (Maidenhood, Chastity, and Es-
pousal), and seven barbicans (Meekness, Charity, Absti-
nence, Chastity, Poverty, Patience, and Ghostly Joy). From
the midst of the highest tower there springs a well that fills
all the ditches. It is the well of Grace.

[16] Monk of Sawley's version of Grosseteste's *Chasteau d'amour,*
printed in *The Minor Poems of the Vernon Manuscript,* Part I, ed. C.
Horstmann (E.E.T.S. 98, 1892), p. 416, ll. 291–300.

[17] Ibid., Vernon version, p. 374, ll. 761–4.

[18] *Cursor Mundi,* Göttingen and Cotton versions, ll. 9885–6
(E.E.T.S. 59, 1875), pp. 568–9.

After its exposition of the allegory, the poem returns to the outer narrative (following from the Fall) of the Redemption, by a brief account of the Incarnation and Passion of Christ and the Harrowing of Hell. It ends with the Resurrection and Ascension: the story is closed with a brief prayer.

Out of this rigid, frigid affair, Langland seems to have picked some elements in the structure of his poem, enough, indeed, to make me feel certain that he knew it in one of its several versions. He was struck by the image of an allegorical castle, for instance, and used it twice in his own work. On one occasion he too made it serve as an allegory for the human body when he tells us of the *Castle of Caro,* the home of *Anima.* But instead of pursuing it into crenellations, baileys, barbicans, and other allegorical absurdities, or basing it upon a heart of rock, he leaves it airy and elemental. In this passage there is no touch of symbolism: it is purely in the tradition of Prudentius, except that instead of epic machinery he employs romance machinery, with a touch of medieval science:

> Of erthe and eir it is mad, medlit togideris:
> With wynd and with watir wittiliche enioynede.
> Kynde hath closid thereinne, craftily withalle,
> A lemman that he louith lik to hymselue.
> *Anima* heo hatte: to hire hath enuye
> A proud prikere of Fraunce, *Princeps huius mundi,*
> And wolde wynne hire awey with wyles yif he mighte.
> Ac Kynde knowith this wel and kepith hire the betere. . . .
>
> (A x. 3–10)

These are correspondences that work by light suggestion, rather than by didactic enumeration, and they are helped by the ease and elegance of the alliteration and rhythmic variableness: all the thoughts make part with the rest of Langland's poem, particularly the association of Kynde with the Creator, and the cunning of his creation, of which we hear much more later:

> He is the pyes patroun and putteth it in hire ere,
> That there the thorne is thikkest to buylden and
>   brede. . . .
>
> (B xII. 227–8)

Princeps huius mundi throws in a neat allusion to the Gospels, yet one in keeping with the general feeling of gallantry and *panache* that the imagery calls for, as well as with the serious under-thought. This is how an allegorical idea can be put to a fanciful, poetic use, without disaster.

But Langland was also able to use it, crenellations and all, in a more visionary way: it comes immediately after a passage in which his fancy had failed him—the description of the pilgrimage to Truth through the Ten Commandments. A journey through a landscape can be made to correspond with a pilgrimage in moral life, as Bunyan's more successful imagery shows, but obedience to the Commandments cannot be worked into the scheme, because they are not features in scenery to be passed or bypassed in succession; they are supposed to be with us during the entire journey: for this reason, if for no other, lines like these are otiose, one of fancy's failures:

> Two stokkis there stonde, but stynte thou not there:
> Thei hote stele nought, ne sle nought: strik forth be
>   bothe.[19]

(A VI. 63–64)

But suddenly we come upon another castle; and here, since it is not an image for a human body, but of the Tower of Truth, the architectural elements are brought into play and make imaginative correspondence:

> Thanne shalt thou come to a court, cler as the sonne.
> The mot is of mercy the Maner al aboute,
> And alle the wallis ben of wyt to holde wil theroute;
> The kirnelis ben of Cristendom that kynde to saue,
> And boterasid with beleue so other thou best not sauid:
> Alle the housis ben helid, hallis and chaumbris,
> With no led but with loue and loughnesse, as breth-
>   eren of o wombe.
> The tour there Treuthe is hymself is vp to the sonne:
> He may do with the day-sterre what hym dere likith:
> Deth dar not do thing that he defendith.
> Grace hattith the gateward. . . .

(A VI. 72–82)

Once again the language leaps easily from one alliteration to another with a varying dance and the opening of the whole poem is recalled in the line "The tour there Treuthe is hymself is vp to the sonne."

In the lines that follow this we have a kind of pun that

---

[19] Quotations from the A Text are taken from the edition by G. Kane (London, 1960), with spelling slightly modified.

gives the double significance of God's power over the stars themselves, and of his control over Lucifer, Death, and Hell. With a characteristic turn from the outer to the inner life, we are then admitted by Grace to see that our pilgrimage to Truth is a pilgrimage into our own hearts:

> And if Grace graunte the to go in this wise,
> Thow shalt see in thi-selue Treuthe sitte in thine herte,
> In a cheyne of charyte, as thow a childe were. . . .
>
> > (B v. 615–17)

These are some of the unique ways in which Langland's mind worked in his "makings"—the unforeseeable turn inwards to find the Kingdom of Heaven within, as well as in a court as clear as the sun, and the touching-off of half-explicit echoes from the Bible or from other passages in his own poem. The chain of charity recalls the bond of peace, and the child-image reminds us that we must become as little children to enter the Kingdom of Heaven. That Truth and Love are naturally seated in the human heart he has told us already: to know it instinctively "it comseth bi myght, and in the herte there is the heuede and the heigh welle" (B I. 161–2).

His treatment of the Four Daughters of God gives us another glimpse of *Piers Plowman* in the "making." In *The Castle of Love* (in whatever version) they are intolerable prigs; Mercy tells the king her father:

> > "Vnderstond," quath heo, "fader myn!
> > Thow wost that I am doughter thyn,
> > And am ful of Boxumnes,
> > Of Milce and of Swetnes,
> > And al Ich habbe, fader, of the." [20]

No Pharisee in the Temple could have spoken better, no, nor Goneril or Regan.

Langland does not make Daughters of God of these four phantoms: he simply thinks of them as "wenches," while creating for their appearance an atmosphere of darkness pierced by supernatural light: of all this the Dreamer is an eye-witness:

> What for fere of this ferly and of the fals Iuwes,
> I drowe me in that derkenesse to *descendit ad inferna*.
> And there I sawe sothely, *secundum scripturas*,
> Out of the west coste, a wenche, as me thoughte,

[20] Vernon version, ll. 325–9.

Cam walkynge in the wey; to helle-ward she loked.
Mercy hight that mayde, a meke thynge withalle,
A ful benygne buirde and boxome of speche.
Her suster, as it semed, cam softly walkynge,
Euene out of the est, and westward she loked,
A ful comely creature: Treuth she highte. . . .
Eyther axed other of this grete wonder,
Of the dyne & of the derknesse, and how the daye rowed,
And which a lighte and a leme lay befor helle.

(B xviii. 110–24)

Here, with the mixture of allegory and symbolism, there is
the further mixture of a homely naturalism with mystery.
What more natural than two wenches meeting when they are
out for a walk? What more mysterious than the light lying
over the darkness of Hell? Mercy and Truth are allegories,
East and West are symbols. The choice of the word *wench* is
the daring of poetry, to startle us with the familiar in the
ambience of the fantastic. It makes a gothic kind of contrast,
like the lewd motif in some misericord, that heightens the solemnity of a chancel, as if by shock-tactic. The way the
wenches talk is in keeping with this idea: they talk slang:

"That thow tellest," quod Treuth, "is but a tale of waltrot:
For Adam and Eue, and Abraham with other
Patriarkes and prophetes that in peyne liggen,
Leue thow neuere that yone lighte hem alofte brynge,
Ne haue hem out of helle. Holde thi tonge, Mercy!"

(B xviii. 142–6)

The mixture of high comedy with a high mystery in the conversation of these wenches is of a piece with what we are told
of Abraham and Moses when they came upon the man who
fell among thieves:

Feith had first sighte of hym, ac he flegh on syde,
And nolde nought neighen hym by nyne londes lengthe.
Hope cam hippyng after, that hadde so ybosted . . . ;
Ac whan he hadde sighte of that segge, asyde he gan
    him drawe,
Dredfully, by this day! as duk doth fram the faucoun.

(B xvii. 57–62)

Within the perfect seriousness of the story, the farce of Hope
hopping, of Moses behaving like a duck, of Abraham dodg-
ing the encounter by nine ridges of plough-land, makes a

homeliness in the holiness, as the wenches and their collo-
quialisms do in the mystery. It brings things down to earth.
This may perhaps be the best way of approaching the supernatural; it is at least a good way: we may see it in a modern
example:

> VLADIMIR: There's a man all over for you, blaming on
> his boots the faults of his feet. (*He takes off his hat again,
> looks inside it, feels about inside it, knocks on the crown,
> blows into it, puts it on again.*) This is getting alarming.
> (*Silence. Vladimir deep in thought, Estragon pulling at
> his toes.*) One of the thieves was saved. (*Pause.*) It's a
> reasonable percentage. . . .[81]

While he gives humanity to the Four Daughters by slang,
Langland gives transcendence to Christ by thinking of him as
a voice in a light: light speaks in a darkness that compre-
hends it not:

> "What lorde artow?" quod Lucifer, *"quis est iste?"*
> "Rex glorie," the lighte sone seide,
> "And lorde of myghte & of mayne and al manere vertues:
>   *dominus virtutum:*
> Dukes of this dym place, anon vndo this yates,
> That Cryst may come in, the Kynges sone of Heuene."
> And with that breth helle brake, with Beliales barres:
> For any wye or warde, wide opene the yatis.
> Patriarkes and prophetes, *populus in tenebris,*
> Songen seynt Iohanes songe, *ecce agnus dei.*
> Lucyfer loke ne myghte, so lyghte hym ableynte.
> And tho that owre lorde loued, into his lighte he laughte.
>   (B XVIII. 314–24)

Between the comedy that gives animation to the four
wenches and the mystery of light that gives transcendence to
Christ comes the strangest figure in the whole poem, a Book,
seen as a person. The Book is the Bible and, so far as that
goes, is not an invention: it speaks an astonishing prosopo-
peia, some of the most visionary lines in the poem: it appears
from nowhere and disappears as soon as it has said its say,
like a mystical Jack-in-the-Box: the Dreamer sees that it has
something comic and treats it with the same earthy noncha-
lance as he treats God's wenches and at the same time with
even more poetry in what it is given to say. It is a perfect

[21] S. Beckett, *Waiting for Godot* (London, 1956), p. 11.

illustration of the grotesque in medieval art: partly ridiculous, partly sublime, even a little mad, by our standards, perhaps:

> Thanne was there a wighte with two brode eyen,
> Boke highte that beupere, a bolde man of speche.
> "By Godes body," quod this Boke, "I wil bere witnesse,
> That tho this barne was ybore, there blased a sterre . . .
> And alle the elementz," quod the Boke, "herof bereth witnesse,
> That he was God that al wroughte, the walkene firste shewed:
> Tho that weren in heuene token *stella comata*,
> And tendeden hir as a torche to reuerence his birthe:
> The lyghte folwed the Lorde into the lowe erthe. . . .
>
> (B xviii. 228–39)

In all that I have discussed in Langland's way of "making" there is a sense of the union of opposites, whether in space and time, allegory and symbol, familiar and fantastic, comic and sublime: it also has some of that solidity which Bunyan, in *The Author's Apology for his Book* that prefaces *The Pilgrim's Progress,* thinks fitting to religious poetry:

> Solidity indeed becomes the Pen
> Of him that writeth things divine to men.

The divine is apprehended as reality through every image he could find or invent in his material and mental world, and he brings them all together in the only context that can effortlessly hold such contradictions, the context of dreams. What he achieves is best expressed in terms of what Blake has to say of allegory and vision that is to be found among his additions to a catalogue of his pictures for the year 1810, and which therefore antedates the publication of Coleridge's more famous utterance on what is virtually the same theme, in the thirteenth chapter of the *Biographia Literaria*. Indeed it not only antedates, but goes beyond it: for although Coleridge makes a similar distinction between a work of fancy and one of imagination (and they might both have used Prudentius as an example of the former and Langland as an example of the latter) yet Blake adds an assertion that the Imagination shows us truth, a step which Coleridge is not so incautious as to take. It shows us something about the nature of reality. For this further claim he might again have instanced Langland, had he known his poetry, with even more commendation than he gives to Bunyan, when he says:

> Vision or Imagination is a Representation of what Eternally Exists, Really & Unchangeably. Fable or Allegory is Form'd by the daughters of Memory. Imagination is surrounded by the daughters of Inspiration, who in the aggregate are call'd Jerusalem. Fable is allegory, but what the Critics call The Fable, is Vision itself. The Hebrew Bible & the Gospel of Jesus are not Allegory, but Eternal Vision or Imagination of All that Exists. Note here that Fable or Allegory is seldom without some Vision. Pilgrim's Progress is full of it . . . but Allegory & Vision ought to be known as Two Distinct Things, & so call'd for the Sake of Eternal Life.[22]

Falstaff thought of the sun as a fair hot wench in flame-colored taffeta: and I think Langland would almost have been capable of such a flight of fancy; but he would more readily have echoed Blake in saying:

> "What," it will be Question'd, "When the Sun rises, do you not see a round disk of fire somewhat like a Guinea?" O no, no, I see an Innumerable company of the Heavenly host crying, "Holy, Holy, Holy is the Lord God Almighty." I question not my Corporeal or Vegetative Eye any more than I would Question a Window concerning a Sight. I look thro' it & not with it.[23]

It is perhaps necessary to add that Langland was a Christian poet (in fact the greatest of English Christian poets) and that he was not writing, nor did he wish to write, "pure poetry" (if there is such a thing). The tides that move in his writing are religious, which means that not all his powers are amenable to "aesthetic" principles. To be able to release the forces of Christian feeling in poetry is not a common gift, as any one can see who reads *Hymns Ancient and Modern.* Not everyone that says "Lord, Lord" can do it: but Langland could, and to read him as "pure poetry" is like trying to read the Bible as merely literature, to hear the *Sanctus* of the *Mass in B Minor* as merely music, or to take a Grünewald altarpiece from its altar and put it in a museum—that is, it is bet-

---

[22] *The Writings of William Blake*, ed. G. Keynes (London, 1925), iii. 145.
[23] Ibid., p. 162.

ter than not reading it at all. In thinking of these things it is well to ponder a phrase from the hymn, which, according to the *Apocryphal Gospel of St. John*,[24] was sung by Jesus and his disciples at the Last Supper, before they went out into the Mount of Olives:

> Divine Grace is dancing,
> Dance ye all!
> Ye who are not dancing
> Know not what we are knowing.

[24] The passage here quoted is taken from the version made by Gustav Holst for his *Hymn of Jesus*. See also M. R. James, *The Apocryphal New Testament* (Oxford, 1955), p. 253.

The Art of Preaching
and Piers Plowman

A. C. SPEARING

Piers Plowman is one of the most fascinating, and also one of the most difficult, of fourteenth-century poems. Its difficulty does not lie primarily in individual passages; for what could be more attractively accessible to the modern reader than the grotesquely heightened realism of this description of Avarice?

> And thanne cam Coveytise; can I hym noughte
>   descryve,
> So hungriliche and holwe Sire Hervy hym loked.
> He was bitelbrowed, and baberlipped also,
> With two blered eyghen as a blynde hagge;
> And as a letheren purs lolled his chekes;
> Wel sydder than his chyn thei chiveled for elde;
> And as a bondman of his bacoun his berde was
>   bidraveled.
> With an hode on his hed, a lousi hatte above,
> And in a tauny tabarde of twelve wynter age,
> Al totorne and baudy, and ful of lys crepynge;
> But if that a lous couthe have lopen the bettre,
> She sholde noughte have walked on that welche,
>   so was it thredebare.
>
> (B V 188–99) [1]

And what could be more immediately moving than the Dreamer's humble reply to a rebuke from Conscience?

> "That ys soth," ich seide, "and so ich byknowe
> That ich have tynt tyme, and tyme mysspended;

Reprinted by permission of Barnes & Noble, Inc., from CRITICISM AND MEDIEVAL POETRY by A. C. Spearing. (1964).

[1] *Piers Plowman* quotations are from *The Vision of William Concerning Piers the Plowman in Three Parallel Texts,* ed. W. W. Skeat (Oxford, 1886). There are three main texts of the poem, called A, B, and C, and probably representing different versions written by the same author (William Langland) in the course of his life. I normally quote from the latest text, C.

And yut ich hope, as he that ofte haveth chaffared,
That ay hath lost and lost, and atte laste hym happed
He bouhte such a bargayn he was the bet evere,
And sette hus lost at a lef at the laste ende,
Suche a wynnynge hym warth thorw wordes of hus
    grace; . . .
So hope ich to have of hym that is almyghty
A gobet of hus grace, and bygynne a tyme
That alle tymes of my tyme to profit shal turne."

                                        (C VI 92–101)

The difficulty is not here, for nothing could appeal more directly than the joke about the louse or the piercing humility
of the word "gobet." The difficulty in *Piers Plowman* is
where it so often is with medieval poems: in the problem of
organization, *dispositio. Piers Plowman* is a very long poem
—in each of the complete versions, called the B- and C-texts,
it has over seven thousand lines—and it is a poem in which
the modern reader will almost certainly get lost. Like *The
Book of the Duchess,* it is a dream-poem, a poem presented
to us as the experience of an "I" who is never fully in control
of what happens to him. But Langland's Dreamer finds more
to baffle him than the sudden appearance of a little dog or a
"man in blak" in the forest: "helped" by authorities with
whom he is usually at cross-purposes, he is engaged in an immense quest whose object is never quite clear—for the question "Who is Piers Plowman?" is never asked and seems incapable of being answered. And yet the poem ends with the
promise of a further and perhaps never-ending continuation
of the quest:

    "By Crist," quath Conscience tho, "ich wol bycome a
        pilgryme,
    And wenden as wide as the worlde regneth,
    To seke Peers the Plouhman, that Pruyde myghte
        destruye."

                                        (C XXIII 380–83)

It is as if the bafflement of the Dreamer were a reflection of
that of the poet; and certainly *Piers Plowman* gives a
stronger impression than almost any other medieval poem of
being a "spontaneous overflow of powerful feelings."

Piers Plowman begins with the Dreamer falling asleep in
the Malvern Hills; like *Sir Gawain and the Green Knight,*
this poem belongs to the West Midland "Alliterative Revi-

val," but while *Sir Gawain* comes from the Northwest, *Piers Plowman*, as the initial setting suggests, belongs to the Southwest. The Dreamer dreams that he is in a "fair feld ful of folke" (C I 19), situated between a tower and a dark valley; an image, fairly clearly, of the world, "Myddelerde" as Langland calls it elsewhere, placed between heaven and hell. Suddenly the people in the field are replaced by rats and mice, and he sees an enactment of the familiar fable of "belling the cat." Next a beautiful and awe-inspiring lady appears—"Ich was aferd of hure face, thauh hue faire were" (C II 10)—and the Dreamer asks her the first of what is to be an interminable series of questions: "what may thys be to mene?" (C II 11). She is called Holy Church, and she explains that the tower is the dwelling of Truth; and in fact the first part of the poem, which is usually called the *Visio*, resolves itself into a quest for Truth. Truth is another name for God Himself, and it eventually emerges that He dwells in the human heart:

> And yf Grace graunte the to go yn thys wise,
> Thow shalt se Treuthe sytte in thy selve herte,
> And solace thy soule, and save the fro pyne.
>
> (C VIII 254–56)

But this knowledge is arrived at by the most devious route conceivable, through visions of the trial of Lady Meed (payment or reward, either just or unjust), a sermon by Reason, the confessions of the Seven Deadly Sins, and the first appearance of Piers himself, a plowman who agrees to guide the community to Truth if they will first help him to cultivate his half-acre. Piers receives what seems to be a pardon from Truth Himself, the text of which is simply:

> *Qui bona egerunt ibunt in vitam eternam:*
> *Qui vero mala, in ignem eternum.*
>
> (C X 287)

> [Those who do well shall go into eternal life,
> while those who do evil shall go into eternal fire.]

But doubt is cast on whether this is really a pardon at all. Now the direction of the poem changes, and the quest for Truth becomes a quest for the quality of "Do-well" suggested by the pardon. The Dreamer seeks for three aspects of this quality, namely Do-well, Do-better, and Do-best, and in the second part of the poem, called the *Vita*, he makes enquiries about these three of a whole host of allegorical figures such as Intelligence, Study, Scripture, Learning, and so on, and also of such non-allegorical figures as some friars and a learned but greedy Doctor of Divinity. After many such encounters, he eventually achieves a vision of the Crucifixion and Harrowing of Hell, in which Christ appears as a knight dressed in the armor of Piers the plowman. This vision might make a triumphant conclusion to the poem; but instead the direction again changes, and the Dreamer is returned from the historic events of the period of the Incarnation to the world of his own day, where a barn called Unity, built by Piers, is being attacked by the deadly sins, and at the same time the Dreamer is being attacked by Old Age and Death. Defeat seems imminent; but the poem ends, as we have seen, with the promise of a new quest.

When the course of events in *Piers Plowman* is summarized briefly in this way, the poem sounds like the most confused phantasmagoria conceivable—a nightmare rather than a dream. And not even a single nightmare, for the Dreamer has waking intervals, and in these too he sometimes meets allegorical figures, and sometimes indeed it is not clear whether he is supposed to be dreaming or awake. It is true that certain themes seem to recur throughout the poem—images of pilgrimage and plowing, for example, or formulas such as the seven deadly sins—but despite these "foretastes and echoes" [2] it appears impossible to call the method of the poem anything more complimentary than "kaleidoscopic": [3] the same elements may recur in different combinations, but the combinations seem to bear only an arbitrary relation one to another. It hardly needs arguing that the *ars poetica* is unlikely to give us any help towards grasping the principle of structure of such a work, for we have seen that *dispositio* is a topic about which the rhetoricians say little. If, however, we turn to consider the *content* of *Piers Plowman,* we find (except in the case of Piers himself) not something peculiar and baffling, but something much more familiar. It has been shown by Professor G. R. Owst that in its content *Piers Plowman* is extremely close to the sermons of medieval preachers. The ideas of the poem, even when they sound, as they sometimes do, most revolutionary, most closely related to the surges of revolutionary feeling that un-

[2] Nevill Coghill, "The Pardon of Piers Plowman," *Proceedings of the British Academy* XXX (1944), p. 312.

[3] E. M. W. Tillyard, *The English Epic and Its Background* (London, 1954), p. 164.

derlay the Peasants' Revolt and the Lollard movement, are in fact "in perfect accord with . . . the most commonplace orthodox preaching of the times, indeed a perfect echo in every respect of the Church's message to the world." [4] This can be taken as established; but in other respects too *Piers Plowman* displays its closeness to the medieval sermon. The poem contains certain passages which are explicitly described as sermons. In passus C VI Reason, "revested ryght as a pope," delivers a sermon "byfor al the reame" (ll. 112, 114). Again, in C XIII we find the following passage:

> "He seith soth," quath Scripture tho, and skypte an hy,
>   and prechede, . . .
> Of here teme and of here tales ich took ful good hede;
> Hue seide in here sarmon selcouthe wordes:—
> *"Multi* to a mangerie and to the mete were sompned,
>   And whan the peuple was plener come the porter unpyn-
>   nede the gate,
>   And plyghte in *pauci* pryveliche, and leet the remenant go
>   rome."

> (C XIII 40, 44–48)

Although Scripture's sermon itself is not reported, but only its "teme"—Matthew xxii 14—expanded sufficiently to recall the whole parable in which it occurs, the passage suggests some interest on Langland's part in the art of preaching. The "teme" or *thema* is what we should now call the text of the sermon, and the "tales" or *exempla* are a regular feature of medieval sermons, and one strongly recommended by the writers of *artes praedicandi*. Langland's interest in preaching shows itself more pervasively throughout his poem. We might expect the many personified abstractions who appear in it to do so in order to take part in an allegorical action which would demand some effort of interpretation from the reader; but in fact they appear most often simply as preachers. They do not have to be interpreted allegorically themselves, but are more likely to *use* the medieval preacher's technique of allegorical exegesis on Scriptural texts. Thus in passus C XI Intelligence explains Matthew vii 18 ("A good tree cannot bring forth evil fruit, neither can a corrupt tree bring forth good fruit") as referring to illegitimate children. The poem is largely made up of such expository, sermon-like speeches. It

4 G. R. Owst, *Literature and Pulpit in Medieval England* (Cambridge, 1933), pp. 548–49.

contains specifically narrative passages, of course, but even when the poet seems most deeply engaged in narrating some action "really" seen in his visions, he is always ready to turn aside to homiletic discourse. He does this, for example, in the Harrowing of Hell episode, when, to Satan's accusation that it is Lucifer's lies that have brought about the misery of the fallen angels, he adds a general disquisition on lying, only to pull himself up apologetically with

> A lytel ich overlep for lesynges sake,
> That ich ne segge as ich seih, suynge my teme!
> (C XXI 360–61)

The poet's apology for not simply "saying as he saw" shows his awareness of his own tendency to let narrative slide across into homily. And indeed, when we think back over *Piers Plowman* after reading it, we find it difficult to distinguish narrative from homily; even so vivid an action as the Harrowing of Hell leaves behind it the impression of being an *exemplum* illustrating some larger argument.

Facts such as these suggest, I think, that it may be useful to examine medieval teachings on the art of the sermon to see whether they can give us any help in understanding *Piers Plowman;* and help will most be needed in grasping the *dispositio* of the poem. On the face of it, *Piers Plowman* does not seem to possess either a single coherent argument or a single coherent plot; indeed, one might borrow a remark of Dr. Johnson's about Samuel Richardson, and say that if you were to read Langland for the story your impatience would be so much fretted that you would hang yourself. Perhaps then a study of the *ars praedicandi* might help us to see how to read Langland.

There can be little doubt that Langland would have been familiar with the art of preaching either directly or indirectly. [5] The *ars praedicandi,* unlike the *ars poetica,* played no part in medieval education, but it was well known in England. Owst has pointed out that "tracts by Englishmen on the formal art of preaching . . . are so numerous from the second half of the thirteenth century onwards, that the practice might almost be looked upon as a speciality of our pulpits." [6] The two *artes praedicandi* I shall be referring to are both by Englishmen of

[5] Compare Elizabeth Salter, *Piers Plowman—An Introduction* (Oxford, 1962), pp. 26 ff.

[6] G. R. Owst, *Preaching in Medieval England* (Cambridge, 1926), p. 314.

the early fourteenth century: the *De modo componendi sermones* of Thomas Waleys, and the *Forma praedicandi* of Robert de Basevorn. But Langland would not have had to study these tracts themselves in order to grasp the principles of the art of preaching. He would simply have had to listen to a number of sermons in which those principles were reflected; and nothing can be more certain than that a medieval man, with Langland's deep interest in religious problems, would have heard thousands of sermons preached in his lifetime. Sermons in the Middle Ages were listened to, at least by the "judicious" among their congregations, with a keenly appreciative and critical attention. Indeed, a convenient way into our subject may be to quote a comment made by an educated listener of the late twelfth century on a sermon he had heard preached. The listener was one Peter of Cornwall, who had heard a sermon given at a synod by a preacher called Gilbert Foliot. He afterwards wrote about it as follows: "The whole sermon was varied by certain *distinctiones,* adorned with flowers of words and sentences, and supported by a copious array of authorities. It ran backwards and forwards on its path from its starting-point back to the same starting-point." [7] What this makes clear, first, is that for a medieval listener the art of the sermon was genuinely an art. It goes without saying that the preacher's ultimate goal was practical, not artistic—the moral and spiritual improvement of his congregation. But within the limits set by this purpose, an aesthetic organization was possible, and might be appreciated by the listeners, or at least by some of them. There is some evidence, too, that with the growth of a class of educated laymen, congregations had become more exacting by the fourteenth century than they were in Peter of Cornwall's day.[8] A second point emerging from Peter of Cornwall's comment is that he seems to have been struck by Gilbert Foliot's use of a particular method of composing a sermon—a method which involved great complexity of structure, and a special kind of circling or spiralling movement. This method was a new one when he heard it—hence his evident surprise and delight—and it is one of two methods distinguished by the *artes praedicandi.* The writers on preaching divide sermons into two

[7] Quoted by R. W. Hunt, "English Learning in the Late Twelfth Century," *Transactions of the Royal Historical Society* 4th s. XIX (1936), pp. 33–34.

[8] See Beryl Smalley, *English Friars and Antiquity in the Early Fourteenth Century* (Oxford, 1960), pp. 28–29.

types: the "ancient" type and the "modern" or "university" type. The "ancient" type of sermon is descended from the homilies of the early Church, and in it, as Thomas Waleys puts it, "the whole gospel passage that is read in the Mass is taken as the *thema,* and the whole of it is expounded." [9] In other words, the *dispositio* of this type of sermon is provided by the Scriptural passage discussed; the preacher will simply go through the passage verse by verse. Thus the "ancient" sermon has no distinctive structure of its own, needs no art of preaching to explain it, and hence is discussed no further by the writers of *artes praedicandi.* It is the "modern" or "university" type with which they chiefly concern themselves. This is based not on a long Scriptural passage but on a "short *thema*"— usually a single verse or part of a verse—and the resulting sermon is remarkably elaborate in structure. The first mention of the *thema* is followed by a transitional section, called the *prothema,* linked to it either by its sense or by repeating some of its words, and leading to a prayer. Then, in a section called the *introductio,* the *thema* is taken up again, and it is divided into a number of parts. This number is most often three, and each part now has to be explained rationally and confirmed by one or more Scriptural authorities, which will also if possible be in verbal concord with the part to which they are attached. This process of *divisio, declaratio* (explanation), and *confirmatio* provides the main framework of the sermon, but there may also be further subdivisions, which will again require confirmatory texts, and all these parts will be linked together by an elaborate system of verbal "correspondences" (*correspondentia*), before finally being brought together again in the *thema* itself.

Clearly, sermons constructed on this plan would be enormously complex in structure, and one might expect that they would be appreciated only by learned, "clerkly" listeners (such as Peter of Cornwall). This seems to have been broadly true; the assumption of the *artes praedicandi* is that their readers will wish to preach in Latin. But they insist that the schemes they set out are not to be followed rigidly in every detail. Thomas Waleys remarks: "I should judge it not only unnecessary but also impossible to deal with all the types and methods of preaching followed by modern preach-

---

[9] Ed. Th.-M. Charland, *Artes praedicandi* (Paris and Ottawa, 1936), p. 344. All further quotations from Waleys and Basevorn are taken from this edition, from which page-numbers are given as references.

ers, for you will hardly find two, among those who preach sermons composed by themselves, who are identical in all ways in their manner of preaching" (Charland, p. 329). And in fact we can find many surviving sermons written in English which are influenced in their structure by the "university" method, but which do not follow it in every detail. They were often intended to be preached to a mixed congregation of clergy and layfolk, educated and illiterate people; and we may note that the repetitive patterning of the "university" method, which would offer aesthetic pleasure to the upper layers of such an audience, would also serve to hammer home the main points of the preacher's message to the lower layers.[10] Such sermons borrow from the *ars praedicandi* not a complete scheme but a general principle of structure: a method of organization by which a sermon, instead of depending on the "plot" of some Scriptural (or other) extract for its *dispositio*, becomes an independent meditation closely and constantly related to a single *thema*. And within this larger structure there will be an interweaving of sub-themes, involving frequent reappearances of the same sets of words and ideas. The analogy which immediately comes to mind for such a *dispositio* is drawn not from literature but from music: it is there that we find forms of structure based on the recurrence, variation, transposition, and re-creation of certain fundamental thematic material. This analogy was current in the Middle Ages; in the early fourteenth century someone complained that just as plainsong was being superseded by more complex musical forms, so the plain old-fashioned type of sermon was being superseded by preaching whose main appeal was aesthetic.[11] And indeed in the twentieth century it has become a familiar idea that works of literature might have a structure analogous to that of musical compositions. Mr. T. S. Eliot, for example, has written that

> The use of recurrent themes is as natural to poetry as to music. There are possibilities for verse which bear some analogy to the development of a theme by different groups of instruments; there are possibilities of transitions in a poem comparable to the different move-

[10] For examples of such sermons, see *Three Middle English Sermons,* ed. D. M. Grisdale (Kendal, 1939) and *Middle English Sermons,* ed. W. O. Ross, Early English Text Society 209 (London, 1940).

[11] See Smalley, pp. 42–43.

ments of a symphony or a quartet; there are possibilities
of contrapuntal arrangement of subject-matter.[12]

And Eliot has explored these possibilities in the group of his
poems called *Four Quartets*. It is surely suggestive that a
modern scholar, Professor Nevill Coghill, has applied the musical analogy to *Piers Plowman* itself, remarking that the
"foretastes and echoes" in the poem "resemble the tentative
statement of a theme by one group of instruments in an or-
chestra, taken up and developed later in the symphony by another." But Coghill goes on to declare that the analogy is imperfect, "for the musical composer effects it by a conscious
technique of musical artifice, by utter skill; there is no reason
for thinking that these echoes and foretastes in Langland
are placed where they are to suit an exact theory of
composition." [13] We have seen, however, that just such a
theory of composition was available to Langland in the *ars
praedicandi*. To see what use he made of it, we must now
turn back to *Piers Plowman*.

We saw that one thing that particularly struck Peter of
Cornwall when he heard a "university" sermon for the first
time was the way in which "it ran backwards and forwards
on its path from its starting-point back to the same starting-
point." A sermon of the "university" type will begin with a
thema, and the result of all its elaborate art of variation will
be to return us to the same *thema,* but with an enriched understanding of its significance. (In this respect, one might
add, the *ars praedicandi* provides a paradigm for any literature based on an immutable revelation. The preacher or poet
of Christian orthodoxy cannot leave us with an original message of his own: his aim must be to revitalize for us a commandment whose very familiarity may have deadened it as a
motive for action.) Now, like a sermon, *Piers Plowman* returns us at its conclusion to the point at which it began, but
this starting-point is seen at the end with a deepened understanding. The poem begins with the field full of folk, a symbol of "modern life." This field reappears later as Piers's
half-acre, and the poem ends with the same field, but it is
now seen as a field of a different kind—a battlefield. The initial innocence of Langland's Dreamer has been superseded by
experience, the experience of the poem. The world was dis-

[12] T. S. Eliot, "The Music of Poetry," in *On Poetry and Poets* (London, 1957), p. 38.

[13] Coghill, *loc. cit.*

played at the beginning of the poem as a scene of lively but incomprehensibly confused bustle and activity, full of baffling anomalies:

> Somme putte hem to plow and pleiden ful seylde,
> In settyng and in sowyng swonken ful harde,
> And wonne that thuse wasters with glotenye destroyeth.
> Somme putte hem to pruyde and parailede hem therafter,
> In contenaunce and in clothynge in meny kynne gyse;
> In praiers and in penaunces putten hem manye,
> Al for the love of oure lorde lyveden ful harde,
> In hope to have a gode ende and heven-ryche blysse; . . .
> And somme chosen cheffare; they chevede the betere,
> As hit semeth to oure syght that soche men thryveth.
>
> (C I 22–29, 33–34)

But at the end this field is seen through wiser and sadder eyes as a scene in which the lines of battle between good and evil, between the plowman and pride, are drawn up all too clearly.[14] Thus the most fundamental sequence of *Piers Plowman*—its movement from the present, through a timeless journey among abstractions and a visit to the historic events of the Incarnation, back to a present which is seen more clearly—can be understood in terms of the *ars praedicandi*. However, the scope of the poem taken as a whole is of course much greater than that of any normal sermon. It has no single occasion, and is developed on the basis of no stated Scriptural text; it is concerned with subjects so wide as to be barely definable—first with "Truth" and then with the whole problem of how to live. The poem is so fiercely concerned with action rather than doctrine that its theme can hardly be formulated, but only embodied in a living and acting person –the enigmatic figure of Piers himself, who becomes eventually the human means by which the triumph of the Resurrection is achieved. In all this Langland's work has no connection with the art of preaching. But if we wished to sum up the poem's subject in a *thema breve*, it would not be misleading to choose part of Matthew xix 16: "What good thing shall I do, that I may have eternal life?" [15] Piers, the ultimate goal, the embodiment of all the Dreamer's longings, is approached through "What good thing shall I do?"—that is,

[14] Cf. R. W. Frank, *Piers Plowman and the Scheme of Salvation* (New Haven, 1957), p. 96.

[15] Cf. R. W. Chambers, *Man's Unconquerable Mind* (London, 1939), p. 124.

through inquiry after Do-well. And Do-well, by a process corresponding to the threefold *divisio* of the "university" sermon, is extended into Do-better and Do-best. There have been many scholarly attempts to identify single and distinct meanings for each member of this triad: it has been argued that the three stand for laymen, clergy, and bishops, or for the active, contemplative, and mixed lives, or for the purgative, illuminative, and unitive ways of mysticism. But the fact is surely that Langland defines the three in different ways at different stages of his poem, and the *divisio* is simply part of the technique of preaching, a device which (to quote a recent critic) "enables the poet to give twofold or threefold answers about the good life when necessary." [16] Significantly, the *artes praedicandi* recommend comparison as a means of *declaratio* and also as a means of amplifying a sermon with subdivisions; Basevorn gives, as one example among several, this: " 'Take away the rust from silver, and there shall come forth a most pure vessel' [Proverbs xxv 4, Douai version]. The pure vessels are the laity, the purer the clergy, the purest the bishops" (Charland, p. 293). The "Do-well" *thema* is stated very early in *Piers Plowman,* in Holy-church's speech in the second passus:

> Alle that worchen that wikkede ys, wenden thei shulle
> After hure deth-day and dwelle ther wrong ys;
> And alle that han wel ywroght, wenden they shulle
> Estwarde to hevene, evere to abyde
> Ther treuthe is, the trone that trinite ynne sitteth.
>
> (C II 130–34)

This is of course the same doctrine as that of the "pardon" sent to Piers. Do-well itself emerges first as part of a similar antithesis between the good and the wicked—the Dreamer supposes that the friars must know "Dowel and Do-uvele, wher thei dwellen bothe" (C XI 17). It is soon divided into a triad by comparison, when Thought tells the Dreamer that "Dowel and Dobet . . . and Dobest the thridde / Beth thre fayre vertues" (C XI 76–77). Towards the end of the poem there is a final statement of the original *thema breve* in its original antithetical form, but now modified by the idea of paying one's debts:

> And what persone payeth hit nat, punysshen he thenketh,
> And demen hem at domesday, bothe quyke and dede;

16 Frank, *op. cit.,* p. 42.

The gode to the godhede and to grete joye,
And wyckede to wonye in wo withouten ende.
(C XXII 195–98)

Up to a point, then, *Piers Plowman* considered as a whole can be seen as constructed according to the principles of *ars praedicandi*. But these principles may help us to read the work in detail, as well as to grasp its *dispositio*, for baffling transitions, changes of direction, and a use of recurrent themes are characteristic of the poem's local development as well as of its overall structure. To illustrate this it will as usual be best to take a particular example, a passage of medium length which does not follow an obvious path of development. A suitable passage, as it happens, is one of those explicitly described as sermons in the poem: the sermon preached by Reason, dressed as a pope, to the whole community in passus C VI. The C version of this sermon is rather different from the B version, and on the face of it less coherent, so we may hope that reference to the methods of the sermon will also help us to understand the purpose of the C-revisions. At the beginning of his sermon, Reason (referring to the many outbreaks of plague that occurred in the fourteenth century)

Prechede, and provede that thuse pestilences
Was for pure synne, to punyshe the puple.
(C VI 115–16)

He connects these "pestilences" with another natural disaster sent by God, "the south-west wynd on Saterday at eve" (117)—probably a particularly memorable storm that occurred in 1362—and then, after bidding "wastours go worche and wynne here sustinaunce" (127), Reason starts giving more particular advice. He refers to various typical figures (such as "Purnele" who ought to give up expensive trimmings on her clothes), and then finally

He bad Bette go kutte a bowh other tweye,
And bete Beton thermyd, bote hue wolde worche.
He charged chapmen to chasten here children,
And lete no wynnynge forwene hem the while thei ben yonge;
For ho so spareth the spring spilleth hus children;
And so wrot the wise, to wissen us alle,
Qui parcit virge, odit filium.
(C VI 135–40)

Thus Reason takes up again the theme with which he began
—that of punishment—and this issues in the text from Proverbs xiii 24: "He that spareth his rod hateth his son." (The
sermon has not begun with a text, perhaps because its occasion is not a particular day in the Church year but a particular social situation.) There now follows in the C-text a section which in B occurs not in Reason's sermon, but in a quite
different part of the poem—a Speech by Learning in passus **B
X**. This section praises the unworldly life "in cloistre other in
scole" (154), attacks selfish clerics, and goes on to threaten,
in a passage that mingles political with apocalyptic prophecy,

> Ac yut shal come a kyng and confesse yow alle,
> And bete yow, as the byble telleth, for brekyng of youre
>   reule.

(C VI 169–70)

Thus the theme of punishment recurs again, and by paying
attention to the thematic method of the *ars praedicandi* we
can begin to see what Langland was about when he borrowed
from B X. The same theme comes up yet again at the very
end of the passage shifted from B:

> For the abbot of Engelonde and the abbesse hys nece
> Shullen have a knok on here crounes, and incurable the
>   wounde;
> *Contrivit dominus baculum impiorum, virgam*
> *dominanciam, plaga insanabili.*

(C VI 177–78)

The confirming text here is a conflation of Isaiah xiv 5–6:
"The Lord hath broken the staff of the wicked, and the scep-
tre of the rulers. He who smote the people in wrath with a
continual stroke, he that ruled the nations in anger, is perse-
cuted, and none hindereth." In the form used by Langland,
this text repeats in *virgam* (rod, staff) the key word of the
previous text from Proverbs.

Immediately after this reference to the oppression of the
oppressors, the whole direction of the sermon seems to be
changed. The line "And sitthe he consailed the kyng hus comune to lovye" (181) initiates a series of particular exhortations directed to the various members of the community who
are supposed to make up Reason's congregation. The
"riche/ And comuners" (183–84) are exhorted to hold together in "unite" (190), and warned against the pride which
caused Lucifer to destroy the "holy commune" (187) of

heaven. The Pope is exhorted to "have pyte of holy-churche" (192) and to see that kings are given "pees for here penaunce" (196). Finally pilgrims are exhorted to seek "seint Treuthe" rather than "seint Jame and seyntes of Rome" (198–99). Here the sermon ends with the conventional *Qui cum patre et filio* (200). This last series of exhortations may appear to be disconnected from the rest of Reason's sermon, though it can easily be seen how the references to "unite" and "seint Treuthe" fit it into the greater sermon of the poem as a whole. If we look at it more closely, however, we find that it does have links with what has gone before. Its ideas of community and mutual love can be referred back to the earlier passage on cloisters and schools:

> For in cloistre cometh no man to chide ne to fighte;
> In scole ys love and lownesse and lykyng to lerne.
>
> (C VI 155–56)

And the (as it were, earthly) "comune" which was in heaven before the rebellion of Lucifer can be connected with the (as it were, heavenly) community of the cloister or school on earth:

> For yf hevene be on thys erthe other eny eyse for saule,
> Hit is in cloistre other in scole, by meny skyles ich fynde.
>
> (C VI 153–54)

Finally, in wishing that kings should have "pees for here penaunce," Reason not only prepares the way for the confession of the Seven Deadly Sins (which immediately follows his sermon), but also takes up again the threat to selfish clerics, who have been told earlier that the king will "putte yow to youre penaunce, *ad pristinum statum ire*" (172). Thus although the sermon may appear on a first reading to be utterly confused (especially in the C Version), we have now seen that it possesses a tenuous but definite thematic organization. It proceeds with a circling or spiralling motion which constantly brings it back to the theme of punishment or "penaunce" as its main source of continuity. The reader may feel that the last connections in particular are fine drawn, and that they might be the result of chance, especially since Langland has taken over a passage from B X with little alteration; but it must be emphasized that such connections are exactly what the *artes praedicandi* would lead us to expect. We have found a sort of organization in Reason's sermon, but it must be admitted that the sermon also has a sort of disorganization; and this too, I believe, can be traced to the art of preaching.

It is only in a paradoxical sense that an independent *art* of preaching is possible. Art is a form of display, but the preacher must preach, as Waleys puts it, "not in order to show off . . . but for the praise of God and the edification of his neighbor" (Charland, p. 330). His immediate aim, especially perhaps when he is preaching to his lay neighbors, will clearly be edification. Horace recommends a mixture of the *utile* and the *dulce,* the useful and the pleasing, as the best recipe for literature, but for the *artes praedicandi* the *utile* comes first, and in fact the very words *utile* and *utilitas* run through them like a refrain. Basevorn expresses his disapproval of the more elaborate arrangements of *correspondentia* by saying that one type is "more ingenious than useful" and that another is "useless." He commends a method of constructing sermons according to which the preacher begins by choosing "three subjects which he supposes to be greatly useful to the listeners" on the grounds that it is "extremely useful and efficacious, and intelligible among simple people in any vernacular language" (Charland, pp. 302, 306, 314). Waleys tells us that when a sermon is intended for the common people, the "ancient" method "is not only easier for the preacher himself, but also more useful for the listener." The *divisio* is not made, as some suppose, "only for its ingenuity," but for its utility: "It is useful for the preacher . . . It is very useful indeed for the listener." And later Waleys observes that the "infinite" multiplication of *divisiones,* though easy for the preacher, "deforms the sermon and renders it insipid and not easily intelligible to the listener" (Charland, pp. 344, 370, 370–71). Here the aesthetic vocabulary—*deformat* being, in context, the antonym of *decorat*—is itself employed in the service of *utilitas*. We find in the *ars praedicandi* the paradox of a utilitarian aesthetic, a literary theory which despises its own techniques.

This theory can be seen at work most clearly in the use of the digression. For the *ars poetica,* it will be remembered, the digression is a purely artistic device; its function is summarized by Geoffroi de Vinsauf's remark that "digression at once amplifies and decorates the subject-matter" (Faral, p. 274). *Piers Plowman* contains many digressions, but their function usually seems to be rather different from this. Langland normally digresses in order to clear up some difficulty in argument, or more simply because he has unexpectedly thought of something important to say. Among many examples of this, one might mention the digression on lying in C XXI, which was discussed above, and the "sermon" of Ymagynatyf (Recollection) in C XV, which is generally concerned with learning, but rambles to take in a description of the Nativity, an explanation that the unlearned thief crucified with Christ is lowest in heaven, and a warning that only Nature knows everything. Now digression of this sort had been defended long before the fourteenth century by St. Gregory, as being appropriate to religious discourse. He uses the image of a river to explain his view, and, we may note, also invokes the concept of *utilitas*:

> Anyone who speaks about God should consider it necessary to search out whatever will correct the behavior of his listeners; and he will be following the proper method of exposition if, when an opportunity for edification occurs, he profitably [*utiliter*] turns away from what he was originally saying. For the commentator on sacred writ should behave like a river. Now if a river, as it is flowing in its bed, runs alongside hollow valleys, the force of its current is turned into them at once; and when it has filled them up sufficiently, it immediately pours back into its bed. There is no doubt that the commentator on holy writ should act just like this: whatever subject he is dealing with, if he happens to find at hand an occasion for appropriate edification, he should as it were turn aside the flood of his eloquence towards that nearby valley; and then, when he has poured enough into it, he should fall back into the channel of his prepared speech. [17]

This river image seems strikingly appropriate to *Piers Plowman,* with its combination of urgent pressure and unforeseen direction. It is borrowed by Basevorn, along with the usual criterion of *utilitas,* to describe *digressio.* He says that digressions should not normally be too long or too remote from the main subject, but that it may be necessary to be prolix where teaching is concerned. "And thus, as Gregory recommends . . . , as the water of a river flows in wherever it finds low places, so sometimes an authority needs to be turned aside so that things that are useful may

---

[17] *Moralium libri,* Epistola cap. II, ed. J.-P. Migne, *Patrologia Latina* LXXV, col. 513.

be said by the way" (Charland, p. 297). Here, as in the matter of *divisiones,* Waleys shows a fuller realization of the paradoxical nature of this aesthetic. He too argues that if a preacher thinks of something edifying to say, even though it is outside his chosen theme, he should say it, and he continues: "Nor in that case is it to abandon the art of preaching if one digresses from the theme; indeed it is to keep most strictly to the art of preaching" (Charland, p. 356). A variant manuscript reading sharpens the paradox by substituting *artissime* (most artistically) for *certissime* (most strictly). Waleys goes on to argue that if a poet follows his art most closely by breaking its metrical rules "so that his meaning may be clearer and fuller," surely a preacher must act similarly? Langland seems to share this attitude towards his art. Of his skill as a poet there can be no question, and yet when Recollection says accusingly to the Dreamer "thow medlest the with makynges, and myghtest go sey thi sauter" (B XII 16), the Dreamer accepts the rebuke as true. For Langland perhaps a contempt for "mere" art was a condition of artistic achievement.

Before we leave the subject of the *dispositio* of *Piers Plowman,* it may be interesting to turn from the theorists of the art of preaching to the practice of a great medieval preacher, perhaps indeed the greatest preacher of the Middle Ages: St. Bernard. We find St. Bernard treating the *ars praedicandi* in practice as an art of improvisation. In the course of his great series of sermons on the Song of Songs, he will casually remark halfway through an exposition, "And another sense [of the text] occurs to me; I had not thought of it before, but I cannot pass it by." Again, in interpreting the text "Thy name is as ointment poured forth," he comments: "Now why is it called ointment? For I have not yet said this. I had begun to say it in a former sermon, but there suddenly came up something that seemed to need preaching about." [18] The last phrase—*aliud quod praedicandum videbatur*—has a charming simplicity: how often in reading *Piers Plowman* we feel inclined to explain an unexpected transition by the sudden occurrence to the poet of "something that seemed to need preaching about!" And Bernard begins his very next sermon with a statement in which he defends his methods as a preacher, and which gives us a vivid insight into the whole ethos of preaching in the Middle Ages. He begins by remind-

[18] Sermones IX 9 and XV 5, ed. Migne, *ibid.,* CLXXXIII, cols. 818 and 846.

ing the quick-witted among his listeners, who may be getting impatient at the slowness of his exposition of the Song of Songs, that "I also have a duty towards slower people, and indeed especially towards them; for I am not concerned nearly so much to explain words as to influence hearts. My duty is both to draw water and to give it to people to drink, and this is not to be done by discussing things hastily and cursorily, but by careful commentary and frequent exhortation." Here we find the active concern for the needs of the congregation that is characteristic of the *ars praedicandi*. On this occasion the congregation is a mixed one, and so, because the end of preaching (to influence hearts) must always override its method (to explain words), the less intelligent must be provided for. *Piers Plowman* too seems to be directed at an audience of mixed intellectual capacity, and similar provision is made for this. In passus C XX, for example, the doctrine of the Trinity is carefully explained through two separate analogies, one more and the other less difficult. The first and simpler analogy is that of a hand, and its functional purpose as a mnemonic is made clear by the remark with which it is introduced:

> And if kynde witt carpe her-agen and other kynne thouhtes,
> Other heretikes with argumens, theyn honde thou hem shewe!

> (C XX 109–10)

The second analogy, more difficult and more poetic, is that of a taper, composed of an intricately interrelated wax, wick, and flame. It is true, St. Bernard continues, that he has not finished in two days an exposition (he calls it "that shady forest, lurking with allegories") which he had expected to complete in one. But, like a man looking at a mountainous landscape from a distance, he was not able to see into the valleys and woods before he came to them. Langland's position must have been very similar, as he embarked on his poem, also a shady forest with allegories lurking in it, and involving difficulties he could hardly have foreseen when he confidently introduced the supreme authority of Holychurch to answer all the Dreamer's questions in the very first passus. St. Bernard concludes by asking, with admirable panache,

> For example, when we were discussing the calling of the Gentiles and the rejection of the Jews, how could I have foreseen that the miracle of Elisha would suddenly

spring out in the middle of them? But now, since we
have come upon this subject accidentally, a short delay
must not worry us, so long as we return eventually to
the subject we interrupted, for that contains just as
much spiritual nourishment. After all, hunters and
hounds often find that they have to abandon the quarry
they had originally started in order to pursue another
which appears unexpectedly.

This image of the preacher and his congregation as a hunter
and his hounds, who cannot carry out a course of action
foreseen in every detail, but must follow whatever quarry
they happen to rouse, is again one which it is tempting to
apply to *Piers Plowman*. Certainly, in reading the poem, one
has the impression that the poet is engaged in a contest
against an unpredictable opponent.

In general, what this passage from St. Bernard suggests is
that his art as a preacher, elaborate and considered as it is,
must nevertheless always include an important element of
spontaneity. And this will lead him not simply into graces beyond the reach of art, but sometimes into pieces of non-art,
produced in response to demands more important than those
of literary criticism. This seeming contradiction, of an art
that embraces its own negation, is expressed by the preaching
theorists, who put forward, along with an intricate formal
patterning for the sermon, the warning that this patterning
must always be disregarded if necessary. And the contradiction is found embodied in Langland's poem, at once magnifi-
cent and impoverished, a work which seems to hang—sometimes uncomfortably and, for the literary critic, disturbingly
—at the point of balance between organization and chaos.
We have seen, I think, that, so far as the *dispositio* of *Piers
Plowman* is concerned, an awareness of the art of preaching
as Langland's contemporaries conceived it can usefully suggest to a modern reader what kinds of organization and what
kinds of disorganization he is to look for in the poem. It remains to consider briefly the poem's local stylistic detail.

The style of *Piers Plowman*, compared with that of other
alliterative poems, such as *Sir Gawain and the Green Knight*,
tends to be bare and lacking in any specifically poetic diction.
Here too we may find the influence of the *ars praedicandi*,
which expresses a traditional Christian suspicion of any kind
of ornament. Waleys ridicules sermons full of the rhyming
endings typical of medieval Latin artistic prose, because, he
says, such heightenings "obstruct the purpose of a sermon,

since, while the external ears are excessively occupied with the sweetness of the voice, the inward ears of the heart gain less from the excellence of the matter and meaning, just as those who take great pleasure in singing attend less to the matter that is being sung" (Charland, p. 373). Basevorn opposes those who say that "preaching ought not to glitter in the deceptively gorgeous robes of rhetorical colors," and he cites St. Bernard's sermons as examples of the proper use of eloquence. But he insists all the same that edification must come first. Modern preachers, he says, introduce into their sermons "much that, as it seems to me, belongs more to ingenuity and to vanity than to edification" (Charland, pp. 248, 244). A similar attitude of mind seems to be at work in *Piers Plowman.* One can claim, I think, that Langland usually produces his most impressive poetry at the crucial points in the development of his poem, and that this poetry is all the more convincing for being won out of inquiry and exposition on a deliberately prosaic and unliterary level. Nevertheless, it must be admitted that *Piers Plowman* contains many long passages of sense—excellence of matter and meaning—which only rarely deviate into poetry. The stylistic devices that stand out most prominently in the poem are various kinds of verbal repetition—the simplest type of rhetorical ornament. This is not in the least surprising, of course; such devices, as we have seen, play a large part in the *ars poetica,* and they are commonly used in medieval literature generally. This is what one would expect of a literature largely composed to be read aloud. The use of such devices, however, would seem to be particularly encouraged by the utilitarian ethos of the *ars praedicandi,* with its strong emphasis on the preacher's effectiveness in relation to his audience. Repetition is necessary, on the lowest level, as a means of emphasizing or clarifying an important point, and so Waleys tells the preacher, "if there are any points that are to be strongly emphasized, do not only say them once with great emphasis, but drum them into the congregation two or three times" (Charland, p. 335). We often find in *Piers Plowman* verbal repetitions of the kind that would result from following such instructions—repetitions serving simply to underline something that not even a simple listener can be allowed to miss. For example, when Lady Meed makes her first appearance, she is described as follows:

Ich lokid on my lyft half as the lady me tauhte,
And sauh a womman, as yt were, wonderlich *riche* clothed.

Hue was purfild with peloure, non purere in erthe,
And coroned with a corone—the kynge hath no betere.
On alle hure fyve fyngres *rycheliche* yrynged,
And theron rede rubies and other *riche* stones.
Hure robe was *ryccher* than ich rede couthe;
For to telle of hure atyre no tyme have ich nouth.
Hure araye with hure *rychesse* ravesshede myn herte.

(C III 8–16)

Here we have a fine example of amplifying *descriptio,* which includes, in the penultimate line, the typical rhetorical device of *occupatio*—a refusal to say what one might say. But the most prominent feature of the description is the repetition of different forms of the word "rich" (a device which the *artes poeticae* recognize as *adnominatio* or *polyptoton*), and this repetition serves to underline the most important fact about Lady Meed, that she represents a form of wealth, attractive and perhaps ostentatious. A little later, when a closer definition of Meed is necessary, Theology says in her defense that she is nearly related to Amends, a lawful form of payment, and this point too is underlined by a repetition:

For Mede is moillere—*Amendes was here dame.*
Thouh Fals were hure fader and Fykel-tonge hure syre,
Amendes was hure moder by trewe mennes lokyng.
Withoute *hure moder Amendes* Mede may noght be
    wedded.

(C III 120–23)

Repetition could hardly be more functional, more obviously a matter of the preacher's need to make things clear to his listeners; but elsewhere in the poem one can find the same device extended from the functional to the poetically creative. For example, in the triumphant speech of Christ to Lucifer as He breaks hell open and lets out the suffering souls, there are thickly clustered repetitions of the word *drynke:*

The biternesse that thow hast browe, now brouk hit thy-
    self;
That art doctour of deth, *drynk* that thow madest!
For ich, that am lord of lyf, love is my *drynke,*
And for that *drynke* todaye deyede, as hit semede;
Ac ich wol *drynke* of no dich, ne of no deop cleregie,
Bote of comune coppes—alle Cristene soules;
Ac thi *drynke* worth deth, and deop helle thy bolle.

Ich fanht so, me fursteth yut for mannes soule sake;
  Sicio.
May no pyement, no pomade, ne presiouse *drynkes*
Moyste me to the fulle, ne my thurst slake,
Til the vendage valle in the vale of Josaphat,
And *drynke* ryght rype most—*resurreccio mortuorum.*

(C XXI 404–15)

Here the use of words is daringly imaginative, for the image
of drinking has grown from a fusion of two different ideas—
that of the Devil as a doctor brewing evil medicines, and that
of the offering of a bitter drink to the parched Christ on the
cross. We cannot say that Langland could have learned to use
words thus from the *ars praedicandi,* or from any other
source; but he may at least have been encouraged by the repetitive nature of sermon structure and style to allow his
powers to develop along this path.

There is a more obvious influence from the art of preaching in a different and more distinctive kind of verbal repetition that Langland uses. We have seen how the texture of
ideas and images in a "modern" sermon, and equally in *Piers
Plowman* considered as a whole and in shorter parts of it such
as Reason's sermon, is one of thematic interweaving. Now the
same pattern is often repeated on a still smaller scale in the
style of *Piers Plowman,* where a number of different *words* are
interwoven just as ideas and images are interwoven on a larger
scale. When the Dreamer asks a character called "Liberum-
Arbitrium" (Free Will) "What is holychurche, frend?" the
answer is "Charite," but this simple reply is then expanded as
follows:

Lyf, and *Love,* and *Leaute* in o *byleyve* and *lawe,*
A *love*-knotte of *leaute* and of *leel byleyve,*
Alle kynne cristene clevynge on on wyl,
Withoute gyle and gabbynge, gyve and selle and lene.
Love lawe withoute *leaute,* lowable was it nevere;
God lereth no lyf to *love* withoute *leel* cause.
Jewes, Gentiles, and Sarrasines jugen hemselve
That *leeliche* thei *byleyven,* and yut here *lawe* dyverseth;
And on god that al bygan with goode herte thei honoureth.
And either *loveth,* and *bilevith* in on lord almyghti.
Ac oure lorde *loveth* no *love* bote *lawe* be the cause;
For lechours *loven* agen the *lawe,* and at the laste
  beeth dampned:

> And theeves *loven,* and *leaute* haten, and at the laste beeth
>   hanged:
> And *leelle* men *loven* as *lawe* techeth, and *love* therof arys-
>   eth,
> The which is hefd of Charite, and hele of mannes soule.
>   (C XVIII 126–40)

In this passage of fifteen lines a number of different repe-
tends, all beginning with the letter *l,* are interlocked: some
form of the root *love* is repeated eleven times, *lawe* six times,
and *leaute, byleyve,* and *leel* four times each. And the repetition has a special purpose: to enrich our conception of "charity" by *re-creating* it from its component elements of love,
belief, and lawfulness or justice (*leel,* lawful, giving the noun
leaute). Liberum-Arbitrium uses words rather as a juggler
uses his balls: several words are tossed so rapidly from hand
to hand that they seem to merge into a single entity—charity.
This really is a distinctive use of a device which in itself is
very common. Comparison with other types of verbal repetition may make this clear. We have just seen how verbal repetition can be used simply to underline an important point. It
may also be employed more subtly, as an aid to analysis or
definition of whatever it is that is repeated; Chaucer, for instance, sometimes employs verbal repetition in this analytic
way. Thus in *The Wife of Bath's Tale,* a knight is forced to
marry an ugly old woman, whom he despises for her ignoble
birth as much as for her lack of physical attractiveness. But
this wife of his lectures him on the subject of *gentillesse*
(nobility) in a speech in which the words *gentil, gentillesse,*
and *genterye* are repeated twenty-one times in sixty-eight
lines (*Canterbury Tales,* III 1109–76). The purpose of her
speech is to define true *gentillesse* by distinguishing between
the nobility of title which men receive from their ancestors
and the nobility of behavior that comes from God alone.
This "analytic" use of verbal repetition contrasts very
strongly with that in Liberum-Arbitrium's speech. The latter
might rather be called "synthetic," for its purpose is to *create*
"A love-knotte of leaute and of leel byleyve"—to fuse a variety of elements into a whole which is felt to be richly mean-
ingful, but which could hardly be defined in conceptual
terms.

In this chapter I have not aimed at an "interpretation" of
Piers Plowman in any way comparable with the account of
Sir Gawain and the Green Knight offered in chapter 2. *Piers*

Plowman seems to me an immensely more difficult poem, and, despite the great quantity of scholarly work that has been done on it, it appears that we are still at the stage of having to make up our minds what *kind* of poem it is. I have therefore done no more than to try to suggest some ways in which an acquaintance with the medieval art of preaching might usefully affect the expectations brought to *Piers Plowman* by a modern reader. But the remarks in the last paragraph on the "synthetic" effect of certain examples of verbal repetition suggest some comments on the way in which the local style of the poem reflects the poet's whole purpose. We saw how this was so in the case of *Sir Gawain and the Green Knight*—how the poem's central conception of *cortaysye* was expressed in Gawain's distinctive mode of speech—and an analogous relation between style and purpose can be seen in *Piers Plowman*. The effect of potent vagueness generated by Liberum-Arbitrium's speech is rather typical of *Piers Plowman* in general: despite the work of various modern scholars, the poem seems to give up very little of itself to attempts at theological analysis or at the separation of its meaning into a variety of allegorical layers. The conceptual vagueness is central to Langland's religious vision, and why this should be so may appear most clearly from a comparison with a modern religious poet, Mr. T. S. Eliot. We have said earlier that the writer whose religious scheme is that of Christian orthodoxy is in a peculiar position. He cannot offer any radical novelty of doctrine: his "originality" must consist not in the creation of new religious concepts but in the re-creation of the old so that they may be apprehended with new force. The kind of re-creation that is necessary will vary from age to age according to the nature of the most powerful destructive forces at work on religious language and thought in the immediate past. Eliot has written religious poetry in a post-Romantic age—an age, that is to say, when the force of religious terms has been dissipated because they have been used recklessly in non-religious contexts. Words such as "divine" or "eternal," for example, have been deprived of all precision, indeed almost of all meaning, in normal speech and thought, by having been employed in a loosely emotive sense, as mere intensifiers, in the common language of nineteenth-century poetry. Thus Eliot's task has been to avoid too ready an invocation of familiar concepts, to skirt round them warily, using methods borrowed from the *via negativa* of mysticism:

>   Neither flesh nor fleshless;
> Neither from nor towards; at the still point, there the
>   dance is,
> But neither arrest nor movement. And do not call it fixity,
> Where past and future are gathered. Neither movement
>   from now towards,
> Neither ascent nor decline.   ("Burnt Norton")

In such poetry, as Dr. F. R. Leavis has written,

> Familiar terms and concepts are inevitably in sight,
> but what is distinctive about the poet's method is the
> subtle and resourceful discipline of continence with
> which, in its exploration of experience, it approaches
> them.[19]

This is the kind of religious poetry that a discriminating twentieth-century reader is likely to admire most readily, but it is not at all the kind he is likely to come upon in Langland's work. If in Eliot's age the religious sensibility has been in greatest danger from Romanticism, in Langland's age the great peril seems to have been scholasticism. The thirteenth century had been a period in which vast and comprehensive systems of theology and philosophy were built up on a basis of careful definition and minute distinction; the supreme example is the work of St. Thomas Aquinas. In the fourteenth century these systems, based on a synthesis of faith and reason, began to give way under the attacks of Ockham and his followers, and the intellectual atmosphere generally was one of criticism and logic-chopping. We can plausibly guess from *Piers Plowman* that for Langland it seemed as though the scholastic impulse in its decay was reducing the method of precise intellectual distinction to a frivolous habit of mind, a kind of uncontrollable mental tic that was obscuring the fundamental motives of Christianity as a way of life. The Dreamer of *Piers Plowman* is presented as a kind of amateur scholastic, searching for *Do*well, without realizing that by satisfying a merely intellectual curiosity he will come no nearer to goodness in action.[20] Thus at the beginning of the *Vita* he is seen in disputation with the friars, parodying the very jargon of scholastic philosophy: " '*Contra*,' quath ich as a clerke, and comsede to dispute" (C XI 20). Later in his

---

19 *Education and the University*, p. 88.
20 Cf. John Lawlor, "The Imaginative Unity of Piers Plowman," *Review of English Studies* n.s. VII (1957), 113–26.

quest he is rebuked by Liberum-Arbitrium for a similar wish to distinguish and dispute. Liberum-Arbitrium has explained that he is called by various other names according to his functions—"soul," "mind," "memory," "love," and so on—and the Dreamer has jokingly said that he is like a bishop who is called *presul, pontifex, metropolitanus,* "And other names an hepe, *episcopus* and *pastor*." Liberum-Arbitrium takes up the silly joke with surprising vehemence, and uses it to show what deep roots the wish to know by intellectual distinctions may have, and what grave consequences it may lead to:

> "That is soth," he seide, "now ich seo thy wil,
> How thow woldest know and conne the cause of alle here names,
> And of myne, yf thow myghtest, me thynketh by they speche!"
> "Ye, syre," ich seyde, "by so that no man were agreved,
> Alle the science under sonne and alle sotile craftes
> Ich wolde ich knewe and couthe kyndeliche in myn herte."
> "Thanne art thow inparfyt," quath he, "and on of Prydes knyghtes;
> For suche a luste and lykynge Lucifer fel fro hevene."
>   (C XVII 206–13)

The Dreamer gains his fullest understanding of Do-well by his vision of the Crucifixion and Harrowing of Hell, where he does not interrupt but simply observes this supreme example of goodness in action. Not the *"contra"* of the scholastic but a patient silence is the means to true philosophy; and indeed the Dreamer has already been told this by Ymagynatyf when, by thrusting in with a philosophical question, he has brought one of his visions to a sudden end (C XIV 184–231). It is a paradox perhaps that if the Dreamer were *not* an amateur scholastic, always demanding reasons and picking arguments, the poem would not exist at all. The tension between argument and submission is part of the essential nature of *Piers Plowman;* but the poem's central effort, despite the use it makes incidentally of scholastic methods, is directed against the making of intellectual distinctions and towards the building up of large, theologically undefined ideas which will have the power to stir men's emotions and move them to action. The supreme example of the poem's suggestive indefiniteness is of course the plowman himself, with his different roles as peasant, secular ruler, Christ's human nature, and the ideal

pope, and with his mysterious appearances and disappearances. We have said that such an imaginative construction lies
beyond the reach of any teaching the *ars praedicandi* can
offer. But Langland's purpose is also expressed in the interweaving and fusing of themes in the whole poem, and of
words in its style; and these are techniques which the medieval art of preaching can certainly help us to understand.

Gawain and the Green Knight

LAURA HIBBARD LOOMIS

THE HERO OF *Gawain and the Green Knight (GGK)*[1] is likened to a pearl beside a pea (vs. 2364), and so might the poem itself be reckoned among its contemporaries. It moves over an almost flawless structure as smoothly as supple skin over the bones of the hand. With the exception of Chaucer's *Troilus and Criseyde*, no other Middle English romance approaches its artistic and spiritual maturity, its brilliant realism, its dramatic vigor, its poetic sensitivity to nuances of word and mood, its humor, its nobility of spirit.

This treasure of Middle English poetry exists in only one manuscript (British Museum, Cotton Nero A X), dated by the handwriting of its one scribe and the costumes of its rather crude illustrations about 1400.[2] The romance has 2,530 lines written in stanzas running from twelve to thirty-eight long lines of unrhymed alliterative verse, each stanza concluding with a "bob and wheel" of five short rhyming lines.[3] The author's mastery of alliterative phraseology predicates a close acquaintance with antecedent alliterative poems, but the extent of his indebtedness to earlier English verse or of his own

Reprinted from ARTHURIAN LITERATURE IN THE MIDDLE AGES, ed. R. S. Loomis, by permission of the Clarendon Press, Oxford. (1959).

[1] All references to *GGK*, unless otherwise indicated, are to the edition by Sir I. Gollancz, re-edited by M. Day and M. S. Serjeantson, EETS (1940); bibliography, pp. lxvii–lxxii. Other editions are by J. R. Tolkien and E. V. Gordon (T & G, Oxford, 1925, 1930, 1936); and by E. Pons (Paris, 1946, with French translation). For recent renderings into modern English see T. H. Banks (New York, 1929); K. Hare (London, 1946, 1948); M. R. Ridley (London, 1950, 1955); Gwyn Jones (London, 1952).

[2] A facsimile of the manuscript was published with an introduction by Sir. I. Gollancz, EETS, 1923. For description of manuscript see *GGK*, pp. ix ff., and R. S. and L. H. Loomis, *Arthurian Legends in Medieval Art* (New York, 1938), pp. 138 f., with illustrations of miniatures (figs. 389–91). On scribal matters see Greg in *Library*, xiii (1933), 188–91, and Oakden, ibid. xiv. 353–8.

[3] J. P. Oakden, *Alliterative Poetry in Middle English*, i (Manchester, 1930), pp. 177 f., 218, 251–5, 266. See *GGK*, p. lxviii; T & G, pp. 118–21.

influence on later verse is still largely undetermined.[4] His poetic preeminence, however, his outstanding artistry, have been searchingly studied and praised since 1839 when, in his *Syr Gawayne,* Sir Frederick Madden first published the poem.

The manuscript contains three other poems which, because of close similarities in vocabulary, phrasing, style, and spirit to *GGK,* have led to a general belief in their common authorship.[5] From different interpretations of the exquisite, elegiac-seeming *Pearl,* the homiletic *Patience* and *Purity (Cleanness),* and *GGK,* conjectural biographies and personalities have been built up for the poet, and several identifications have been proposed.[6] None of them, however, has won acceptance, and the identity of the "Master Anonymous" remains a mystery. Was he a monk, a minstrel, a learned clerk, an official in some lordly household, or himself a man of rank and wealth?[7] In any case he wrote as one familiar with courtly life, its pleasures, luxuries, arts, and ways.[8]

[4] Oakden op. cit. ii, *passim.* For relation to Alliterative *Morte Arthure* and *Awntyrs of Arthur* see Chap. 38 above; to *Carl of Carlisle* and *Turk and Gawain* see Chap. 37 above. For theories about relation of *GGK* to *The Green Knight* see G. L. Kittredge, *Study of GGK* (Cambridge, Mass., 1916), pp. 125–35, 282–9; Hulbert in *MP,* xiii (1915–16), 49 ff., 461 f.; O. Löhmann, *Die Sage von GGK, Albertus Univ. geisteswissenschaftliche Reihe,* xvii (1938), 24–36. For relation to *Wars of Alexander* see *GGK,* pp. xiii–xviii; for connection of *GGK,* vss. 2414 ff., with *King Alisaunder* see King in *MLR,* xxix (1934), 435 f. For possible influence of *GGK* on Chaucer's *Squire's Tale* see Chapman in *MLN,* lxviii (1953), 521–4; Whiting in *Medieval Studies,* ix (1947), 230 ff. For the influence of *GGK* on a poem by Humphrey Newton (d. 1536) of Cheshire, see Robbins in *MLN,* lviii (1943), 361–6; *PMLA,* lxv (1950), 249–81; Cutler in *JEGP,* li (1952), 562–70.

[5] *GGK,* pp. x–xiii; *Purity,* ed. R. J. Menner (New Haven, 1920), pp. xix–xxvii; Oakden, op. cit. i. 72–87, 251–3; ii. 88–93; 393 ff.; D. Everett, *Essays on Middle English Literature* (Oxford, 1955), pp. 68–96. The attribution to one author has been questioned for reasons more ingenious than convincing by J. W. Clark in *JEGP,* xlix (1950), 60 ff.; *MLN,* lxv (1950), 232 ff.; *MLQ,* xii (1951), 387 ff.

[6] For proposed identifications see *GGK,* pp. xviii f. For notable perceptive comments on the poet's nature, learning, background see *Pearl,* ed. C. Osgood (Boston, 1906), pp. xlvii–xlix; H. L. Savage, *The Gawain-Poet* (Chapel Hill, 1956), ch. i.

[7] Despite the poet's piety and knowledge of biblical and theological matters, his secularity has been increasingly emphasized. See *Pearl,* ed. Osgood, pp. lii–liv; T & G, p. xx. Oakden, op. cit. i. 257–61, thought him a retainer of John of Gaunt; Savage, op. cit., pp. 206–13, would assign him to the household of John's French brother-in-law, Enguerrand de Coucy, of whose chivalric character and English experiences, 1363–77, Savage (pp. 99–117) thought he detected some reflections in *GGK.* But the content and genesis of the poem seem best accounted for by the literary sources.

[8] For the poet's knowledge of music see Chapman in *PMLA,* xlvi (1931), 177–81; for courtly manners and sports see discussion below.

The realistic references in *GGK* to North Wales, Anglesey, and the wilderness of Wirral in Cheshire (vss. 697–701) are unusual. The scenic descriptions, the extensive use of words of Scandinavian origin, the dialect, all place the author's home in the northwest Midland area.[9] The detailed account of the so-called Green Chapel and the great castle near by have suggested even more precise localizations.[10] The architecture, the costume, the armor, so accurately described, are appropriate to a date between 1360 and 1400, and of the four poems in the manuscript *GGK* is considered the latest.[11] Though no one has succeeded in connecting the green girdle worn as a baldric by the knights of Arthur's household (vss. 2515 ff.) with any historic order of chivalry, Gawain's wearing a costume like that of a knight of the Garter (vss. 1928 ff.) and the insertion of the Garter motto after the close of the poem have tempted some to think that the author wrote under the patronage of a knight of that order, renowned for chivalry and possessed of estates in the northwest Midlands, where the poet was at home.[12]

The romance, according to vss. 31–36, was heard "in toun," but was also known to the author in a book (vs. 690). He proposes to tell it in "letteres loken," that is, in alliterative verse.

Sources and Analogues

The main framework of the plot is known as the Challenge

[9] Southern Lancashire, Cheshire, and Derbyshire have been suggested for the poet's home. For bibliography see *GGK*, p. lxviii, and Menner in *PMLA*, xxxvii (1922), 503–26; Serjeantson in *RES*, iii (1927), 327 f.; Oakden, op. cit. i. 82–87; Savage, op. cit., pp. 128–33.

[10] Tolkien and Gordon (p. 94), following Madden, accepted Volsty Castle and the neighboring Chapel of the Grene, Cumberland. Oakden, op. cit. i. 257 f., proposed John of Gaunt's castle of Clitheroe, Lancs. Mabel Day (*GGK*, p. xx) identified the Green Chapel with a small, rocky "cave projecting from a hillside" at Wetton Mill, Staffs., but confused it with Thor's cave (Thursehouse), a huge cavern in a cliff a mile away, which could not possibly fit the poet's description (vss. 2178–83). The supposition that the Green Chapel was a megalithic barrow (*GGK*, note to vs. 2172) is questioned by Brewer in *Notes and Queries*, cxciii (1948), 194 f.

[11] *GGK*, p. xiii; T & G, pp. xx–xxii; Brett in *MLR*, xxii (1927), 451–8; Savage, op. cit., pp. 8, 141 f., 222.

[12] Connection of the poem with the Order of the Garter was maintained by I. Jackson in *Anglia*, xxxvii (1913), 393–423; Cargill and Schlauch in *PMLA*, xliii (1928), 118–23; and by Savage, op. cit., *passim* (see especially pp. 146 ff. for a list of Garter knights with West Midland holdings). For those opposed to the Garter connection see Menner, *Purity*, pp. xxvii ff.; Hulbert in *MP*, xiii. 710–18; T & G, pp. xx, 117.

or the Beheading Game, and into this has been skilfully fitted a second major element called the Temptation. The earliest version of the Challenge is found in *Bricriu's Feast (BF)*, a composite Irish saga of the eighth century extant in a manuscript antedating 1106.[13] The saga contains, in fact, two variants of the Challenge (*BF*, p. 99) and refers to other book versions. The first, or "Terror," version is shorter and more archaic; the second, the "Champion's Bargain," is more elaborate. In each a shape-shifting enchanter challenges Cuchulainn and two other Ulster heroes, likewise contending for the championship, to exchange with him a decapitating blow. Twice the challenger is decapitated but walks away with his head and returns the next day, his head restored to its place. Cuchulainn alone keeps his part of the bargain, and after receiving one or more pretended blows from the challenger's axe, he is acclaimed the champion. When this legend passed out of Ireland, it lost its most primitive and savage elements, and, somewhat rationalized and simplified, it passed eventually into several Arthurian romances. Of these, *GGK* has preserved by far the largest number of features which go back to some form of the Irish saga.[14]

In a fundamental study Kittredge summarized the Challenge as it appeared in these romances.[15] The earliest extant French version forms part of the so-called *Livre de Caradoc*,[16] included in the First Continuation of Chrétien's *Perceval* . . . Though the hero of the Challenge is Caradoc, not Gawain, it presents the closest correspondence to *GGK*. Both poems transform the court of Ulster into that of Arthur, and refer to his custom of waiting for a marvel to happen;[17] alike they mention the queen's presence and describe the challenger, not, as in the Irish, as a huge and hideous churl (*bachlach*), but as a tall knight who rides into Ar-

---

[13] *Fled Bricrend* or *Feast of Bricriu (BF)*, ed. G. Henderson (London, 1899), with English translation; Kittredge, op. cit., pp. 9–26.

[14] A. Buchanan in *PMLA*, xlvii (1932), 328 f.; R. S. Loomis, *Wales*, pp. 77 f.

[15] Kittredge, op. cit., pp. 26–74. . . . Kittredge's argument that the "Champion's Bargain" was the sole source of the Challenge was refuted by Alice Buchanan, loc. cit., pp. 316–25.

[16] For texts of the Challenge see *Continuations of the Old French Perceval*, ed. W. Roach (Philadelphia, 1949–55), i. 89–97; ii. 209–19; iii. 141–56.

[17] Sixteen romances tell of this custom. Chrétien's *Perceval*, ed. Hilka, p. 668; J. R. Reinhard, *Survival of Geis in Medieval Romance* (Halle, 1933), pp. 182–95. The reference in *Caradoc* may well have been borrowed from a more original part of the *Perceval*. See *Continuations*, ed. Roach, i. 232; ii. 371; iii. 196.

thur's hall. Both offer parallels to the Irish challenger's grim proposal, his taunting the courtiers with their hesitancy, his decapitation, and his departure. Both tell how the challenge is accepted, not by three successive heroes as in the Irish, but by one, who is described as Arthur's nephew and who modestly speaks of himself as the most foolish of knights. Both romances remark that anyone accepting such a challenge would be mad; both speak of the grief of the knights and ladies for the hero; both add to the Irish hero's protest against the challenger's delay in striking a taunt as to his cowardice; both change the interval of a day between the challenger's decapitation and his return to a year. Long before the Irish antecedents of the Challenge had been discovered the likeness between the episode in the *Livre de Caradoc* and *GGK* led to the belief that this French romance was the immediate source of *GGK*.[18] But Kittredge's conclusion that they were independent versions of a lost French story seems justified, for only thus could those Irish features which are found exclusively in one poem or the other be accounted for.

Among the Irish elements to be found in *GGK* but not in *Caradoc*, Kittredge (pp.32–34) and others have noted the following: the challenger's size, his fierce eyes, silence as he enters the hall, his great axe (in *Caradoc* a sword), his high praise of the court, his exit carrying his head, not, as in *Caradoc*, replacing it on his shoulders. To these Irish elements, still preserved in *GGK*, another may well be added. In *GGK* alone the Challenger is named Bercilak (vs. 2445); as the Green Knight he plays the *same role*, is the *same character*, as the Challenger in the "Champion's Bargain." There he is repeatedly called a *bachlach* (churl), a trisyllabic word in Irish.[19] Changed in transmission, its meaning lost, the Irish common noun seems to have survived in the English name and best explains its origin.

Though so much in *GGK* was thus ultimately derived

---

[18] M. C. Thomas, *Gawain and the Green Knight, A Comparison with the French Perceval* (Zurich, 1883), pp. 34–68. See criticism in *R*, xii. 376; J. L. Weston, *Legend of Sir Gawain* (London, 1887), pp. 88 ff.

[19] Hulbert established in *Manly Anniversary Studies* (Chicago, 1923), pp. 12–19, the manuscript reading as Bercilak, and identified the name with that of Bertelak, Bercelai, emissary of the False Guenièvre in the prose *Lancelot*. The reading was accepted by T & G, p. 114, R. S. Loomis in *Celtic Myth and Arthurian Romance* (New York, 1927), found its origin in Irish *bachlach*. Roland Smith in *JEGP*, xlv (1946), 16 ff., questioning this derivation, proposed a hypothetical Irish form *Bresalach*, meaning contentious, and sought to relate the Green Knight to figures outside the Ulster cycle and without any connection with the head-cutting episode.

from the "Champion's Bargain," other elements came from the "Terror" version, also found in *Bricriu's Feast*.[20] In this tale the hero and his two rivals are not tested at the royal court but, journeying into a wild region, stop at a house and receive a guide from their host. They go to Terror, a shape-shifter, who proposes the head-cutting test. Three times, like the Green Knight, he makes a feint with his axe at the hero's neck. The corresponding features in *GGK*, especially the placing of this testing episode away from Arthur's court, establish the influence of the "Terror" version upon the romance.

Besides the *Livre de Caradoc*, only one other French text provides a version of the Challenge which is significant for *GGK*, namely *Perlesvaus* . . . [21] The Challenge is here set not in a palace hall, but in a Waste City, and its hero is Lancelot. Though differing widely in other respects from *GGK*, it offers three noteworthy resemblances: the challenger whets his axe with a whetstone (1. 6674) as the hero approaches to fulfill his bargain; the hero shrinks from the blow; he is sharply rebuked.[22] These parallels, supplemented by resemblances in phrase, again argue for literary borrowing, whether directly by the English poet or through a French intermediary.[23]

Thus we have three closely related Arthurian versions of the Challenge or Beheading Game. Since they do not agree as to the name of the hero, there is no certainty as to whether Caradoc, Lancelot, or Gawain was the first of Arthur's knights to meet a head-cutting challenger. It is remarkable that the challenger in no version antedating *GGK* appears as a green giant, clad in green and riding a green horse.[24] Expla-

---

[20] Kittredge, op. cit., pp. 97–101; D'Arbois de Jubainville, *Cours de Littérature Celtique*, vi (Paris, 1892), pp. 132–5.

[21] *Perlesvaus*, ed. Nitze and others, i. 136–8, 284–6; discussed ii. 281–3.

[22] Kittredge, op. cit., pp. 52–61, noted the weakening in this episode of the supernatural element.

[23] See *GGK*, pp. xxxi ff., for phrasal parallels. Nitze noted (*Perlesvaus*, ii. 3) that the Bodleian manuscript of *Perlesvaus* was once owned by Sir Brian Fitzalan of Bedale, Yorks. Possibly this very manuscript was read by the *GGK* poet.

[24] No extant French text before the prose *Perceval* printed in 1530 (Roach, *Continuations*, i, p. xxxii) supports Kittredge's belief (pp. 32, 140) that the challenger wore green in an early form of the *Livre de Caradoc*. For him, as for Hulbert (*MP*, xiii. 456 ff.), the challenger was green because in folklore green is often a fairy color. R. S. Loomis in *Arthurian Tradition*, p. 279, n. 7, explains the color as due to the ambiguity of the Irish and Welsh adjective *glas*, meaning either grey or green, and points out that Curoi, the Irish prototype of the Green Knight, was repeatedly referred to as "the man in the grey mantle,"

nations for this greenness have been sought in mythology, folk ritual, and folklore,[25] but since the ultimate sources of the Challenge—the two tales incorporated in *Bricriu's Feast* —provide no support in the way of hints of vegetation rites or concepts, and since in *GGK* the Green Knight and his other self, Bercilak, have only mid-winter associations,[26] his greenness there can hardly be due to vegetable traits.

Fitted into the framework of the test by decapitation is another test—the three successive temptations to which Gawain is subjected by the wife of the Green Knight. Though the finesse with which these scenes were developed was the poet's own contribution, yet the situation itself, the aggressive wooing of a reluctant young man in bed by a lovely lady— was already employed by romancers in the twelfth century. It is easily recognizable in the *Lanzelet* of Ulrich von Zatzikhoven,[27] which . . . he translated from the Anglo-Norman shortly after 1194.

Lanzelet and two companions are welcomed at the castle of Galagandreis, a rich forester. Their host's daughter arrays

---

though the word *glas* is not the word chosen. See Buchanan in *PMLA*, xlvii (1932), 327–30. No historic person seems to have been called the Green Knight. But two fourteenth-century Englishmen, Sir Ralph Holmes and Simon Newton, were known as the Green Squire. See Braddy in *MLN*, lxvii (1952), 240 ff.; Highfield in *MedAev*, xxii (1953), 18–23. Highfield studies an important West Midland family of Newtons of the type which might have produced the author of *GGK*. See above, n. 4, for the Cheshire Humphrey Newton (1536) who used *GGK*.

[25] E. K. Chambers in his *Medieval Stage* (Oxford, 1902), i. 117, 185, and Nitze in *MP*, xxxiii (1936), 351–65, derive the Challenge from vegetation ritual or myth. Speirs in *Scrutiny*, xvi (1949), 270–300, urged that a ritual underlying the story and "the poet's belief in its value as myth is what gives the poem its life." This ignores both the power of individual genius and the evidence of the Irish stories of the Challenge, the sources of *GGK*, which are not easily susceptible to interpretation as vegetation ritual. Even more reckless is the statement of Francis Berry in *The Age of Chaucer* (Pelican Book, 1954, p. 158) that the poet's awareness of "the generic forces of life . . . realizes itself in the Green Knight; . . . his reckless vigor and amorality of life . . . testify to an assumption that moral behavior . . . is subservient to and dependent on something more primary—creative energy. Gawain and his society humbly come to terms with the Green Knight."

[26] Loomis, *Arthurian Tradition*, pp. 208 ff., 230 ff., 280 ff., derived certain episodes in Arthurian romance from Irish texts preserving mythic concepts of sun and storm gods. These sometimes survived as dramatic or picturesque features, but it is to be doubted whether the French authors or the *Gawain*-poet who introduced such elements were conscious of their mythical origin and significance.

[27] Ulrich von Zatzikhoven, *Lanzelet*, trans. K. G. T. Webster (New York, 1951), pp. 34–43, and notes 37, 43.

herself sumptuously and at night tempts each of the three knights in turn in the most wanton manner. The story anticipates *GGK* in its emphasis on her elaborate dress and her young beauty, in the way she sits beside each sleeping knight and wakes him, in her offer of a gold ring and its rejection, in her urgent plea to hear talk of love, and in her frank proposals. The outcome of the temptation scenes differs from that in *GGK* since, though Lanzelet's companions repel the lady's advances, Lanzelet himself is easily persuaded. None the less, the lady's behavior and conversation are similar enough to those of Bercilak's wife, though on a much lower level, as to suggest that the two poems were following the same original pattern. The Anglo-Norman source of *Lanzelet* also anticipated *GGK* in making Galagandreis, like Bercilak, a notably human figure; despite warnings of his cruelty, he performs kindly services for his guests, and has almost nothing of the supernatural, gigantic, or imperious qualities of other notable hosts in Arthurian romance.[28] Of special interest is the challenge which he issues to Lanzelet the morning after the temptation scenes—a challenge to throw knives at each other in alternation. It is as truly a *jeu parti* as the beheading by alternation in *GGK* and *Bricriu's Feast*,[29] and provides the earliest instance of the combination of the Challenge theme with that of the Temptation.

The *Lanzelet* version did not include the strange feature which Kittredge (pp. 79 ff.) pointed out in other Arthurian romances as well as in *GGK*, namely, that the temptress was the wife of the host and that she wooed at her husband's wish.[30] One of these, *Yder*, offers a striking parallel, representing the lady of the castle as making violent love, at her husband's order, to the hero as he lies in bed in the hall.[31] In other analogues cited by Kittredge her role is passive; she is constrained by her husband or father to admit the guest to her bed in order to test him. This situation presents, as Mabel Day has remarked, but a shadowy likeness to *GGK*. Equally

---

[28] For these figures, see Kittredge, op. cit., Index, Imperious Host; Loomis, *Arthurian Tradition*, chap. xlvii.

[29] Kittredge, op. cit., pp. 21–23, 219–21, mentioned the combat in *Lanzelet* only as an instance of dueling by alternation and said nothing of the related Temptation.

[30] Kittredge summarized (pp. 83–101) analogues to the Temptation in *Ider, Carl of Carlisle, Chevalier à l'Epée, Hunbaut*.

[31] *Iderroman*, ed. H. Gelzer (Dresden, 1913), vss. 185–510, and p. lv.

remote from it are two repellent Temptation tales in Latin and French versions of the *Vitae Patrum*.[32]

A significant analogue to the Temptation occurs in the Vulgate *Lancelot* and has been proposed as perhaps "the immediate cause for the insertion of Morgain la Fée into the English poem." [33] This enchantress, who in the course of the French narrative thrice attempts to seduce Lancelot in vain,[34] sends her damsel, a younger self as it were, to effect the same end. Three times the girl employs her amorous arts on the recumbent hero. From this episode, with the instigating background figure of Morgain and the foreground figure of the young, active seductress, it is but a step to the two figures in *GGK,* the aged Morgain,[35] prime mover in the plot, and the agent of temptation, Bercilak's young wife. She was, no less than Bercilak, a servitor of the resident goddess who sat highest at their table (vs. 1001), who had already forced him to enact the Green Knight's cruel part, and who, presumably, also forced him to order his wife to tempt their guest (vss. 2446–63). No wonder that the young wife was at heart Gawain's "enmy kene" (vs. 2406). Despite his moral sensitivity, the poet imputes no moral obloquy to the lordly pair who yet were helpless in the power of that malignant goddess. The might of Morgan le Fay (vs. 2446) was, for Gawain himself, a sufficient explanation and exculpation for all that he had endured and made him able to part from the Green Knight on most friendly terms.

The concept of Morgain as an evil enchantress, a witch, had appeared in Hartmann von Aue's *Erek* by 1190; her origin in Celtic mythology and the amazing diversity of her roles in medieval romance have been studied by Lucy Paton

[32] E. von Schaubert, "Der englische Ursprung von *GGK*," *ES,* lxii (1923), 330–446. These tales have been widely but uncritically quoted as true analogues. The author's low estimate of the English poet's skill is almost unique. See *YWES,* iv (1923), 52.

[33] Hulbert in *Manly Anniversary Studies,* p. 18.

[34] H. O. Sommer, *Vulgate Version,* iv. 123–8; v, 91–93, 215–18; *Spec.,* xx (1945), 186.

[35] Kittredge (pp. 131–5) and Hulbert in *MP,* xiii. 454, regarded Morgain as a late and poorly integrated element in *GGK,* mainly because she, though a supernatural person, failed in her purposes and did not foresee her failure. But in medieval romance enchanters and enchantresses often suffer defeat. Baughan in *ELH,* xvii (1950), 241–51, defended Morgain's role by the untenable argument that she had sent the Green Knight to purge Arthur's court of moral evil, and that the Beheading Game was "an apotheosization of chastity." Likewise unrealistic is the conclusion of J. F. Eagan in *The Import of Color Symbolism in GGK* (St. Louis, 1949), p. 83.

and R. S. Loomis.[36] Her wanton traits reappear in many amorous and related Arthurian figures; as we have seen, there are the temptresses in *Lanzelet* and *Yder*, and the splitting of Morgain's personality into two selves in the Vulgate *Lancelot*. The author of *GGK*, apparently familiar with this older dichotomy, has effectively contrasted the goddess, grown old and wrinkled, with the young beauty who is at once Morgain's other self and agent,[37] but who has also a personality of her own.

The earliest example surviving in medieval fiction of a Temptation approximating in curious ways that in *GGK* is to be met in the *mabinogi* of *Pwyll*, attributed to the eleventh century.[38] Arawn, a huntsman and an otherworld king, like the Green Knight himself (vs. 992), arranged that Pwyll should be lavishly entertained in his absence in his palace and lie with his own wife as a test of his chastity and loyalty.[39] At the year's end Pwyll, like Gawain, was required to meet a supernatural enemy at a river-crossing. The differences between *Pwyll* and *GGK* forbid any thought of direct literary connection, but undeniably *Pwyll* offers the oldest example of a traditional story pattern in which carnal temptation, whether passively or actively offered, and a Hospitable Host who constrains wife or daughter to tempt a guest, are recurrent themes. It not only anticipates the conjunction of these and other elements in *GGK* and its analogues, but it at least suggests, as they do not, in its mysterious figure of Arawn and in the Welsh folklore connected with him, a clue to the mid-

[36] L. A. Paton, *Studies in the Fairy Mythology of Arthurian Romance* (Boston, 1903), chap. vii, on the Chapelle Morgain in the Val sans Retour; R. S. Loomis in *Spec*, xx (1945), 183–203; reprinted in *Wales*, pp. 105–30; Loomis, *Arthurian Tradition*, index *sub* Morgain; Hulbert, in *Manly Anniversary Studies*, pp. 16 ff.; T & G, notes on vss. 2452, 2460.

[37] *Sire Gauvain et le Chevalier Vert*, ed. E. Pons (Paris, 1946), p. 74, on Morgain as a foil to Bercilak's wife.

[38] *Mabinogion*, trans. G. and T. Jones, Everyman's Lib., pp. 1–9; for date see p. ix. In *JEGP*, xlii (1943), 170–81, and in *Wales*, chap. vi, R. S. Loomis detected in *Pwyll* four features also combined in *GGK*: the royal huntsman-host; the hero's resistance to the temptation presented by the host's fair wife with the latter's connivance; the anniversary combat; its localization at a river crossing. For other cases of the influence on Arthurian romance of traditions in *Pwyll* see Loomis, *Arthurian Tradition*, index *sub* Pwyll.

[39] These are precisely the virtues tested in *GGK*. In *Pwyll* Arawn's wife, on learning that it was her husband's friend, not her husband, who had slept chastely beside her, said to Arawn, "Strong hold hadst thou on a comrade for warding off fleshly temptation and for keeping faith with thee." Cf. Gawain's fears (vss. 1775 f.) that "he should commit sin [i.e. lechery] and be a traitor to that man."

winter associations of Bercilak and his connection with Morgain la Fée.[40] In *Pwyll* the still half-mythic Arawn hunts with fairy hounds, wears gray wool, and engages in annual combats with Havgan (Summer-White)—an apparent reminiscence of the strife of summer and winter. In Welsh folklore Arawn also identified with that Wild Huntsman who, in Welsh as in European folklore, rode with his dogs on the winter winds. As late as 1276 it was remembered by Adam de la Halle that Morgain la Fée had once had for lover Hellekin, chief of the "chasse furieuse," "le gringneur prinche qui soit en faerie." Before this date, then, the wanton Morgain was associated with a wild huntsman of whom, perhaps, some faint traditional trace remains in the wintry world of Bercilak, in the fury of his three hunts, in the occasional wildness of his manner (vs. 1087). But in any case Bercilak as regal host and mid-winter huntsman, as tester, through his own wife, of a hero, as a shape-shifter, finds an ancient prototype in the Welsh Arawn.

The Challenge and the Temptation, then, originated as entirely distinct stories. Who was responsible for their fusion into one of the best plots in medieval fiction? [41] We have seen that both elements appear combined in *Lanzelet,* and that this form of the Temptation, if read in the Anglo-Norman source of *Lanzelet,* may even have provided some suggestions for the *Gawain*-poet. But in other respects *Lanzelet* differs so widely from the English poem (and from *Bricriu's Feast,* with its early versions of the Challenge) that it cannot be regarded as the model for the combination in *GGK.* It is, therefore, still an open question whether the English author derived the Challenge and the Temptation from separate lost French texts (as well as the *Caradoc* version of the Challenge and the *Perlesvaus* version of the Temptation) and fitted the two stories together; or whether he found this highly artistic combination ready made by some French poet of unusual talent. Even if the latter alternative could be proved correct, one can hardly doubt that the English poet found large scope for his own genius in the adaptation of the plot to his special purposes and ideals.

He may well, indeed, have provided the one plot element which is completely non-Celtic in origin. The mutual promise

---

[40] *JEPG*, xlii. 181–3; Loomis, *Wales*, pp. 81–85.

[41] See A. C. Baugh, *Literary History of England* (New York, 1948), pp. 236–8; G. Kane, *Middle English Literature* (London, 1951), pp. 73–76; *Sire Gauvain*, ed. Pons, p. 15.

of Bercilak and Gawain, to give each other what each has won at the end of each day, motivates a whole series of consequences. The motif of an Exchange of Winnings, as Hulbert demonstrated,[42] appeared in a medieval Latin poem known as the *Miles Gloriosus*. A poor knight becomes the partner of a rich citizen; they agree to exchange their winnings. The citizen's faithless wife becomes the knight's mistress and gives him of her husband's treasure. The husband, suspicious, tries thrice to trap the knight, but is ultimately driven forth from his own home. This fabliau, now thought to have been written about 1175 in the Loire valley,[43] could have contributed nothing but the exchange idea to *GGK*. No other Arthurian narrative makes any use of the motif, and the deftness with which it is integrated into *GGK* bespeaks the English poet's skill in design and his sensitive perception of character. Gawain, facing the deadly head-cutting test, keeps the protective girdle given him by Bercilak's wife. He breaks his promise and presently suffers deep shame and remorse. The poet, aware of weakness even in the noblest, thus saves his hero from a "schematic perfection" and humanizes him by his fault and his pain. This treatment of the Exchange motif can hardly be due to anyone but the Englishman who so deliberately fashioned his whole story to a "fine issue" and a finer end.

Literary Art

The artistry which is revealed in the construction and style of *GGK* is exceptional. Kittredge noted (p. 4) passages which must be considered, because of their individuality, the poet's own. They include the traditional yet original passage on the seasons; the elaborate account of Gawain's arming, so precise and so contemporaneous in detail; the spirited hunting scenes equally exact and expert; the courtly dialogues between Gawain and his temptress, which reveal such delicacy of characterization. This sophisticated familiarity with varied aspects of aristocratic life and thinking prompts the question whether it was due to observation only or came from the inti-

---

[42] *MP*, xiii. 699 f. The text of the *Miles* is published by G. Cohen, *La Comédie Latine en France au XIIe Siècle* (Paris, 1931), i. 181–210.
[43] E. Faral, *Les Arts Poétiques du XIIe Siècle et du XIIIe* (Paris, 1924), pp. 3–6; F. J. Raby, *History of Secular Latin Poetry in the Middle Ages* (Oxford, 1934), ii. 65 ff.

mate awareness of one who had been born to high estate and "gentilesse." [44]

The poem bears witness not only to the author's acquaintance with earlier romances in French and English,[45] but also to his awareness of literary types. He speaks of his creation as a "laye" (vs. 30). The decapitation of the Green Knight is compared to the playing of an interlude (vs. 472), a short dramatic performance introduced between the courses of a banquet.[46] Indeed, *GGK* seems to interfuse the well-knit, romantic matter of the former type with the dramatic manner of the latter. It keeps the unified structure of the Breton lais, and, like them, concerns itself with marvels and an exclusively aristocratic world.[47] But in preserving their pattern, the *Gawain*-poet transformed their fragile charm. Almost alone among poets before 1400, he told of winter with all its harsh rigors, its freezing rain and snows, its howling winds. He conjured up the sense of cold with an intensity hardly matched till Keats wrote the *Eve of St. Agnes*. He laid his scene realistically in the English north country, on heath and crag and in tangled forests of hoar oaks, hazel, and hawthorn. He swept through this wilderness three great hunts that seem transcripts from life. He breathed into courtliness the naturalness of fine, happy people, rejoicing, even joking together. Here, in truth, and at its best, is "merry England," splendid, stalwart, joyous, with its great Christmas and New Year feasts and frolics, inspirited by wine and mirth.

The *Gawain*-poet not only made of his romance a lai but also, in its dramatic effectiveness, something of an interlude, with which, as his own reference shows, he was familiar. Scenes are sharply set; speeches reveal character; gestures and bearing are indicated with lively verisimilitude. The Green Knight, enacting the role of the Challenger, does so with all the gusto of an accomplished mummer. He rolls his red eyes, wags his great beard, boasts and taunts derisively,

[44] G. Mathew, "Ideals of Knighthood in Late-Fourteenth Century England," *Studies in Medieval History Presented to F. M. Powicke* (Oxford, 1948), pp. 354–62, notes similarities between the Chandos Herald's characterization of the Black Prince and that of Gawain in *GGK*.

[45] Hulbert noted in *Manly Anniversary Studies*, pp. 16–19, that with two exceptions all the names in *GGK* occur in the French *Vulgate* romances. See also C. O. Chapman, *Index of Names in Pearl, Purity, Patience, and Sir Gawain* (Ithaca, N.Y., 1951).

[46] L. B. Wright in *MLN*, xl (1926), 96–100, and below, p. 538, n. 3, on interludes at banquets.

[47] Garrett, "The Lay of *GGK*," *JEGP*, xxiv (1925), 125–34.

makes, after his decapitation, a tremendous, noisy exit.[48] Though at first he seems almost gigantic (*half etayn,* vs. 140), actually he towers only by a head or so over other men (vs. 332). Apart from his green hue and separable head, he is represented as a fine, handsome, human figure. Later, at the Green Chapel, when he has finished his final testing of Gawain, he drops on the instant his role of magic horror and becomes again the gallant, benevolent Bercilak, full of warm goodwill. Though no moment in medieval romance surpasses in eerie terror that in which he held up his severed head and its eyes opened on Arthur's stricken court (vs. 446), he is primarily described, not as a supernatural being, but as a man acting a part. The gruesome incident of his decapitation is dismissed by Arthur himself, as no more than a play, the device of an interlude (vs. 472). Like Chaucer in the *Franklin's Tale* (vs. 1140),[49] similarly indulging in a bit of rationalizing over the dramatic illusions of skillful magicians, the *Gawain*-poet was inclined to minimize marvels. He jokes a little about those Gawain encountered on his terrible journey; it would be too "tore" (hard, vs. 719) to tell a tenth of them; anyway the fighting with giants and trolls was not so bad as the winter weather! He derisively pictured Morgain la Fée, though he called her a goddess, only as an ugly, squat, old lady.

As an artist the *Gawain*-poet had the habit of close visual observation and an exceptional sense of form, proportion, and design. As a connoisseur familiar with costly things and courtly taste and custom, he pauses to describe exquisite trifles of embroidery or jewelery, rich fabrics, fine armor. He dwells on the architectural details of the great castle that Gawain first sees shimmering through the distant trees, then in all the glory of its chalk-white, many-towered magnificence. The poet accents social sophistication; manners are polished, talk is an art. The conversations between Gawain and the lady suggest the advances, the retreats, of a courtly dance. Within the set pattern of perfect courtesy, wit meets wit; a gracious comedy of manners is enacted. Temptation is offered to Gawain and refused largely in the tone of light social badinage. One has but to read other society romances [50] in Mid-

---

[48] Elizabeth Wright in *JEGP,* xxxiv (1935), 157–63.

[49] For illustration of an *entremets* presented at the French court in 1378 see L. H. Loomis in *Spec,* xxxiii (1958), 242–55. The illumination accords with Chaucer's description (*Franklin's Tale,* vss. 1140–51) of the arts of "subtile tregetours."

[50] S. F. Barrow, *Medieval Society Romances* (New York, 1924), Appendix. The English *William of Palerne,* though commissioned by

dle English to recognize the difference between them and the greater elegance, the more assured touch, of the *Gawain*-poet. Moreover, in this romance, unlike many others, there is no inchoate rambling, no waste. The episodes move directly from cause to consequence and individual act and character are finely linked. Situations are repeated, but with skillful, deliberate variety and contrast. Court scenes at royal Camelot are different from those at Bercilak's castle; the three temptations of Gawain have subtle differences of tone and temper; the three hunts, whether they have allegorical significance or not, are as different from each other as are the hunted beasts; each hunt implies expert familiar knowledge.[51] The rich indoor revels, whether at Arthur's court or Bercilak's castle, are effectively alternated with cruel winter realities without, and so is the gay fellowship indoors with Gawain's stark loneliness as he goes by desolate crags to seek his death.

The romance has superlative art in its fashioning; it is mature, deliberate, richly seasoned by an author who never suggests minstrel servility or even compliment to those who hear him.[52] He wrote in his own way and apparently for his own delight in a provincial dialect and in the alliterative verse which belonged to that same north country which he pictured with such startling vigor.

But above all else the romance has a quality of spiritual distinction comparable to that in the *Pearl*. Piety, devotion, purity of thought, are natural to it. Gentle meditations occur, on Troy's vanished glory, on the swift passing seasons with all their yesterdays, on the pentangle [53] as symbol of the endless interlocking of the knot of truth. Richly informed about the lovely things of life, the poem is without asceticism or intolerance. It has no mysticism; Gawain is called the Virgin's

---

Humphrey de Bohun, Earl of Hereford, has, in comparison with its French original, a homely tone. L. A. Hibbard, *Medieval Romance in England* (New York, London, 1924), pp. 214–23. Even Chaucer's *Troilus* is less consistently courtly than *GGK*.

[51] Savage in *JEGP*, xxvii (1928), 1–15; Savage, *The Gawain-Poet*, pp. 13, 32–48, 224.

[52] There are references to a listening audience in vss. 30, 624, 1996. For Chaucer's use of such minstrel tags as "I yow telle" and "be stille," see *Sources and Analogues of the Canterbury Tales*, ed. Bryan and Dempster (Chicago, 1941), pp. 496–503. Like Chaucer, the *Gawain*-poet may well have expected his work to be read aloud. Such expressions may echo a minstrel convention, but they do not prove minstrel authorship.

[53] On the pentangle see Hulbert in *MP*, xiii. 721–30; R. S. Loomis in *JEGP*, xlii, 167–9; Savage, *Gawain-Poet*, pp. 158–68; Ackerman in *Anglia*, lxxvi (1958), 254–65.

LAURA HIBBARD LOOMIS

knight (v. 1769), but he sees no vision, goes on no holy quest. Its deep concern is not with evil, but with good. In this Gawain, the blithe young embodiment of chivalry at its best,[54] goodness is made manifest and radiant, but not, as in Galahad of the Grail romances, a supernatural virtue touched by a mysterious divinity. The "fine issue" of his story is not that he fell into vulgar sin, but that he failed to keep goodness perfect. Moral earnestness could hardly go farther.[55] Gawain's confession of his fault in breaking his word to save his life reveals a deep sense of Man's responsibility for his every act, no matter how deadly the betraying circumstance. For the author, as for William of Wykeham, "Manners [in the sense of morals] maketh Man." Integrity knows no compromise. Wholeheartedly Gawain recognizes this rigorous truth and contrition overwhelms him. Unlike other Arthurian heroes, he returns to Arthur's court, not in conventional glory, but in self-confessed shame. Yet, as noted above, that shame gave him new grace, and the Round Table achieved a new nobility by its act of compassionate fellowship. Henceforth all the knights will wear as a baldric the green girdle that was, to Gawain, the mark of his shame.[56] No other medieval poet, save Wolfram von Eschenbach, has so transformed traditional romantic materials by the grace of his own spiritual insight, or given them more enduring significance.

[54] Cf. B. J. Whiting, "Gawain, His Reputation, His Courtesy, and His Appearance in Chaucer's *Squire's Tale*," *Medieval Studies,* ix (1947), 189–254.

[55] Mabel Day in *GGK,* p. xxxv, thought the story "the vehicle of a great moral lesson." Baugh strangely remarked (op. cit., p. 236) that it was "in no sense a story told to enforce a moral."

[56] Kittredge, op. cit., pp. 139 f., rejected the girdle as a feature of Celtic origin, but see R. S. Loomis in *JEGP,* xlii. 149–55.

Pearl

DOROTHY EVERETT

PEARL STANDS MUCH farther apart from other Middle English writings than *Sir Gawain*. Though its form is influenced by the familiar dream convention, and though it is thoroughly medieval in spirit and workmanship, yet as a whole it is unlike any other Middle English poem. In some respects it is nearer to *Lycidas* than to anything else in English, for—without prejudice to the controversial question of whether or not *Pearl* is an elegy—it begins, like *Lycidas,* by lamenting a loss; from this the poet is led on to consider certain spiritual and moral problems, and he finally reaches understanding and acceptance of God's will. Like *Lycidas, Pearl* is cast in a conventional literary form, is built with scrupulous artistry and expressed in highly charged language—language, that is, selected and ordered for particular ends. Though the differences between the two poems are, of course, many and important, they are essentially of the same order.

So far as *Pearl* is concerned, there is much in this statement that needs justification, and it would be well to begin by outlining the poem as impartially as possible. It opens with praise of the pearl which the poet has lost in an "erbere," [1] and he tells how, on going back to the spot, he finds it covered with so many sweet flowering plants that he is overpowered by their fragrance and falls asleep. He passes in spirit into a marvelous country and, on the other side of a river, he perceives a maiden clad in gleaming white garments set with pearls. He recognizes her. "I knew hyr wel, I hade sen hyr ere," [2] "Ho wat [3] me nerre Þen aunte or nece"; [3] and he begins to question her: "What fate has carried away my jewel and plunged me in such grief?" (249–50). The maiden re-

Reprinted from ESSAYS ON MIDDLE ENGLISH LITERATURE by Dorothy Everett (ed. Kean), by permission of the Clarendon Press, Oxford.

[1] "herb garden."

[2] "I knew her well, I had seen her before" (164).

[3] "She was nearer to me than aunt or niece" (233).

bukes him, saying that he has no cause for grief, for, though she was but young when she departed, her Lord the Lamb took her in marriage and crowned her queen.

The dreamer cannot believe this, for surely Mary is the Queen of Heaven. But the maiden explains that in heaven no one dispossesses any other, and all are kings and queens; and then, as he protests that she is too young to be a queen, she relates the parable of the workers in the vineyard to show that the first shall be last, and the last first. The dreamer still protests, for this means that he who works less receives more. The maiden replies that there is no question of more or less in God's kingdom; His grace is enough for all. The sinner who repents finds grace, why not the innocent who never sinned? "When such knock there upon the dwelling, quickly shall the gate be unlatched for them," (727–8). In the kingdom of heaven is endless bliss, the pearl of great price, which the merchant sold all that he had to purchase. In answer to the dreamer's further questions, he is permitted to see the New Jerusalem and, in the streets of it, a procession headed by the Lamb. In the throng that followers Him he sees his "lyttel quene."

Longing to be with her, he is about to start into the stream, but he suddenly awakes, to find himself back in the "erbere." Though full of grief at his banishment from the fair country of his vision, he cries:

> If hit be ueray and soth sermoun,
> Þat þou so strykeʒ in garlande gay,
> So wel is me in þys doel-doungoun,
> Þat þou art to þat Prynseʒ paye [4]

He reflects that, had he been more submissive to God's will, he might have come to know more of His mysteries, and he ends by offering up his vision to God, praying that God may "grant us to be the servants of His household and precious pearls for His pleasure."

This summary is perhaps sufficient to suggest the nature of the appeal made by *Pearl*, but it cannot convey the qualities which make it an outstanding example of poetic art.

In this poem, as in all great poems, form and content are not separable; and both are evident alike in the smallest detail and in the conception and shaping of the whole.

[4] "If it is indeed sober truth that thou movest thus in a gay garland, then I am content, in this prison of grief, that thou art to the Prince's pleasure" (1185–8).

As in *Sir Gawain and the Green Knight,* the matter of *Pearl* is ordered so as to form a pattern. Naturally the means by which this is done here differ from those employed in the narrative poem, and the pattern is all-embracing, as it is not in *Sir Gawain.* Of the twenty equal sections of the poem [5] the first four are mainly devoted to presenting the dreamer's state of mind and to description of the dream-country and of Pearl herself; argument and exposition occupy the central twelve sections, and the last four again contain description, this time of the New Jerusalem, and end with the poet's reflections. This pattern is emphasized by the echoing of the first line of the poem, "Perle, plesaunte to prynces paye," [6] in the last, "Ande precious perleʒ vnto his pay." The metrical scheme, which subdivides the poem into smaller sections and at the same time links all its parts into a continuous sequence, forms a second pattern, subsidiary to the main one but concurrent with it. There are 101 stanzas of twelve four-stressed lines, rhyming a b a b a b a b b c b c. Two or more of the stresses are usually marked by alliteration. The stanzas fall into groups of five, the same refrain being used in the last line of each of the five, and it is thus that the poem is divided into the twenty equal sections, though section XV, exceptionally, contains six stanzas. A key word or phrase in the refrain is always echoed in the first line of the following stanza; this means that the sections are linked to one another, since a significant word is repeated, in the first line of each new section, from the refrain of the preceding one. The echo between the first and last lines of the poem gives the effect of a completed circle, intended perhaps to suggest the idea of the pearl, which in 1. 738 is called "endeleʒ rounde." [7]

The same stanza form, and the linking, are found elsewhere in Middle English, in some lyrics in the Vernon MS, for instance; but nowhere else is there anything like this complex scheme, nor is the stanza handled with such mastery. This poet makes good use of the natural break after the eighth line, and, within the line, he allows himself freedom in the use of alliteration and varies the rhythm and the number of syllables. Thus, within the rigid metrical scheme of the whole, the line, its smallest unit, is flexible. The following stanzas, one descriptive, one argumentative, illustrate some of these characteristics. They also illustrate what appears to be a

[5] Indicated by initial capitals in the manuscript.
[6] "Pearl, a precious thing for the Prince's pleasure."
[7] "endlessly round."

general practice, the greater use of alliteration in description:

> The dubbemente of þo derworth depe
> Wern bonkeȝ bene of beryl bryȝt;
> Swangeande swete þe water con swepe,
> Wyth a rowande rourde raykande aryȝt;
> In þe founce þer stonden stoneȝ stepe,
> As glente purȝ glas þat glowed and glyȝt;
> As stremande sterneȝ, quen stroþe men slepe,
> Staren in welkyn in wynter nyȝt;
> For vche a pobbel in pole þer pyȝt
> Watz emerad, saffer, oþer gemme gente,
> Þat alle þe loȝe lemed of lyȝt,
> So dere watȝ hit adubbement.[8]

> Grace innogh þe mon may haue
> Þat synneȝ penne new, ȝif him repente,
> Bot wyth sorȝ and syt he mot hit craue,
> And byde þe payne þerto is bent.
> Bot resoun of ryȝt, þat con not raue,
> Saueȝ euermore þe innossent;
> Hit is a dom þat neuer God gaue,
> Þat euer þe gyltleȝ schulde be schente.
> Þe gyltyf may contryssyoun hente,
> And be þurȝ mercy to grace þryȝt;
> Bot he to gyle þat neuer glente,
> As innoscente is saf by ryȝte.[9]

The refrains are the most difficult part of this scheme to
manage, but on the whole the poet is amazingly successful

---

[8] "The beauties of those precious deeps [i.e. deep waters] were
pleasant banks of bright beryl; swinging softly, the water swept with a
whispering voice, flowing straight on. In the depth there lay bright
stones that glowed and glittered like lights through glass; shimmering
like stars, which, while men on earth are sleeping, gleam in the heavens
on a winter night. For every pebble set there in the pool was an emer-
ald, sapphire or precious gem so that all the water shimmered with
light, so splendid was its adornment" (109–20).

[9] "Grace enough may that man have who sins afresh, if he will repent; but with sorrow and lamentation he must crave it and endure the
pain that is bound with it. But Reason, Who cannot swerve from justice, evermore saves the innocent. It is a judgment that God never gave
that ever the innocent should be discomfited. The guilty man may cling
to contrition and by mercy be drawn back to grace—but he who never
turned aside to sin, being innocent is saved by right" (661–72, emend-
ing MS *at* to *as*, and MS & to *by* in the last line.)

with them. Often they appear to fit naturally into his train of
thought, but when necessary he will vary them slightly. The
emphasis which certain words receive from so much repetition is rarely misplaced; indeed, most of the reiterated words
and phrases are so essential to the poem as a whole that,
taken in order, they almost form a key to its contents. There
are some sections, certainly, in which the repetition seems
mechanical, and others in which the meaning of the repeated
word or phrase has to be ingeniously stretched to fit every
context in which it is used. Yet the poet can make a poetic
virtue even of this kind of ingenuity, or of something very
closely akin to it. In Section VIII the refrain word "cortasye," is used to mean, not only "courtesy," "courtliness," but
"generosity," "benevolence," and, as critics have pointed out,
it is sometimes almost a synonym for "grace" (divine favor
or condescension). No one of these meanings fits every context in this section, but the poet uses now one, now another,
while keeping all the time some reflection of the basic meanings "courtliness," "courtesy," and its implications. This is
achieved by the use of many words such as "queen," "king,"
"emperor," "empress," "court" which are naturally associated
with "courtliness" and "courtesy." So the lesson of Section
VII—that though Mary is Queen of Heaven, she is also
Queen of Courtesy, and none who comes there is, or feels
himself to be, dispossessed, but each is "king and queen by
courtesy"—is doubly conveyed by clear statement which can
be intellectually apprehended and by all the associations of
the word "courtesy."

Such exploitation of the association of words is a marked
feature of the whole poem and takes many forms, from mere
word-play, dependent on similarity of sound, as in the line
"So is hys mote wythouten moote." [10] to the vividly metaphorical language of the following lines:

> I loked among his meyny schene
> How þay wyth lyf wern laste and lade [11]

or of these:

> For þoȝþou daunce as any do,
> Braundysch and bray þy brapeȝ breme,

[10] "So is His dwelling without spot" (948).

[11] "I gazed among His radiant following [and saw] how they were
loaded and weighed down with life" (1145–6).

When þou no fyrre may, to ne fro,
Þou moste abyde þat he schal deme.[12]

Some words already have poetic or literary associations
which are of value to the context in which they are used. So,
"douth," having dignified associations from its use in old heroic poetry, but having lost the precise significance of the Old
English "duӡuþ," [13] is at once impressive and mysterious
enough to be used of the hosts of hell, earth, and heaven that
gaze upon the Lamb (839–40). In writing of his longing for
the Pearl the poet evokes, by the word "lufdaungere," [14] mem-
ories of the separation of lovers, and of the love-longing so
often described by poets of the *Roman de la Rose* tradition.
Especially in descriptive passages, his phrasing is full of
echoes; and it is here that they have most value, for in all his
descriptions the poet is attempting to present something tran-
scending ordinary human experience. In the description of
the maiden, he calls to his aid conceptions of feminine beauty
by using terms from the romances, and throughout the opening descriptions there are reminiscences, verbal and otherwise, of the Garden of Love in the *Roman de la Rose*. The
flowers on the spot where Pearl was lost are, like those in the
Garden of Love, fragrant spices known for their healing properties; and the trees, the birds, the river of the country of
the poet's vision could not fail to remind his readers of that
beautiful garden. Yet the details—the "flaumbande hweӡ" [15]
of the birds, the tree-trunks "blwe as ble of ynde,"[16] the em-
eralds, sapphires, and other gems that lie at the bottom of the
stream—are peculiar to this description and less realistic than
those in the *Roman*; for this land is more remote from normal experience than the Garden of Love and surpasses it in
beauty. At one point the poet compares the banks of the river
to "fyldor fyn," [17] normally associated with jewelry or, in simile, with golden hair, and the effect of this fantastic comparison is to convey the splendor of the banks and at the
same time their unreality. To the modern mind, however, the

---

[12] "For, though you skip about like any doe, rush to and fro, and
bray out your fierce wrath, when you can go no further, forwards or
backwards, you must put up with what He decrees" (345–8).

[13] "a band of noble retainers."

[14] "separation in love" (11). "Danger," in the *Roman de la Rose,*
comes between the lover and the beloved.

[15] "flaming colors."

[16] "blue as indigo."

[17] "fine gold thread."

associations with nature evoked by some of the poet's similes
are probably more effective—the comparison, for instance, of
the precious stones glinting through the water to stars that
shine on a winter night,[18] or of the sudden appearance of the
procession of Virgins to the rising of the moon:

> Ryȝt as þe maynful mone con rys
> Er þenne þe day-glem dryue al doun,
> So sodanly on a wonder wyse
> I watȝ war of a prosessyoun.[19]

More than any secular book it is the Bible that fills the
poet's mind and imagination. When he describes his distress,
"My herte watȝ al wyth mysse remorde, As wallande water
gotȝ out of well," [20] he is recalling the Psalmist's "Sicut aqua
effusus sum"; at the words of the Lamb, "Cum hyder to me,
my lemman swete, For mote ne spot is non in þe" (763–4),
the maiden is invested with the associations of the Song of
Songs ("et macula non est in te. Veni de Libano sponsa
mea ..."). In the central portion of the poem the poet
makes constant appeal to the authority of the Bible, buttress-
ing his argument by passages drawn from it. The ease with
which he passes from one part of it to another is an indication both of his familiarity with it and of the alert independence of his mind. In Section XIV and the beginning of XV,
where the maiden is replying to the dreamer's question "Quat
kyn þyng may be þat Lambe?, [21] her answer is a tissue or
reminiscences of Isaiah liii, of the Gospels, of the Book of
Revelation and of other passages, all coordinated into a coherent and moving statement.

However closely dependent on the Bible the poet may be,
he always follows his own line of thought. The parable of the
workers in the vineyard, which is a close paraphrase of Matthew xx. 1–16, is interpreted in a way that is relevant to the
argument and, so far as is known, unique; and, in the description of the New Jerusalem, the poet makes his own
choice of details from the Book of Revelation and presents
them in his own order.

With the parable of the pearl of great price (Matthew xiii.

18 See n. 8.

19 "Even as the mighty moon rises before the gleam of day has quite
descended thence, so suddenly, in a miraculous way, I was aware of a
procession" (1093–6).

20 "My heart was all stricken with grief [so that I was] like rushing
water pouring from a stream" (364–5).

21 "What kind of thing may that Lamb be?"

45–46), from which the symbolism of the poem largely derives, it is not the Bible alone that the poet has in mind, but
in addition various interpretations of it. The parable is alluded to and partly paraphrased in ll. 729–32, just after the
reference to Jesus calling the little children to Him, and the
implication would seem to be that the precious pearl (the
"spotless pearl" in the words of the poem) means innocence.
But at the same time it means the kingdom of heaven, the
reward of innocence, for ll. 729 ff. state explicitly that the
pearl which the merchant sought is "the joy that cannot
cease" which is found in the kingdom of heaven, and in the
next stanza (lxii) the maiden shows in what respects the
pearl resembles that kingdom. She finally identifies it with the
pearl she wears upon her breast which, she says, her Lord the
Lamb placed there in token of peace. Of the many interpretations of the pearl of great price which might have been familiar to the poet. Gregory's statement that "margarita vero mystice significat . . . dulcitudinem coelestis vitae," or that of
Petrus Chrysologus that the pearl is "vita aeterna," may lie
behind his thought here; and there may even be a hint at the
interpretation, used in Usk's *Testament of Love*, that the
pearl of great price means grace. The poet shifts to yet another interpretation in the first line of stanza lxiii, when the
maiden herself is addressed as the "spotless pearl." Here he is
probably thinking of St. Bonaventura's "Bonae margaritae
sunt omnes sancti." It is evident that in this passage the poet
is playing upon various ideas connected with the pearl of
great price in much the same way as he plays upon the meanings of the word "cortasye," and he sums up the complex
symbolism of the passage in the lines which the dreamer addresses to the maiden:

> "O maskeleʒ Perle in perleʒ pure,
> Þat bereʒ", quod I, "Þe perle of prys . . ." [22]

It is likely that, to a medieval lover of poetry, many of the
passages that have been quoted in the preceding pages would
have conveyed a rather different impression from that which
they make on a modern critic. While not less alive to their
effects, he would at the same time have recognized them as
examples of the rhetorical "figures" and colors which Chaucer's Host begs the Clerk to keep till he composes in the
"high style"; and he would have noticed many others, for

[22] " 'Oh spotless Pearl, in pure pearls, that wears', said I, 'the pearl
of price' " (745–6).

rhetorical devices of all kinds abound in the poem. In *Pearl* as in *Sir Gawain and the Green Knight,* the whole method of composition, including the planning of the poem, is determined by the precepts of the rhetoricians. But, again as in *Sir Gawain*, it is not rhetorical doctrine but the poet's artistic sense that is the ultimate court of appeal. In some of his descriptive passages, where he needs to create an impression of gorgeous beauty, he writes in the "high style" enriching his expression by every means he knows; but when he wishes, he can write simply, with few devices, comparatively little alliteration, and few words that were not in common use. The paraphrase of the parable of the workers in the vineyard is for the most part in this simple style, and a comparison of this passage with the description of the dream-country makes it possible to answer the criticism that the poet's vocabulary is "faulty in too great copiousness." It is obvious that there is "copiousness" where it is in place, but not everywhere.

Another objection might perhaps more legitimately be brought against *Pearl*. It might be argued that a work so meticulously wrought must be lacking in vital force, that such close attention to form and expression cannot be compatible with the creation of poetry that is "the breath and finer spirit of all knowledge." To this the only answer is a personal one. To many readers, the present writer among them, the human emotion manifested in the poem appears to be its driving force and its motive. Whether the poet is describing his grief, or wrestling in argument, or realizing the joy of those who follow the Lamb, there is an urgency and a passionate sincerity in his writing which forbids one to regard it as a mere exercise in the poetic art. This has been widely felt, even though there has been no general agreement about the nature of the poet's loss or the meaning of his poem.

These are problems still in dispute, and possibly incapable of final solution, since it will not do to argue that, because the poet makes us feel a sense of loss, Pearl must represent a real child and cannot be the allegorical representation of some virtue or, as has even been suggested, of the poet's own soul in a state of perfection. For men have grieved for such losses as much as for the loss of a child. Yet, on the whole, it seems most satisfactory to assume that the poem was inspired by the death of a loved child, not necessarily a daughter or a sister, for the line "Ho[23] watʒ me nerre[24] þen aunte or nece"

23 "She."
24 "nearer."

need not imply blood relationship. The poet's grief is intensified by his uncertainty about her fate, for she died too young to please God by works or even to pray (484). In the vision that is granted him, he is convinced, both by argument and by the sight of his "lyttel quene" in the New Jerusalem, that she is saved and that she is among those who follow the Lamb; and with this reassurance he is able to resign himself to God's will.

R. Wellek has shown that the child's fate could have presented a real problem at the time when *Pearl* was written.[25] Though belief in the salvation of the baptized child through free grace was widely held from the time of Augustine, yet the matter was still under discussion in the fourteenth century. The reaffirmation by Thomas Bradwardine (d. 1340), in *De Causa Dei contra Pelagium,* of the doctrine of salvation by grace, against those who held the Pelagian heresy of salvation by merit, points to an interest in fourteenth-century England in matters fundamentally connected with this. Hence the poet's anxiety to know what had happened to the child, and his concern with the nature of grace, are understandable. Clearly the maiden's answer, that the innocent who have been baptized (626–7) are saved. "For Þe grace of God is gret innoghe," [26] is not, as one critic has suggested, unorthodox; and it would appear that R. Wellek was right in maintaining that there is nothing unorthodox, either, in the high position in heaven which is assigned to the child. The intellectual and spiritual struggle presented in the poem is not waged against orthodox beliefs; rather, it is a struggle to accept the teaching of the Church by one who wishes to do so, but is beset by doubts.

The battle, must, of course, have been won before the poem was written, since it is the poet who, in the person of Pearl, provides the answers to his own difficulties. But it is not the least of his powers as a poet that he conveys the agony of the struggle as if it were still to win. There is a close parallel to the *Divina Commedia* here. Small as the scale of *Pearl* is compared with Dante's poem, the method is essentially the same. In both, the process of enlightenment is presented by means of a dialogue between a mortal seeking it and a celestial being, once a loved mortal, who now pos-

25 "*The Pearl:* an interpretation of the Middle English Poem," *Studies in English by Members of the English Seminar at the Charles University,* iv (Prague, 1933).
26 "enough."

sesses knowledge, by virtue of her position in heaven. In both, the poet has, as it were, split himself into two, so that he can present at once his ignorance and uncertainty and his knowledge and confidence; and since his serene confidence, and even his power to understand, was not achieved unaided, but was the result of divine revelation both direct and through the teaching of the Church, the person of the instructor is rightly represented as insusceptible of human emotion, remote and incomprehensible, while the person of the instructed remains human and prone to emotion, and for that reason able to arouse emotion. Though the dialogue form is often used in medieval literature to convey instruction, the similarity here is unusually close; and it is between something so fundamental to each poem that it affords far better grounds for thinking that the poet of *Pearl* knew the *Divina Commedia* than some of the lesser parallels that have been cited.

If this be the right way of looking at the poem, there is little point in the old argument as to whether *Pearl* is an elegy or an allegory. Though it has, of course, elegiac and allegorical elements in it, it is not to be comprehended by either term, and it could with as much justice be called a homily, a debate (*disputatio*), or a vision of the other world. None of these labels, by itself, is any more illuminating than the bare terms "elegy" or "pastoral" would be, if applied to *Lycidas*.

This brings us back to the starting-point and by now it should have become clearer in what respects *Lycidas* and *Pearl* are alike and in what they differ. Perhaps the most surprising thing is the marked similarity of their conclusions. The vision of the Catholic poet of *Pearl* ends where the Protestant Milton's does.:

For Lycidas your sorrow is not dead,
. . . but mounted high
Through the dear might of him that walked the waves . . .
And hears the unexpressive nuptial Song,
In the blest Kingdoms meek of joy and love,
There entertain him all the Saints above,
In solemn troops and sweet Societies.

Courtesy and the Gawain-Poet

D. S. BREWER

ALL VIABLE SOCIETIES necessarily practice some forms of
self-control and mutual help among their members, some
forms of decency and gracefulness in daily social intercourse.
This necessity in part took the form, in medieval European
feudal society, of courtesy. Courtesy, the virtue of courts, as
such, is a medieval European invention, like universities and
nation-states and other notable institutions. "Courtesy" came
to be a characteristic of much medieval literature. Modern
literature has seriously attacked concepts like courtesy, and
the generalizing words which denote them, and modern life,
has tended to follow literature. The favorable connotations
quite recently given to the word "aggressive" suggest our different set of values. So the first justification of the present
subject is historical and analytical. Here is a concept which
was once very important in literature, and of which many
traces still survive in our general culture. It deserves investigation.

We soon find a bewildering variety of interpretations of the
word, though not, alas, that full and general history the word
and concept deserve. It is clear that "courtesy" really contains
a whole family of meanings, each related to others, but, as
with other families, in some cases not necessarily in harmony
with each other. It is first necessary to see what are the specific structures of meaning attributed to the word in individual instances. In English, apart from Spenser, the word has
been most significantly used by the great poet—or poets—who
wrote the group of late fourteenth-century poems in British
Museum Manuscript Cotton Nero A X. . . . One of these
poems, *Sir Gawain and the Green Knight,* is now widely
known as one of the great achievements of English literature.
Pearl, another of the group, is in the opinion of those who
know it as great as *Sir Gawain*. The two others, *Patience* and
Cleanness, still almost unknown, are very delightful and interesting poems. So that an account, even if inadequate, of

Reprinted from PATTERNS OF LOVE AND COURTESY, ed. J. Lawlor,
by permission of Edward Arnold (Publishers) Ltd., and the author.

courtesy in these poems, however objectionable or antiquated
the concept may seem, is justified on grounds of cultural history and analysis. But I should be deceiving the reader if I
did not also confess that I find courtesy as a quality in itself
attractive and desirable. I do not mean I hanker after medieval ways of life and thought. The present, besides being all
we have, is much to be preferred. Nor do I think we can take
over meanings from the past without both conscious and unconscious translation. But the actual quality and content of
thought and feeling in these poems, of which courtesy is an
important part, seem to me to be of high value in themselves,
so far as we can understand them, and to be worth preserving
because they enhance the pleasure and value of life now. It
goes without saying that "what the poems say" is the product
of a verbal art of a most sophisticated kind which deserves
elaborate commentary.[1] But my chief aim in this essay is to
explore part of the pattern that the poet's art has created,
rather than to make an analytical technical criticism of the
poetic processes.

Perhaps I may be forgiven by those who know all these
poems well if a few words of explanation come first. It is a
paradox that four of the most splendid poems in English
should exist in a single rather scruffy manuscript with some
poor-quality illustrations. So slender are the physical threads
which bind the literary culture of the past to us. It is still not
proved that all four poems are by one author, though most of
those who have worked on them think they are.[2] I do not
propose to rehearse the arguments, which are detailed and
technical, and to which reference can be found in the editions. *Gawain* and *Pearl* have been edited several times, *Patience* twice, and *Cleanness* thrice, one of which editions entitled it *Purity*.[3] The title *Purity* was chosen because the meta-

[1] *Sir Gawain* has received some: see M. Borroff's *Sir Gawain and
the Green Knight: a stylistic and metrical study* (New Haven, 1962).
Mr. J. A. Burrow's *A Reading of Sir Gawain and the Green Knight* is
announced but not available at the time of writing.

[2] Professor Morton Bloomfield, in an important article surveying *Gawain* studies, *PMLA* LXXVI (1961), reminds us that the question is
still not settled.

[3] The following editions are used in this essay: *Sir Gawain and the
Green Knight*, ed. Gollancz, Day and Serjeantson, Early English Text
Society 210 (1940); *Pearl*, ed. E. V. Gordon (Oxford, 1953); *Patience*,
ed. I. Gollancz (London, 1913) and H. Bateson (Manchester, 2nd. ed.,
1918); *Cleanness*, ed. I. Gollancz, 2 vols. (Oxford, 1921 and 1933);
Purity, ed. R. J. Menner, Yale Studies in English LXI (New Haven,
Conn., 1920). *Pearl, Cleanness, Patience* were edited together; R. Mor-
ris, *Early English Alliterative Poems*, E.E.T.S., O.S. 1, 1864.

phorical implications seemed clearer (and, of course, all these titles are editorial). But the poet takes "cleanness" in its simplest most physical sense as the basis of his metaphor, and uses the word as often in the poem in this as in the metaphorical sense. The word "purity" has to my feeling an air of urban refinement and delicacy alien to the aristocratic courtesy of the poet, who is plain-spoken in these matters, so that *Cleanness* is the title I prefer.

For convenience I assume that the same poet, whom I refer to as the *Gawain*-poet, wrote all four poems. They were certainly all written about the same time and place. They group themselves together in various similarities not only of phrase and reference but in quality of mind. Although they are part of the same alliterative tradition as *Winner and Waster* and *The Parlement of the Three Ages* and numerous other poems, they are clearly by a different author. Only *St. Erkenwald* [4] is now sometimes attributed to him in addition to the main four, but it is not a poem in which courtesy as a word or a concept is significant, and I express no opinion about its authorship. It would not damage my arguments if it could be proved that more than one author wrote the Cotton Nero A X poems, but it does seem easier to suppose only one. Since he was a great poet, his poems differ from each other and he did not materially repeat himself. It is natural to suppose the simpler poems are the earlier. The simplest and shortest, the most bookish, with least apparent experience of the courtly life, is *Patience*. It is strongly personal in its conclusions, as if the poet were exhorting himself to keep his courage up. *Cleanness* is longer, a little more complex, still with a certain tension as of a personal inner problem to solve. *Pearl* is, at least ostensibly, highly personal, in that the poet, as most but not all critics think, represents himself as a father mourning his dead daughter. It has a complexity and a certain detachment of treatment which make it very moving, and which can only be the product of a mature mind and art. *Sir Gawain* is the least personal and the most complex, and has the widest general appeal. It may or may not have been written after *Pearl,* but it will be convenient to consider it last.

How does the poet portray courtesy in these poems? We should consider his actual usages before imposing our own ideas of what courtesy was upon him.

[4] Ed. H. L. Savage, *Yale Studies in English* LXXII (New Haven, Conn., 1926).

Patience, after sixty lines of prelude on the need for patience, which take in the Beatitudes on the way, paraphrases the story of Jonah, as a rather surprising *exemplum.* The point is that God was patient both with Jonah and the city of Nineveh, and the poet takes the lesson to himself, to encourage himself to be patient in bearing poverty, and to do the will of God; that is, to act in accordance with reality, with "how things are." *Courtesy* as a word at first sight comes in oddly here. Jonah, pitched on to the shore of Nineveh with great reluctance by God's agency, via the whale's noisome belly, has to preach God's wrath. He is so successful that the people repent and God forgives them. Jonah is furious. God has let him down. So yet again he remonstrates with the Lord. "Well knew I thy courtesy," he says bitterly—I knew well you were soft, and *that's* why I didn't want to come. The words that go with "courtesy" are interesting here; they are part synonyms, part members of the associative field of the word.

> Wel knew I þi cortaysye, þy quoynt soffraunce,
> Þy bounté of debonerté & þy bene grace,
> Þy longe abydyng with lur, þy late vengaunce;
> & ay þy mercy is mete, be mysse neuer so huge.

> 417–20

"Wise sufferance," "kindly grace," "long endurance with loss," "delayed retribution," are all, of course, aspects of patience, conceived in rather theological terms as attributes of a long-suffering God of mercy. "Wisdom" is also important. On the other hand, "Bounty of debonerté," words frequently applied to God in the fourteenth century, have also more courtly associations. Ladies are asked for "bounty," and have "debonerté" attributed to them; and both ladies and God are frequently asked for "mercy." "Cortaysye" in this passage actually refer to the biblical Latin *clemens,* which the contemporary Wycliffite version translates *meke and merciful.* Thus *cortaysye* is a word describing a relationship between persons, here God and mankind. The relationship is not between equals; it is from high to low. Yet it is marked by warmth which may be greater than the merit of him who receives it, even though it must be earned. In one sense, courtesy is undiscriminating, since it is not exclusive to one person. It is not, in fact, to be equated with romantic love, settled upon one object, though it is close to love. As applied to God in these few lines it is very much like Grace. Yet it is conceived in terms of secular relationship. A reinforcement of these characteristics of the word is found in the parallel words of the king of Nineveh who repented, though for obvious reasons he is not so irritated with God as Jonah is: "Who can know if the sound of our repentance may please the Being," he says,

> Þat is hende in þe hyȝt of his gentryse?
>
> 397–8

—"who is *hende* in the height of his nobility?" *Hende* is a curious word,[5] but here, from the context and on empirical grounds, one can see its equivalence to "courteous." The king continues,

> I wot his myȝt is so much, þaȝ he be mysse-payed,
> Þat in his mylde amesyng he mercy may fynde.
>
> 399–400

God has nobility, power, mild gentleness, mercy—he has power to hurt, yet will do none—this is what it is, for the poet, to be *hende*. The word is the English equivalent of the French-derived "courteous." In this poem the poet seems to use the English word *hende* for the more concrete adjective, and the French word *cortaysye* for the more abstract noun —a situation that is still in general not unfamiliar. But the associations of power, nobility, graciousness, of both *hende* and "courteous," are the same. And in each case the poem makes the general meaning of the words "drift" towards the concept of patience.

In *Cleanness* the idea of courtesy is used more consciously by the poet to give force to the special concept of the poem. *Cleanness* is much longer than *Patience* and consists of a series of stories, told at very varying length. The poem illustrates that associative principle of literary and linguistic construction which is so important in both language and literature, and which has been almost totally neglected by modern critical theory and criticism.[6] The stories illustrate various aspects of cleanness, or rather, of uncleanness and its destruction in the Flood, Sodom, and the death of Belshazzar. The poet in his preliminaries presents God very clearly as a king

---

[5] See note on *Hende*.

[6] As a principle of language, see R. Jakobson, "Two Aspects of Language" in R. Jakobson and M. Halle, *Fundamentals of Language*, The Hague, 1956. The only critic who has used the principle in literary studies appears to be A. M. F. Gunn, *The Mirror of Love* (Texas, 1951).

in his court, and in so doing strikes, perhaps for the first time, the major image that underlies all his poetry—the court. The court may be good, like Arthur's in *Sir Gawain*, or the instrument of evil, like Belshazzar's: it may be the image of secular society, or of the Kingdom (significant word) of Heaven. It is always hierarchical, festival, splendid:

> (God) is so clene in his courte, þe kyng þat al weldeȝ
> & honeste in his hous-holde, & hagherlych serued
> With angeleȝ enourled in alle þat is clene,
> Boþe wyth-inne & wyth-outen, in wedeȝ ful bryȝt.
>
> 17–20

Again, in the parable of the Wedding Feast, which the poet proceeds to relate with zest, and where the lord is, of course, a figure for God, the lord is seen as a king or great baron who gives a courtly banquet complete with roast swan and crane in the most liberal fourteenth-century style. Those who are brought to his court from the highways and byways are placed according to their degree by the marshal in hall, and served with meat and noble minstrelsy. The "great lord" of the feast comes out like a cheerful fourteenth-century baron to welcome his guests "and bid them be merry." When he finds the thrall who has not put on his "festival frock," but is wearing clothes stained with work—which must be the mucky toil of the farmyard—he changes his mood terrifyingly, like a fiercely jovial sergeant-major who finds an improperly dressed soldier. The lord calls his tormentors, the man is put in stocks, and set deep in a dungeon. One recalls those dark dungeons, full of the castle sewage, which even now, as they may be seen open and dry by twentieth-century tourists, strike chill on a summer's day, and shadow the mind with the knowledge of suffering. This is the dark underside of glory and praise. The possibility of Heaven creates the possibility of Hell. God in this poem is felt very much as a noble, just, warm-hearted, but therefore also passionate and indeed hot-tempered, feudal lord.

The poet, however, does not use the court as a simple image of the good life, natural or supernatural. He is better grounded in the particularity and actuality of experience than that, as is shown in the description of Belshazzar's court. The court shines with idealized splendor, but it is the court of a tyrant and blasphemer. The associations of festival splendor, reverence, proper hierarchy, are still there, but described with a touch of sarcasm. The feast is held so that dukes and "other dear lords" should come to acknowledge their allegiance and pay reverence, and to revel, and also to look on Belshazzar's concubines, his "lemmans," and "call them ladies" (1365–72). (Lemman, like "wenches" (1423), is almost always a contemptuous word with this poet, as with Chaucer.) The feast is prepared "gluttons to serve" (1505) and there are around many a "boaster on bench," who bib till they are as drunk as the devil (1499–1500). Belshazzar himself gets drunk. Yet the misuse of riches and power is not necessarily a condemnation of them. There is nothing in the poet's description to suggest any condemnation of courtly splendor as such: in itself it is a good, and the poet's natural image of good in this life and the next.

Of course, we today cannot so easily take the medieval feudal court as a type of earthly good life and heavenly splendor, with God as king. It implies many elements of medieval Christian belief that no one can now take to be true. But we are well used to disentangling, say, the literary greatness of Yeats and D. H. Lawrence from much of what they thought true, but which now seems nonsense or an abominable proto-Fascism. We have a well-known doctrine of the symbolic image, and we need find no difficulty in accepting as a singularly potent and valuable image of God, or at least of certain aspects of "reality," the personal splendor and power of the medival king or magnate and his court. "All these," as the poet says, "are signs and tokens," though he goes on, as we cannot, "to believe in yet."

The court in itself, as an image of splendor and power, the greatest that the poet knows, if it were no more, would be only the place of "courtesy." In addition, the court demands a standard of behavior which is central to the poet's concept. That is, although the social grouping, represented by the court, with its external standards and all its ties and obligations between persons, is important, it must be related to inward, subjective, standards. Thus, while, in *Cleanness,* the poet associates the court with simple and literal external cleanliness (a secular and courtly virtue which the poor could not afford and which monks repudiated), he thinks equally of metaphorical cleanness, which is an internal value, and which is indeed superior. Early in the poem he speaks of priests, who ought to be "clean"; immediately he builds multifold significances into his imagery of courtesy:

> Bot if þay conterfete crafte, & cortaysye wont,
> As be honest vtwyth, & in-with alle fylþeȝ,

Þen ar þay synful hemself, sulpe(n) altogeder
Boþe God and his gere, & hym to greme cachen.

                13–16

Courtesy, that is, implies lack of "inward filth"; it is "courteous" for inner values to correspond to outer. In courtesy
external cleanliness signifies inner purity, good manners are a
sign of moral goodness, appearance *is* reality. No hypocrite
can be courteous. (This contrasts with complaints in courtly
poetry, and repeated in Chaucer, of the flattery and lies
found in courts.) The poet's high view of courtesy is rein-
forced by the imposing list of sins that can cause one to "miss
the Creator's court" (177 ff.). But the special sin is "uncleanness," generally conceived, in that it includes Belshazzar's
sacrilege, but seen at its most gross in sexual perversion. The
virtue of cleanness is in this poem made synonymous with
"courtesy." When Christ is born he is known by his cleanness
to be king of nature (1087), which again establishes the
royal power of the concept.

There are yet further associations, only lightly touched on.
There is an association of courtesy with moderation, or "mesure," always implicit perhaps, but explicit where God "knit a
covenant courteously with mankind," in "the mesure of his
mode"—the moderation of his mind (564–5). Moderation
also appears in the courtesy of Lot, when he tries to persuade
the Sodomites who are besieging his gates to go away:

Þenne he meled to þo men mesurable wordeȝ
For harlotes wyth his hendelayk he hoped to chast

                859–60

—he hoped his courtesy would correct them by his moderate
words.

This, like other passages, shows how essential to the relationships demanded by courtesy is *speech*. Courteous words
give comely comfort (512); "hende" speech of the courteous
one heals those who call on him (1098); not all speech is
courteous, but one of the chief ways that courtesy is made
known is with speech. The combination of social sensibility
with inner virtue, on the secular plane, which is one major
characteristic of courtesy, comes out especially clearly here.
And it is associated with education. Courtesy is product of
"nobleye of nurture," though this is not completely disso-
ciated from *nature*. Christ is known by his cleanness as king
of nature, as already mentioned. "And if cleanly he then
came" (referring to his sinless conception) says the poet,

"full courteous thereafter": he hated evil and filth "by no bleye of nurture" (1085–92). Gawain is later to be described as "fine fader of nurture" (*Sir Gawain* 919). Medieval courtly life highly valued eloquent speech. The knight in Chaucer's *Squire's Tale* addresses the king "as art of speech" had taught him. Heroines, like Chaucer's in *The Book of the Duchess* (919 ff.), were both soft of speech and supremely eloquent. The highest value was set on friendly, intelligent, lively, modest speech; courtly culture was a notably oral culture, though it had a manuscript base. All the same, speech is not the only, though it may be the chief, witness of manners. Gollancz notes a curious point of courteous manners attributed to Christ in the poem, though it is not peculiar to the author. In the fourteenth century it was considered impolite to *break* bread, which should only be cut: how should the "king of nature," with his "nobleye of nurture," break bread with his fingers? The answer is that when Christ broke bread it was divided more neatly than could have been done "by all the blades of Toulouse" (1105–8).[7] Nothing illustrates more clearly the assimilation of biblical manners to those of the medieval court.

The "nobility of nurture" retains its Christian quality in the emphasis in this poem on the willingness of Christ in his cleanness to be approached by and to heal the filthy. The poet typically thinks especially of the physically filthy, repulsive lepers, as well as all other sufferers of physical ills, who "alle called on pat cortayse," at whose touch all filth fled, for

So (h)en(d)e watȝ his hondelyng, vche ordure hit schonied.
1101

The movement of courtesy is here from high to low; the internal quality of cleanness is shown in social action.

The cluster, or family, of meanings and relationships within the general concept of courtesy receives further additions and complications in *Pearl*, and the whole poem defines the extent of courtesy. It is difficult to speak temperately of the rich beauty of *Pearl* in thought, feeling and expression—its deep tenderness and pathos, its progressive transformation of pathos into acceptance and resolution, its intellectual force and metrical art. It is little known because of the difficulty of its language, and perhaps because its deepest appeal is to fathers of small daughters, who do not, as a rule, form a large class

[7] *Cf. Early English Meals and Manners,* ed. F. J. Furnivall, Early English Text Society, O.S. 32, 1868.

among the undergraduates on whom, in the last resort, dissemination of this kind of literary culture rests. Perhaps social change will change that, too. But it would be a gross error to think that literature depends for its effect on the audience having had direct experience of what is described. Words themselves can generate experience, or all our studies are vain. Furthermore, the patterns of events, thoughts and feelings conveyed in words, that constitute a work of art, can reflect, or suggest, other patterns, of which the writer may himself have been quite unaware. This consideration is important for *Pearl* because of the arguments about its "real" meaning. The question essentially has been whether the "real" meaning is centered in the ostensible subject, the primary pattern, of a father who is instructed and consoled in a vision by the glorified spirit of his dead daughter; or whether the "real" meaning is centered in some other pattern, that is, in some symbolic meaning represented by but quite different from the ostensible subject. A great work of art is open to many interpretations. But *courtesy,* so important in the poem, is part of the ostensible, primary subject, and I leave arguments about general interpretation aside.[8]

After the poet has told how, in his misery, he fell asleep, we are transported to a land of shining splendor where we meet the girl in gleaming white at the foot of the crystal cliff with its "royal" rays. Such description establishes a setting for courtesy; as soon as the poet sees the girl, his eyes eagerly "question her fair face" (169 ff.), and a "gladdening glory" glides into him, such as he has been little accustomed to. The vision "stings his heart"; he is abashed and stands "as hende as hawke in halle" (184). There is a special poignancy in this. A loving father might well, in those days of authority, expect his daughter to be obedient, quiet, a little in awe of *him.* A grown man naturally governs a little child, and courtesy tends to flow from superior to inferior. But here, though only partially (and the more poetically) sensed for the moment, a reversal of the flow of courtesy takes place. *Hende* can quite well be used of God, as in *Cleanness;* but here in familiar alliterative phrase, commonplace, casual, expressing the tied-down docility of the well-trained bird of prey, it conveys the complementary aspect of *courtesy,* modesty, restraint, quietness, self-negation, receptivity. The situation, with the father in awe before the child, is tenderly ironic. The

---

[8] Some of them are summarized in the edition by E. V. Gordon.

poem proceeds to create more fully the vision of the touch-
ingly slight figure, regally dressed, her golden hair and long
fashionable hanging sleeves, all gloriously adorned with
pearls. She is splendidly crowned, a courtly heroine in a setting of unearthly brilliance. She is the pearl of great price that
was "nearer to him than aunt or niece," whose finding again
brings great joy. They speak, and the dialogue modulates
with great delicacy between his joyous, loving, half-reproach-
ful words (a version of that strange mixture of feelings any
parent will know, arising, in the recovery of a child, from
anxiety and relief) and her unexpectedly reproachful, sober,
though loving, response—a masterpiece of unusual narrative
dialogue. It is she who instructs him, and indeed speaks
sharply to him for his incomprehension. The dialogue is in
itself wonderfully courteous; and yet again an ironic complexity is unfolded when she accuses him of discourtesy. He
is

> much to blame and vncortayse
>
> 303

because he believes "our Lord would make a lie," when our
Lord promised he would raise us after death. The concept of
courtesy here is centered on words, and discourtesy is the
failure to believe a promise; but its special significance is internal, on the failure to regulate properly the mind and heart,
lack of self-control. The father is not, in fact, being "as
hende as hawke in halle." He acknowledges this in apologiz-
ing most courteously:

> Þaȝ cortaysly ȝe carp con
> I am bot mol and manereȝ mysse.
>
> 381–2

He uses the polite second person plural to the child to whom
normally he would use the familiar, casual singular form (as
he does sometimes later). *She* can speak courteously, he admits; *he* is as dust, he lacks manners. It is worth noticing that
she can speak pretty sharply and yet courteously because she
is in a superior position. Her courtesy is not lowliness now
that she is a spirit enskied and sainted. As soon as he excuses
himself in his misery she is warm and forgiving:

> For now þy speche is to me dere.
> Maysterful mod and hyȝe pryde
> I hete þe, arn heterly hated here.
>
> 400–2

An alternation between superiority and inferiority is established when he shows a proper humility, which, in his position, is an essential element in courtesy.

The interplay between the necessary inequalities of courteous relationships now becomes the motif of the section of the poem that follows, but this interplay is also associated with the demand that courtesy makes for a proper regard for others, and hence for a proper equality before God. This paradox of equality within inequality that courtesy requires is again developed in a marvelous piece of narrative dialogue. The Pearl says she has been crowned queen, in blissful marriage with the Lamb. But how, says the poet? He represents himself as then, at that point, having been naively, almost comically, confused.[9] Very apologetically he says, What about Mary, unique as the Phoenix, whom we call "Queen of cortaysye" (421–32)? *Cortaysye* then becomes the link-word of the next group of linked stanzas and the concept is part of their subject matter. There are no supplanters in heaven, and Mary is empress of heaven and earth and hell, for "she is Queen of Courtesy" (440–4). The mutual support the words "Queen" and "Courtesy" give each other, each raising the other's power, is in the context clear enough. Yet it is very difficult to give a precise meaning to the phrase "of cortaysye." As often with this poet, the aura of association does the necessary work, without any precisely defined center of meaning. Perhaps *cortaysye* may be taken here to imply all the network of relationships in heaven, the mutual love and respect that all individuals bear for each other; but since Mary is supreme, her courtesy is particularly the raining down of grace upon others. God's court has this special quality, the Pearl continues, that all there are kings or queens, all are equal, none is envious, none deprives others by his own merit; and yet Mary has the empire over all. The

_____

[9] It would be easy here to make what is now the familiar dichotomy between the simple narrator inside the poem and the subtle poet who is writing the poem but quite outside it, as Henry James in his late novels is outside the internal narrator of his novel. It is a distinction familiar in Chaucer criticism that has helped to clarify much. But the pleasure and poetry here, as actually in Chaucer, comes from the *real* unity of the "internal" narrator and "external" poet. A man recounting his past actions identifies himself, at least partially, with his past self (because of the continuity), yet dissociates himself from his past self, who is a character acting *then* whereas he is speaking *now*. Good raconteurs, again, usually tell stories as if they were personal experience. The achievement of such duality in unity is a rich effect that all the major fourteenth-century European poets were fond of; Machaut, Deschamps, Froissart, Dante, Petrarch, Langland, Gower, Chaucer, certainly practice it.

paradoxical dual relationships between persons, equality and
hierarchy, apparently illogical, yet conveying a profound
truth about human relationships on earth, not to speak of
heaven, is now further illustrated from St. Paul:

> "Of courtaysye, as saytȝ Saynt Poule,
> Al arn we membreȝ of Jesu Kryst:
> As heued and arme and legg and naule
> Temen to hys body ful trwe and tryste,
> Ryȝt so is vch a Krysten sawle
> A longande lym to þe Mayster of myste.
> Þenne loke what hate oþer any gawle
> Is tached oþer tyȝed þy lymmeȝ bytwyste.
> Þy heued hat nauþer greme ne gryste,
> On arme oþer fynger þaȝ þou ber byȝe.
> So fare we alle wyth luf and lyste
> To kyng and quene by cortaysye."
>
>   457–68

This draws on the familiar teaching in I Corinthians xii, that
we are all members one of another, that each person has his
necessary place, just as the various parts of the body have
their necessary parts to play in the whole man. Once again, it
is difficult to give a precise meaning to "of courtaysye." It
looks as if the poet is quoting St. Paul, and Gordon indeed
says that *courtaysye* here means theological *grace*. But there
is, in fact, no word in the biblical text that corresponds with
courtaysye, and Paul is discussing in this passage not divine
grace but unity in diversity, which might indeed be an aspect
of courtesy. The poet agrees there may well be courtesy and
great charity (a reminiscence of the famous following chapter,
xiii, in I Corinthians) among the heavenly host; but he goes on
to distinguish, it seems, another aspect of courtesy, the generosity or beneficence of God in making everyone king or queen
in heaven. This fairness is unfair; it is too generous, since it
rewards equally those who have not suffered on earth, and
those who have suffered much to win heaven. There follows
in reply the parable of the laborers in the vineyard, justifying
the equality of reward. One may perhaps detect here an underlying disregard for the asceticism which men were accustomed to practice, punishing their bodies to attain a heavenly
reward, a disregard natural to the poet who celebrates marriage in *Cleanness* and the courtly life in *Gawain*. But essentially the retelling of the parable is an exploration of relationships between individuals in a group. The regulation of such

relationships is supremely for this poet in this poem the content and function of courtesy. Included in this, courtesy means courteous speech (by which relationships are expressed and regulated): courtly manners, which are the other expression of proper relationships, and which are, of course, in any case largely a matter of speech: and that internal virtue (here in its aspect of faith; in *Cleanness*, of purity; in *Patience*, of patience) which is the central *bien ordonnance* of the spirit, the virtue which the poet above all cherishes. Of this complex, the secular fourteenth-century court provides the physical image, but, as we have seen, there has so far been little or nothing to suggest that, for the poet, courtesy has anything to do with the service of ladies and what is usually, though misleadingly, called "courtly love."

Yet the relationships between men and women, if not of that all-usurping importance sometimes attributed to them now, are obviously of special piquancy, interest, pleasure, and difficulty, since their human variety is built upon the simplest and one of the most powerful biological drives. Much of the traditional literature of courtesy has been concerned with the relationships between men and women . . .

When the poet of *Patience, Cleanness, Pearl,* or his twin brother, took up the subject of the testing of Gawain, he brought to the very front of his mind that image of the secular court which in the other poems is only occasionally evoked, or which remains in the background as a conditioning factor. In the fourteenth-century court there were many ladies, and the poet has been shown to be no ascetic. He had a Spenserian love of virtue, and a Spenserian susceptibility to beauty. Like Spenser, and in accordance with the general trend of courtly literature of his day, he had an idealizing cast of mind, modified by that "heightened realism" which Miss Everett has shown to be an important characteristic of medieval romance.[10]

Courtly life, when treated by such a mind, becomes an elaborate embodiment of courtesy itself. Courtesy becomes both the general element of the poem, seen in the characters' every action, and also, paradoxically, a less generally moralized, more specific part of the courtly life.

The two courts of *Sir Gawain and the Green Knight*, Arthur's and Bercilak's, are each represented as the height of courtesy. The words denoting courtesy, *courteous, hende,* and

[10] D. Everett, *Essays on Middle English Literature* (Oxford, 1955).

their natural associates, *gentle, noble, good, comely, apel*, chime throughout the poem. *Hende* (used of Mary queen of heaven, of Gawain, of the lady, of Arthur) and *cortays*, are especially frequent. Every action within these courts is *courteous*, except only for the Green Knight's uncouth lack of manners when he first enters Arthur's hall. In particular, the way in which Gawain is received at Bercilak's castle on Christmas Eve, with the salutations, and the extremely polite attention paid to his needs, is almost a summary of the romance-ideal of the courteous life, very reminiscent of passages from the Grail-romance *Perlesvaus*.[11] The poet's constant association of court with festival is even a heightening of the normal medieval literary presentation. The whole way of life, again, is thought of as the elaborate product of education, and Gawain, as already mentioned, is "the fyne fader of nurture" (919)—the very origin of this way of life. Courtesy has, as usual, the aura of virtue. The Virgin Mary is "hende" (647), the noble Jesus and St. Julian have "courteously" shown Gawain the way to the castle (775), Gawain "hendely" takes off his helmet to pray (773)—just as he does to thank the Green Knight, incidentally (2408); his "hendelayk" goes coupled with his "honour" according to the lady (1228). In particular, Gawain's courtesy is associated with his virtue in the symbolic device of the pentangle in his shield. The five virtues attributed to him, separate yet inextricably connected like the points of the pentangle, are *franchise*, fellowship, cleanness, courtesy, pity (652–5). Really, all these virtues might be said to be subsumed, in one way or another, under courtesy, as that concept has been built up through the other poems. All five are the socially oriented virtues of a close-knit society, economically assured, where some degree of internalization has developed the normal social need for self-control. The pentangle shows that the meanings of the words are not distinct. We are not to attribute the same kind of precision of meaning to part-oral poetry as we are to the poetry of print. Gawain's five moral virtues are doubtless not analytically set down, and they all mingle with each other.

Nevertheless, within the general *bien ordonnance* suggested by courtesy there does seem to be a more specific area of meaning attributed to courtesy in this poem. That meaning

[11] For a valuable summary of the courtly ideal of behavior in French literature, which has many resemblances to *Sir Gawain*, see H. Dupin, *La Courtoisie au Moyen Âge* (Picard, Paris, 1931).

has to do with good manners, and as with *Pearl* the high
point of good manners is found in courteous speech. Very
early in the action, when Gawain asks to take over the adventure of the Beheading from Arthur, we see Gawain's good
manners brilliantly made clear in perhaps the most courteous
and elaborate speech in the whole poem.[12] Gawain's whole
manner is a vindication of the court where, as the Green
Knight has sneered, "courtesy is known" (263). Gawain's
speech expresses his own self-control and "mesure," his defer-
ence to Arthur and the Queen and the ways of the court, his
boldness and defiance towards the "aghlich mayster," all at
once—a living expression of courtesy.

Gawain's supreme courtesy, and its special expression in
speech, is further emphasized when he arrives at the castle.
Everyone is delighted to know that it is Gawain himself who
is come—the knight who possesses all excellence, prowess, refined manners, who is honored above all others:

916 "Now shal we semlych se sleʒteʒ of þeweʒ
    & þe teccheles termes of talkyng noble;
    Wich spede is in speche, vnspurd may we lerne,
    Syn we haf fonged þat fyne fader of nurture;
    God hatʒ geuen vs his grace godly forsoþe,
    Þat such a gest as Gawan graunteʒ vs to haue,
    When burneʒ blyþe of his burþe schal sitte
      & synge.
    In menyng of manereʒ mere
    Þis burne now schal vs bryng,
    I hope þat may hym here
    Schal lerne of luf-talkyng."

The emphasis here is clearly upon speech. When Gawain finishes dinner he goes to chapel, meets the lord, and his beautiful wife and the ugly old lady with her, in a mutual display
of exquisite manners, proceeds with them to take spices and
play Christmas party games, and so to bed. The following
day, being Christmas Day, the birth of our Lord was joyfully
celebrated with meat and mirth and much joy at a rich and
dainty banquet where the lord of the castle sat by the old
lady and Gawain with the young. Gawain and she took great
comfort of each other's company:

    Þurʒ her dere dalyaunce of her derne wordeʒ
    With clene cortays carp, closed fro fylþe,

[12] Admirably analyzed by A. C. Spearing, *Criticism and Medieval
Poetry* (London, 1964), p. 40.

> [Þat] hor play watȝ passande vche prynce gomen
>   in vayres.
>
>   1012–15

The spotless terms of noble talk, the profit of speech, the significance of pleasant manners, are the general aspects of courtesy: they are specifically shown in "love-talking," the "dear dalliance of private words, with clean courteous conversation, excluding filth."

The deliberate emphasis on "love-talking" is unmistakable. It is equally clear that the concept of courtesy here is narrowed from what it was in *Patience, Cleanness* and *Pearl*, and even from the earlier part of the poem, where it comes close to being identified with the whole chivalric way of life. Yet this narrowing is not an inconsistency. It is characteristic of the poet to emphasize some special element in the general structure of the word's meaning in each of the poems. Nothing in this "love-talking," as both the teller and the tale assure us, was contrary to virtue. It was not the prelude to seduction on Gawain's part, and not indecent, but *very* delightful and *very* polite, and presumably about love, the favorite topic of medieval courtly conversation.

The specific, realistic, social context no doubt to some extent causes the poet to emphasize Gawain's courtly speech. It is that aspect of courtesy which is peculiarly appropriate to that situation, to a knight's social relationship to a lady. There is also a deeper reason. The plot itself depends on the nature of courtly speech. The plot is now to show how Gawain's virtue of courtesy is to be used against him. This is a more subtle parallel to the similar use made of Gawain's virtue of bravery by the lady's husband. The original challenge is an unfair trick, since the Green Knight can manage without his head rather more easily than a mortal man. By the challenge the Green Knight attempts to destroy Gawain, not to mention Guenever, through Gawain's own bravery. Were Gawain not brave he would not have been endangered by the Green Knight's challenge. Similarly, were Gawain not courteous he would not have been endangered by the lady's attempt at seduction. In neither case does it seem justified to think that the poet disapproves of Gawain's virtue.[13]

---

[13] A *modern* view might well be different. It would be perfectly possible from a modern point of view to maintain that, for example, Sir Philip Sidney met his death through criminal folly, and that as a general he ought to have been ashamed of himself for wantonly risking his

When Bercilak has gone hunting and the lady attempts to seduce Gawain the main weapon she employs is words. This is partly the mere effect of the medium, yet not only. The lady is beautiful, sits on his bed, leans over him to pin the bedclothes down on each side. This might have been vividly and concretely described: imagine what a modern novelist would have made of it. In fact, it is only indirectly revealed by the dialogue. A more pictorial description would have placed the story at the level of bedroom farce—in medieval terms, of fabliau—and would have made Gawain look ridiculous.

Gawain is in exactly the same dilemma that another brave "knight" of chastity, Britomart, found herself in. She, like Gawain, came to a luxurious castle where she was most courteously welcomed, Castle Joyous. It was full of comely glee, though all the inhabitants were "swimming deep in sensuall desyres." The lady of the castle, taking the armed Britomart for a handsome knight, fell in love with her and very soon

> she told her briefe
> That, but if she [Britomart] did lend her short reliefe
> And do her comfort, she mote algates dye.
>
> (III.i.53)

Britomart, like Gawain,

> For thy she would not in discourteise wise,
> Scorne the faire offer of good will profest;
> For great rebuke it is, loue to despise,
> Or rudely sdeigne a gentle harts request;
> But with faire countenaunce, as beseemed best,
> Her entertaynd; nath'lesse she inly deemd
> Her loue too light, to wooe a wandring guest.
>
> (III.i.55)

The very similar situation that Spenser portrays with explicit comment, and the very similar temper of Spenser to the *Gawain*-poet, are useful in helping us to see Gawain's situation and in confirming our sense of his dilemma. Puritan as Spenser is, he loves courtesy, and is not particularly shocked by, though he disapproves of, the lady's behavior. Similarly, Gawain does not approve of the lady, but he is bound to be courteous towards her.

---

life. Thus, when the Green Knight turned up in his bullying way at Arthur's feast, if no one had taken any notice of him (!), his plan would have been foiled without all the trouble that was caused.

The lady's first assault is told with great relish for the comedy of Gawain's pretence of sleep, the lady's beauty, the innuendo of her words, and finally her bluntness (1178–1240). That Gawain was ashamed for her (1189), however, is a clear enough indication of what we should think about the situation, even if our own good sense and morality do not tell us. Gawain is "the good man" (1179), but the lady flatters him to the top of his bent, particularly emphasizing his courtesy and that many ladies love him. At the end of her speech she quite bluntly offers him her body,

$$\text{ȝe are welcum to my cors.} \quad 1237$$

It is always embarrassing to refuse a frank offer made with flattery. But Gawain must not be embarrassed or offensive, for that would be discourteous. Gawain cherishes his courtesy, and when a little later the lady hints he is less than courteous he responds quickly, "afraid he had failed in form of his manners" (1295). At the same time, Gawain must not be complaisant, for that, as the story later shows, would be fatal. His reply steers beautifully between discourtesy and what the poet would probably have called, had he cared to specify, "uncleanness."

There are two levels of narration present in this seduction scene. One is that of surface realism. On this level, the lady is a wanton wife who follows, on the whole, normal social convention, but who wishes to evade it in one material particular. She makes pious reference to God (1256) and accepts the social conventions of courtesy that emphasize its verbal quality—the supreme joy of Gawain's company being "to dally with dearly (his) dainty words" (1253). She also accepts as the norm, while trying to evade, the usual conventions of morality. Thus Gawain through his superior courtesy and ingenuity is able to pretend that she is just being very courteous herself; he praises her noble frankness! (1264) Gawain's verbal courtesy here is also the outward and visible sign of his inward invisible integrity, that prevents him betraying his host and also betraying himself. As such this narrative passage might come from a witty, sophisticated, and unusually decent Restoration comedy. The various motives and sanctions are those we might still recognize in ordinary social life.

There is another level, determined by the story structure. The general premise behind the story is the obligation to fulfill a bond, even to a demon. The demon, the Green Knight, wishes to destroy the hero, so he tricks him into a bargain, the Beheading Game. The hero does not know that the demon has a magical attribute: he can survive unimpaired when his head is cut off, as the hero cannot. But the hero, unknown to himself, also has a magical attribute. While he remains chaste the Green Knight cannot harm him. In consequence, the demon gets his wife to try to seduce the hero. In so far as she succeeds in getting him, for any reason, to accept a gift, a sign of love, the hero loses his invulnerability. (If he had accepted the gift of her body he would have become completely vulnerable.) As he accepted only a trivial gift, he received only a nick in the neck. Such is the logic of the story—whether put together by the *Gawain*-poet or not, does not matter. Such a story, like all the best stories, does not depend on realistic logic, psychological motivation, nor development of character (in the sense of personality). It uses role, not *personality* (young man, young woman, enemy, friend, etc.). By its bold non-realistic fantasy it presents human situations, truths, fears and desires, with a vividness and profundity which no realism, no purely abstract formulation, can attain of themselves. The story of Oedipus, in terms of myth, and the life of Christ, in historical actuality (and no doubt mythic formulation), are obvious examples. The story of Gawain at a less exalted level shows in its fantasies that if you keep your nerve you will probably survive. It says that promiscuous sexual intercourse (or perhaps just sex) leaves a man weak and defenseless. Far from associating sex with life it shows the ancient association (repeated daily in our newspapers) between sex and death. Life and all that makes it worthwhile, the story says, depends on the control of sexual desire. Such was the wisdom of our ancestors.

To put such a mythic story into even partly realistic terms almost always leads to minor inconsistencies, as Chaucer in *The Clerk's Tale* and Milton in *Paradise Lost* illustrate. There is always the possibility of a gap, as it were, between the logic of realism and the structure of fantasy, often leading to irrelevant questions, particularly psychological ones. The local realism of speech and behavior in the seduction scenes of *Sir Gawain* may thus lead us to question the motivation of Bercilak and his lady—are they really evil; what was their real aim? There is no answer. The situation, the individual in relation to another, or to a group, controls the effects, and there is a fruitful, often ironic, tension between the "surface" of the story and its underlying structure. The courtesy of Gawain is part of this poet's version of the goodness of the hero. The bridge between the profound but unrealistic fantasy of the story and the social high comedy of the surface realism is created by the common situation, the testing of Gawain. On the social level, the test is one of morals: on the story level, one of survival.

It is also clear that the poet's main interest is in the social and moral level, rather than in the story structure. One may well wonder whether, though he responded to a story whose moral implications were obviously sympathetic to him, he very clearly understood the structure. Surely, Bercilak ought to be more sinister, under his joviality?[14] The poet finds it hard to present evil at any extent, especially in a courtly environment, as *Cleanness* shows. Nevertheless, the underlying story gives a tension to the relationship between Gawain and the lady which it would lack—as Restoration comedy lacks tension—if the mythic structure were absent. And the mythic structure accounts for such a social breakdown as the lady's blunt offer of her body, which is so much at variance with the courteous tone of the rest of her speech.

At last, when the lady goes, she gets a kiss from him, by wondering if he is Gawain indeed, as he has not yet asked for a kiss. As already mentioned, he fears he has been discourteous. She says

> "So god as Gawayn gaynly is halden,
> & cortaysye is closed so clene in hym-seluen.
> Couth not ly3tly haf lenged so long wyth a lady,
> Bot he had craued a cosse bi his courtaysye,
> Bi sum towch of summe tryfle at sum tale3 ende."
>
> 1297–1302

Gawain most courteously says he will kiss at her commandment. What is noticeable here is that the appeal is made to Gawain's regard for his own ideal of behavior: the kiss itself becomes paradoxically impersonal, as later kisses are that have to be begged. When the lady leaves him she has been

[14] J. Speirs, in *Scrutiny*, 1949, repr. in *English Medieval Poetry: the non-Chaucerian Tradition*, 1957, interprets Bercilak as a fundamentally friendly, favorable person, which accords with the tone of presentation, but seems to deny the story structure. In a valuable article, "Magic, Fate and Providence in Medieval Narrative and *Sir Gawain and the Green Knight*," *Review of English Studies*, NS XVI (1965), T. McAlindon illuminates the tradition of jovial demons.

defeated by the very courtesy she has invoked, by Gawain's humility conveyed by delightfully ingenious politeness.

On her next visit, after being made to ask for a kiss (which thus loses any amatory significance from Gawain, and which Gawain can thus easily give up at the Exchange of Winnings with Bercilak), the lady speaks of love again. Of all chivalry, she says, the chief thing that is praised is the "loyal game of love" (presumably a transposed epithet—the game of loyal love), which is "the learning of arms"; knowledge about love is the sort of knowledge good knights have (1512–13). She goes on to give a brief summary of the romances of adventure, how knights have endured hard experiences for their love. But from him that is so courteous she has heard nothing about love. He ought to teach "a young thing," who is so anxious to learn! Or is he ignorant? Or does he think her too dull? Once again, however, she is defeated by her very appeal to his courtesy. His courtesy must compliment her. *She* knows far more than he about love—which is presumably true as well as complimentary. She has to accept the compliment like the fashionable lady she appears to be, and Gawain escapes again.

Perhaps the most interesting general consideration here is the lady's attempt to identify courtesy with love, and Gawain's successful refusal. In a sense the lady is endeavoring to fasten on Gawain the promiscuous sexuality of the Gawain of the late French romances (see note on the Character of Gawain, below). Gawain here, and in the later scene, where he says he has no beloved (1790–1), repudiates the French character. His courtesy is essentially that of the Gawain of the earliest stories.

On her third visit Gawain has had a bad night, anticipating fearfully the fate that apparently awaits him at the Beheading. The lady is much more pictorially described, for the more serious occasion and the resistance made to the previous temptations now allow the poet to increase the tension. She is beautifully but seductively dressed, with very low-cut gown. Gawain is more tempted sexually than ever before. She pressed him so hard, says the poet, that his usual dilemma was even sharper: he must either accept her love or rudely (*lodly*) refuse (1772). Yet the poet does not seem to make an absolute distinction even here between courtesy and chastity. True, he goes on

He cared for his cortaysye, lest craþayn he were,

& more for his meschef, ȝif he schulde make synne
& be traytor to þat tolke þat þat telde aȝt.

1773–5

This certainly suggests a division between courtesy and chastity, and no doubt courtesy is thought of here for a moment in narrow terms of social politeness. But sharp distinctions are not characteristic of this poet's style, and it is not clear either whether the "synne" of adultery is thought of separately, or whether it is merged into the consideration of loyalty to his host. As the narrative and dialogue continues, all three considerations, courtesy, chastity and loyalty, are all equally valued and preserved, as Gawain, "with love-laughing" puts aside all the lady's "speeches of specialty," and tells her he loves no one, and intends to love no one. This she accepts. The point is of some importance because this passage so far has defined Gawain's courtesy in terms of pleasant conversation with ladies, but has again specifically excluded from it any concept of *fine amour*. As the action has proceeded the lady herself, compelled by the demands of the plot, has become discourteous. It has been pointed out that the normal love-conventions, where the knight takes the initiative, have been reversed.[15] But such a reversal is not an attack on, or a rejection of, courtesy. Gawain's courtesy has remained unimpaired, for the humility that is part of it has allowed him to refuse to take the initiative himself, and the lady apparently accepts defeat in calling him "hende of hyȝe honours" (1813). When, as if by afterthought and with much trouble, she eventually persuades him to accept the "magic" girdle, it is clear that he takes it in the hope of saving his own life, though she pretends it is a "love-gift," and the poet actually calls it a "love lace" (1874). Even here, the real failing is not in accepting the girdle, but in failing to give it up according to his bargain with his host. In this respect he failed a little in loyalty, as the Green Knight later says (2366), though this is involved with his relationship with the lady, because he obviously would never have accepted the girdle if he had intended to surrender it later. Since he acted so to save his own life he can reasonably, from his own high standards, describe his failure to hand over the girdle as "cowardice and covetousness," "treachery and untruth" (2379–83). But nowhere does he accuse himself, or the poet accuse him, of discourtesy.

15 See J. F. Kiteley, *Anglia* 79 (1963).

After Gawain has loyally and bravely fulfilled his year-old promise to meet the Green Knight, has withstood the three strokes and the nick in his flesh that pays for the trivial fault in accepting the girdle, the long explanation that follows takes place on the moral, social and realistic plane rather than on the mythic, and some questions, such as those about Bercilak's motivation and true status, are answered rapidly but not clearly. What *is* clear is that Gawain the brave, the good, the courteous, remains an exemplary figure. By all human standards his bravery is unimpaired; so are his chastity and loyalty, which in various ways are aspects of his bravery. So is his courtesy, inextricably connected, as in the pentangle, with his other virtues, but with a special quality of its own. He has maintained the somewhat paradoxical ideal of all medieval knights, as expressed in the lament for Launcelot in Malory, in Chaucer's description of the Knight in the *General Prologue*, in the alliterative *Morte Arthure*, and which indeed goes back to *Beowulf:* the perfect knight is a lion on the field of battle, and a lamb in the hall. Gawain's performance in this poem is an unusually rich and subtle enactment of this familiar and noble ideal.

Yet it has been maintained by several critics that Gawain, and through him, the poet, rejects courtesy at the end of the poem. When the Green Knight explains he knew all the time about his wife's foisting of the girdle upon him, Gawain is shown with a fine dramatic realism condemning himself heartily for his slip. The very tones of exasperated mortification ring in his speech of self-reproach. He is furious with himself. He politely takes off his helmet and thanks the Green Knight—with what restrained bitterness—and commends himself to "that cortays," the lady, and the old lady, too, "mine honored ladies that have thus cleverly tricked their knight" (2412–13). The undertone is bitter: the manner is irreproachably courteous. This might almost be Gawain's last test. He is exemplary still, even if we may permit ourselves a sympathetic smile at him. Then he goes on to say, "but it is not surprising that a fool (i.e. himself) should go mad, and be brought to sorrow by the wiles of women, for Adam, and Solomon, and Samson and David, were all tricked" (2414–19). It is these six lines that have been taken to show the rejection of the whole courtly system based on devotion to women, and to show that Christianity in this poem is conceived of as an essentially ascetic life-denying system. Yet the immediately preceding half-dozen lines in the

same stanza, when he sends his respects to the ladies, have
been as courteous as anything, almost *more* courteous than
anything, Gawain has ever uttered. The half-dozen lines of
traditional anti-feminism would be a feeble denial of the
whole elaborate and virtuous system of courtesy as evolved in
the poem. In truth, they are dramatic and not without a touch
of comedy as wrung from the knight of courtesy by his intense exasperation with himself. In the economy of the poem
they bear much the same relationship to Gawain's courtesy as
his acceptance of the girdle did to his bravery. They constitute the minute flaw that makes his virtue human. Any man,
even as good as Gawain (and who is?), after all he had gone
through might well be annoyed. We believe in Gawain's courtesy the more readily after this brief explosion. Nor should
we exaggerate its discourtesy. After all, no ladies are present
to be offended, and masculine society must be allowed some
freedom of comment when it cannot give offense. Gawain
continues his speech to say that as regards ladies it were a great
delight "to love them well and not to believe them" (2421).
Now, there is nothing in any concept of courtesy that states
that courteous knights should *believe* ladies who try to seduce
them, or indeed, should believe ladies in general under any
circumstances. To love them well and not to believe them is a
courtly paradox, an ironic, half-comic, complexity of behavior very characteristic of the *Gawain*-poet and, of course, of
that fascinating culture which he represents. We do it, and
ourselves, an injustice if we unduly neglect or oversimplify it.
Courtesy is one of its major constituents and pleasures, and
not the least complex. It is an ideal very variously explored
and fully maintained throughout all these remarkable
poems.[16]

No summary of characteristics can do justice to the poet's
rich concept of courtesy, but some principal traits have been
established. Essentially courtesy is for him an ideal of personal integrity (and therefore of mental and spiritual self-
realization), but its quality can only be realized in benevolent
actions or at least speech towards other people. Another way

[16] The view of the *Gawain*-poet's presentation of courtesy put forward here differs from that of other critics, who assume that courtesy
is the same as *fine amour*. See in particular, besides the works of A. C.
Spearing and J. F. Kiteley already cited, the important articles by M.
W. Bloomfield, *PMLA* 76 (1961), and Professor G. V. Smithers,
"What *Sir Gawain and the Green Knight* is about," *Medium Aevum*
XXXII (1964) (which has much other valuable material), and the
brief, brilliant interpretation by E. T. Donaldson in *The Norton An-
thology of English Literature* (New York, 1962).

of putting it would be to say that courtesy consists in loving God and one's neighbor as oneself. The three persons, God, neighbor and self, are for the poet indissolubly linked, which is one reason why he is no ascetic. The general concept is fully realized in delightfully concrete fourteenth-century terms, physical, social and moral. It includes beauty, politeness, humor, self-control, bravery, cleanliness. For our poet it does *not* include *fine amour*, any more than it (apparently) includes, say, almsgiving.

An Historical Note

Courtesy is usually thought to be an offshoot of "love," but this seems to be an oversimplification. A very early use of "courteous" comes in *La Chanson de Roland*, where Oliver, who knows *mesure,* is *curteis,* while Roland fails in courtesy.[17] But there is no doubt that in those significant poems of the troubadours in the early twelfth century, where the new feeling of romantic self-abasing love begins to show itself most clearly, courtesy is understood to be one of the characteristics of love.[18] It would seem most likely that courtesy arose with the new courts of Europe, along with a new feeling about love, a new sense of personal identity, and consequently a different sense of the individual's relations to the group. This complex of new feelings underlay both secular and religious life, but may have started as a secular phenomenon, as the word *courtesy* itself suggests. Such complex changes have complex causes, and to the several that have been already suggested—Classical influence, Arabic influence, economic improvement—I should add, lay literacy, changing the basis of courts from an oral culture to a manuscript culture, where individuality had more expression than in an oral culture, but was still in close *rapport* with the group, unlike the solitary author and reader in a print culture.[19]

By the end of the twelfth century the concept of courtesy was elaborate and widespread through France. According to Dupin it comprised a whole scale of internal and external values, and was most usually associated with love. "One cannot be courteous unless one loves," says Marie de France.[20] There can be no doubt that for some reason there was a new influence of women in the lay secular courts of Europe, and that, as always, this influence had a civilizing effect, especially on that brutal military aristocracy. But the assumption that

---

[17] Pointed out by André Burger, in a review of *The Ethos of the Song of Roland* by G. F. Jones, *Medium Aevum XXXIV* (1965), 53. Burger points out traces of the influence of love and of ladies in *The Song of Roland;* but love and courtesy, though associated, are different things.

[18] A. J. Denomy, "Courtly Love and Courtliness," *Speculum XXVIII* (1953).

[19] *Cf.* M. McLuhan, *The Gutenberg Galaxy* (Toronto, 1962).

[20] *Guigemar,* 59, quoted by H. Dupin, *La Courtoisie au Moyen Age,* p. 93.

love and courtesy *are the same thing* is shown to be histori-cally untrue from the beginning by the example of *La Chan-son de Roland*. We can say no more than that there was a close association. This association was to some extent broken by the writers of the Arthurian Grail romances, like *Perles-vaus,* who are, as Dupin shows, deeply conditioned by the ideal of courtesy, but hostile to secular love. Even in purely secular relationships and behavior courtesy, became very gen-eralized.

Courtesy is indeed complex. I close this note with a quota-tion from the late twelfth-century poem *Guillaume de Pa-lerne,* very popular in its day. A little boy is being taken to court, and he is instructed how he should behave there. It is a passage which could be matched in a good many French and English romances, but it is specially worth noting here, as this poem was translated into English in the middle of the fourteenth century as *William of Palerne,* the first of the poems of the alliterative revival. It expresses that sense of in-dividual integrity in relation to the group, that sense of self-control and moderation, of active good will and kindness to others, which I take to be central to the concept of courtesy; but it has no word of love.

"Si ferés, fix," disit li preudon,
"Car grans biens vos en puet venir.
Si soiés prex du deservir
Et de faire tot son voloir,
Et quanques vos poés savoir
C'on doit a si haut cort faire;
Si soiés frans et debonaire
Et servicables et temprés.
Ne soiés pas desmesurés,
Ne outrageus, fel ne estous,
Et vos faites amer a tous;
Ne de ton droit ne te destort
Nus plus prisiés de toi en cort
Que vos si bien nel deteigniés,
Que tort ne blasme n'i aiés,
Ta parole garde et tes dis
Que tu ne soiés entrepris
Si que blasmer ne vos en sace
Nus hom en rue ne en place.
As povres vos humeliés,
Contre les riches or aidiés.
En cort si haute emperial
Mult i sont cointe cil vassal:
Mult voelent bien que lor paroles
Soient sages u soient foles,
Aient lor lieus, soient oies
Et chier tenues et joies
Nus ne vos i prenge a vo tort;

(The cowherd) seide "þou swete sone,
seþþe þou schalt hennes wende
Whanne þou komest to kourt among þe kete lordes,

& knowest alle þe kuþþes þat to kourt langes
bere þe boxumly & bonure þat ich burn þe loue.
Be meke and mesurabul, nouзt of many wordes,
be no tellere of talis but trewe to þi lord
& prestely for pore men profer þe euer,
For hem to rekene wiþ þe riche in riзt & in skille.
Be feiзtful & fre, euer of faire speche,
& seruisabul to þe simple, so as to þe riche,
& felawe in faire manere, as falles for þi state.

Mais den ton droit te truissent fort
Ne troveras qui li t'apreigne." [21]

So schaltou gete Goddes loue,
& alle gode mennes." [22]

The Character of Gawain

"Character" in a work of literature can usually be placed somewhere on a line between two poles. The one pole is character as role. Using the word "character" simply to denote the personage in the work of literature, we may say that the character appears as role when he (or she) has only generally defined characteristics, which are sufficient for the purpose in hand. Examples of roles are lecherous young students, like those in Chaucer's *Miller's* and *Reeve's Tales*, or brave and good knights, like Troilus, or beautiful and virtuous ladies, like Dorigen in the *Franklin's Tale*. Such characters have their main interest as performers in a series of events, or as part of the situational pattern. At the other extreme, character can be portrayed as personality for its own sake, almost independent of the story or other characters: examples might be Fielding's Parson Adams, many of Dickens's characters, Hardy's Henshaw. The late nineteenth century saw the heyday of character as personality, often drawn with great psychological insight, and we still tend to value this literary achievement higher than almost all others. There is no strict dividing line, but the two types of portrayal are nevertheless usually distinct. Medieval literature very rarely created character as personality. Chaucer merged role with individual personality to some extent in *The General Prologue to the Canterbury Tales,* and with Pandarus, but much less so in the *Tales*. The important thing is to recognize that each type of character portrayal has its own advantages and then not to confuse them. It is pointless to demand personality from the portrayal of Gawain in *Sir Gawain and the Green Knight*. His role is presented with flashes of psychological insight (as is Chaucer's Troilus) but that is a different matter. Gawain is always exemplary in *Sir Gawain and the Green Knight*.

[21] *Guillaume de Palerne*, ed. H. Michelant, Société des Anciens Textes Français (Paris, 1876), ll. 544–73.

[22] *William of Palerne*, ed. W. W. Skeat, Early English Text Society, Extra Series I (London, 1867), ll. 329–40.

Gawain is not always presented quite as the *Gawain*-poet presents him, though he never becomes a unique person. B. J. Whiting has studied his various appearances in medieval literature, and finds that though he is called *courteous* on the whole more often than other knights, his courtesy is never insisted upon so much as in *Sir Gawain and the Green Knight*.[23] Whiting found his presentation fell into three main stages, corresponding with the three main stages of development of the Matter of Britain. First come the chronicle-like accounts of the life and death of Arthur, where Arthur is the central figure and Gawain is his chief knight, the ideal warrior, loyal and honorable. Second come the episodic verse romances, of which the poems of Chrétien de Troyes are an example. Arthur's court is the place of departure and return, but the interest is in the adventures of many different knights. Gawain is always prominent, and often the hero. He has many adventures, military and amorous. He is brave, charming and promiscuous, and consequently welcomed with enthusiasm by almost every maiden he meets. The stories are fantasies of prodigious military and sexual valor:

> Gawain as a lover followed a well-defined pattern: when he met an unattached girl he made love to her; if she rebuffed him he departed; if, as more often, she welcomed his attentions, he also departed, but not so soon. With him, too, out of sight was out of mind. For him a love affair was an exchange of verbal and physical courtesies, and he had no realization of his own unworthiness or the lady's supreme condescension in granting him her slightest favor. If we also remember that, for whatever reason, he did not make love to married women, we understand that Gawain could not be a participant in any game of love played by the rules of the code.[24]

In the third stage, when the verse romances were turned into prose and extended and added to, some authors, especially those of the Grail legend who made virginity the supreme value, blackened Gawain's character. It is this darker character whom we are most familiar with in the middle part of Malory's *Morte Darthur*, and in later treatments like Tennyson's, though Malory cuts out much of Gawain's love-making.

[23] B. J. Whiting, "Gawain: His Reputation, His Courtesy," *Medieval Studies* IX, 1947.
[24] B. J. Whiting, *loc. cit.*, p. 215.

To locate the *Gawain*-poet's treatment of Gawain historically we need to return to the first stage of Arthurian story. Whether or not he knew it, the most striking portrayal of Gawain in English before his own poem is in the alliterative *Morte Arthure*. This poem is based on the chronicle stories of early Arthurian romance, and so, though late fourteenth century in date, represents the first Arthurian stage.[25] It is a poem at the center of the fourteenth-century alliterative revival, and like the others, though proudly provincial, is not ignorant of the king's court. *Morte Arthure* is a stern, pious, poem, with a vein of repellent brutality as well as a hearty enthusiasm for battle. Surely no minstrel wrote this, but a cleric of some great baron's court. The author is patriotic, historically minded, concerned with public affairs. Though Arthur is severely criticized, the author and the assumed audience are decidedly on his side, and one has very much the feeling that the presentation of Arthur has deliberate parallels with Edward III. For all the fantasy of such episodes as Arthur's fight with the giant, the poem gives an extraordinarily vivid sense of infantry war in general and the Hundred Years War in particular. It is a fascinating poem for any middle-aged soldiers and politicians who may be able to read a slightly difficult Middle English dialect: not much likely to attract women and undergraduates. Malory, it will be remembered, used the poem perhaps as the starting-point for his whole work,[26] but changed its tone somewhat, and by inventing episodes brought Sir Launcelot into prominence.

In *The Morte Arthure* Sir Gawain "of the West Marches" (2953) is most prominent, after the King. When the King and his chief knights withdraw to a chamber after the feast it is Gawain who takes in Queen Guenever (233). He is the "warden" of the knights, wins most glory in battle, and is called "father" as a term of respect by the younger knights. When the "good Gawain, gracious and noble" (2851) is outnumbered by the enemy and advised not to fight, he makes a speech that reminds one of Henry V's speech before Agincourt in Shakespeare's play, and he finishes up with an appeal to Mary, "that mild queen." (All this was cut by Malory.) He meets his end in a sortie that he himself recognizes as suicidally reckless. When Arthur finds Gawain dead "the sweet

25 *Morte Arthure*, ed. E. Brock, Early English Text Society (1871), O.S. 8; ed. E. Björkman (Heidelberg, 1915).

26 See my remarks in *Essays on Malory*, ed. J. A. W. Bennett (Oxford, 1963), pp. 46–47.

king swoons," and sweetly kisses the corpse until his beard is as smeared with blood as if he had been cutting up beasts (3969–72). He collects Gawain's blood in a helmet, and vows to Messiah and "Mary, the mild queen of heaven," that he will never hunt at roe nor reindeer, nor handle a hawk nor hold a Round Table, "till thy death, my dear, be duly revenged" (4006).

This poem without love is not without courtesy. *Courteous* itself is used in such collocations as "kind and courteous" (21), "courteous and gentle" (987). The apparatus of the courtly life is gloried in—for example, the rich feast at Christmastime at Caerleon, which calls for comparison with the similar feast in *Sir Gawain and the Green Knight*. Arthur arms himself in a set-piece description (900 ff.) that should also be compared with the arming of Gawain in the later poem (566 ff.). The poem creates a courtly context that is potentially similar to that in *Sir Gawain and the Green Knight*. The highest reach comes with the lament for Gawain's death spoken—and it is a fine touch—by no other than Modred, the traitor who killed him. When a foreign king asks who the mighty fighter was, Modred replies that he was matchless, "Gawain the good," "the most gracious man," "hardiest of hand," "happiest in arms"

> And the hendeste in hawle vndire heuene riche;
> Þe lordelieste of ledinge qwhylles he lyffe myghte,
> ffore he was lyone allossede in londes i-newe.

> 3880–82

"Hendest in hall," a lamb in the hall; a lion in the field, like Launcelot and Beowulf and others. There is no mention of ladies in the poem, apart from Guenever, but there is no doubt of, if no emphasis on, Gawain's courtesy. Here is the basis for the *Gawain*-poet's portrayal of his exemplary knight.

But the lady in *Sir Gawain and the Green Knight* had clearly been reading the romances of chivalry very extensively, and it is from these that *she* takes Gawain's character. This character is not one, as Whiting points out, that cherishes *fine amour*, like Launcelot; it is the character of a man who simply cannot resist any young and pretty woman. The poet, however, leaves this version of Gawain's character entirely in the mouth of the lady. Gawain's courteous *speech* is a natural development of the virtuous earlier Gawain, and of late fourteenth-century ideals of courtly education. The existence of two views of Gawain, so to say, the lady's and the poet's, helps to increase the social tension in the scenes between them. Even in the light of the stories of the promiscuous Gawain, however, the poet is not entirely changing his character; for it seems, according to Whiting, that he never made love to married women.

Hende

Hende is the Middle English form of Old English *gehende,* meaning "near, convenient, at hand." Only rarely, in Scots, does it seem to retain something like this sense in later centuries. Early in the Middle English period in England it developed the further metaphorical senses of "dexterous," hence "clever," and came to be associated occasionally with learning. But at the same time (about 1200) it developed as a general epithet of praise of persons, and was so used extremely commonly, both of human beings and of God and Mary. As such it came into collocation with *courteous,* which had similarly developed a very wide general sense of approval. Although it is difficult to be certain from the necessarily limited number of quotations in OED, it does look as if *hende* was more current in the west and north. The abstract noun with an Old Norse suffix, *hendelayk,* is rare and certainly not found in the south.

(The noun *courtesy* is first recorded in *The Ancrene Wisse* about 1200, but towards the end of the thirteenth, and in the fourteenth century, together with its adjective and adverb, becomes very widespread and often generalized in meaning to mean simply "the good.")

Apart from his early translation, *The Romaunt of the Rose,* Chaucer uses *hende* to suggest an uneducated speaker, like the Host in *The General Prologue* (once), and the Wife of Bath, who uses the word once of "jolly Jankin" the clerk. Chaucer uses it no less than eleven times in referring to "hende Nicholas" of *The Miller's Tale,* in which old-fashioned love-language is used, to put it very simply, to satirize low-class persons aping the (courtly) manners of their betters.[27] Chaucer's aristocratic views clearly made him feel

----

[27] E. T. Donaldson makes a close examination of Chaucer's use of *hende* in a valuable essay, "Idiom of Popular Poetry in 'The Miller's Tale'," *English Institute Essays 1950,* ed. A. S. Downer (New York, 1951). [reprinted above pp. 174–189. ed.]

that *hende* was old-fashioned, provincial, low-class, hackneyed. It is also noticeable that, for whatever reason, *hende* had a strong association with the idea of a "clerk," a student, for Chaucer. In this, as in other ways, he was very different from the *Gawain*-poet.